SCULLION

A Dishwasher's Guide to Mistaken Identity

SOAP

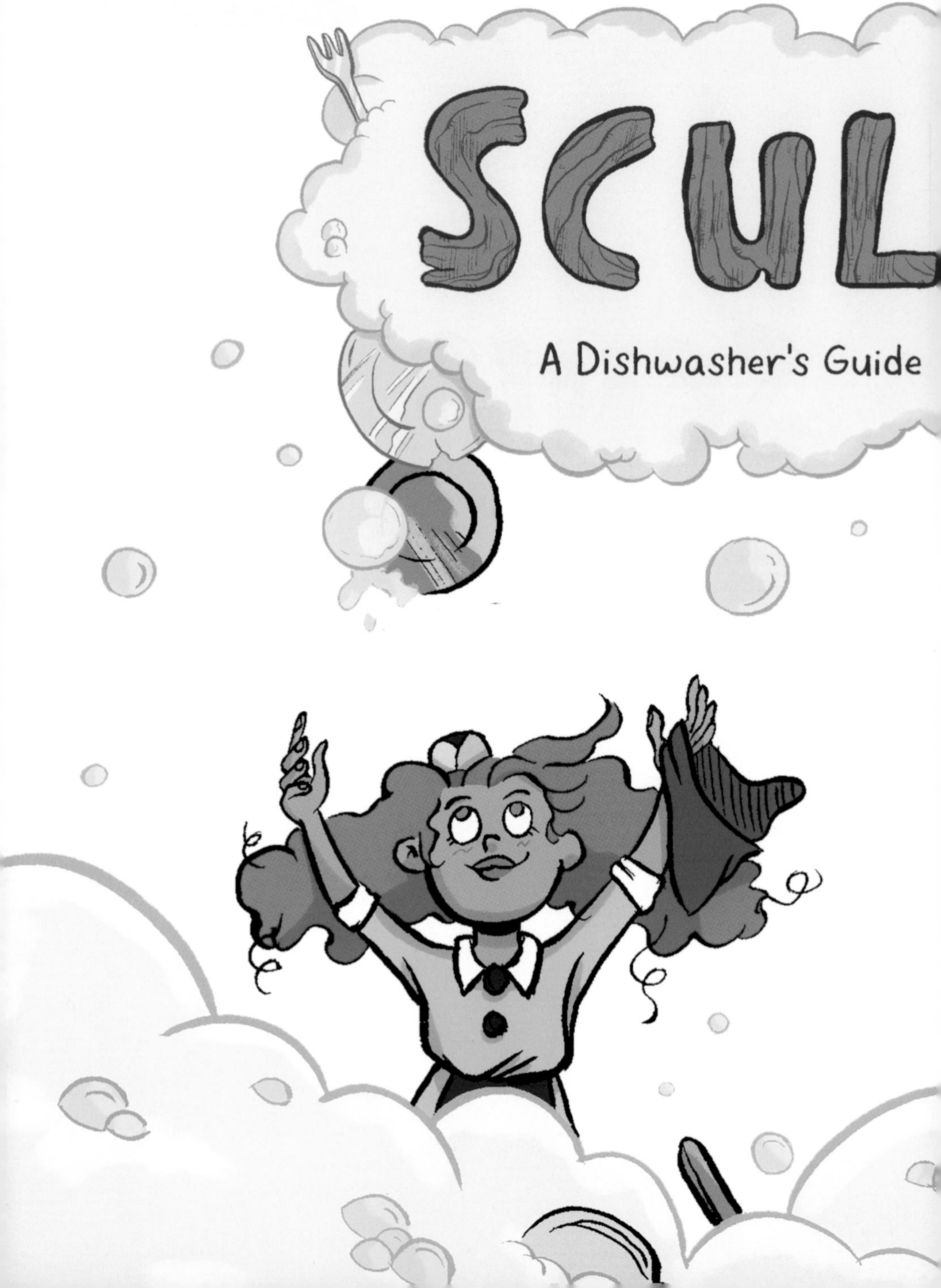
SCUL
A Dishwasher's Guide

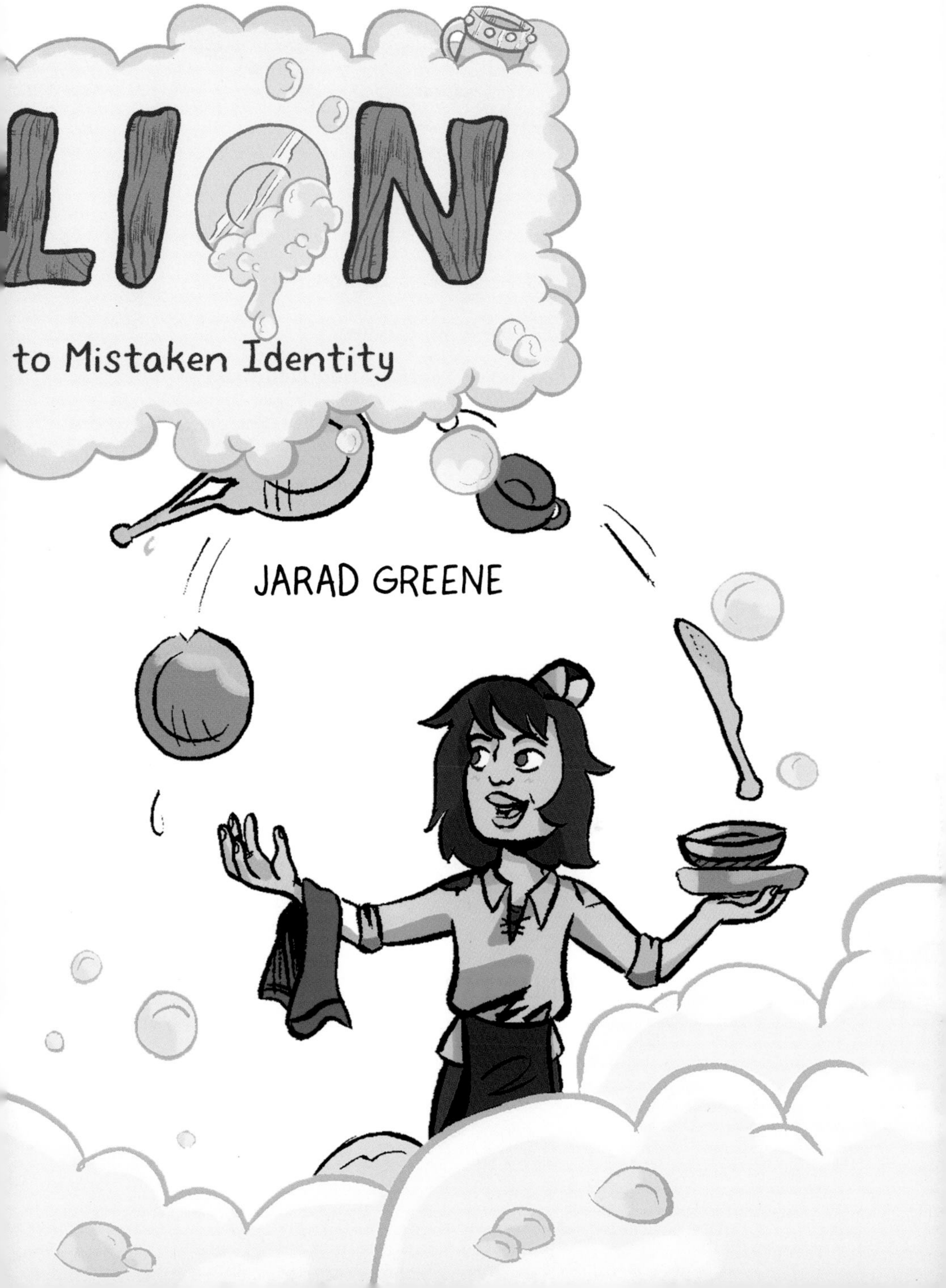

LION
to Mistaken Identity
JARAD GREENE

For Mom, Dad, and Lydia
—Jarad

Written, Illustrated, and Lettered by **Jarad Greene**

Designed by **Sarah Rockwell**

Edited by **Hazel Newlevant** and **Amanda Meadows**

Color flatting assistance by **Steve Thueson, Whiteley Foster,** and **Jess Johnson**

Font designed by **John Martz**

Published by Oni-Lion Forge Publishing Group, LLC

James Lucas Jones, president & publisher Sarah Gaydos, editor in chief Charlie Chu, e.v.p. of creative & business development Brad Rooks, director of operations Amber O'Neill, special projects manager Harris Fish, events manager Margot Wood, director of marketing & sales Jeremy Atkins, director of brand communications Devin Funches, sales & marketing manager Katie Sainz, marketing manager Tara Lehmann, marketing & publicity associate Troy Look, director of design & production Kate Z. Stone, senior graphic designer Sonja Synak, graphic designer Hilary Thompson, graphic designer Sarah Rockwell, junior graphic designer Angie Knowles, digital prepress lead Vincent Kukua, digital prepress technician Shawna Gore, senior editor Robin Herrera, senior editor Amanda Meadows, senior editor Jasmine Amiri, senior editor Grace Bornhoft, editor Zack Soto, editor Steve Ellis, vice president of games Ben Eisner, game developer Michelle Nguyen, executive assistant Jung Lee, logistics coordinator Joe Nozemack, publisher emeritus

onipress.com | lionforge.com
facebook.com/onipress | facebook.com/lionforge
twitter.com/onipress | twitter.com/lionforge
instagram.com/onipress | instagram.com/lionforge

jaradgreene.wordpress.com
facebook.com/JaradGreene
twitter.com/JaradGreene
instagram.com/JaradGreene

First Edition: July 2020
ISBN 978-1-62010-753-9
eISBN 978-1-62010-759-1

Library of Congress Control Number: 2019952827

1 3 5 7 9 10 8 6 4 2

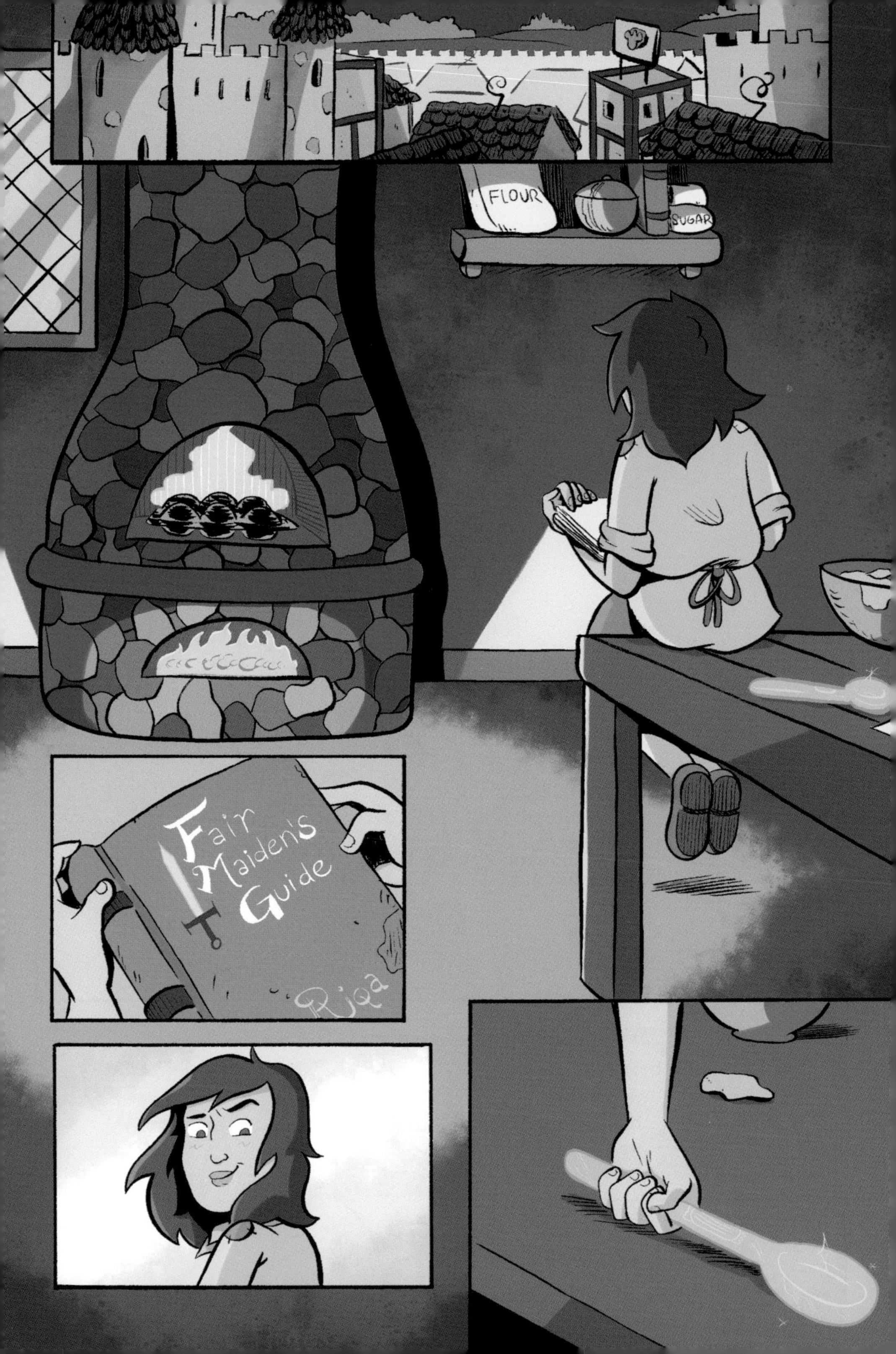
FLOUR
SUGAR
Fair Maiden's Guide
Riqa

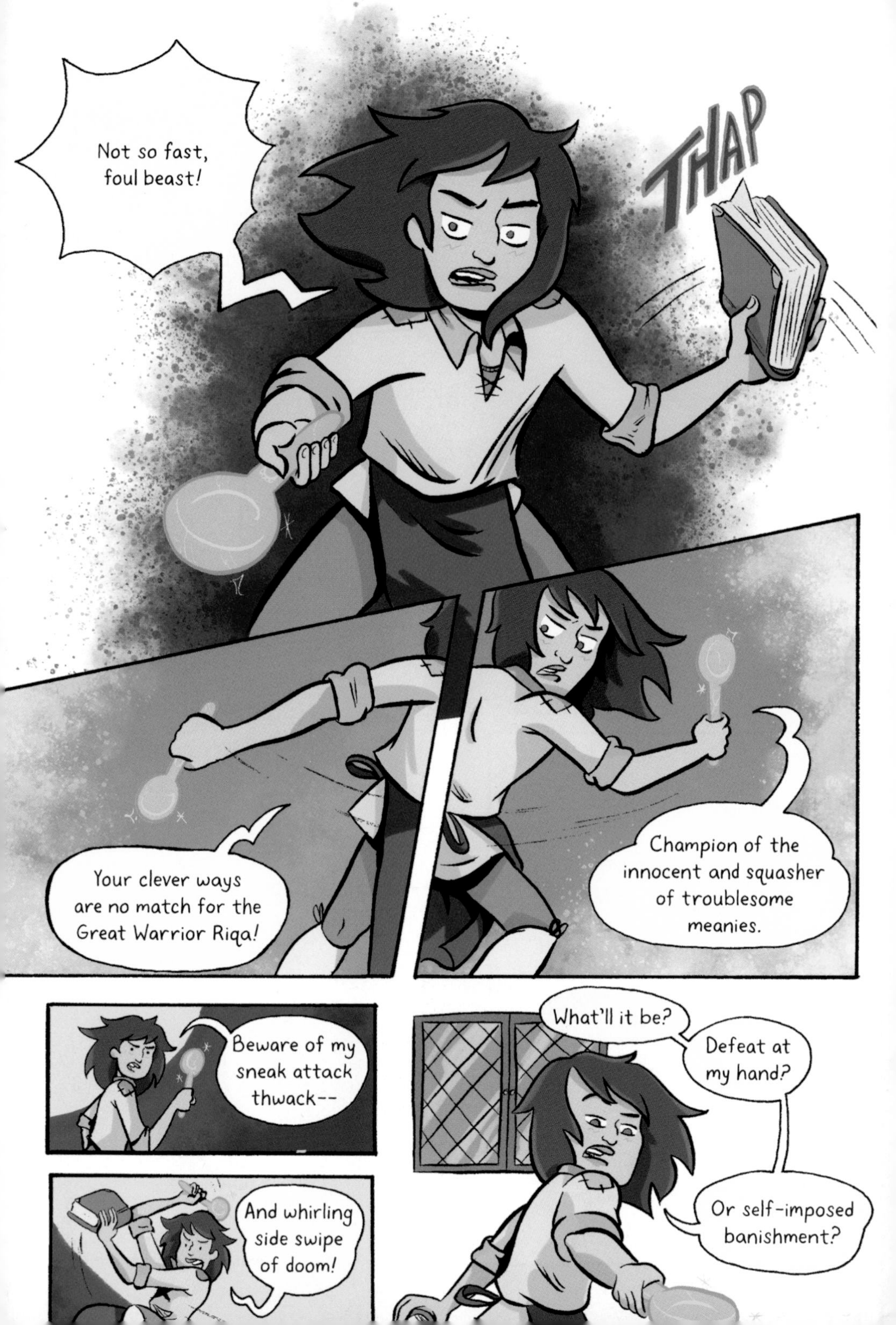

Not so fast, foul beast!
THAP
Your clever ways are no match for the Great Warrior Riqa!
Champion of the innocent and squasher of troublesome meanies.
Beware of my sneak attack thwack--
And whirling side swipe of doom!
What'll it be?
Defeat at my hand?
Or self-imposed banishment?

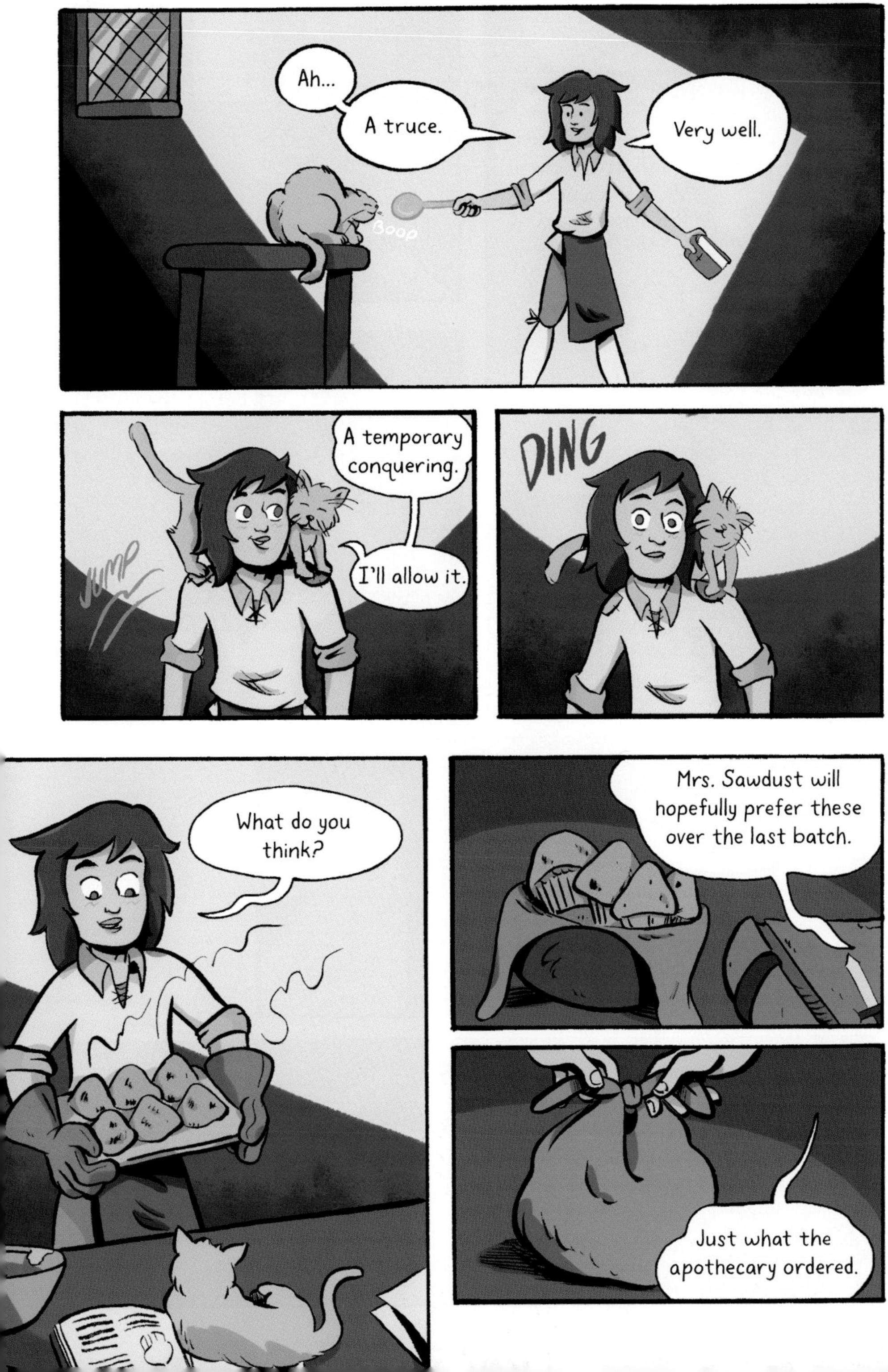

Ah...
A truce.
Boop
Very well.
A temporary conquering.
JUMP
I'll allow it.
DING
What do you think?
Mrs. Sawdust will hopefully prefer these over the last batch.
Just what the apothecary ordered.

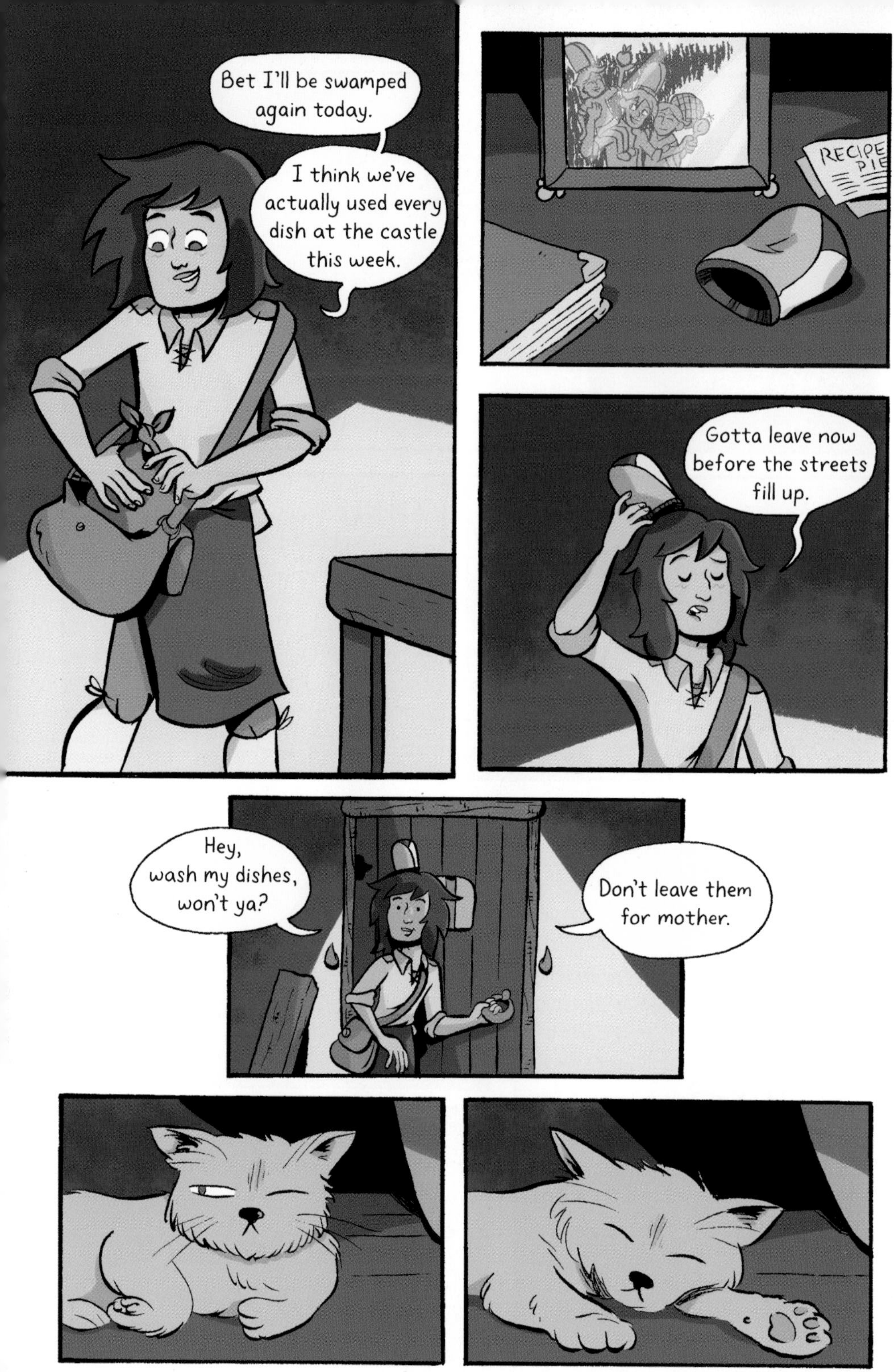
Bet I'll be swamped again today.
I think we've actually used every dish at the castle this week.
RECIPE PIE
Gotta leave now before the streets fill up.
Hey, wash my dishes, won't ya?
Don't leave them for mother.

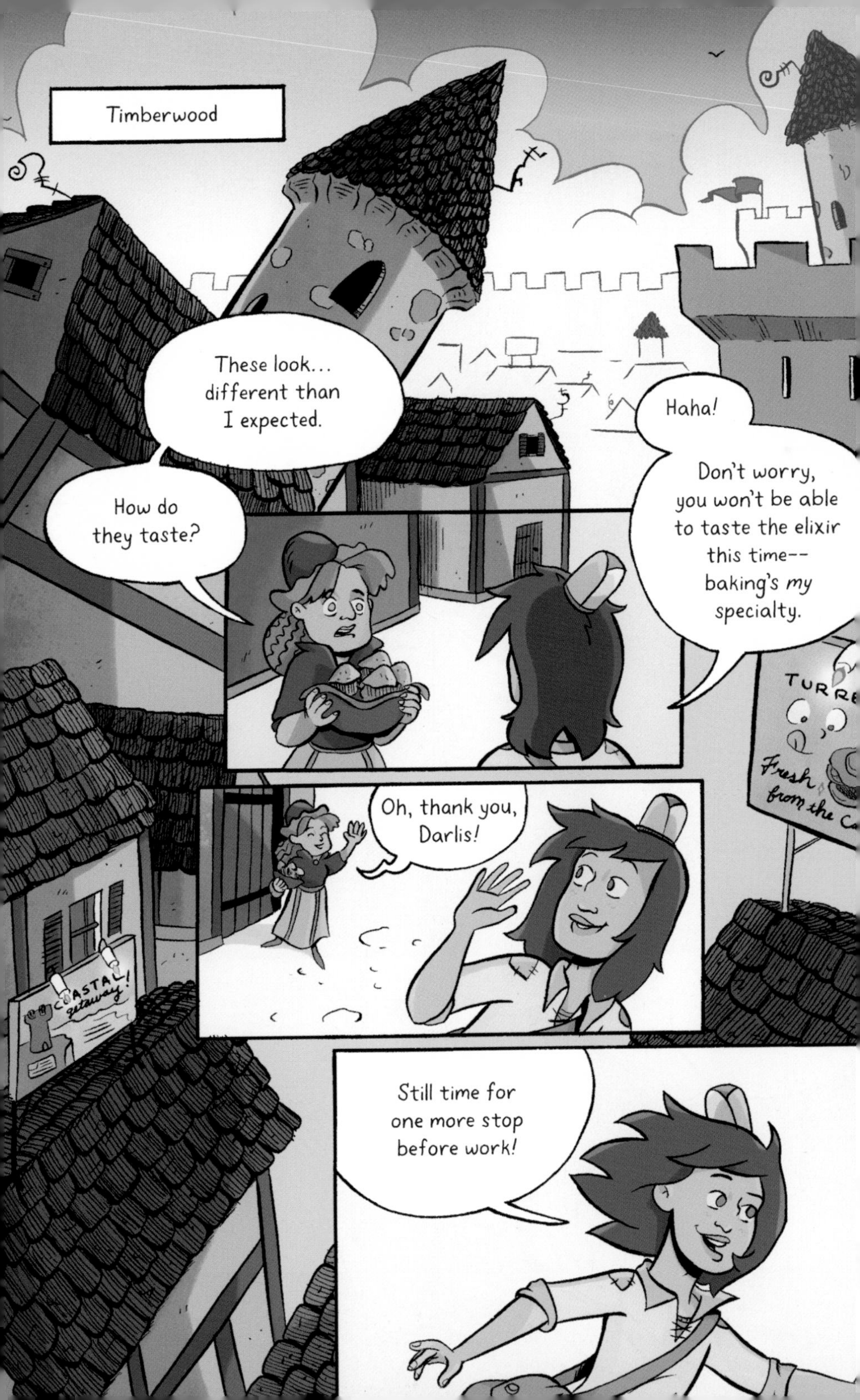
Timberwood
These look... different than I expected.
How do they taste?
Haha!
Don't worry, you won't be able to taste the elixir this time-- baking's *my* specialty.
TURRE
Fresh from the Ca
Oh, thank you, Darlis!
COASTAL getaway!
Still time for one more stop before work!

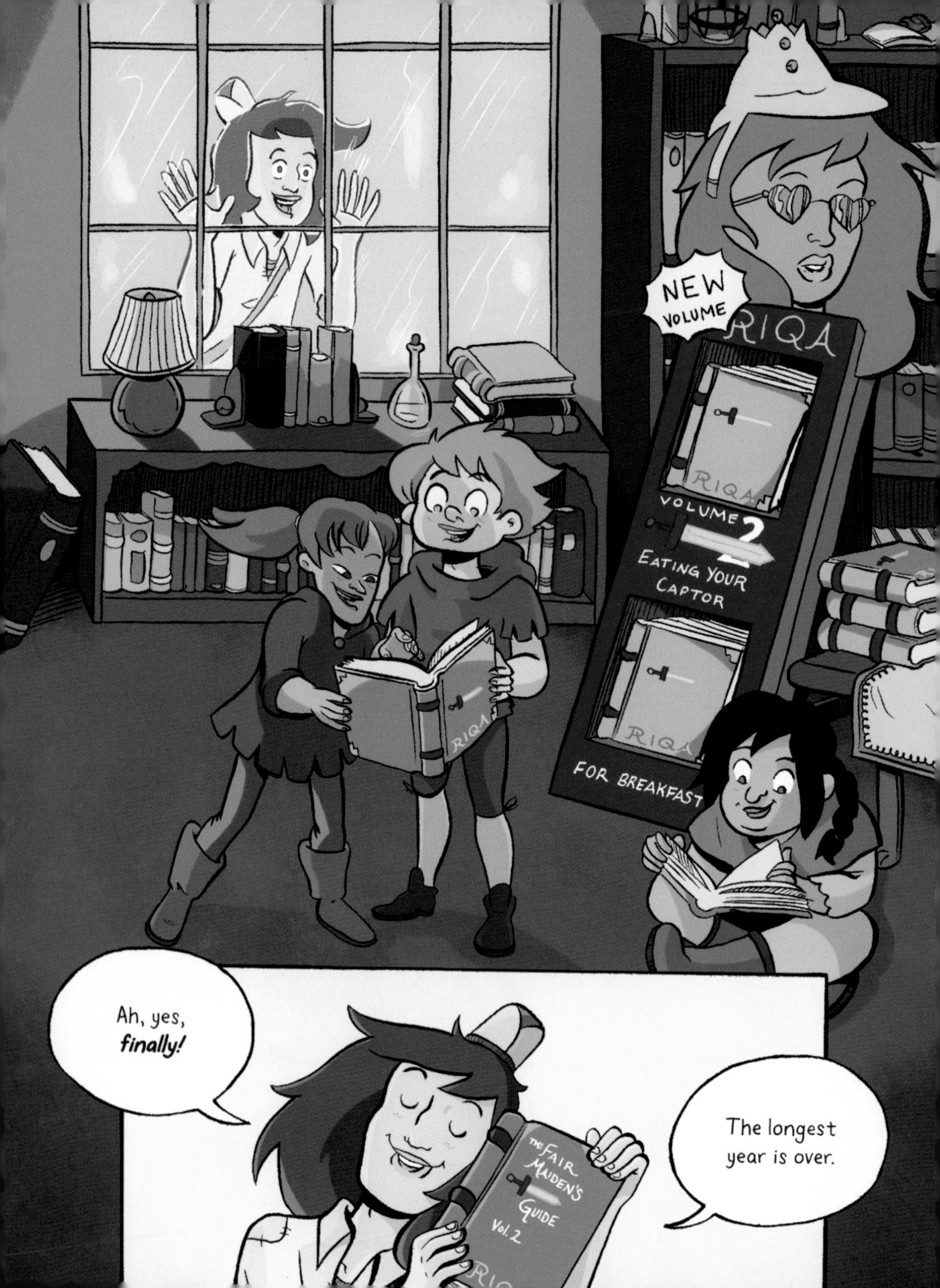
NEW VOLUME
RIQA
VOLUME 2
EATING YOUR CAPTOR
FOR BREAKFAST
Ah, yes, **finally!**
The longest year is over.
THE FAIR MAIDEN'S GUIDE Vol. 2

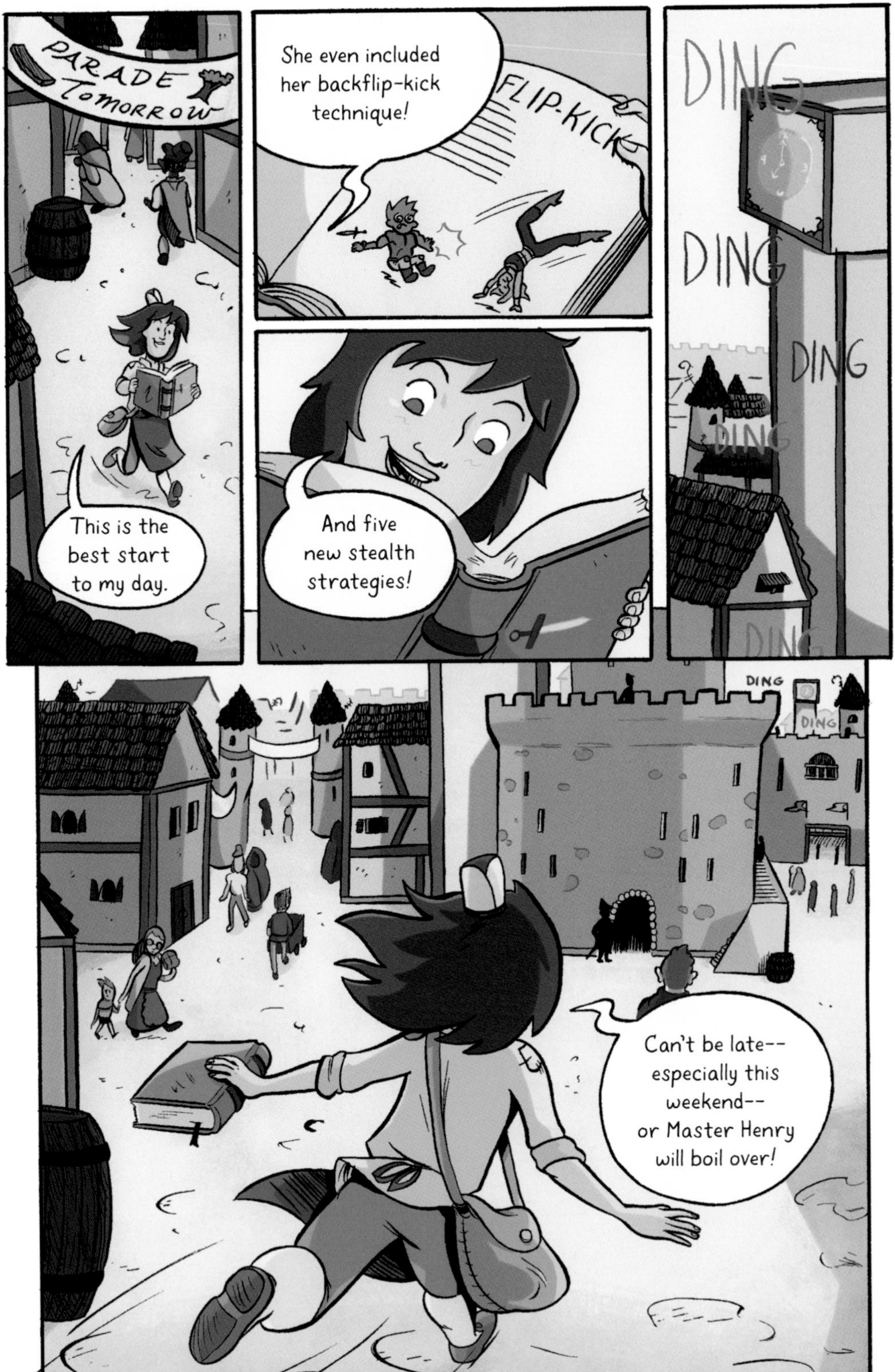
PARADE TOMORROW
This is the best start to my day.
She even included her backflip-kick technique!
FLIP-KICK
And five new stealth strategies!
DING
DING
DING
DING
DING
DING
DING
Can't be late-- especially this weekend-- or Master Henry will boil over!

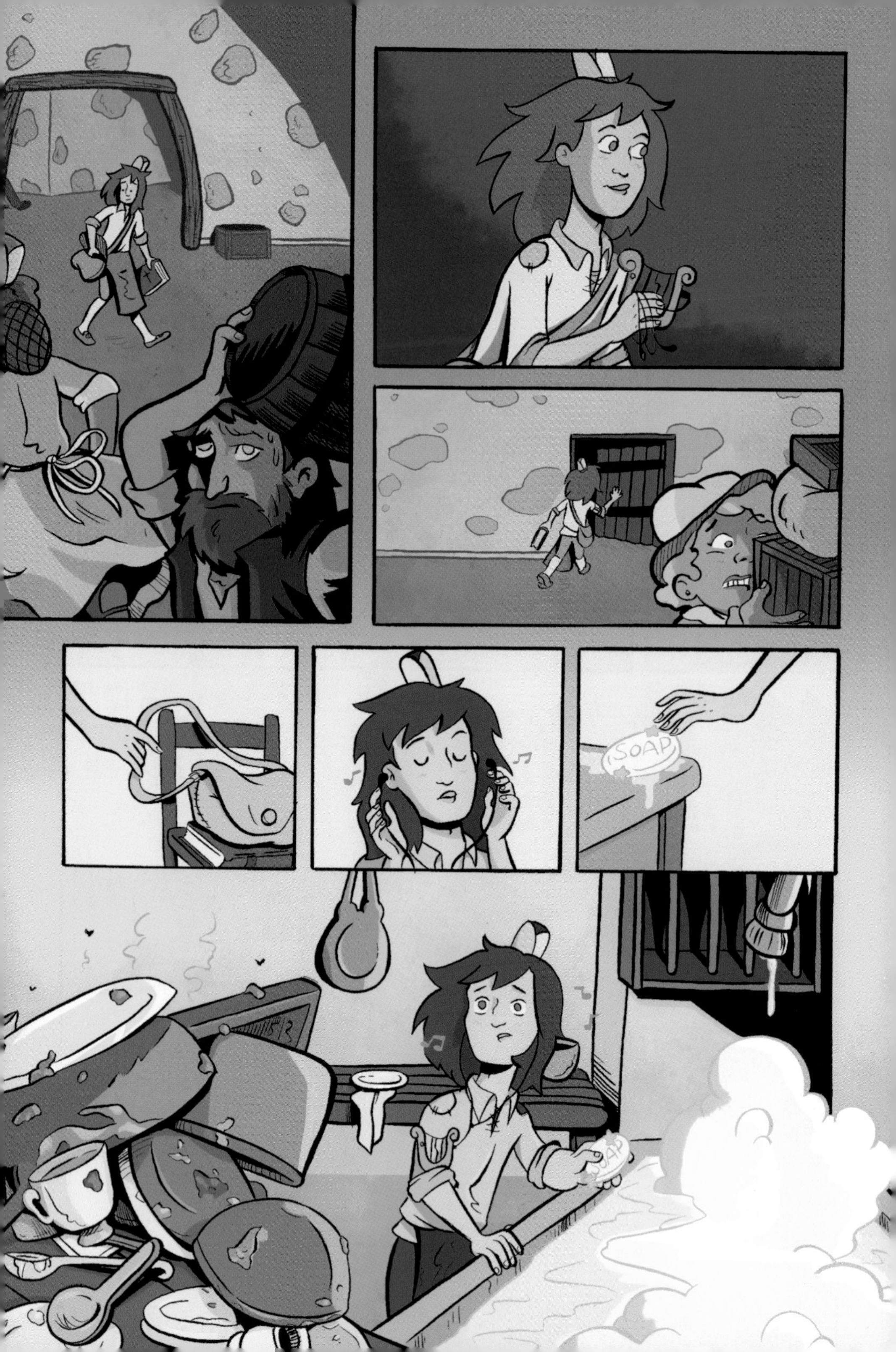
SOAP
SOAP

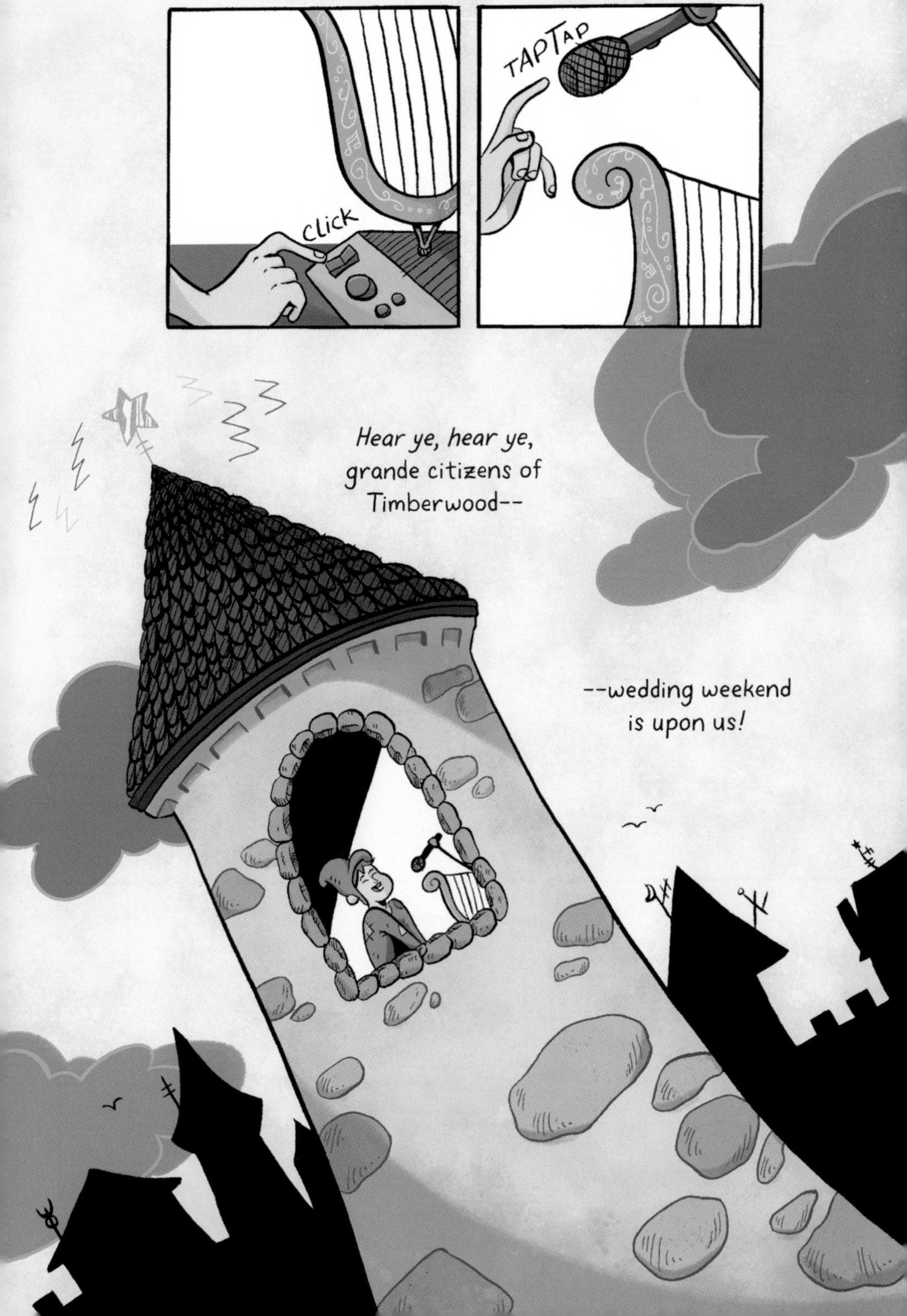
CLICK
TAPTAP
Hear ye, hear ye, grande citizens of Timberwood--
--wedding weekend is upon us!

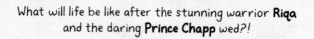

What will life be like after the stunning warrior **Riqa** and the daring **Prince Chapp** wed?!

Who can say?!

--But we'll be your eyes and ears from the towers above, down the hallways, past 1,000 maids dusting--

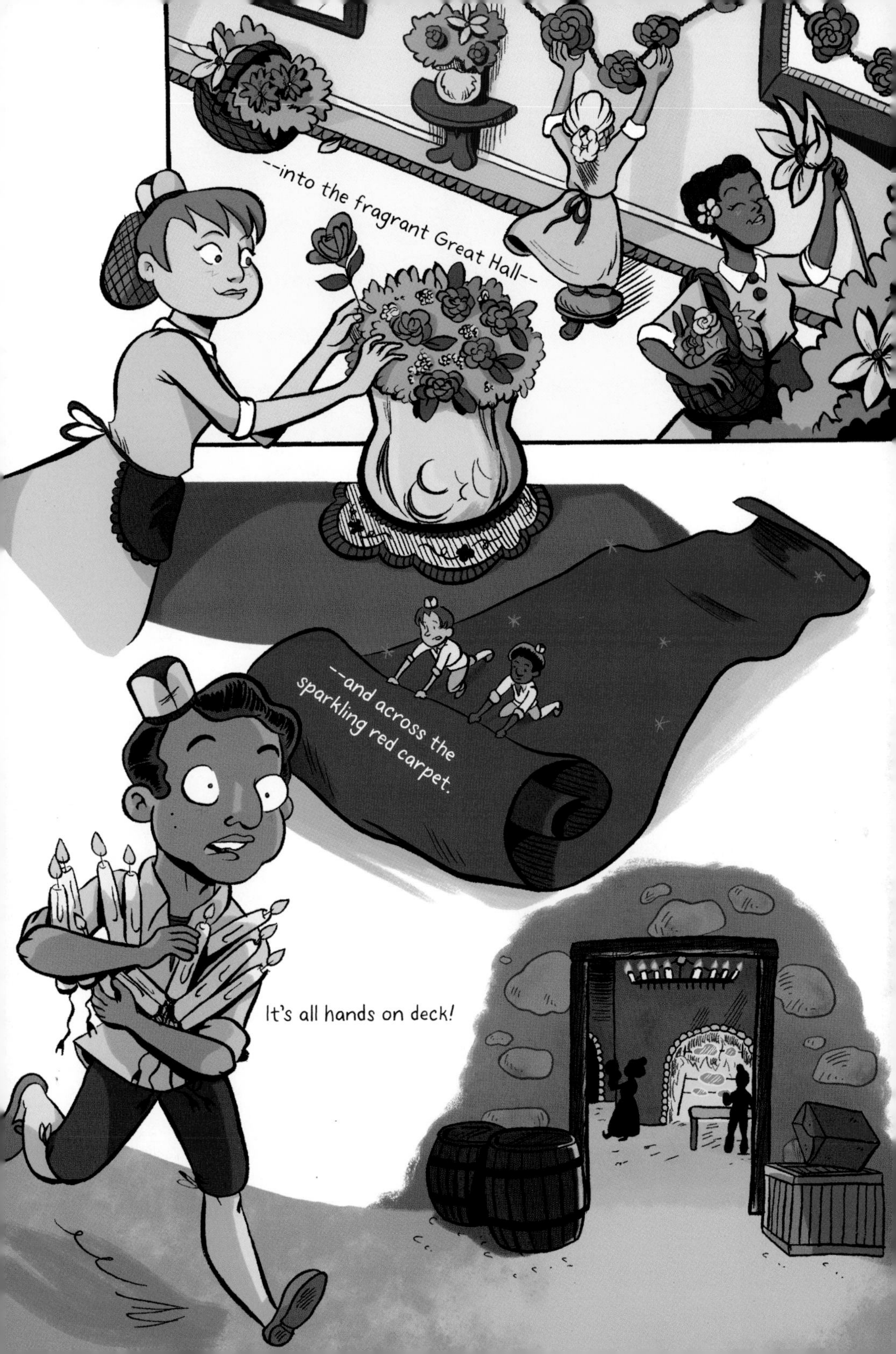
--into the fragrant Great Hall--
--and across the sparkling red carpet.
It's all hands on deck!

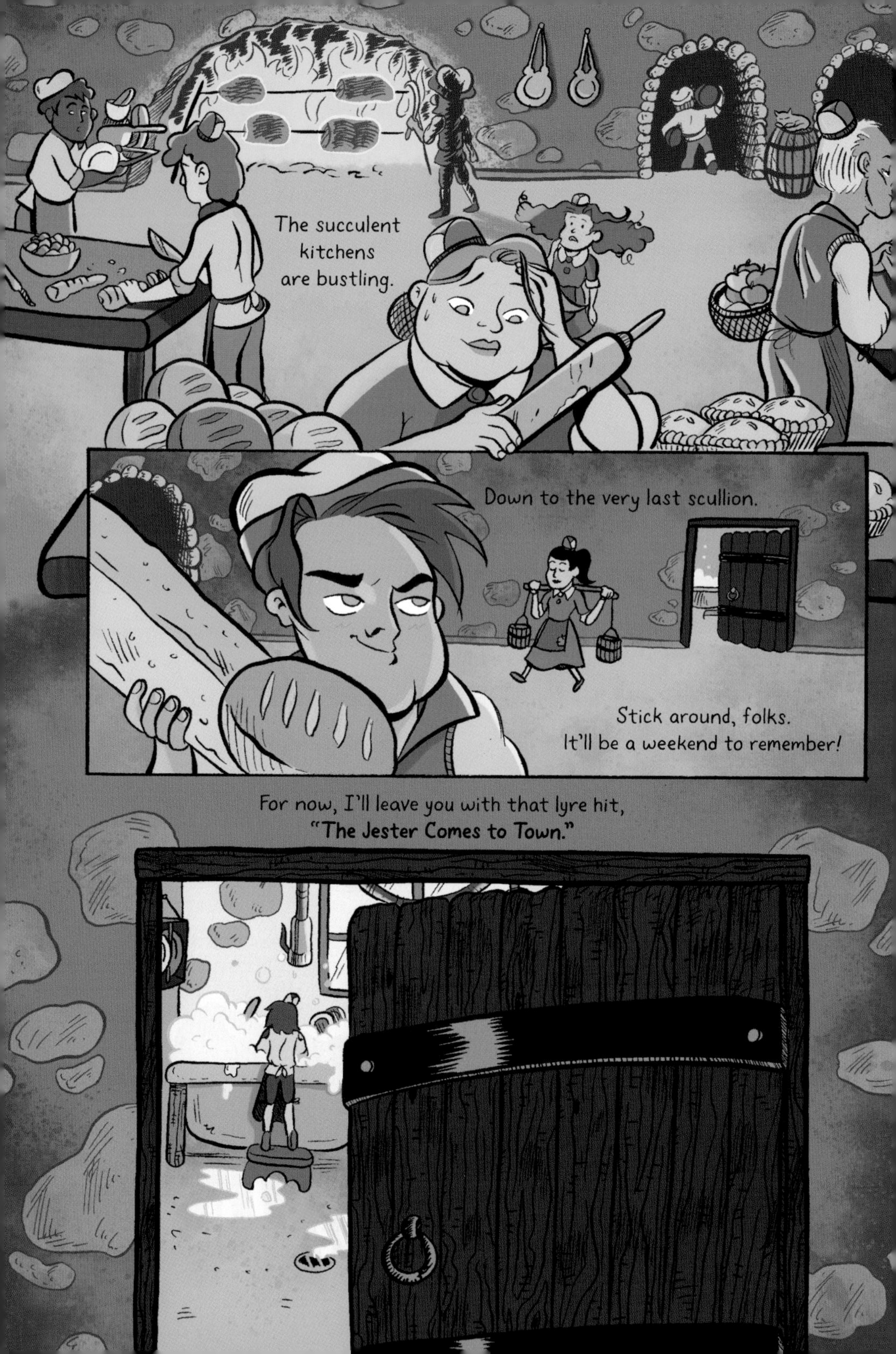
The succulent kitchens are bustling.
Down to the very last scullion.
Stick around, folks. It'll be a weekend to remember!
For now, I'll leave you with that lyre hit, "The Jester Comes to Town."

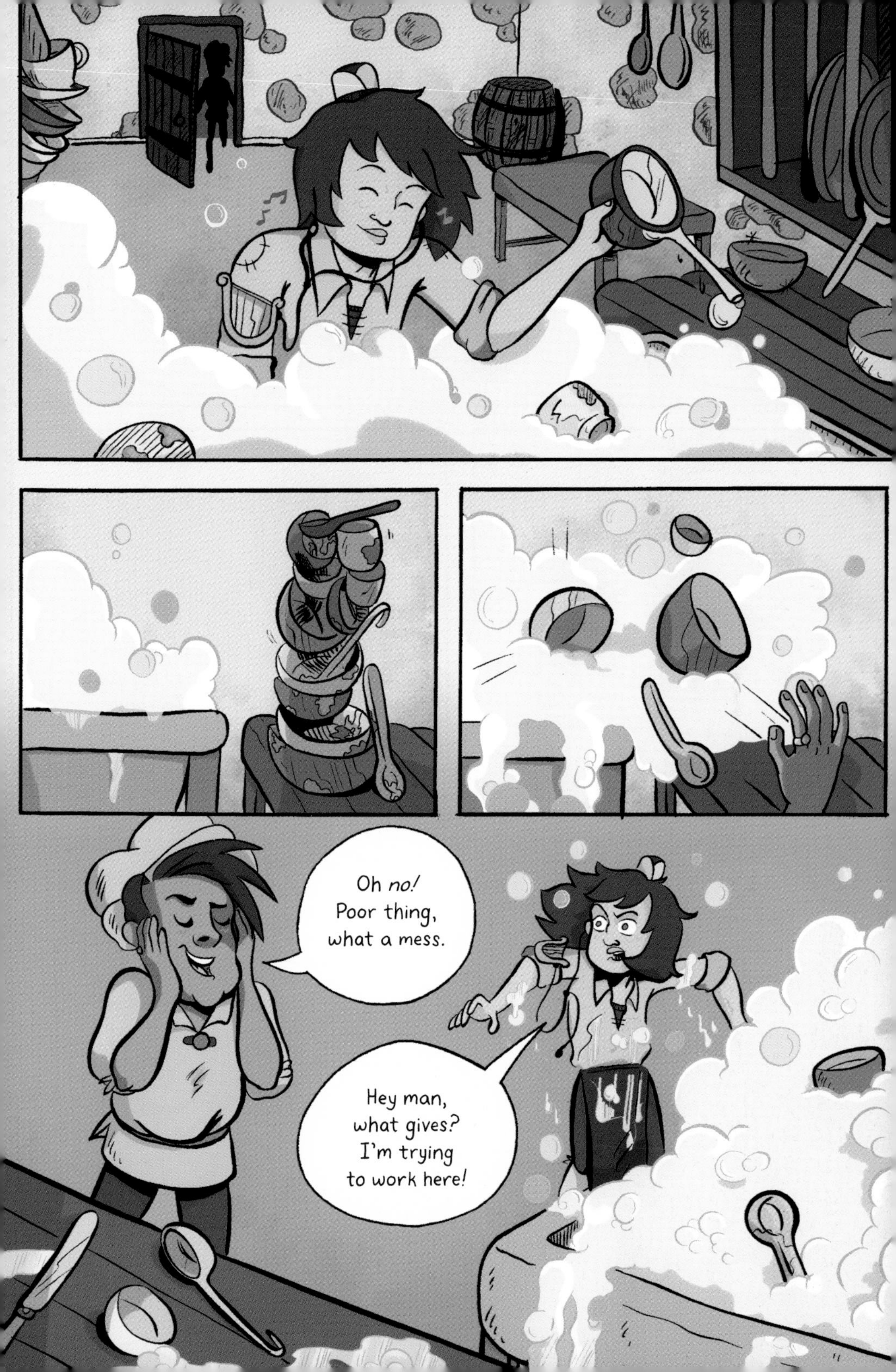
Oh *no!*
Poor thing,
what a mess.
Hey man,
what gives?
I'm trying
to work here!

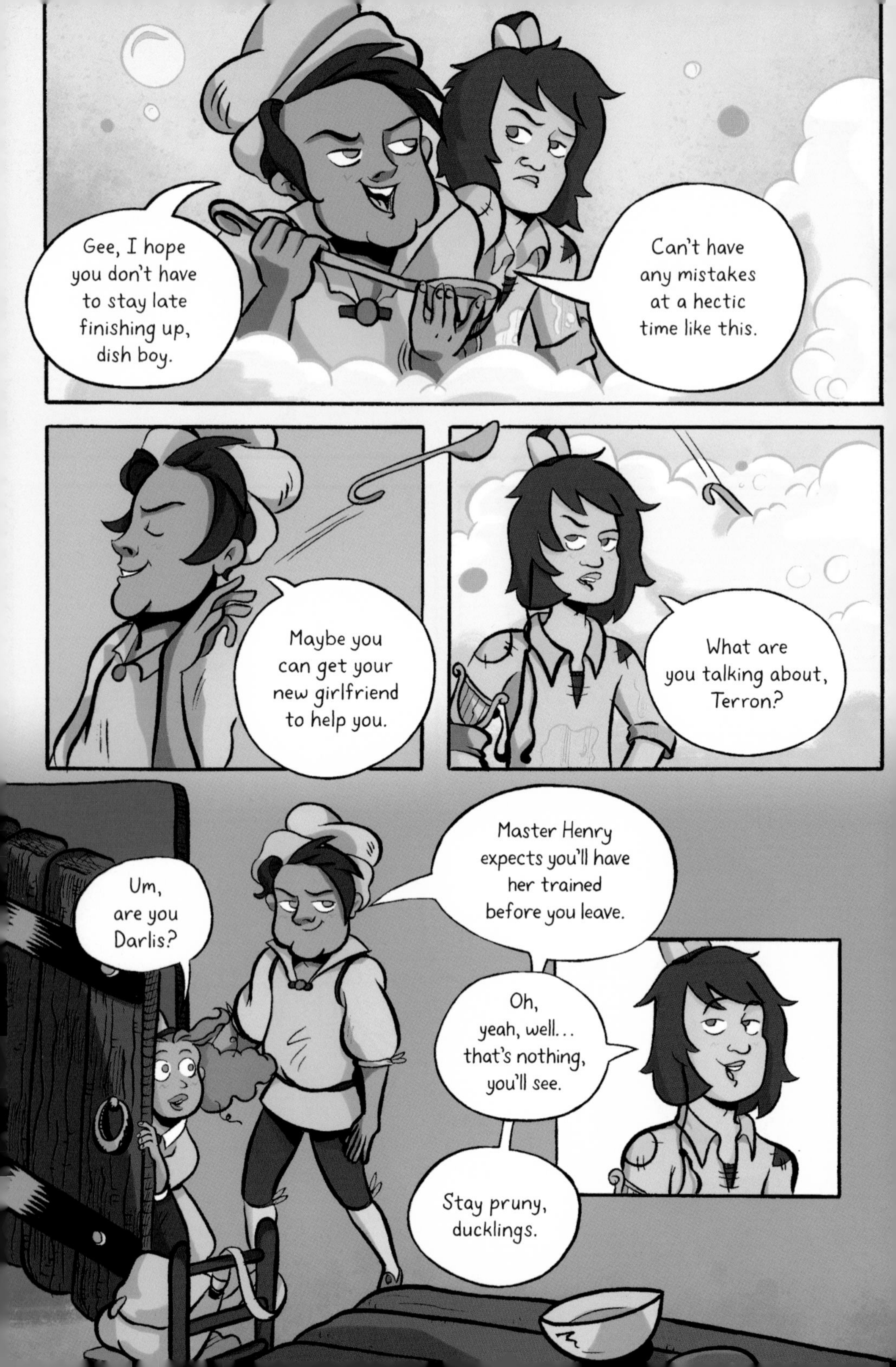
Gee, I hope you don't have to stay late finishing up, dish boy.
Can't have any mistakes at a hectic time like this.
Maybe you can get your new girlfriend to help you.
What are you talking about, Terron?
Master Henry expects you'll have her trained before you leave.
Um, are you Darlis?
Oh, yeah, well... that's nothing, you'll see.
Stay pruny, ducklings.

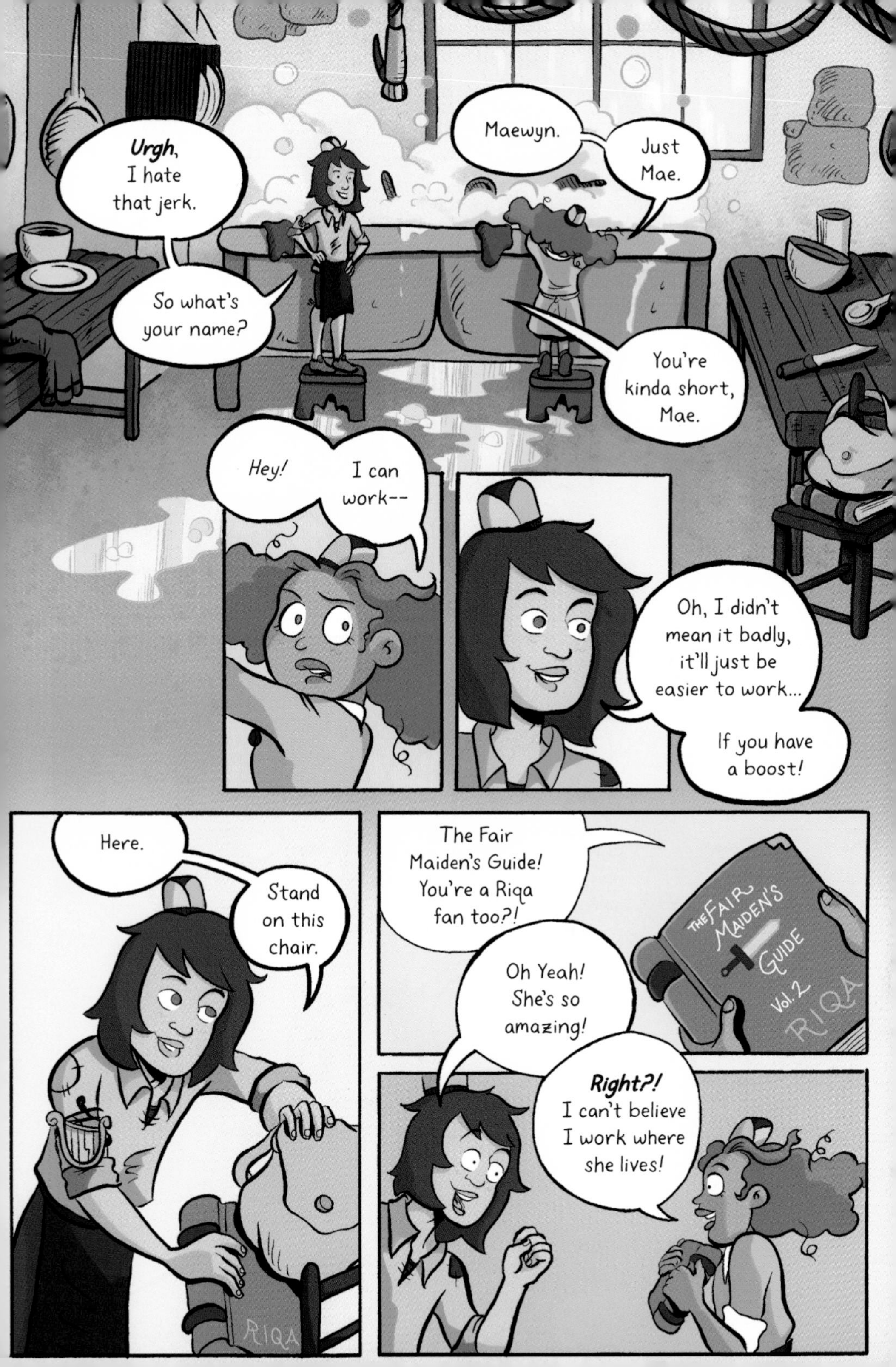

Urgh, I hate that jerk.
So what's your name?
Maewyn.
Just Mae.
You're kinda short, Mae.
Hey!
I can work--
Oh, I didn't mean it badly, it'll just be easier to work...
If you have a boost!
Here.
Stand on this chair.
The Fair Maiden's Guide! You're a Riqa fan too?!
THE FAIR MAIDEN'S GUIDE Vol. 2 RIQA
Oh Yeah! She's so amazing!
Right?! I can't believe I work where she lives!
RIQA

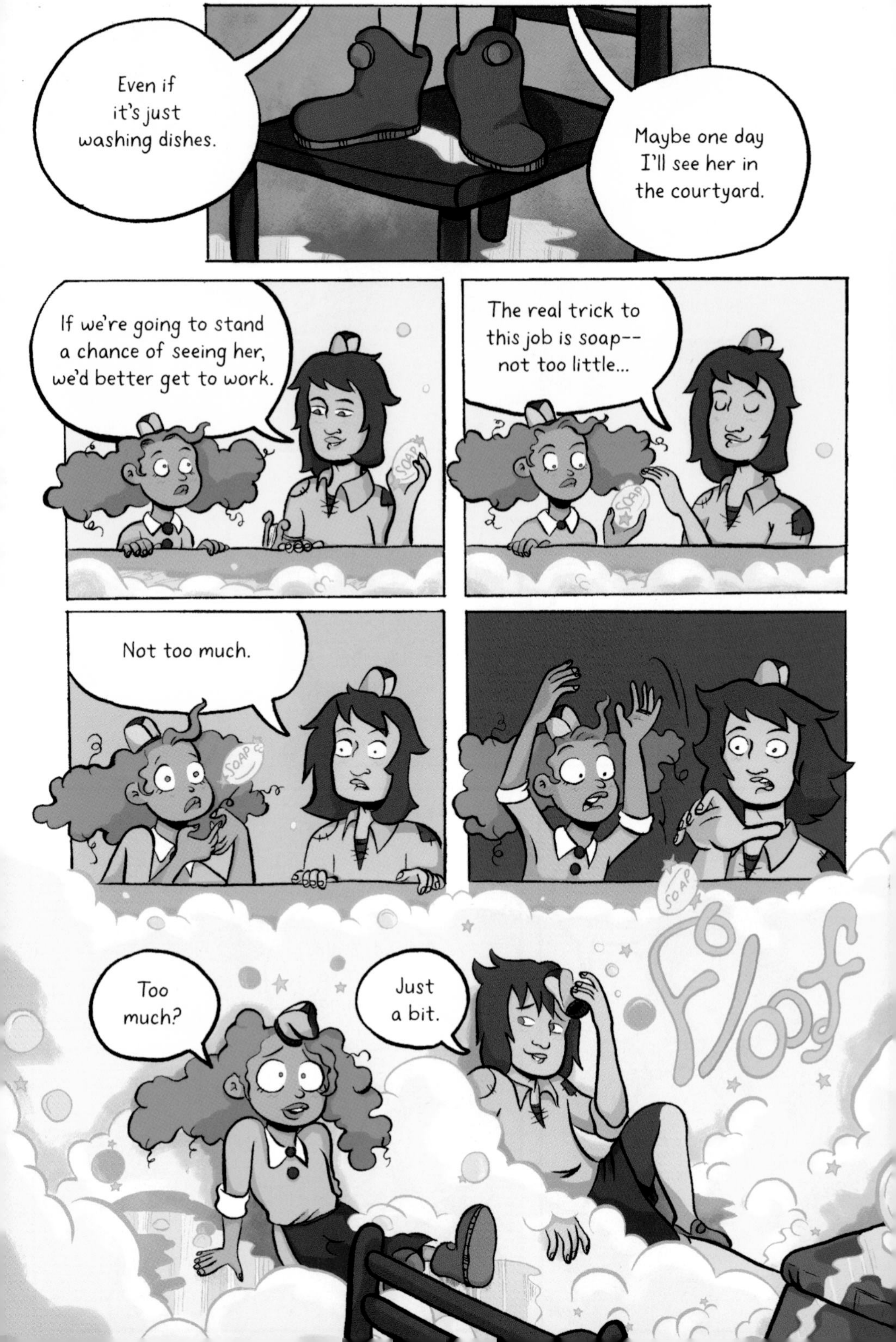
Even if it's just washing dishes.
Maybe one day I'll see her in the courtyard.
If we're going to stand a chance of seeing her, we'd better get to work.
SOAP
The real trick to this job is soap-- not too little...
SOAP
Not too much.
SOAP
SOAP
Floof
Too much?
Just a bit.

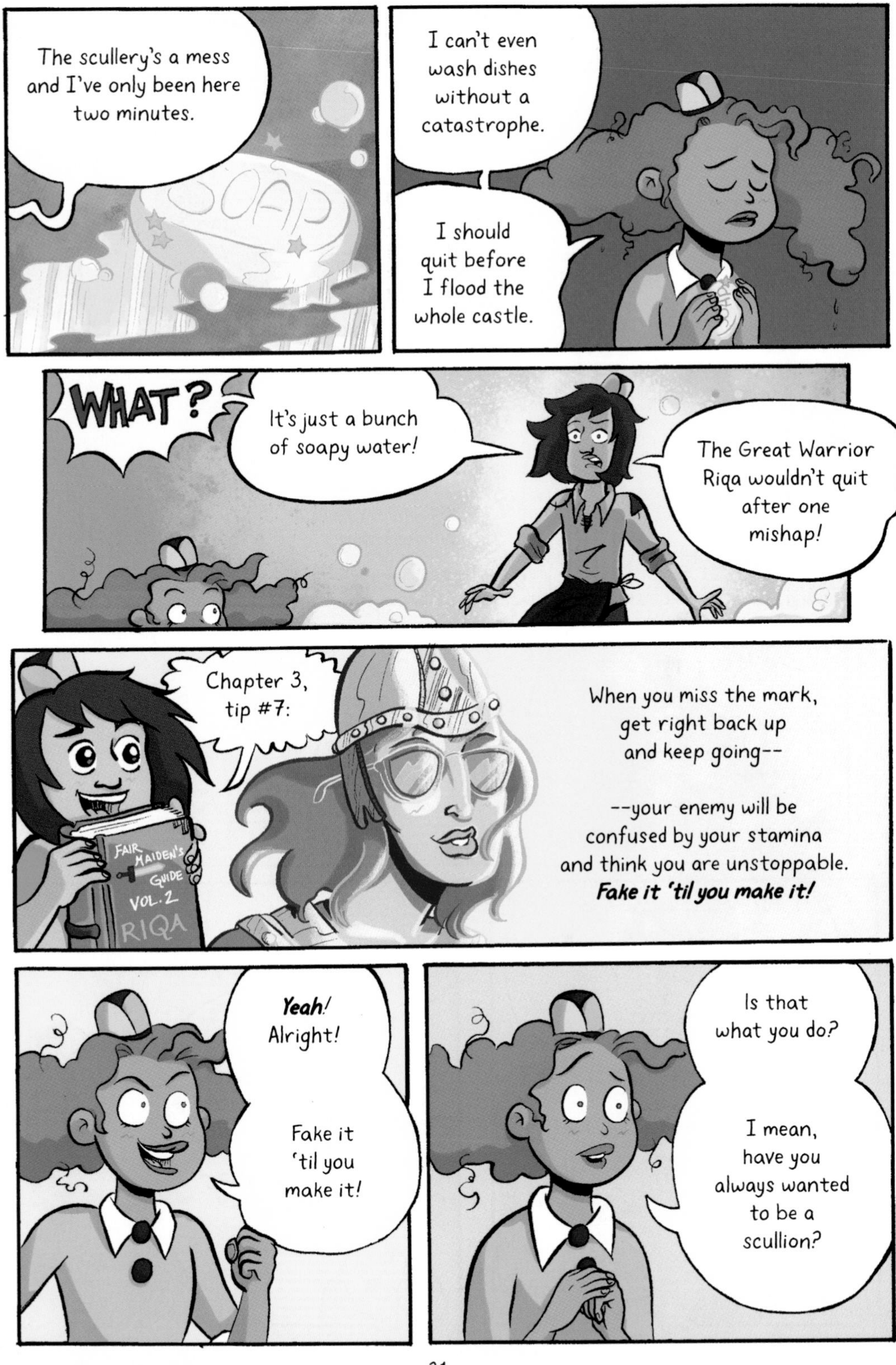

The scullery's a mess and I've only been here two minutes.
SOAP
I can't even wash dishes without a catastrophe.
I should quit before I flood the whole castle.
WHAT?
It's just a bunch of soapy water!
The Great Warrior Riqa wouldn't quit after one mishap!
Chapter 3, tip #7:
FAIR MAIDEN'S GUIDE VOL. 2 RIQA
When you miss the mark, get right back up and keep going--
--your enemy will be confused by your stamina and think you are unstoppable. ***Fake it 'til you make it!***
Yeah! Alright!
Fake it 'til you make it!
Is that what you do?
I mean, have you always wanted to be a scullion?

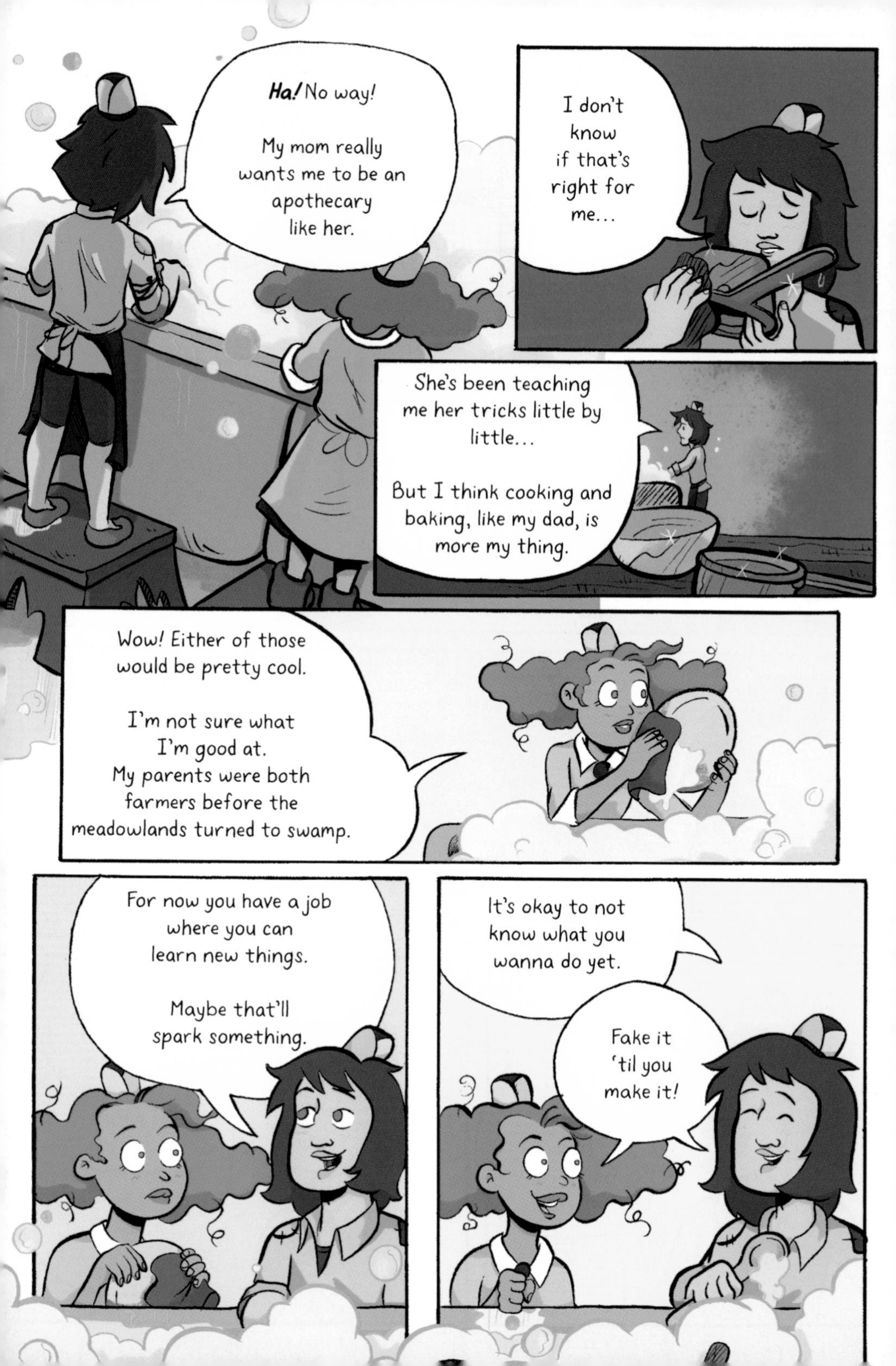
Ha! No way!
My mom really wants me to be an apothecary like her.
I don't know if that's right for me...
She's been teaching me her tricks little by little...
But I think cooking and baking, like my dad, is more my thing.
Wow! Either of those would be pretty cool.
I'm not sure what I'm good at.
My parents were both farmers before the meadowlands turned to swamp.
For now you have a job where you can learn new things.
Maybe that'll spark something.
It's okay to not know what you wanna do yet.
Fake it 'til you make it!

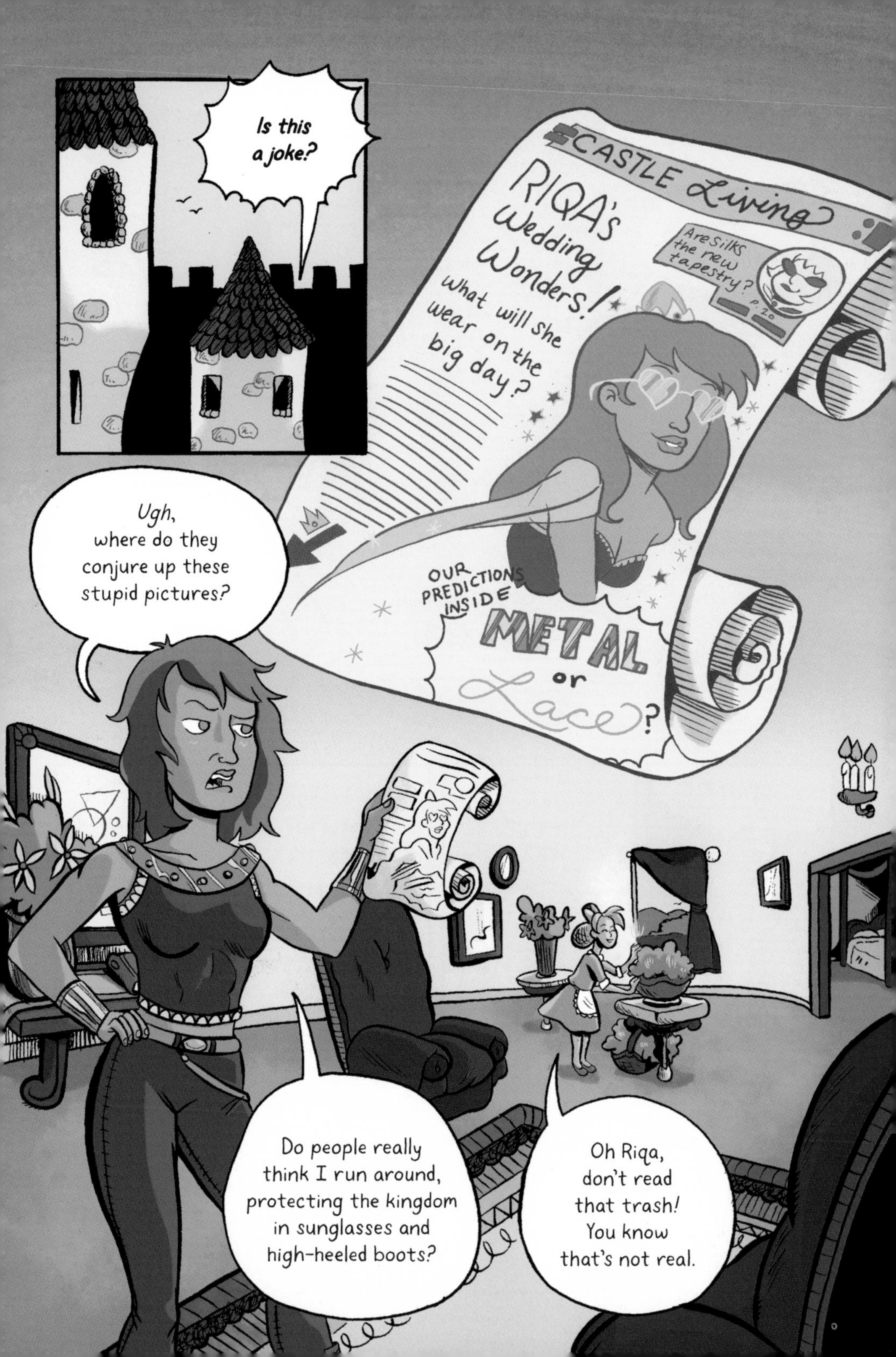
Is this a joke?
CASTLE Living
RIQA's Wedding Wonders!
what will she wear on the big day?
Are Silks the new tapestry?
p. 20
OUR PREDICTIONS INSIDE
METAL or Lace?
Ugh, where do they conjure up these stupid pictures?
Do people really think I run around, protecting the kingdom in sunglasses and high-heeled boots?
Oh Riqa, don't read that trash! You know that's not real.

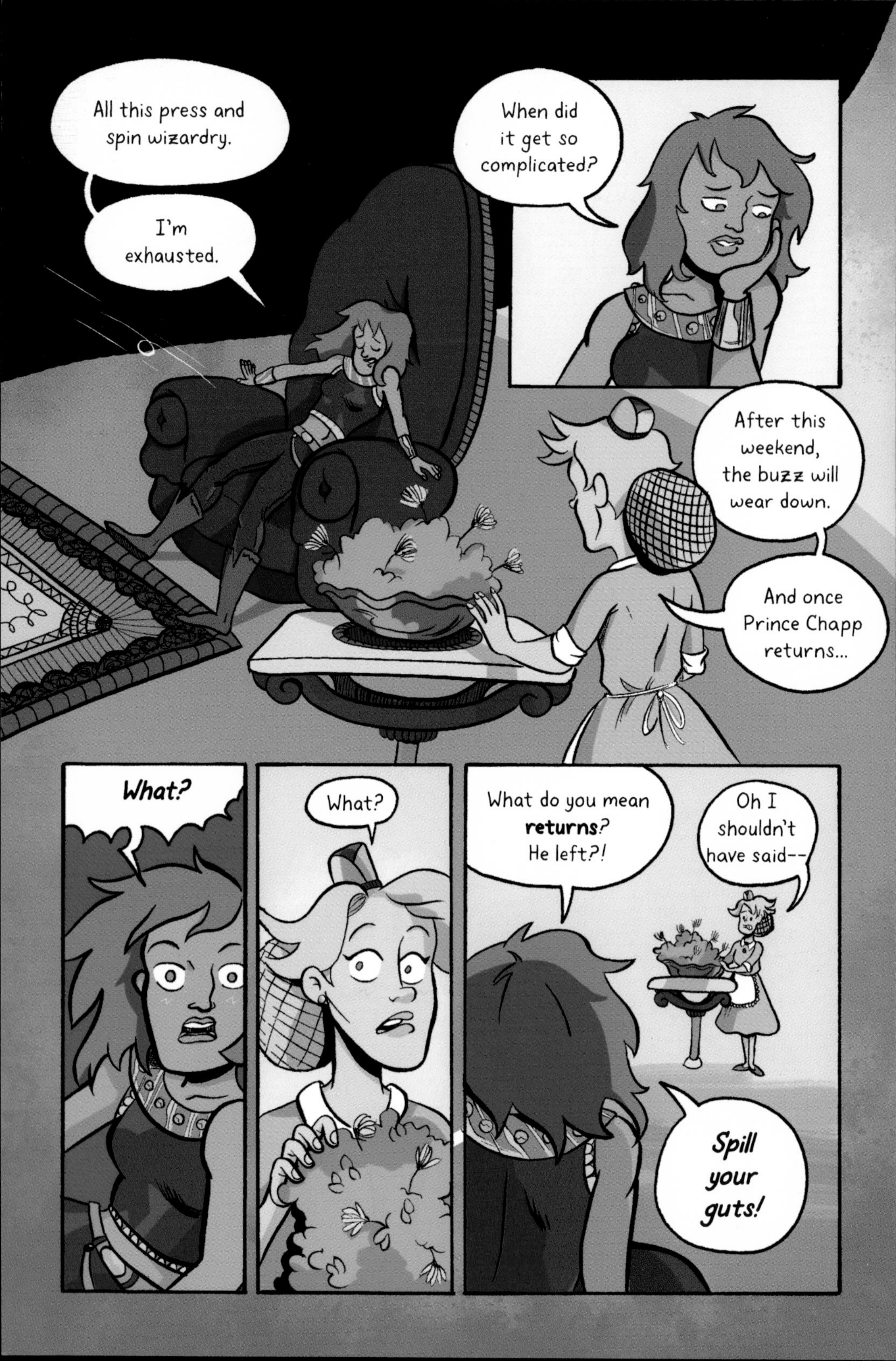
All this press and spin wizardry.
I'm exhausted.
When did it get so complicated?
After this weekend, the buzz will wear down.
And once Prince Chapp returns...
What?
What?
What do you mean **returns**? He left?!
Oh I shouldn't have said--
Spill your guts!

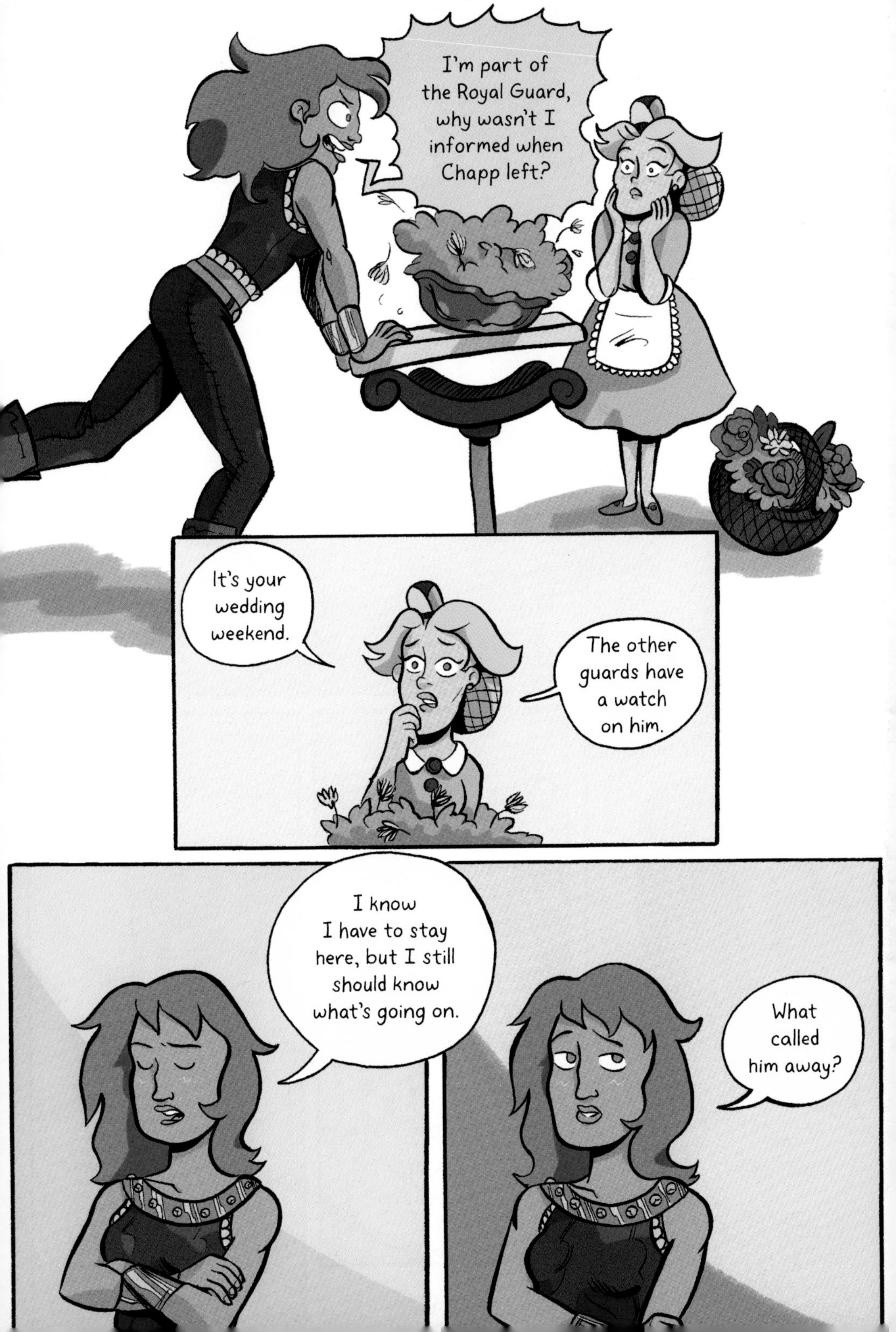
I'm part of the Royal Guard, why wasn't I informed when Chapp left?
It's your wedding weekend.
The other guards have a watch on him.
I know I have to stay here, but I still should know what's going on.
What called him away?

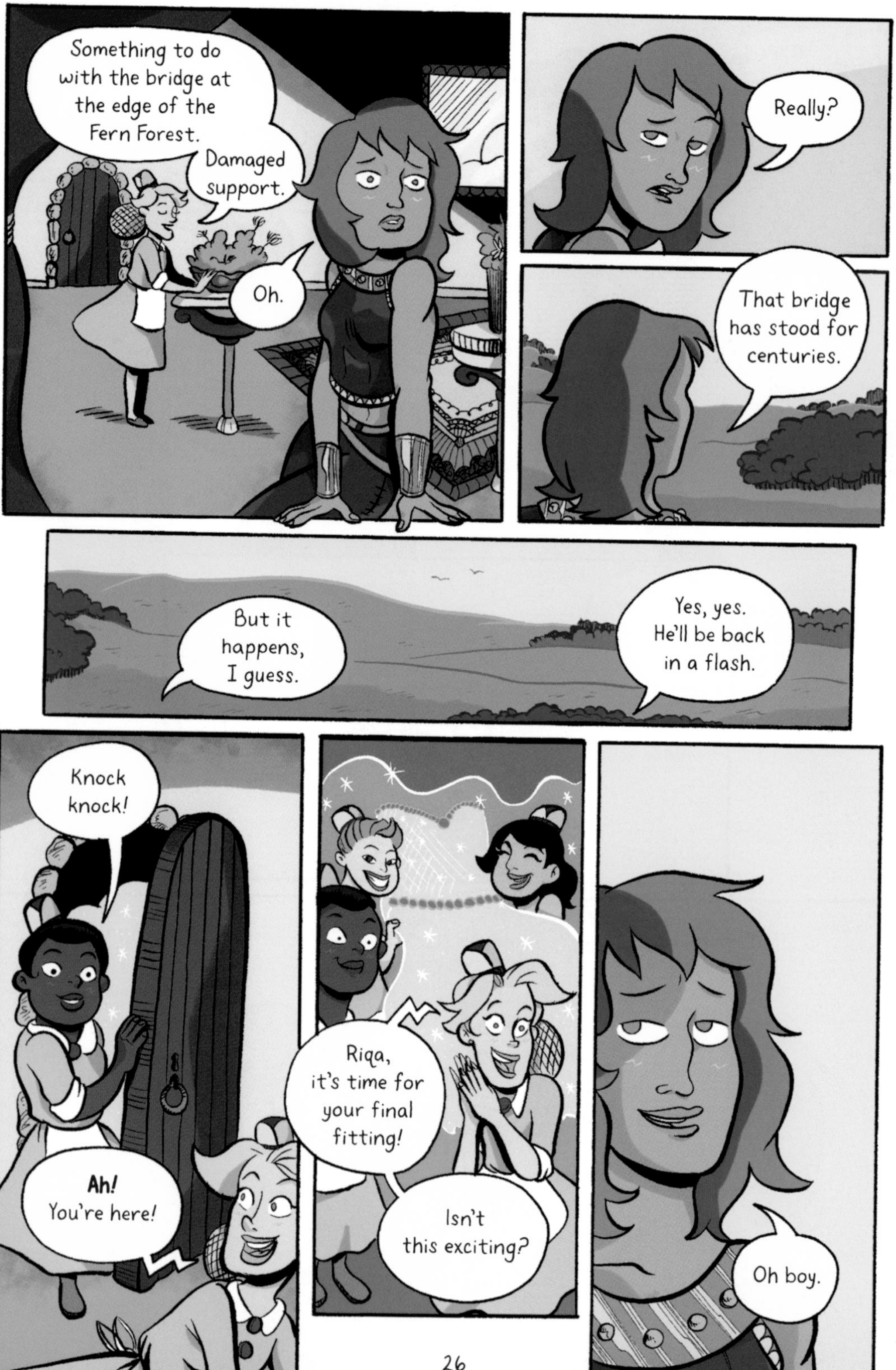
Something to do with the bridge at the edge of the Fern Forest.
Damaged support.
Oh.
Really?
That bridge has stood for centuries.
But it happens, I guess.
Yes, yes. He'll be back in a flash.
Knock knock!
Ah! You're here!
Riqa, it's time for your final fitting!
Isn't this exciting?
Oh boy.

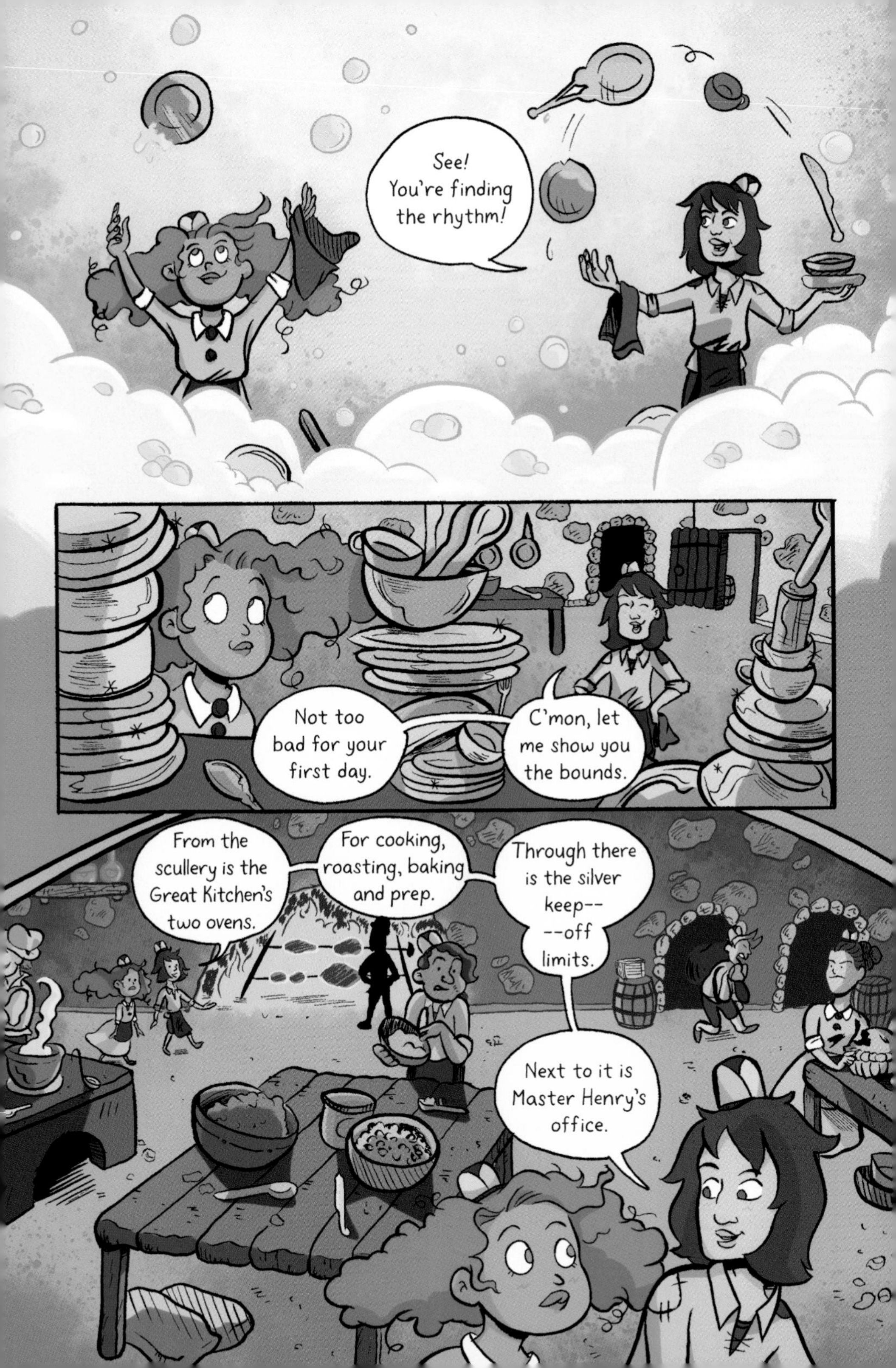

See! You're finding the rhythm!
Not too bad for your first day.
C'mon, let me show you the bounds.
From the scullery is the Great Kitchen's two ovens.
For cooking, roasting, baking and prep.
Through there is the silver keep--
--off limits.
Next to it is Master Henry's office.

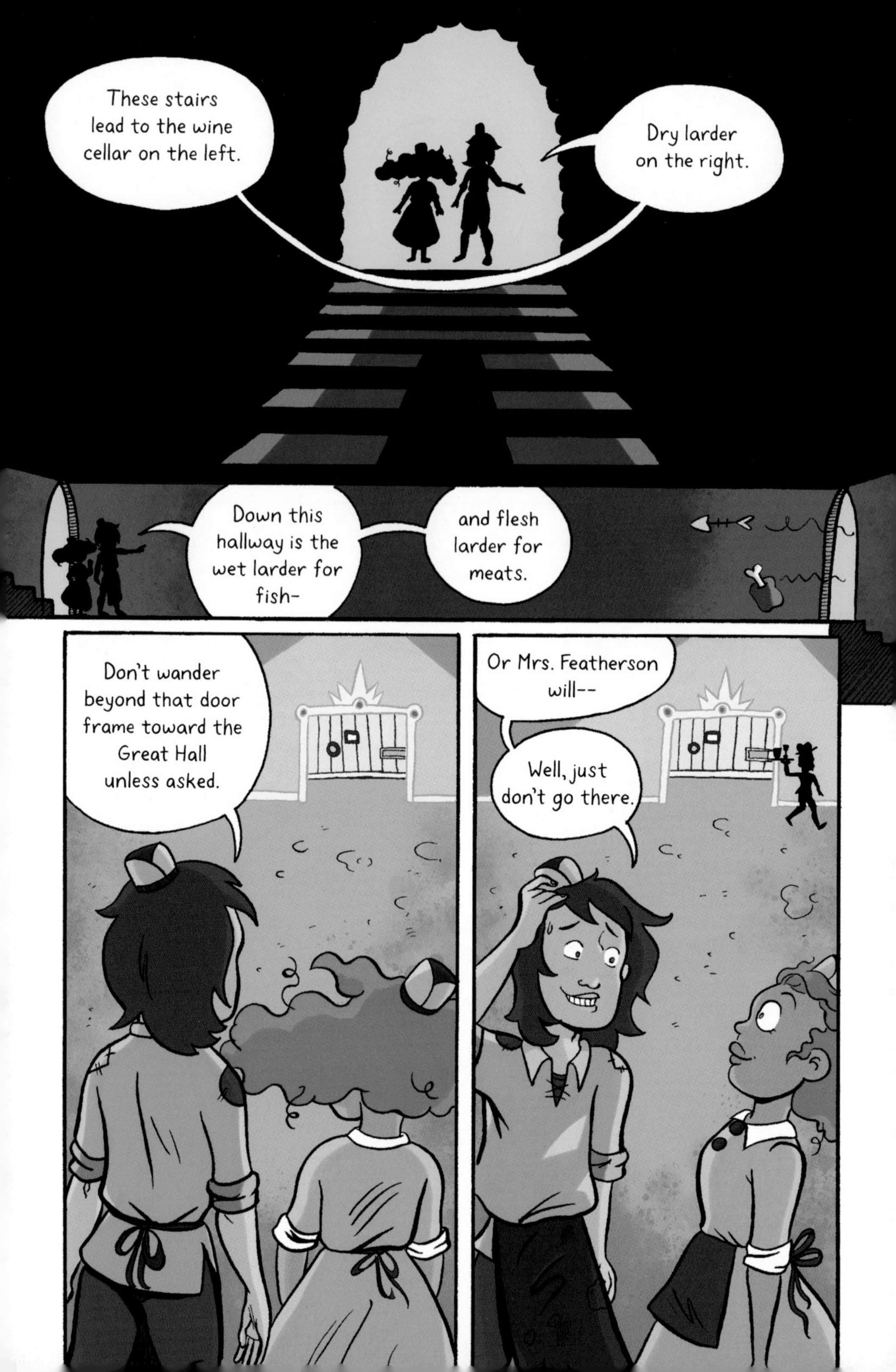
These stairs lead to the wine cellar on the left.
Dry larder on the right.
Down this hallway is the wet larder for fish-
and flesh larder for meats.
Don't wander beyond that door frame toward the Great Hall unless asked.
Or Mrs. Featherson will--
Well, just don't go there.

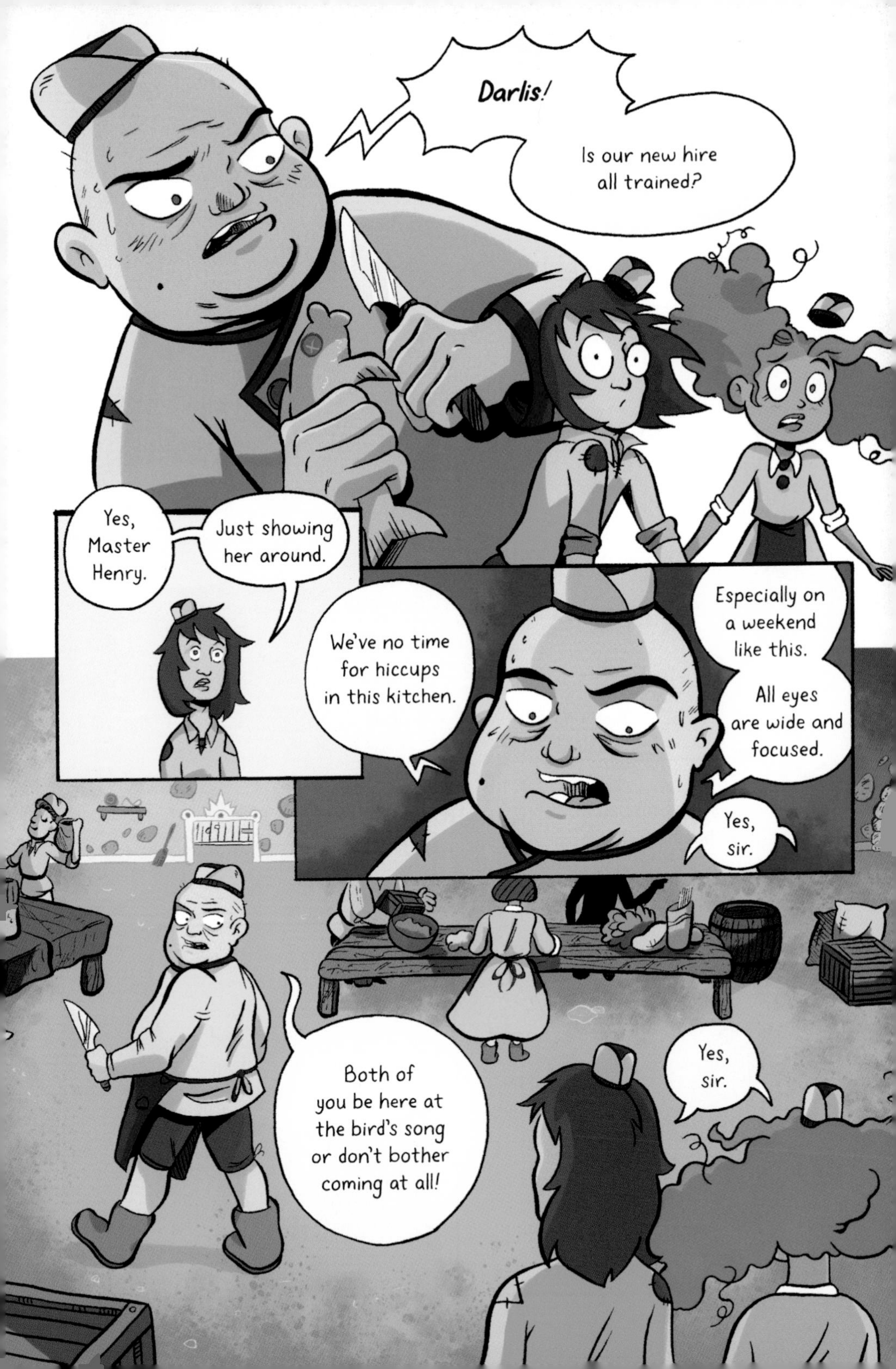
Darlis!
Is our new hire all trained?
Yes, Master Henry.
Just showing her around.
We've no time for hiccups in this kitchen.
Especially on a weekend like this.
All eyes are wide and focused.
Yes, sir.
Both of you be here at the bird's song or don't bother coming at all!
Yes, sir.

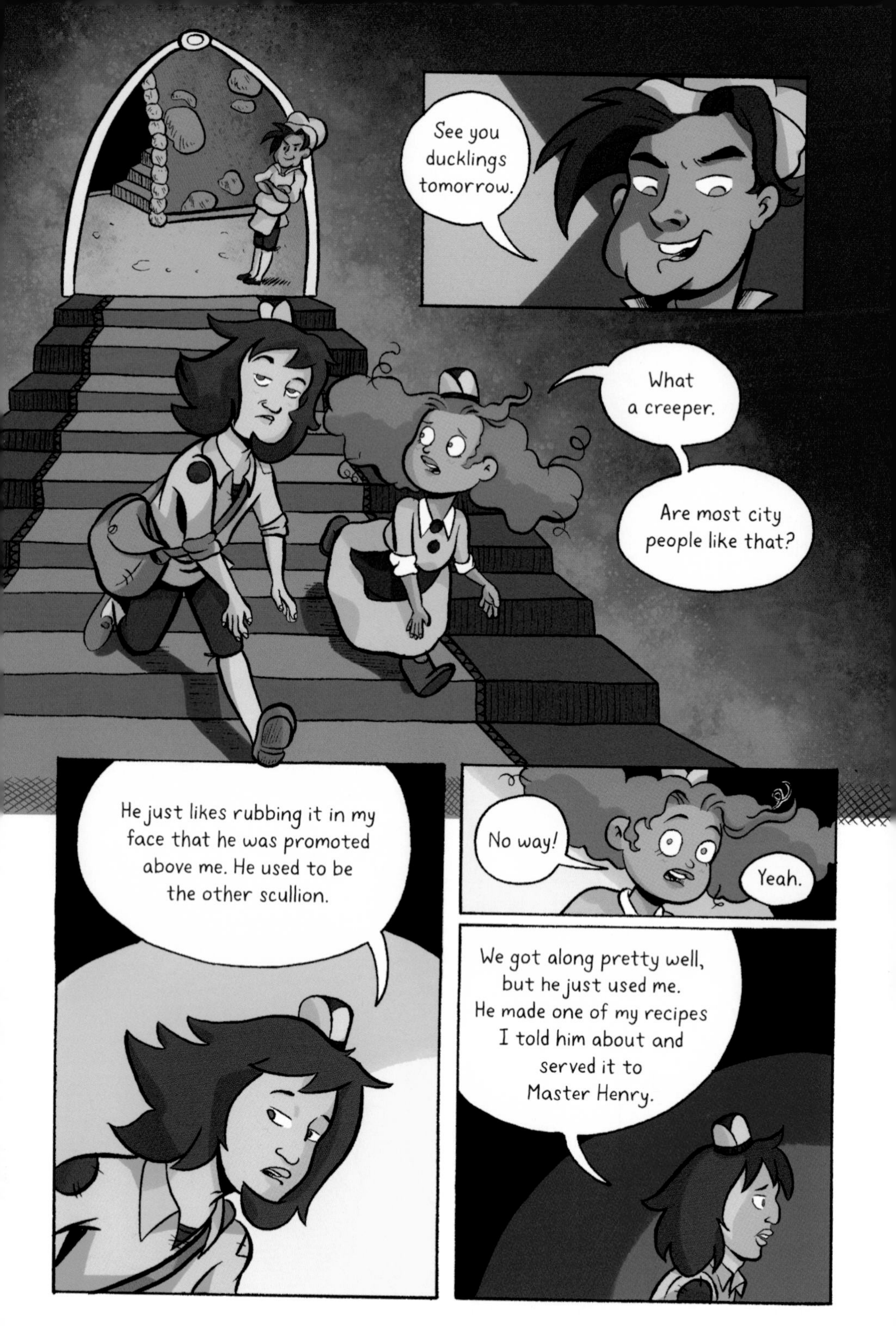
See you ducklings tomorrow.
What a creeper.
Are most city people like that?
He just likes rubbing it in my face that he was promoted above me. He used to be the other scullion.
No way!
Yeah.
We got along pretty well, but he just used me. He made one of my recipes I told him about and served it to Master Henry.

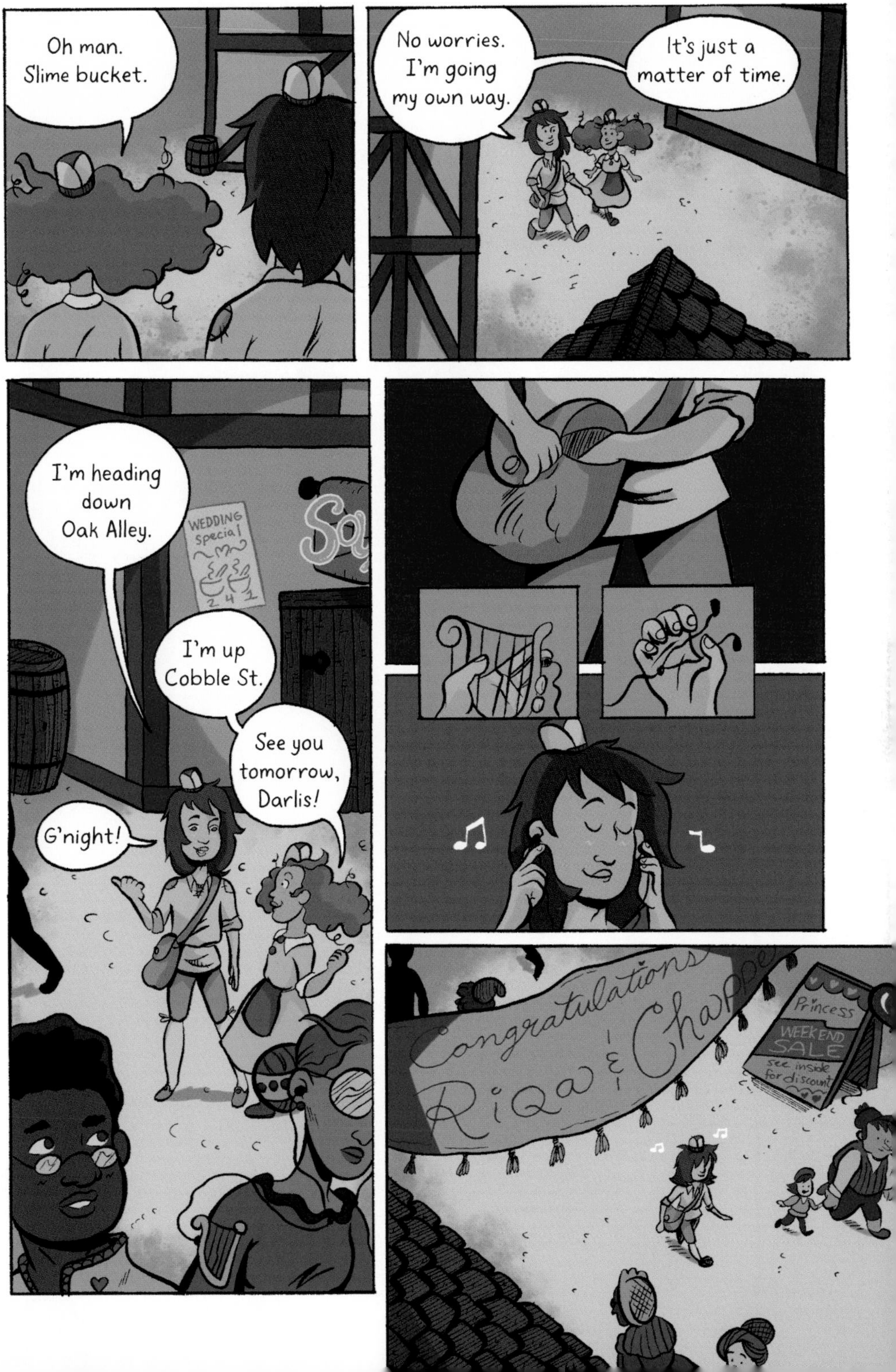
Oh man. Slime bucket.
No worries. I'm going my own way.
It's just a matter of time.
I'm heading down Oak Alley.
WEDDING Special
2 4 1
I'm up Cobble St.
See you tomorrow, Darlis!
G'night!
Congratulations
Riqa & Chappe
Princess
WEEKEND SALE
see inside for discount

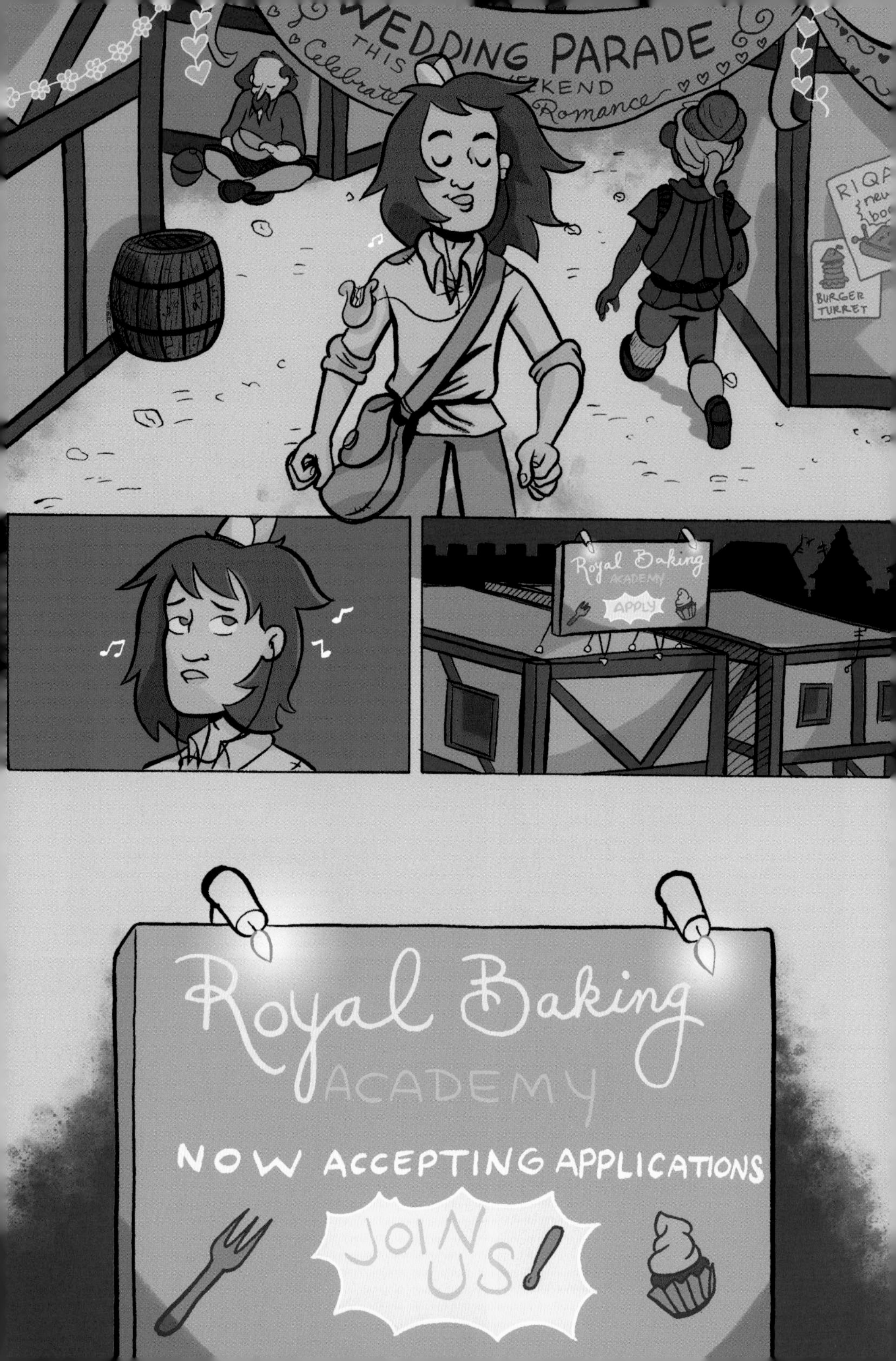
WEDDING PARADE
THIS
Celebrate
Romance
BURGER TURRET
Royal Baking ACADEMY
APPLY
Royal Baking
ACADEMY
NOW ACCEPTING APPLICATIONS
JOIN US!

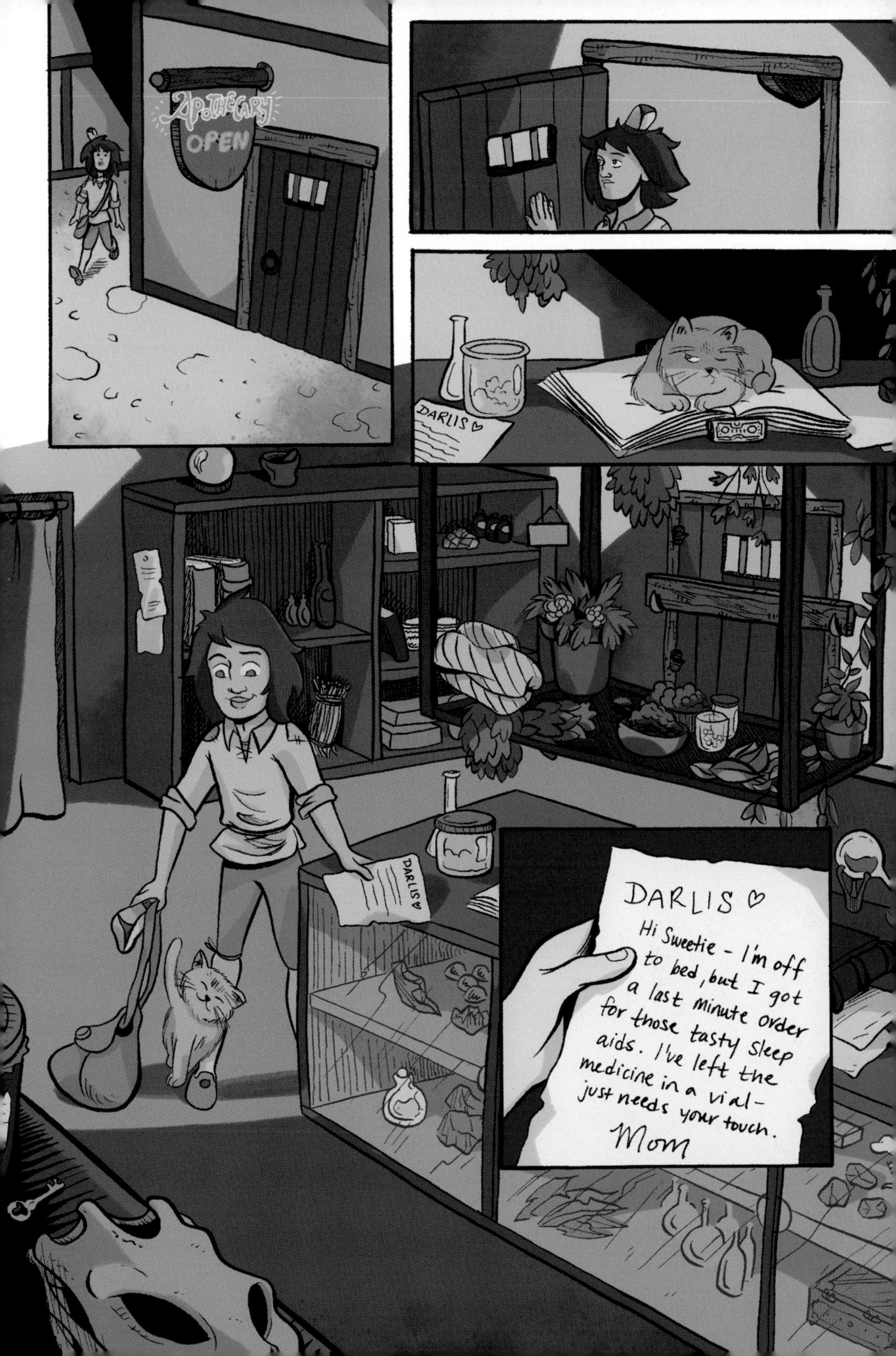
APOTHECARY
OPEN
DARLIS ♡
DARLIS
DARLIS ♡
Hi Sweetie - I'm off to bed, but I got a last minute order for those tasty sleep aids. I've left the medicine in a vial- just needs your touch.
Mom

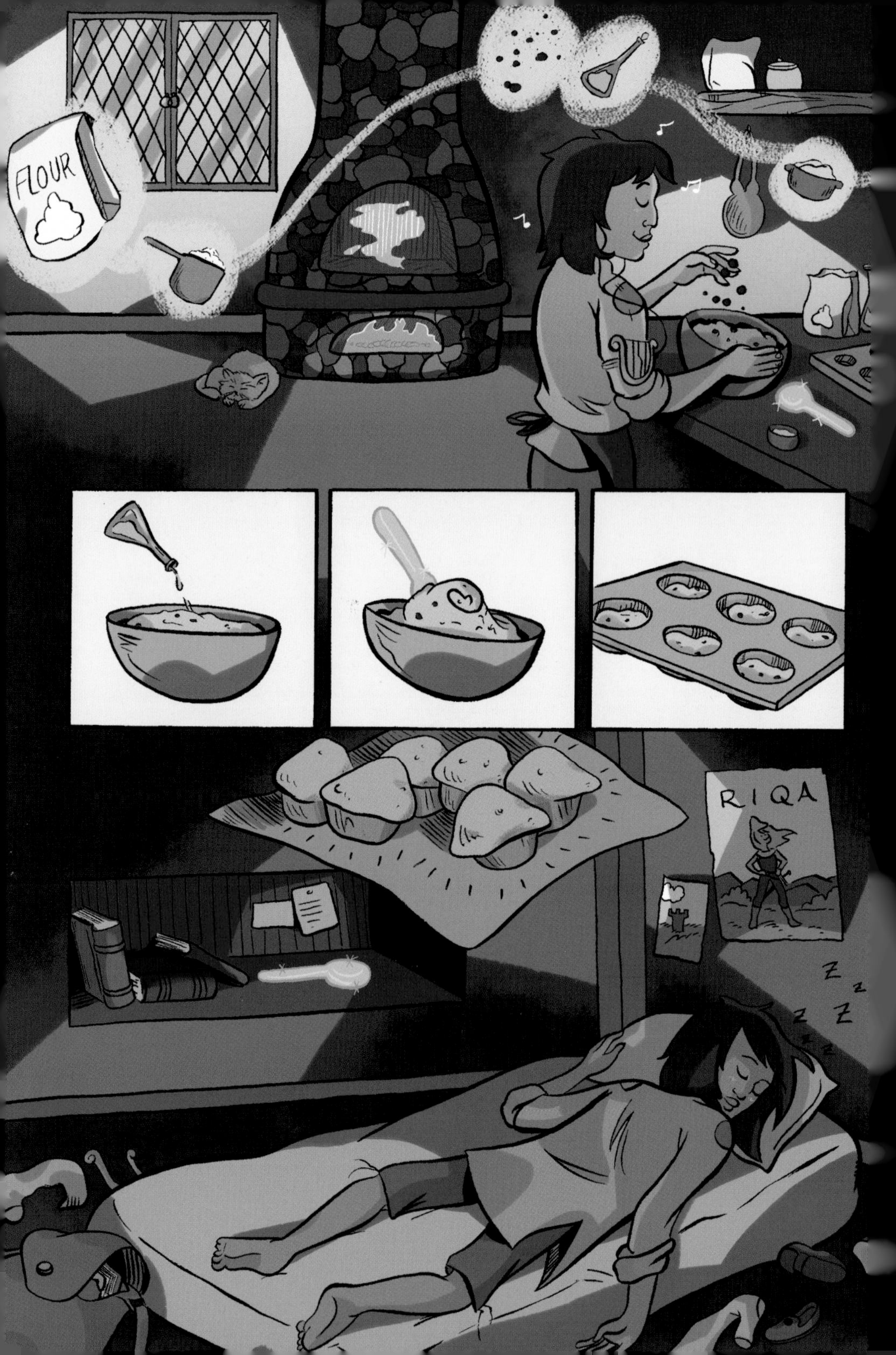
FLOUR
RIQA
Z Z Z Z

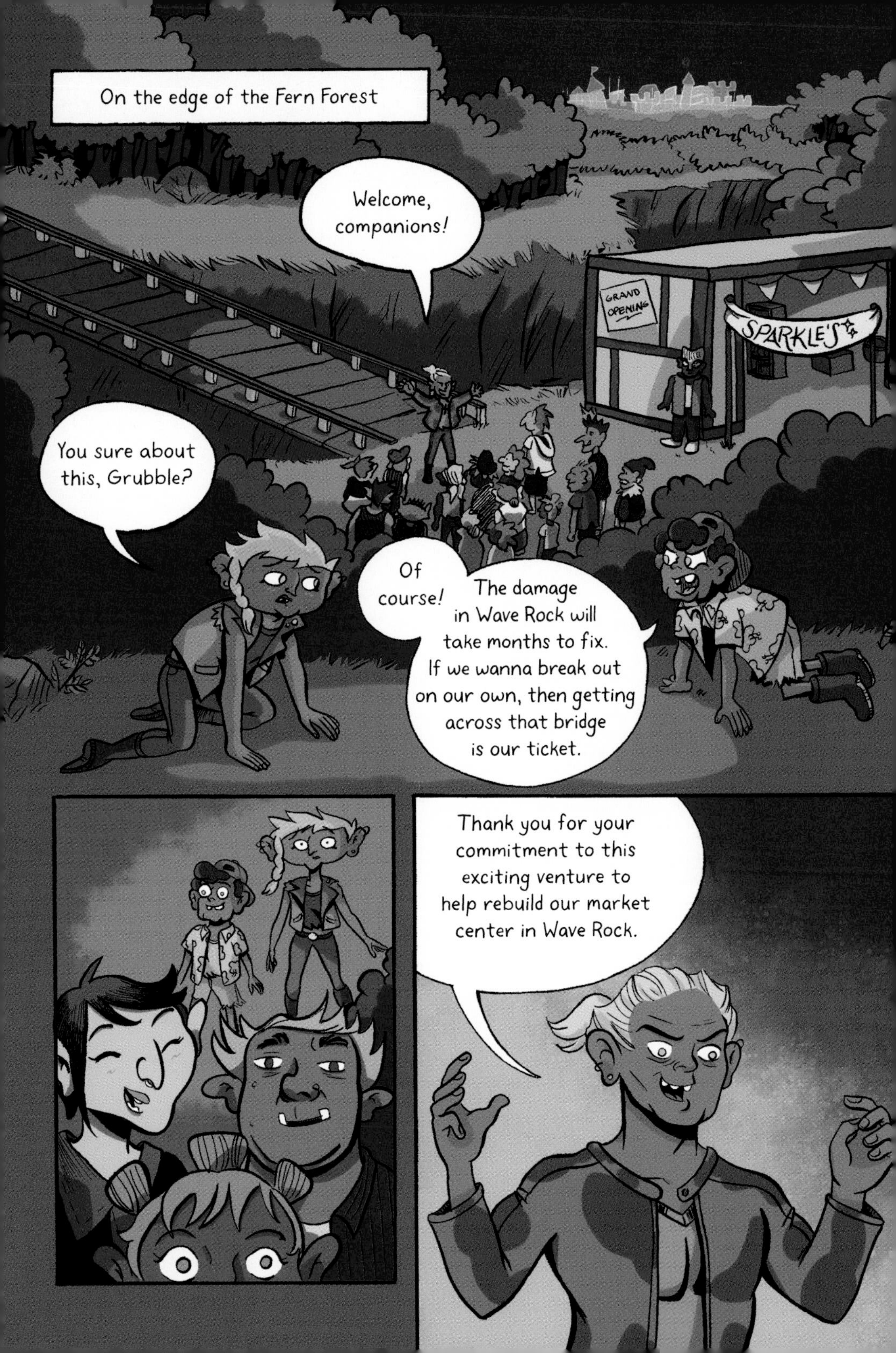
On the edge of the Fern Forest
Welcome, companions!
GRAND OPENING
SPARKLE'S
You sure about this, Grubble?
Of course!
The damage in Wave Rock will take months to fix. If we wanna break out on our own, then getting across that bridge is our ticket.
Thank you for your commitment to this exciting venture to help rebuild our market center in Wave Rock.

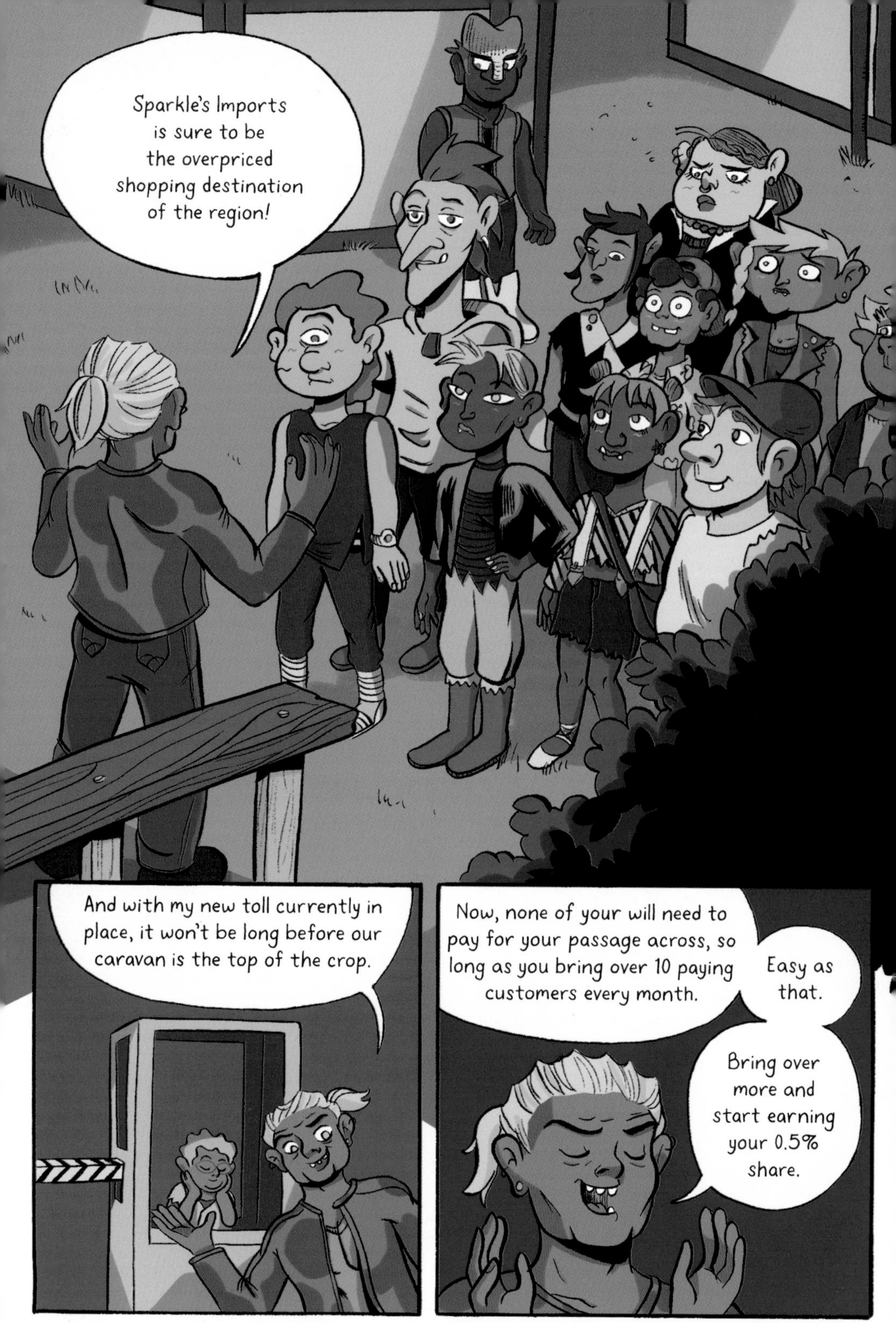
Sparkle's Imports is sure to be the overpriced shopping destination of the region!
And with my new toll currently in place, it won't be long before our caravan is the top of the crop.
Now, none of your will need to pay for your passage across, so long as you bring over 10 paying customers every month.
Easy as that.
Bring over more and start earning your 0.5% share.

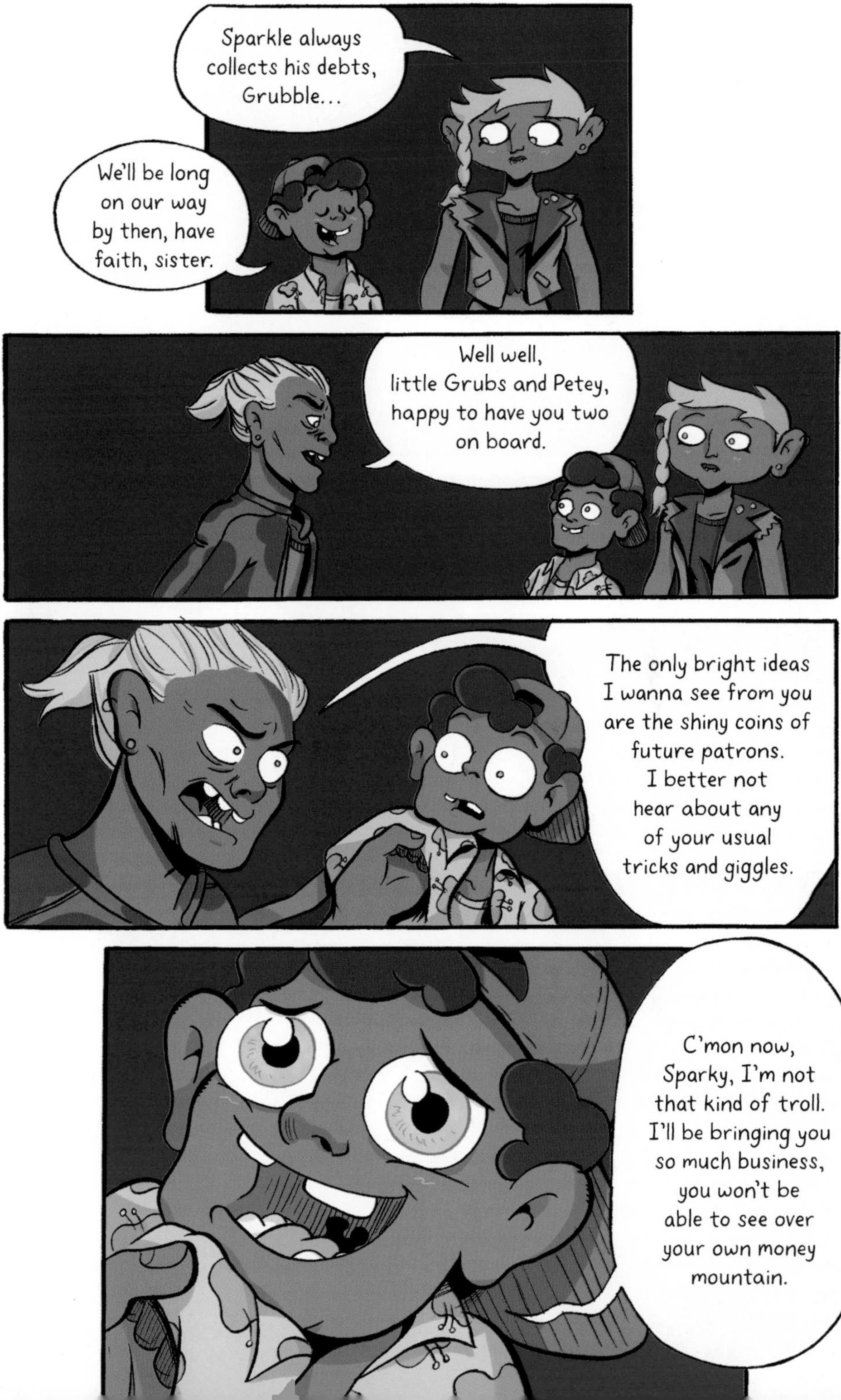
Sparkle always collects his debts, Grubble...
We'll be long on our way by then, have faith, sister.
Well well, little Grubs and Petey, happy to have you two on board.
The only bright ideas I wanna see from you are the shiny coins of future patrons. I better not hear about any of your usual tricks and giggles.
C'mon now, Sparky, I'm not that kind of troll. I'll be bringing you so much business, you won't be able to see over your own money mountain.

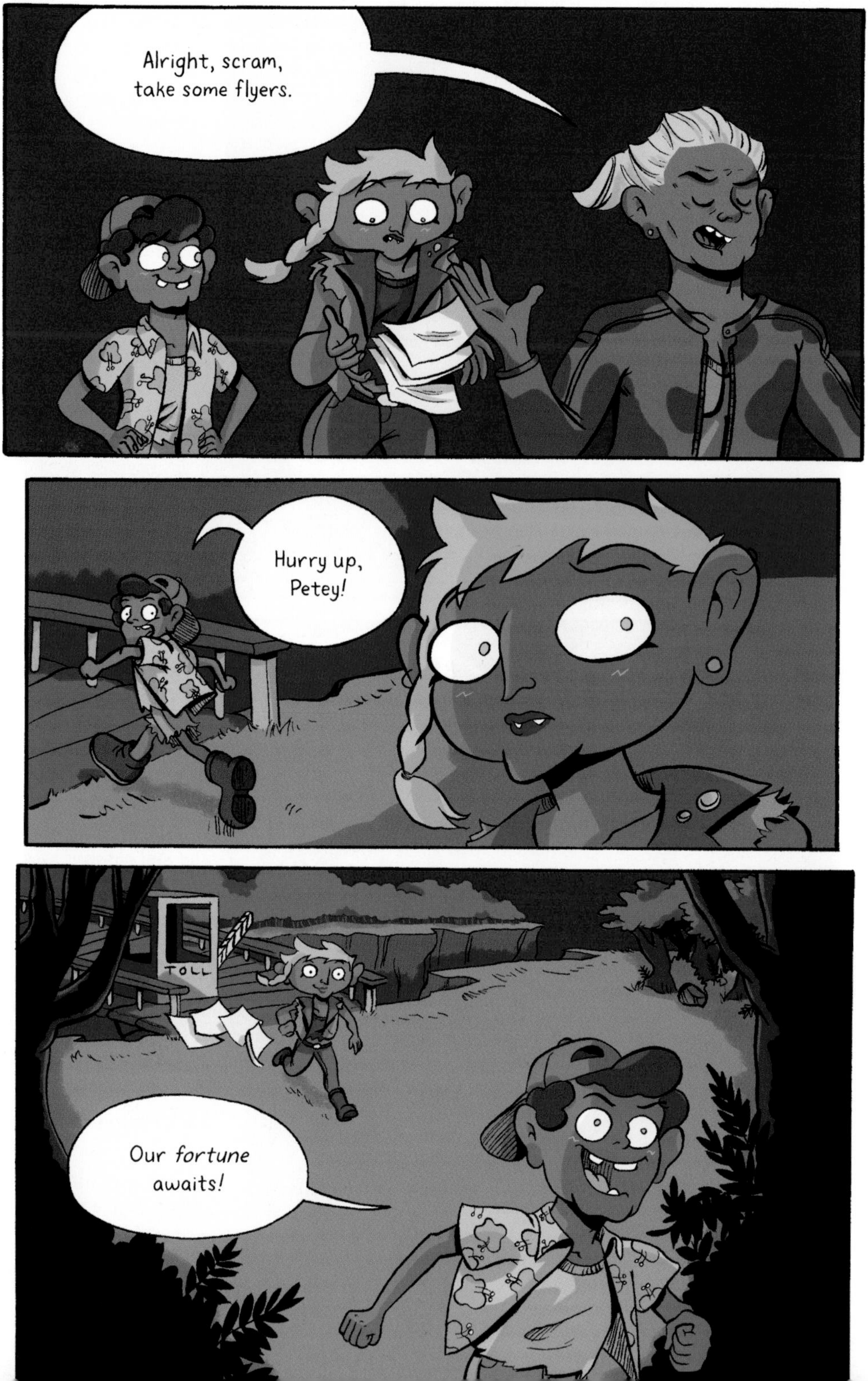
Alright, scram, take some flyers.
Hurry up, Petey!
TOLL
Our fortune awaits!

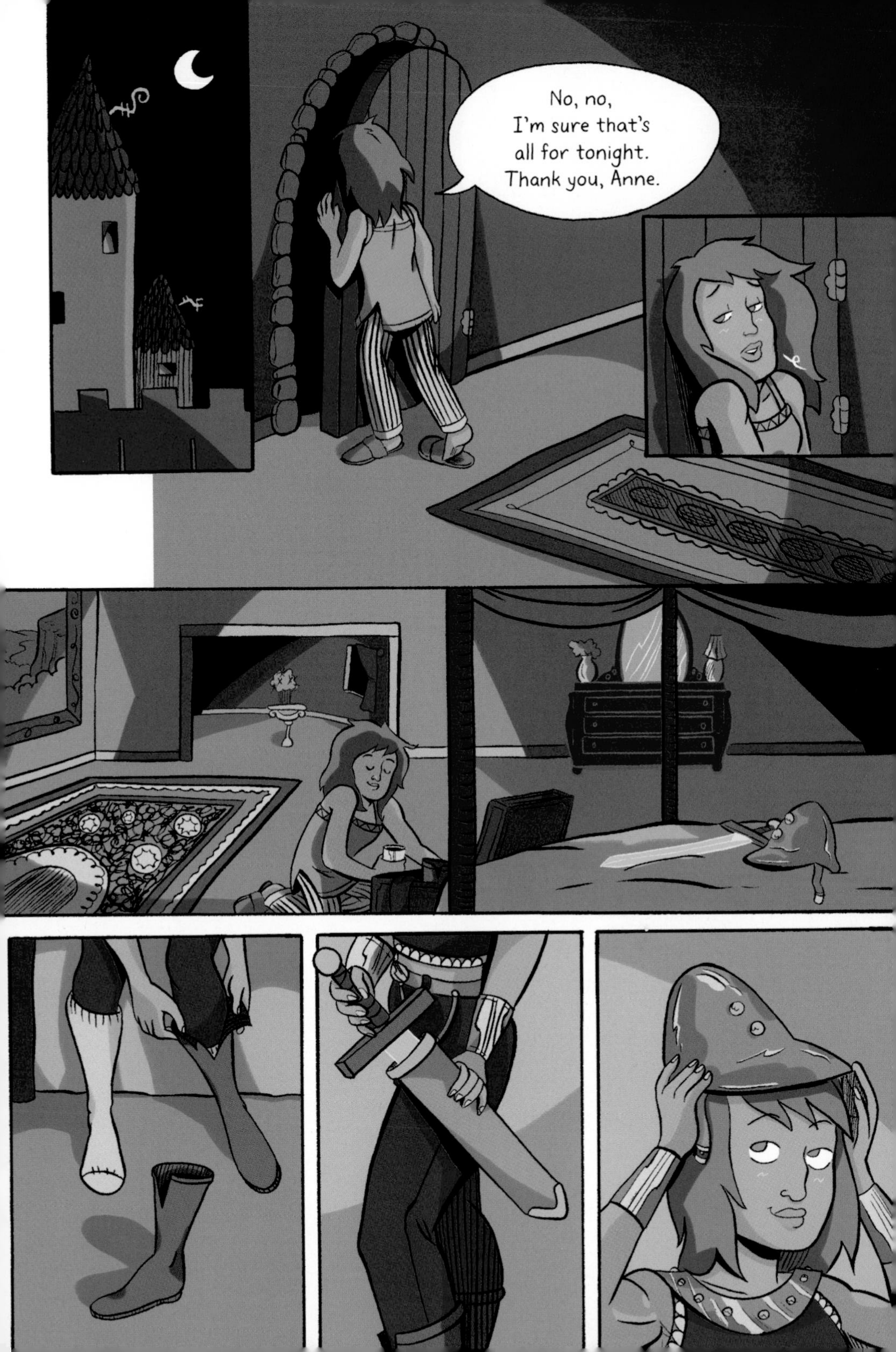
No, no,
I'm sure that's
all for tonight.
Thank you, Anne.

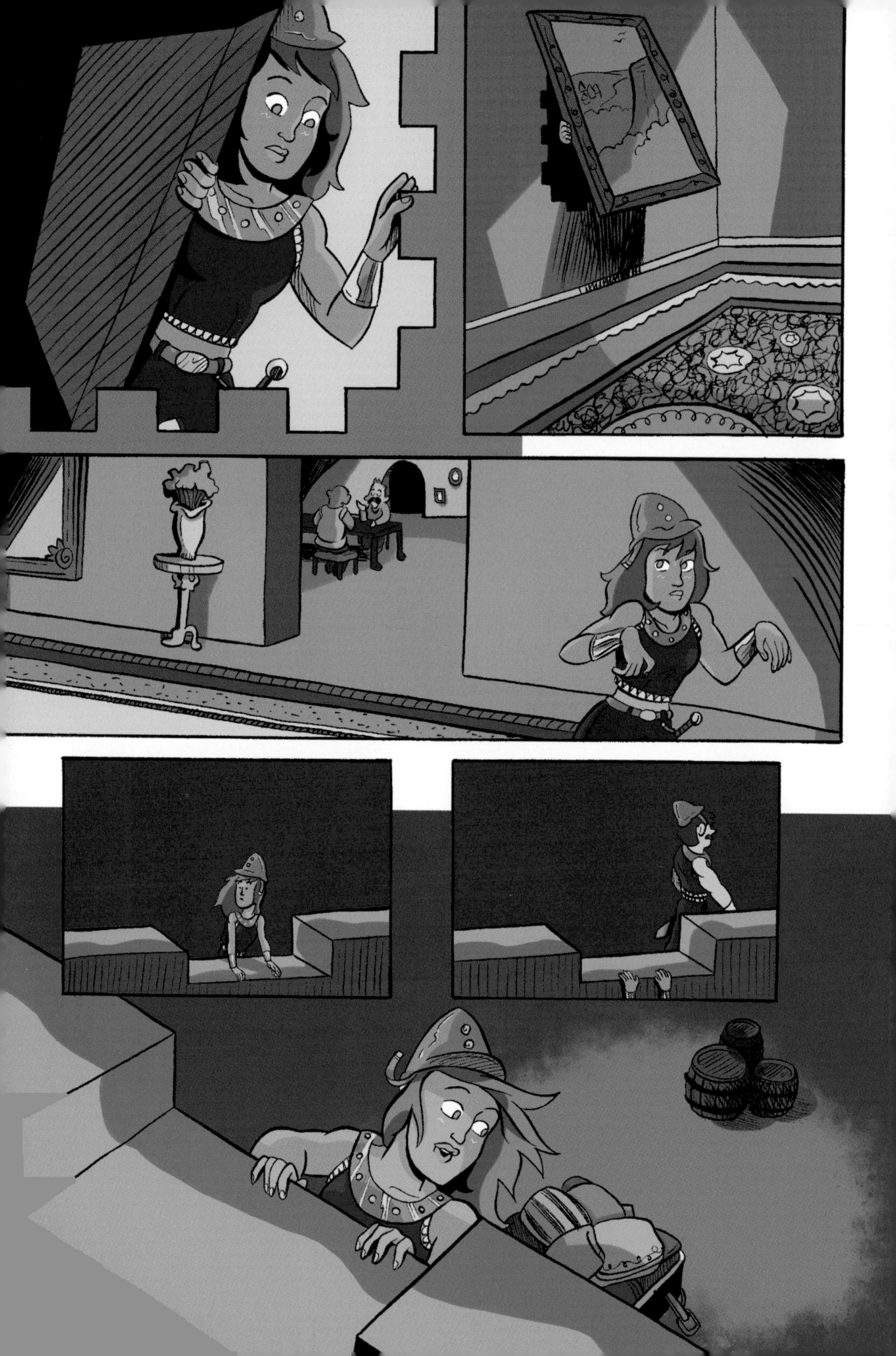

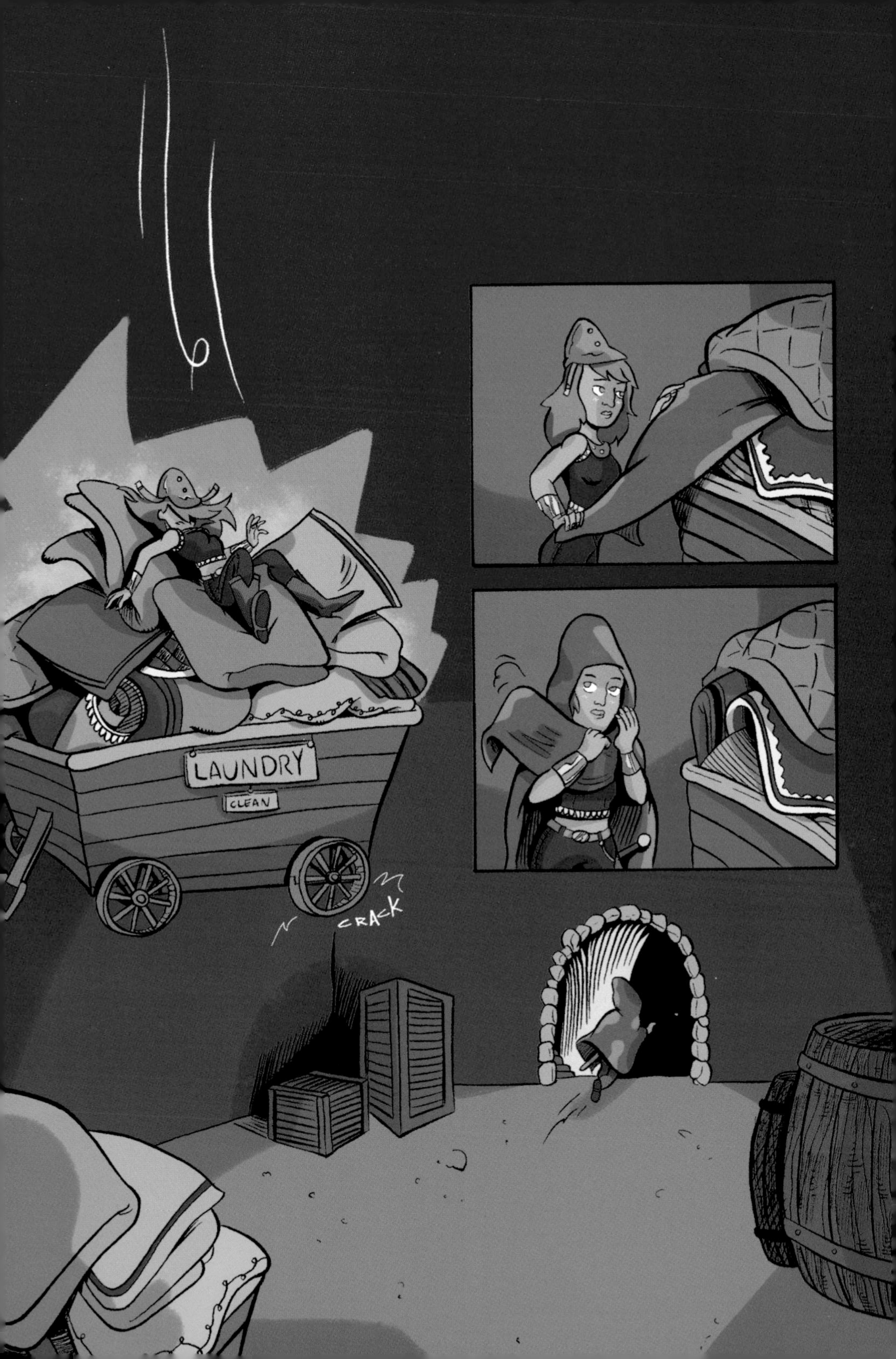

LAUNDRY
CLEAN
CRACK

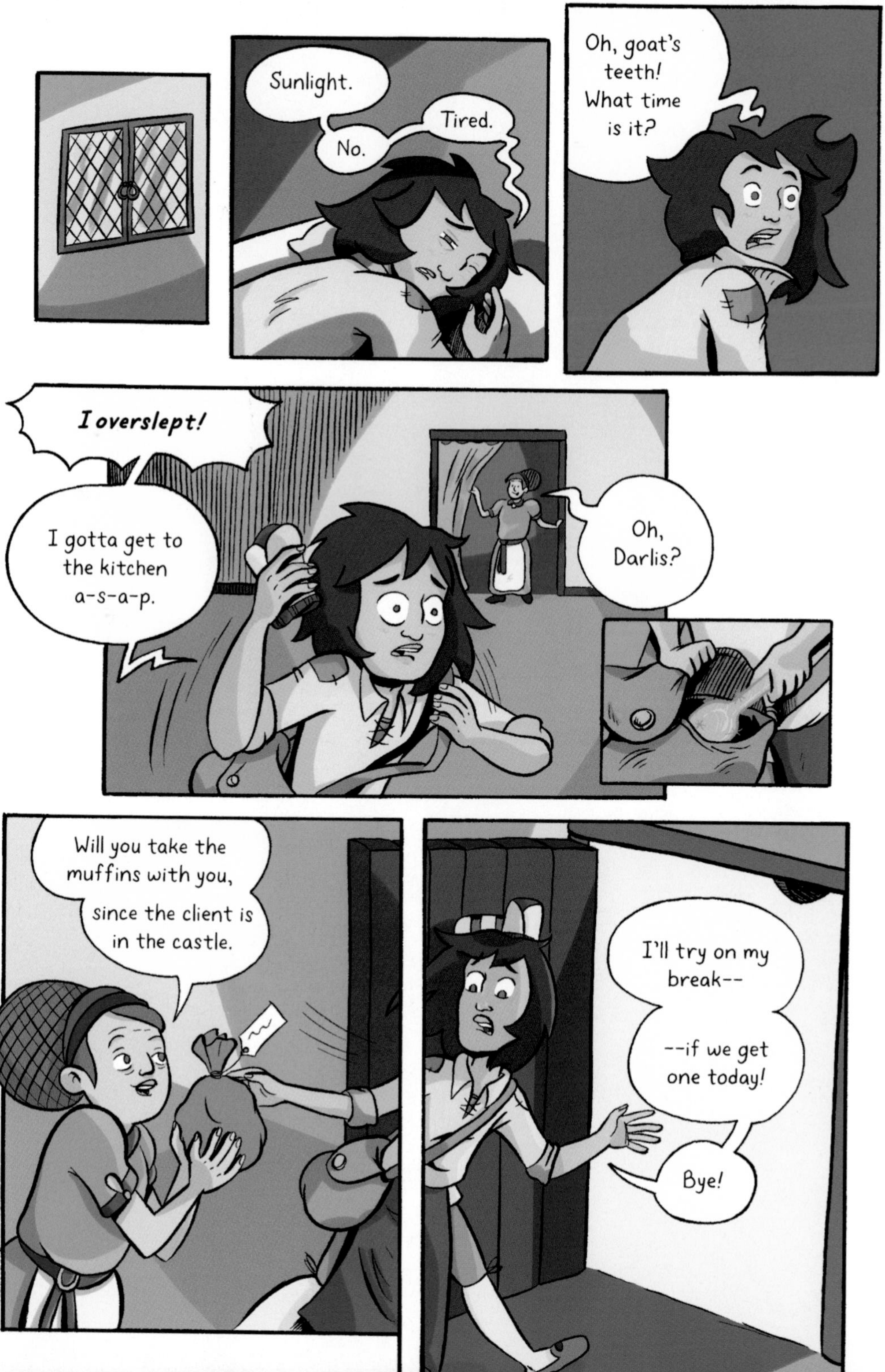
Sunlight.
No.
Tired.
Oh, goat's teeth! What time is it?
I overslept!
I gotta get to the kitchen a-s-a-p.
Oh, Darlis?
Will you take the muffins with you,
since the client is in the castle.
I'll try on my break--
--if we get one today!
Bye!

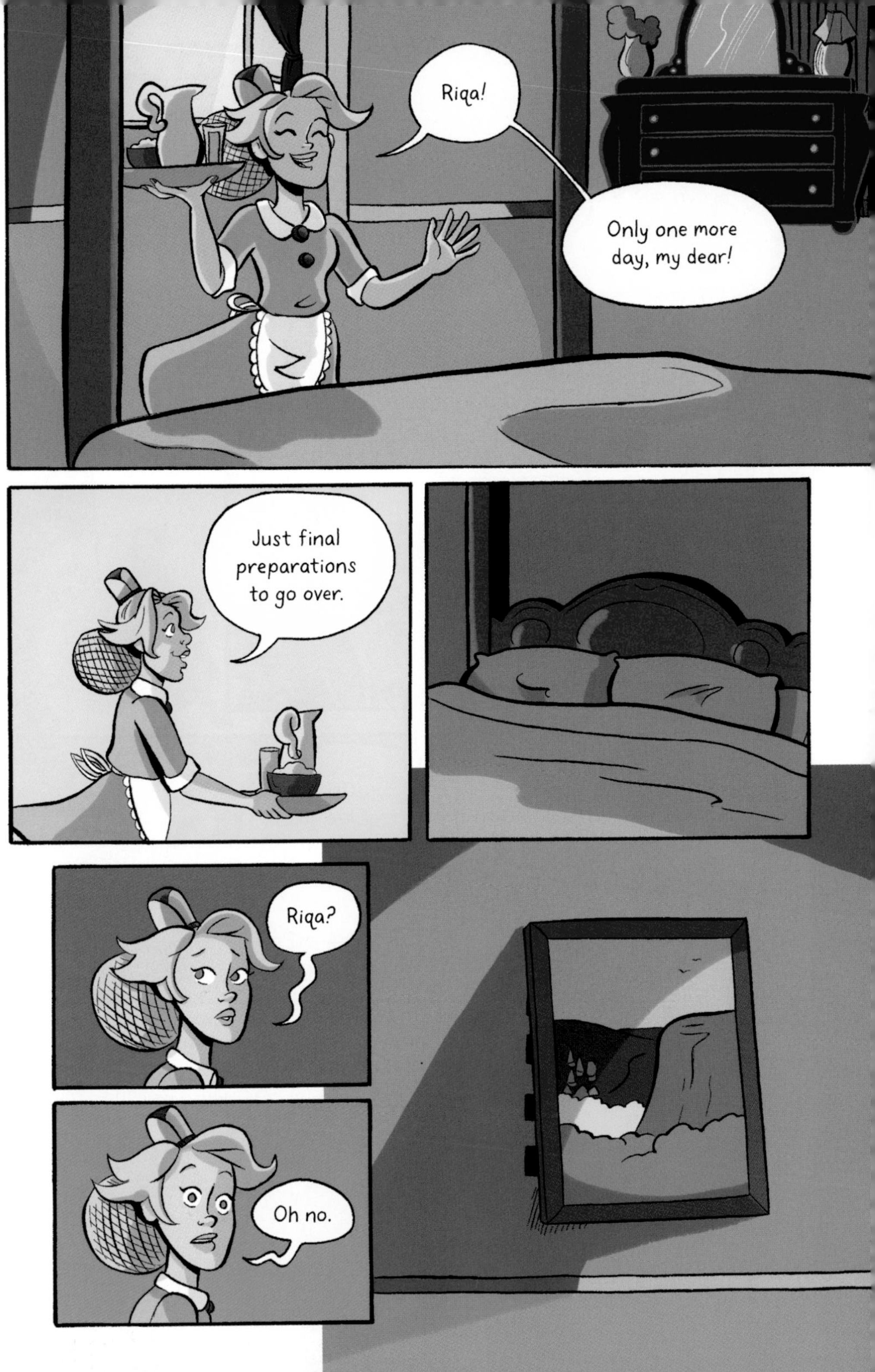
Riqa!
Only one more day, my dear!
Just final preparations to go over.
Riqa?
Oh no.

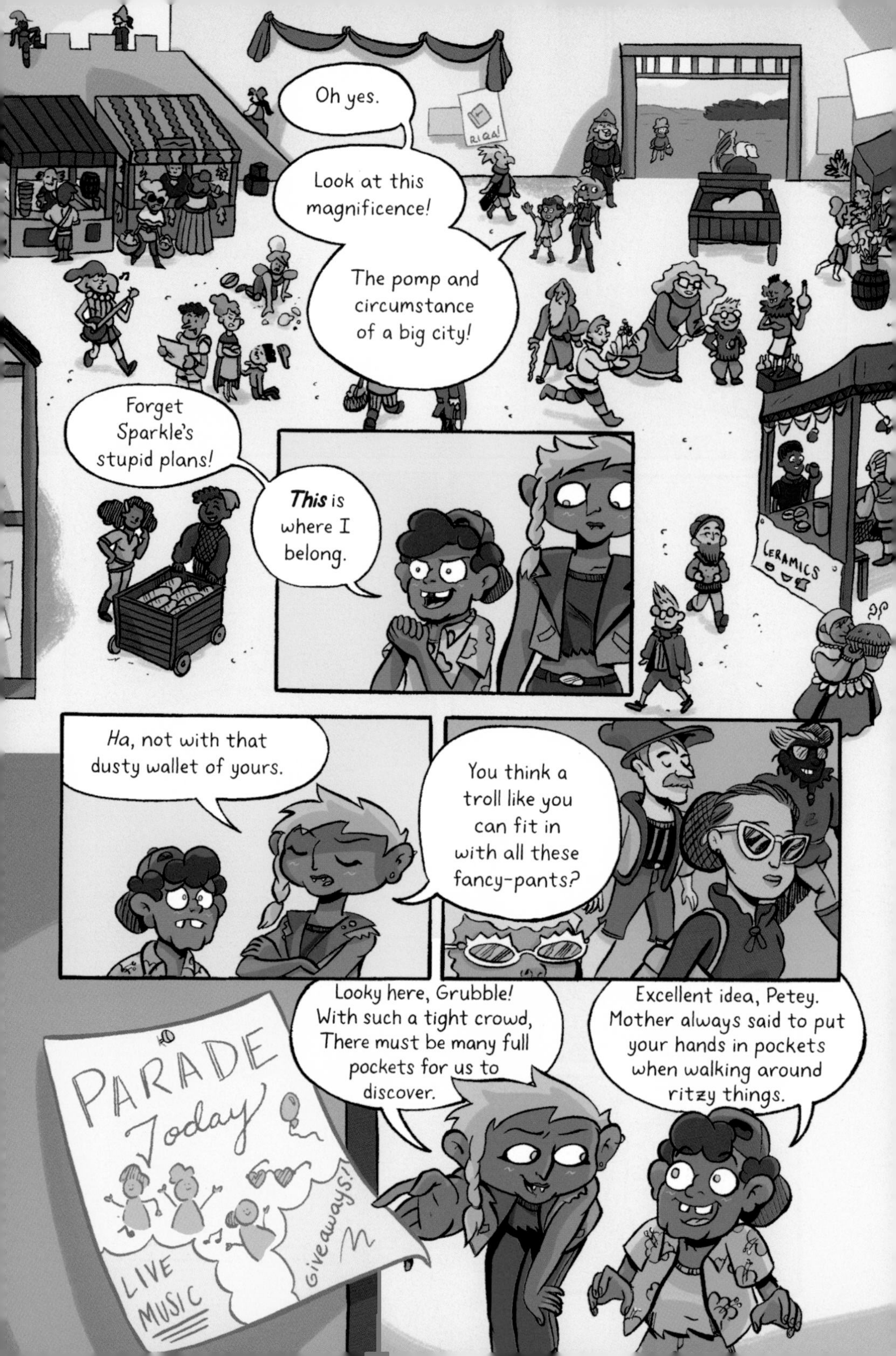

Oh yes.
Look at this magnificence!
The pomp and circumstance of a big city!
RIQA!
Forget Sparkle's stupid plans!
This is where I belong.
CERAMICS
Ha, not with that dusty wallet of yours.
You think a troll like you can fit in with all these fancy-pants?
Looky here, Grubble! With such a tight crowd, There must be many full pockets for us to discover.
Excellent idea, Petey. Mother always said to put your hands in pockets when walking around ritzy things.
PARADE Today
Giveaways!
LIVE MUSIC

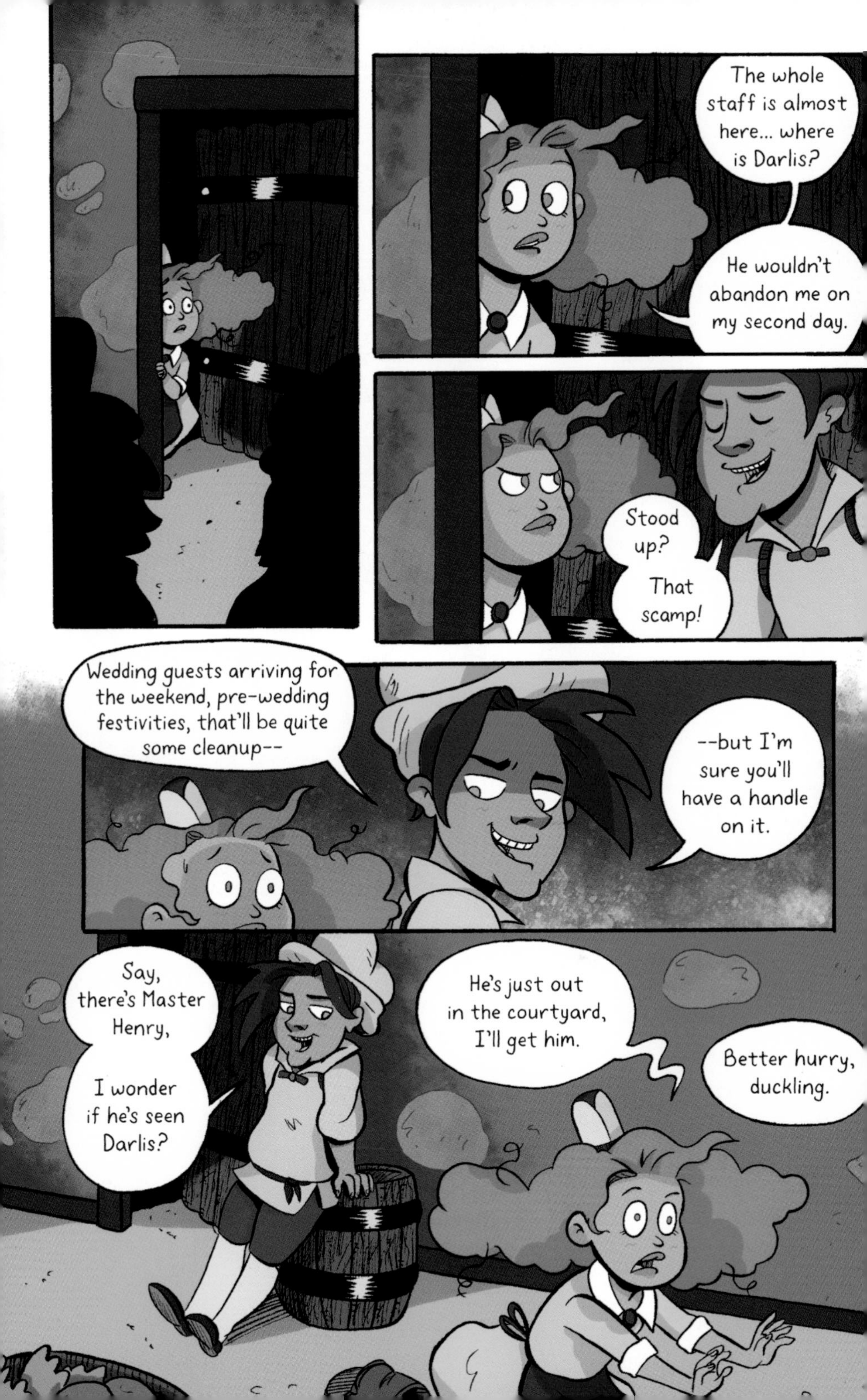
The whole staff is almost here... where is Darlis?
He wouldn't abandon me on my second day.
Stood up?
That scamp!
Wedding guests arriving for the weekend, pre-wedding festivities, that'll be quite some cleanup--
--but I'm sure you'll have a handle on it.
Say, there's Master Henry,
I wonder if he's seen Darlis?
He's just out in the courtyard, I'll get him.
Better hurry, duckling.

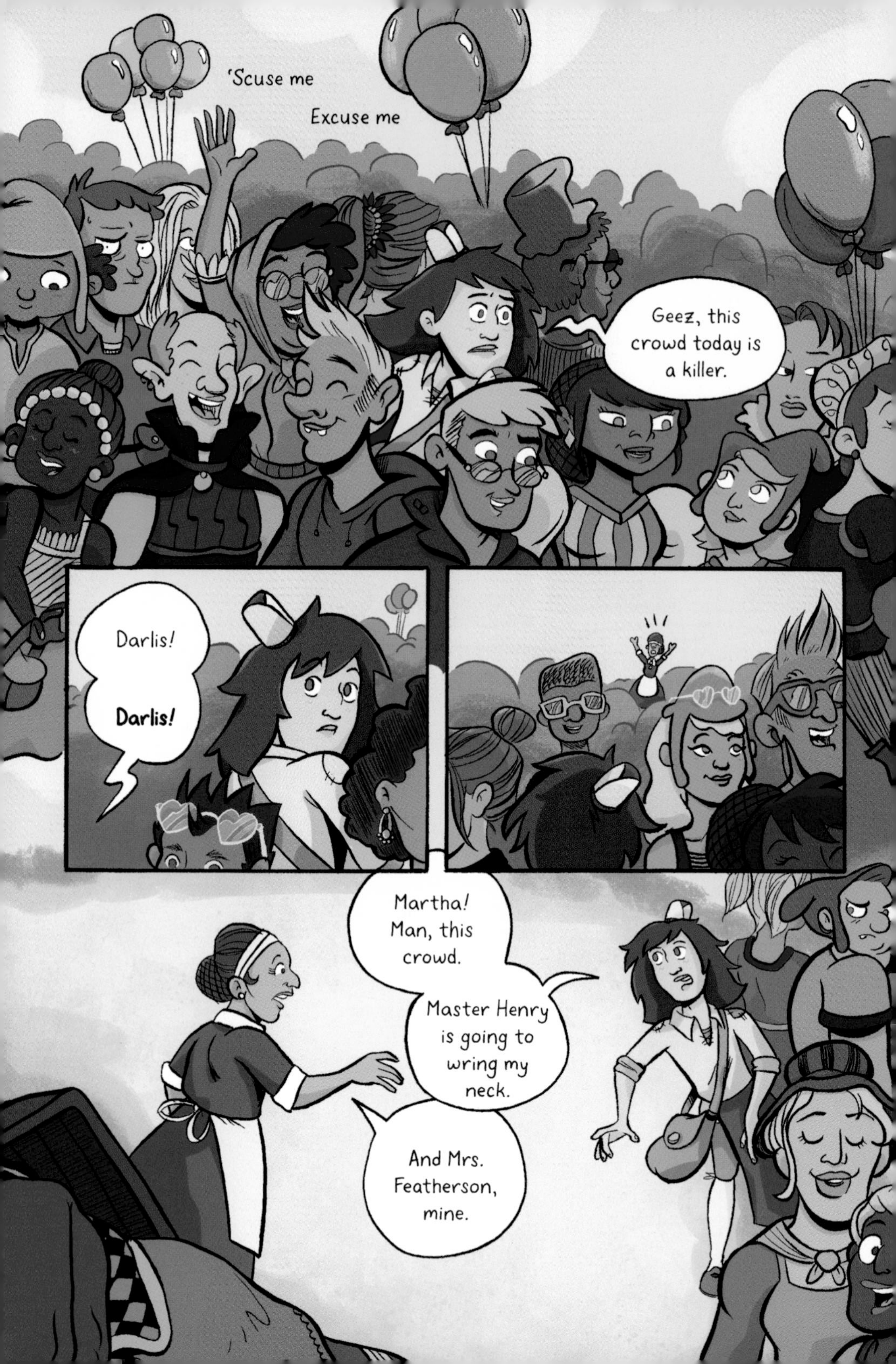
'Scuse me
Excuse me
Geez, this crowd today is a killer.
Darlis!
Darlis!
Martha! Man, this crowd.
Master Henry is going to wring my neck.
And Mrs. Featherson, mine.

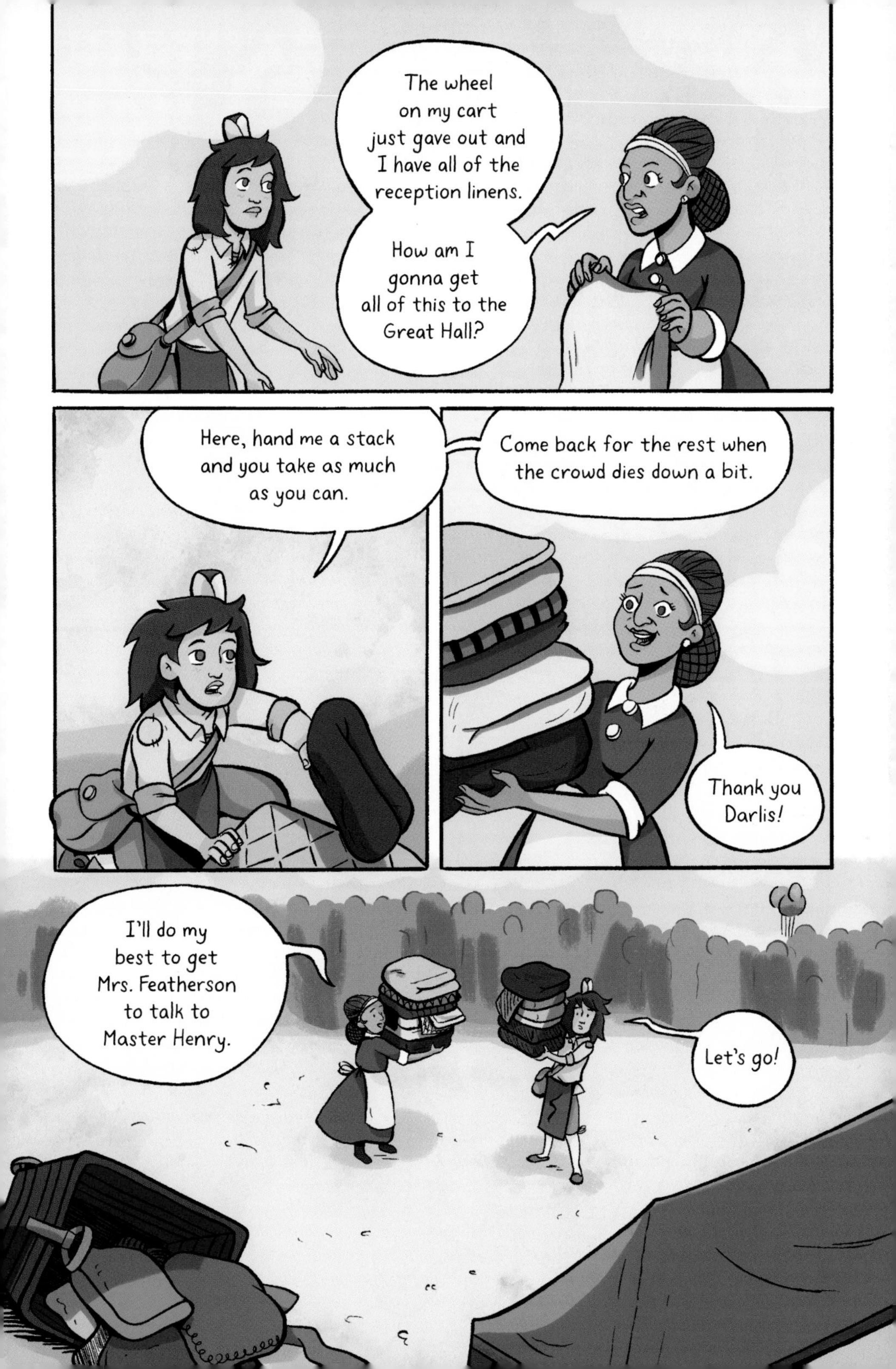
The wheel on my cart just gave out and I have all of the reception linens.
How am I gonna get all of this to the Great Hall?
Here, hand me a stack and you take as much as you can.
Come back for the rest when the crowd dies down a bit.
Thank you Darlis!
I'll do my best to get Mrs. Featherson to talk to Master Henry.
Let's go!

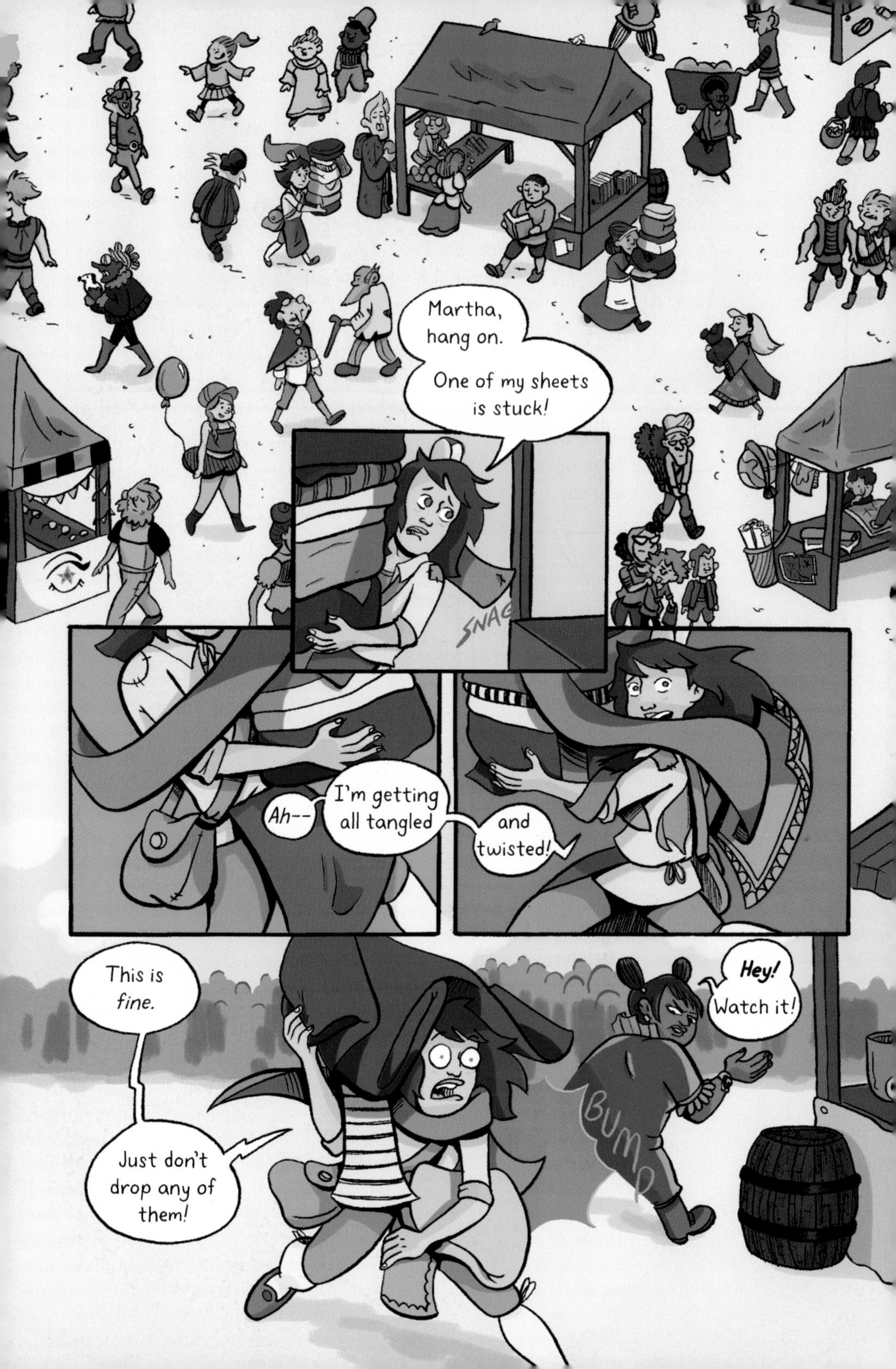
Martha, hang on.
One of my sheets is stuck!
SNAG
Ah--
I'm getting all tangled
and twisted!
This is fine.
Just don't drop any of them!
BUMP
Hey!
Watch it!

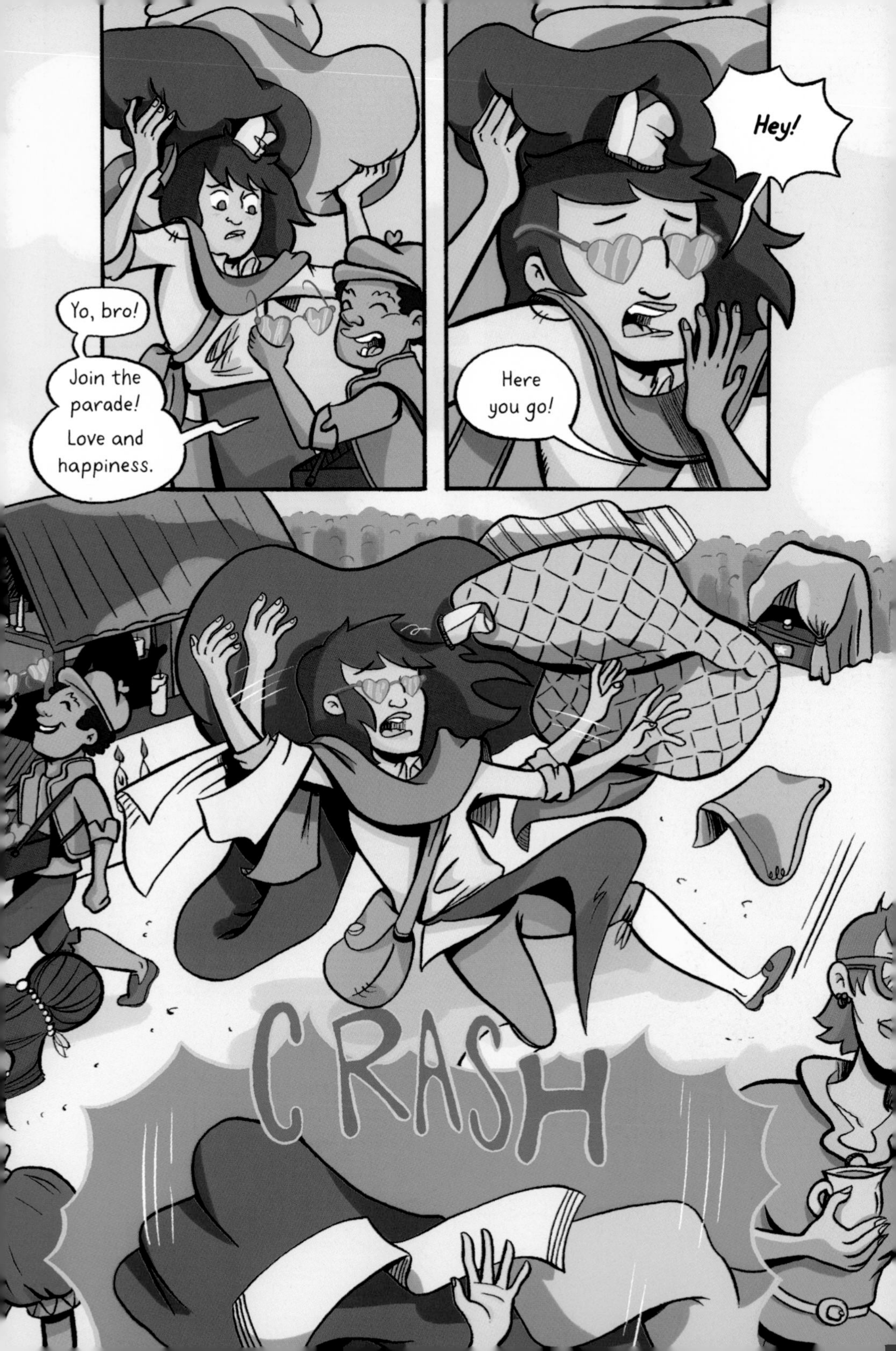
Yo, bro!
Join the parade!
Love and happiness.
Hey!
Here you go!
CRASH

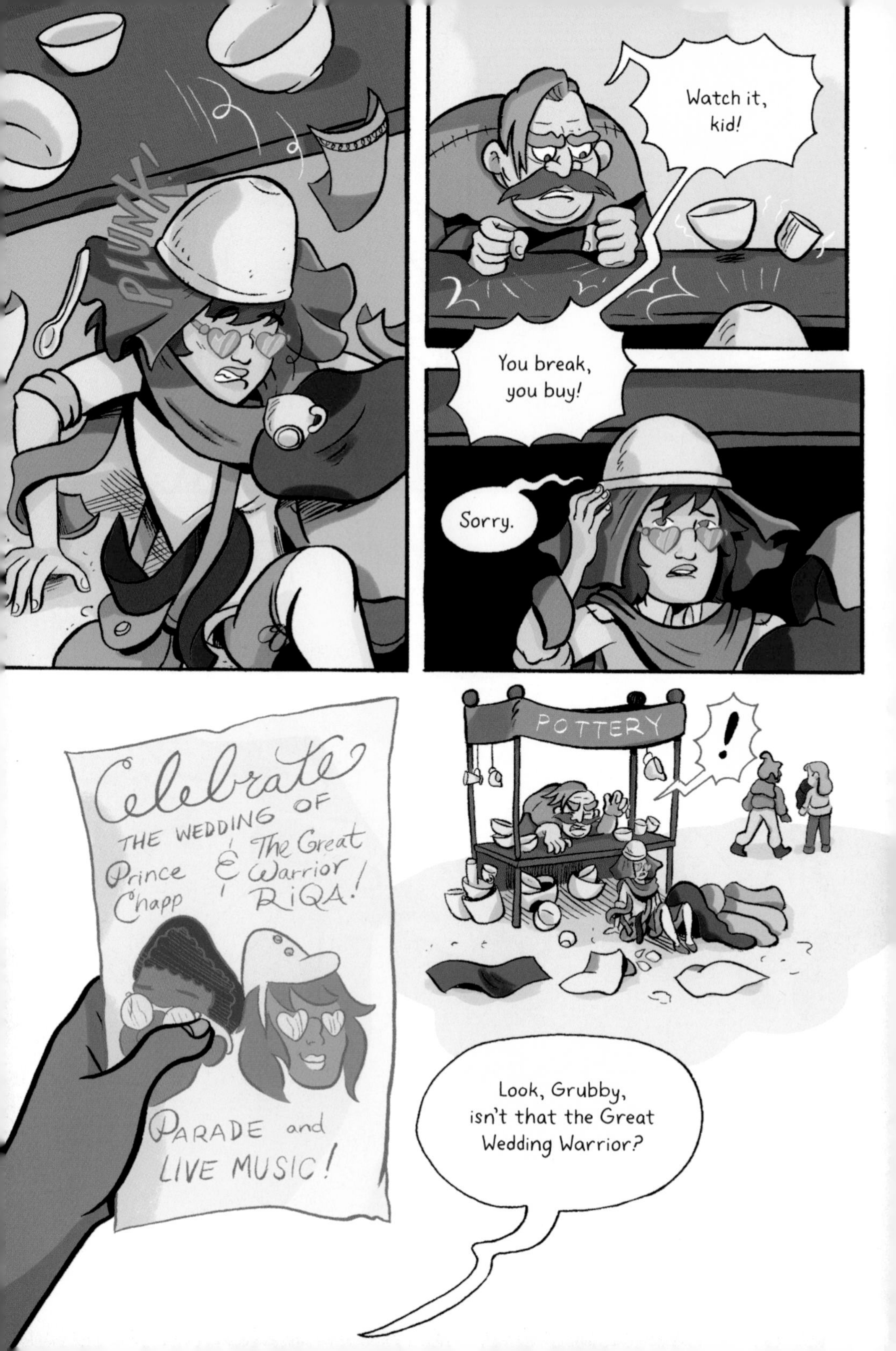
PLUNK!
Watch it, kid!
You break, you buy!
Sorry.
Celebrate THE WEDDING OF Prince Chapp & The Great Warrior RiQA!
PARADE and LIVE MUSIC!
POTTERY
!
Look, Grubby, isn't that the Great Wedding Warrior?

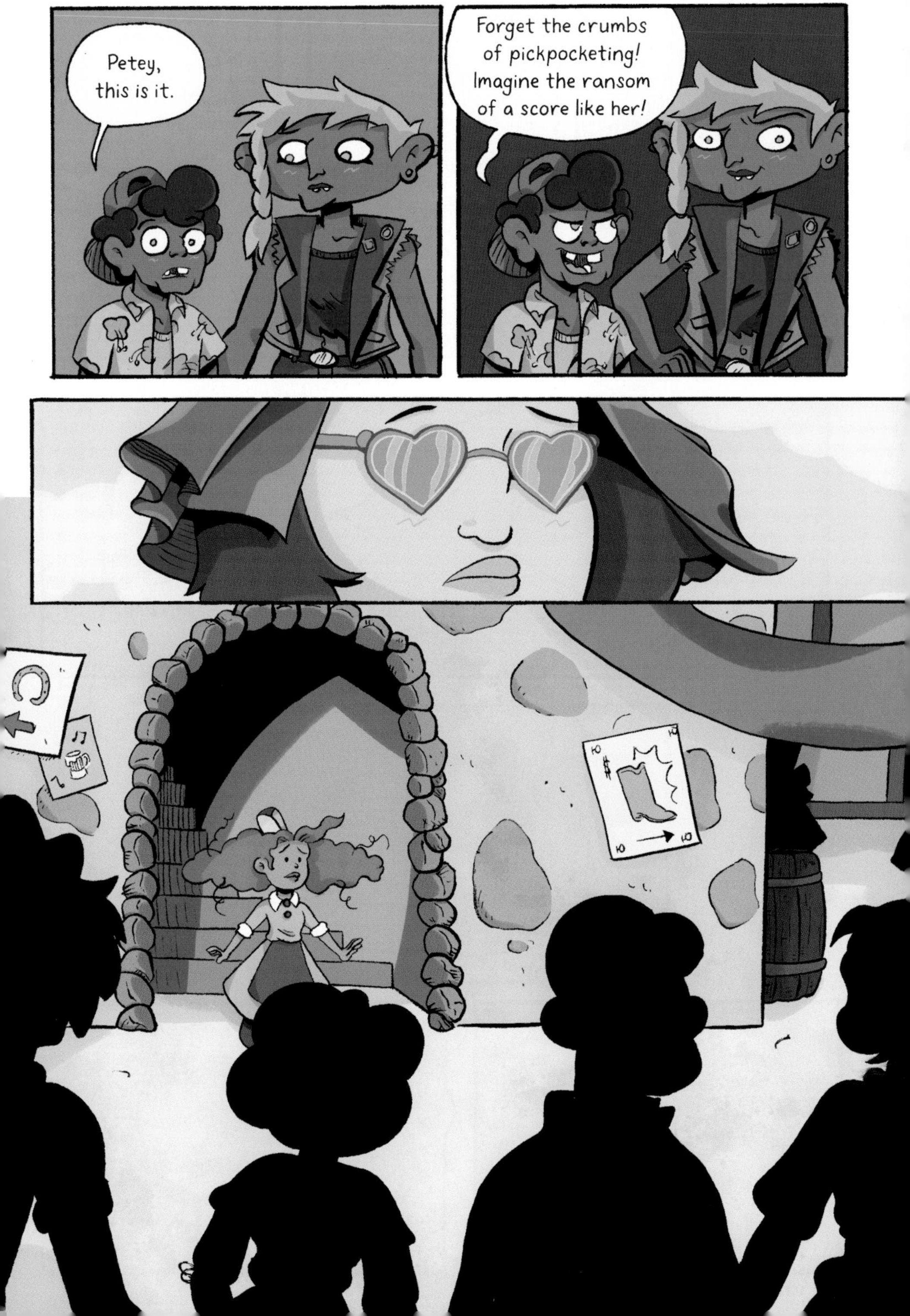
Petey, this is it.
Forget the crumbs of pickpocketing! Imagine the ransom of a score like her!

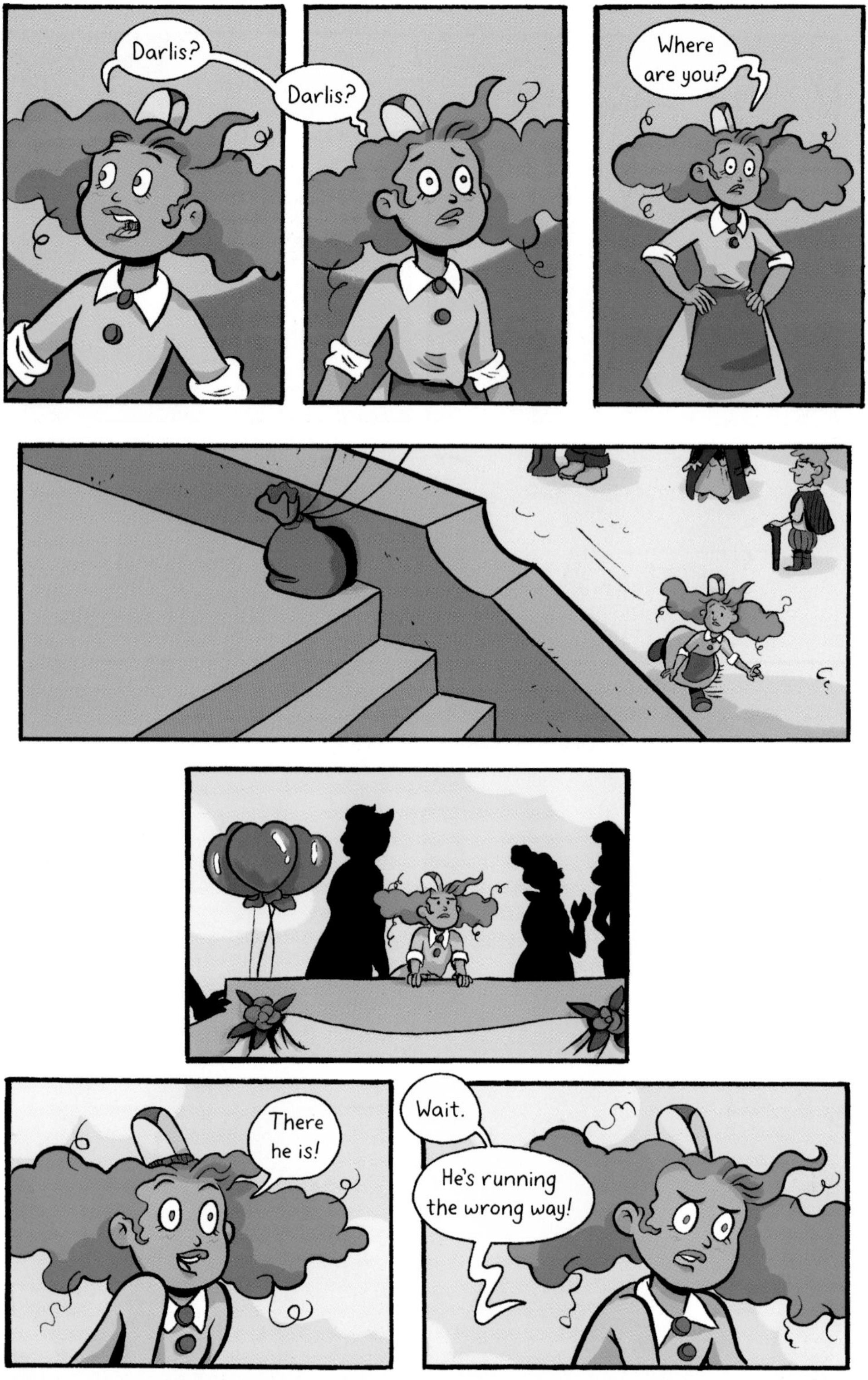
Darlis?
Darlis?
Where are you?
There he is!
Wait.
He's running the wrong way!

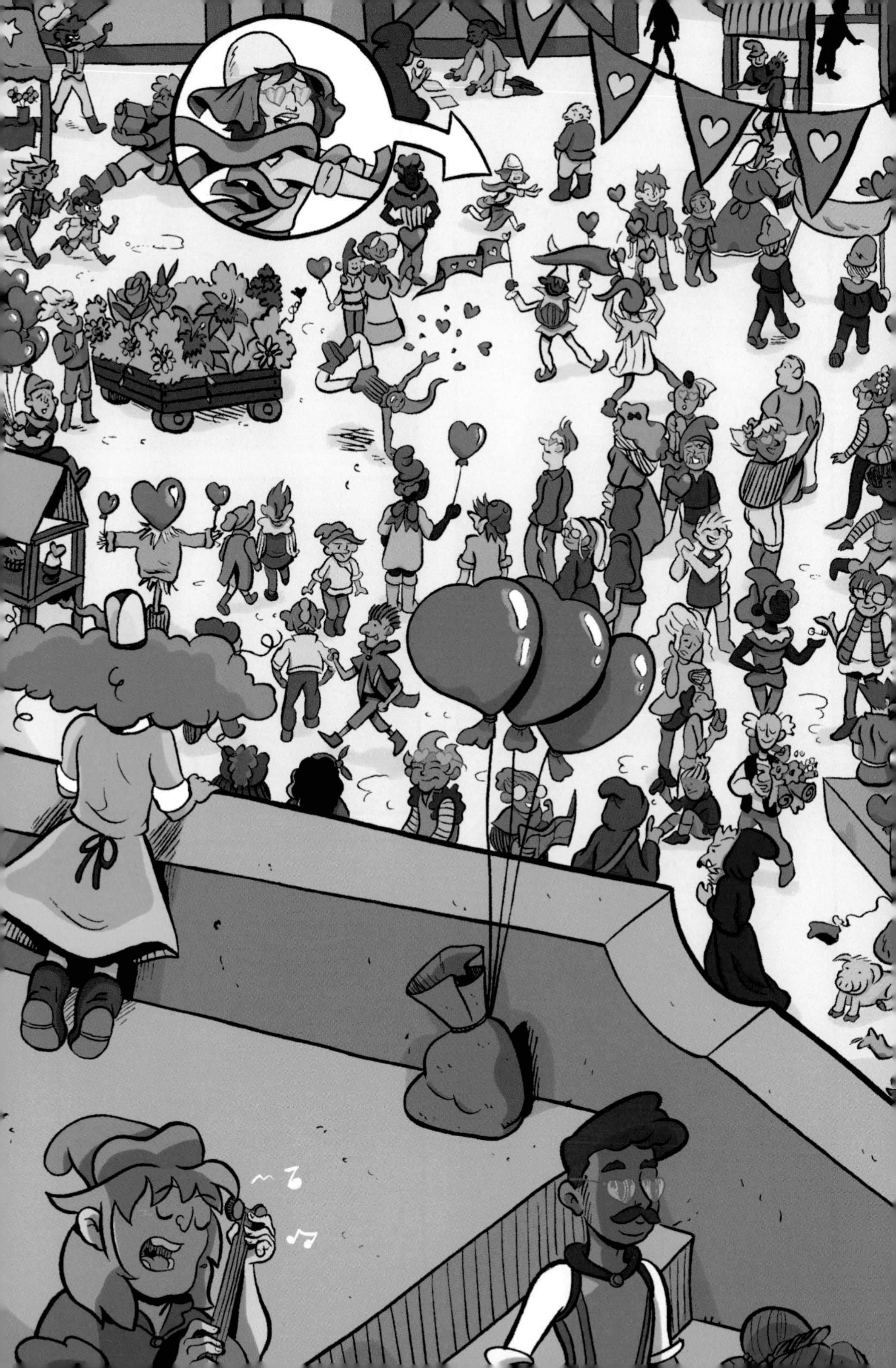

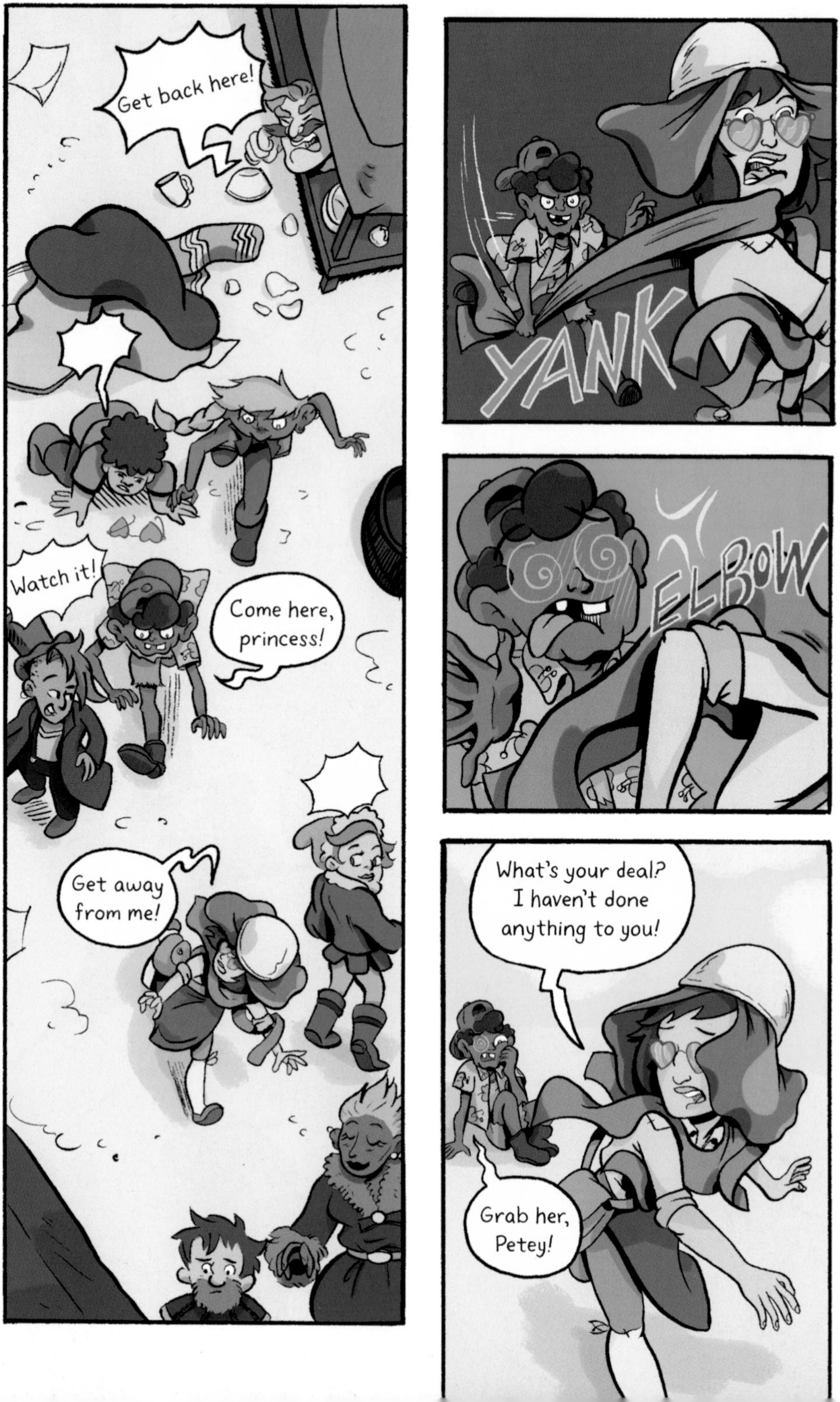
Get back here!
Watch it!
Come here, princess!
Get away from me!
YANK
ELBOW
What's your deal? I haven't done anything to you!
Grab her, Petey!

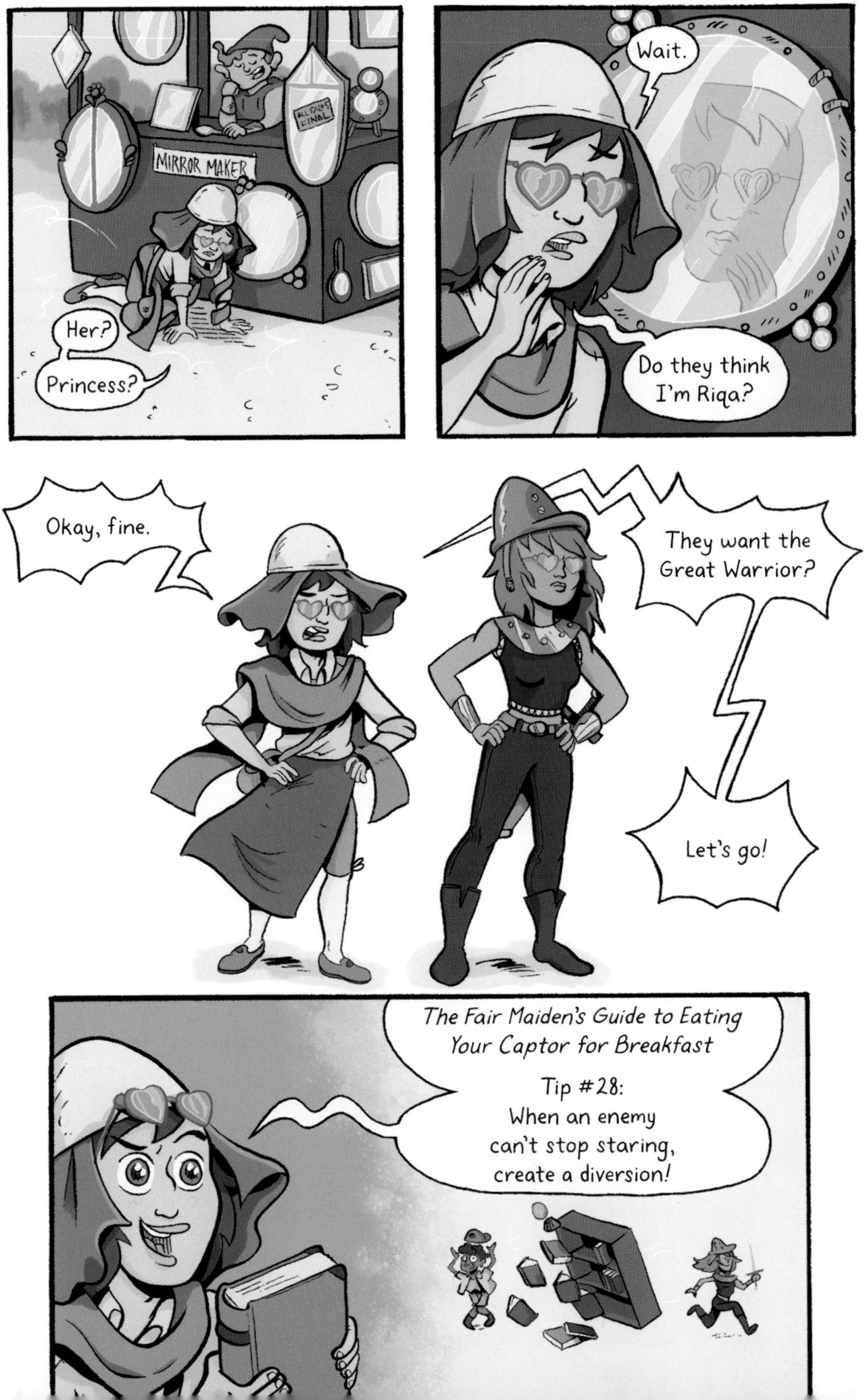
MIRROR MAKER
Her?
Princess?
Wait.
Do they think I'm Riqa?
Okay, fine.
They want the Great Warrior?
Let's go!
The Fair Maiden's Guide to Eating Your Captor for Breakfast
Tip #28:
When an enemy can't stop staring, create a diversion!

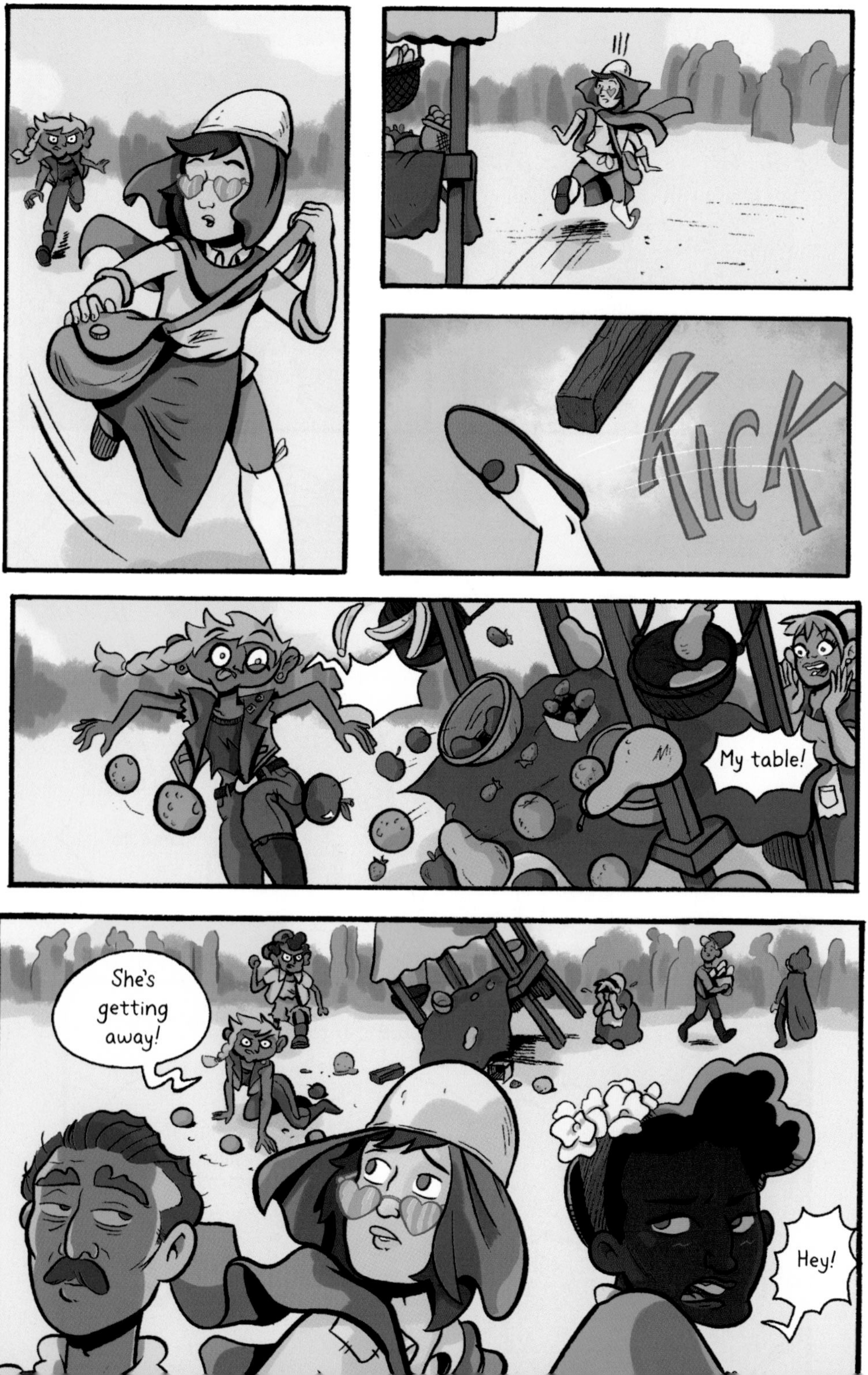
KICK
My table!
She's getting away!
Hey!

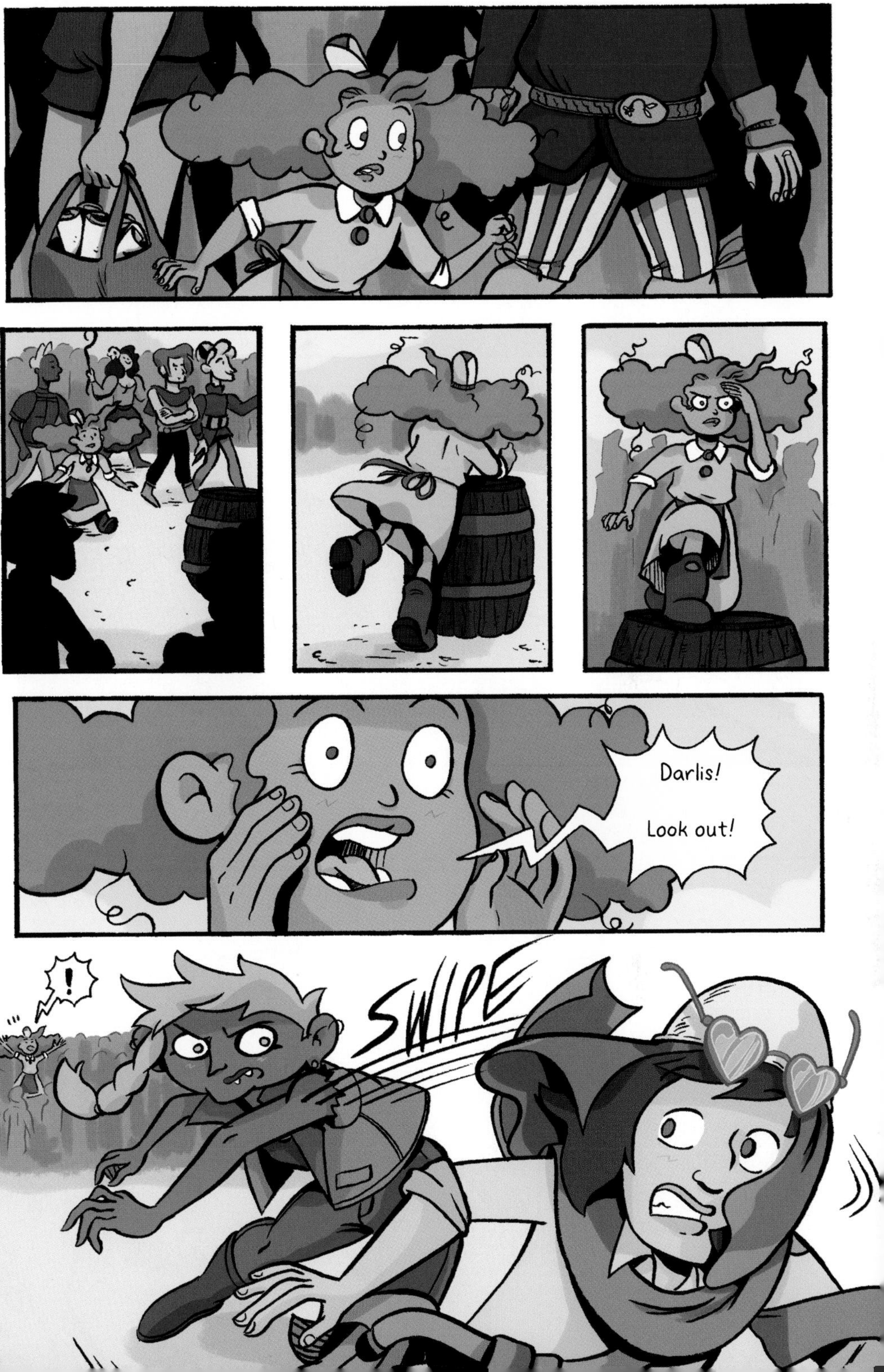
Darlis!
Look out!
!
SWIPE

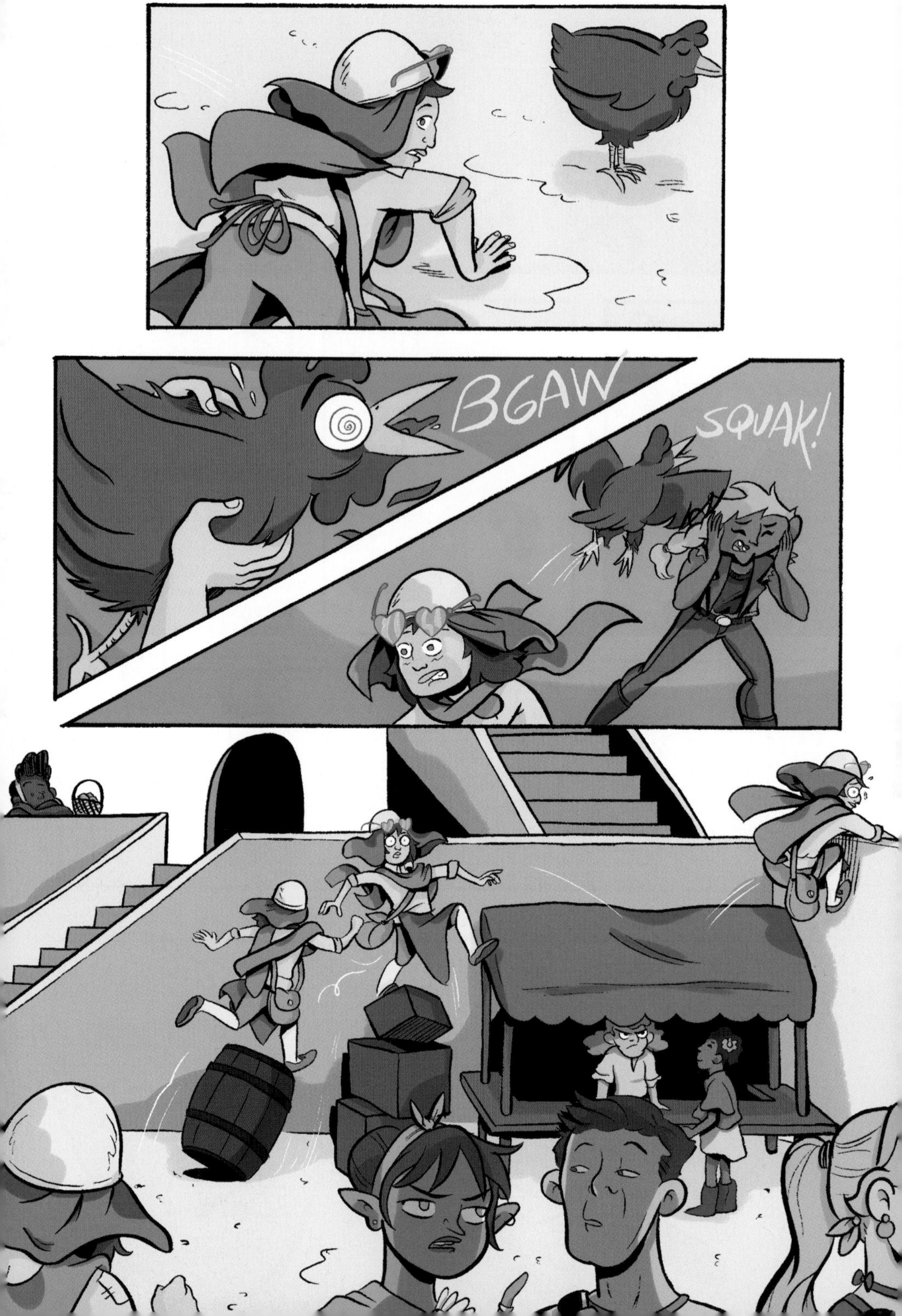
BGAW
SQUAK!

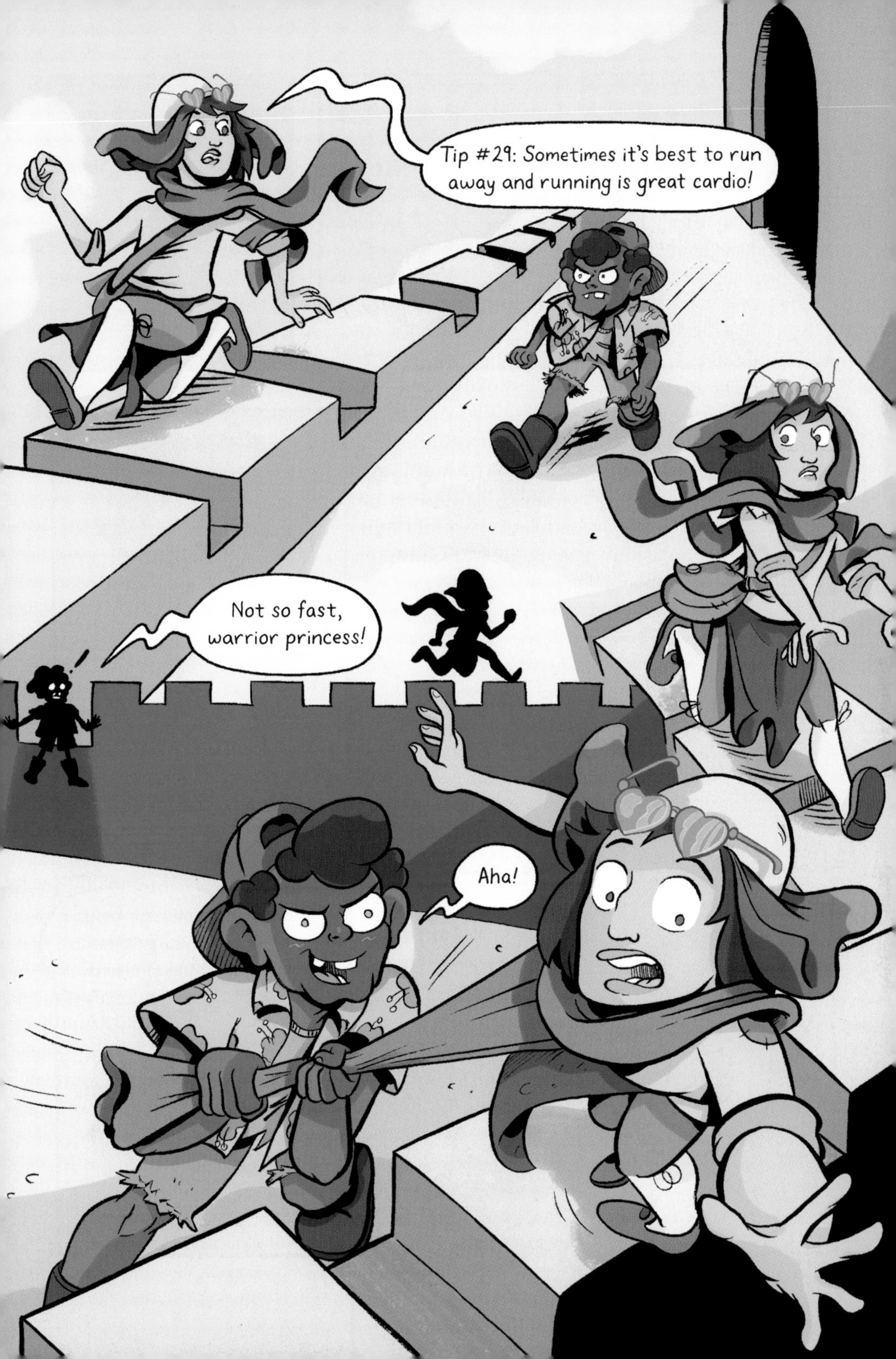
Tip #29: Sometimes it's best to run away and running is great cardio!
Not so fast, warrior princess!
Aha!

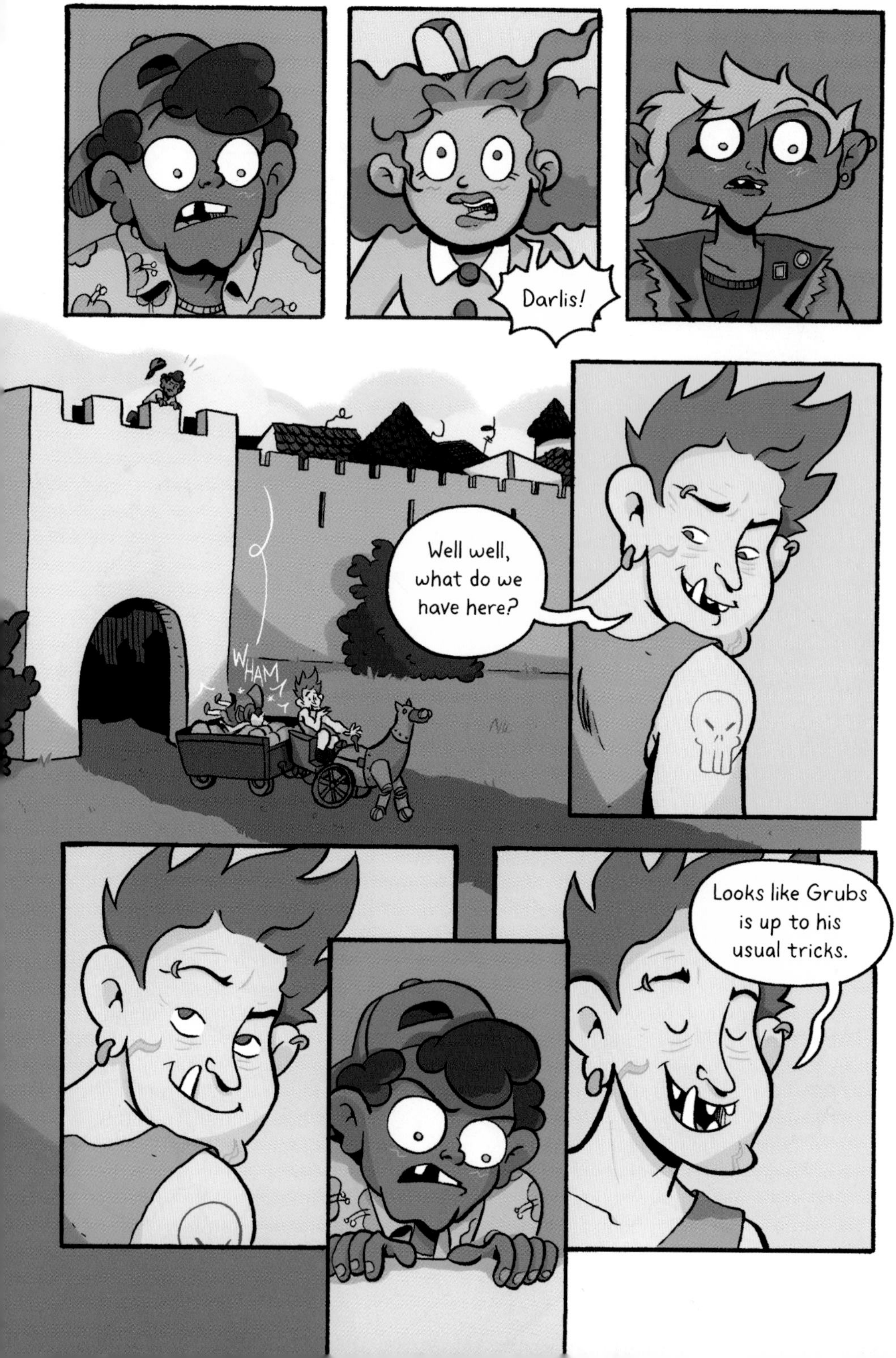
Darlis!
WHAM
Well well, what do we have here?
Looks like Grubs is up to his usual tricks.

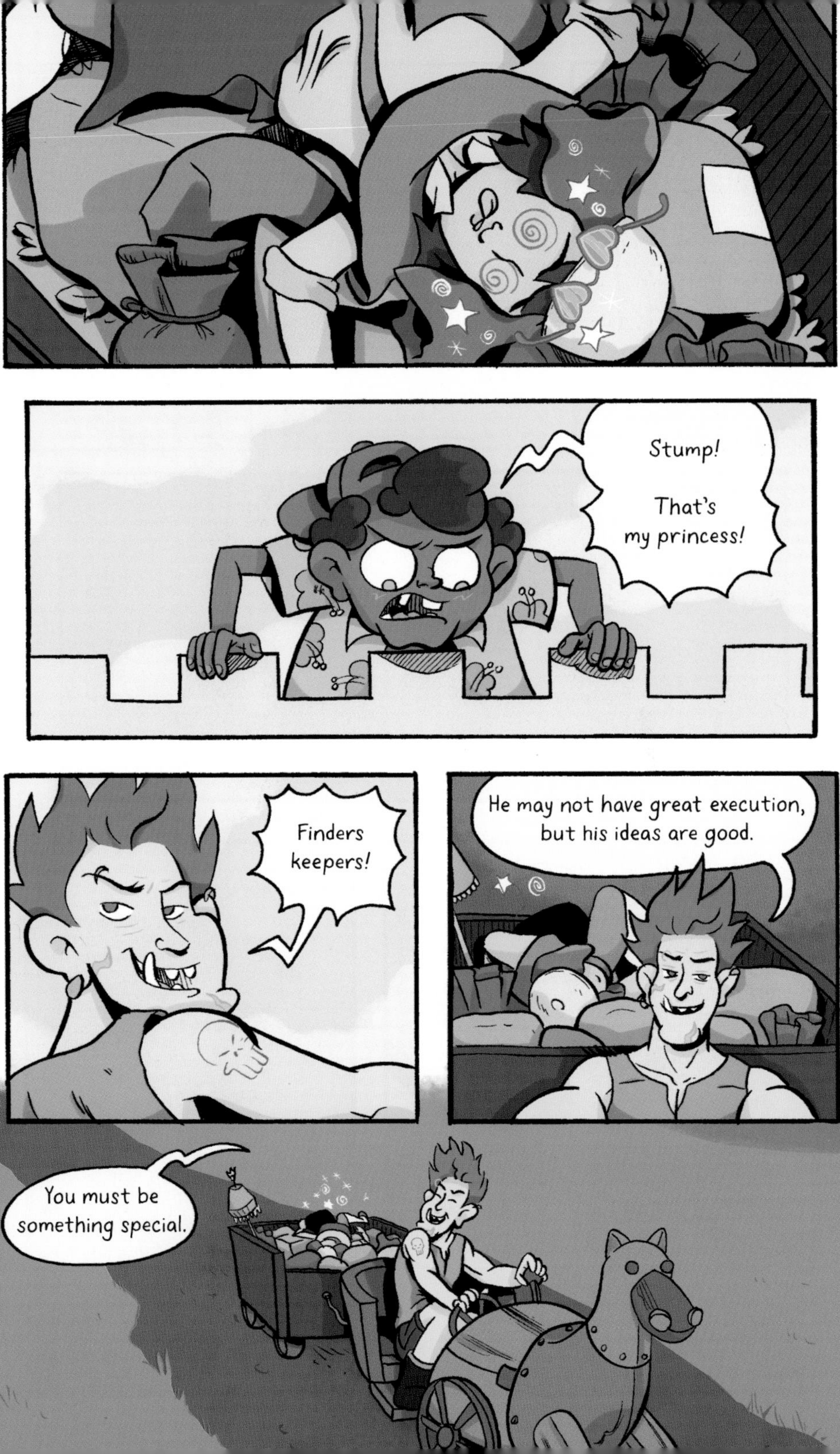
Stump!
That's my princess!
Finders keepers!
He may not have great execution, but his ideas are good.
You must be something special.

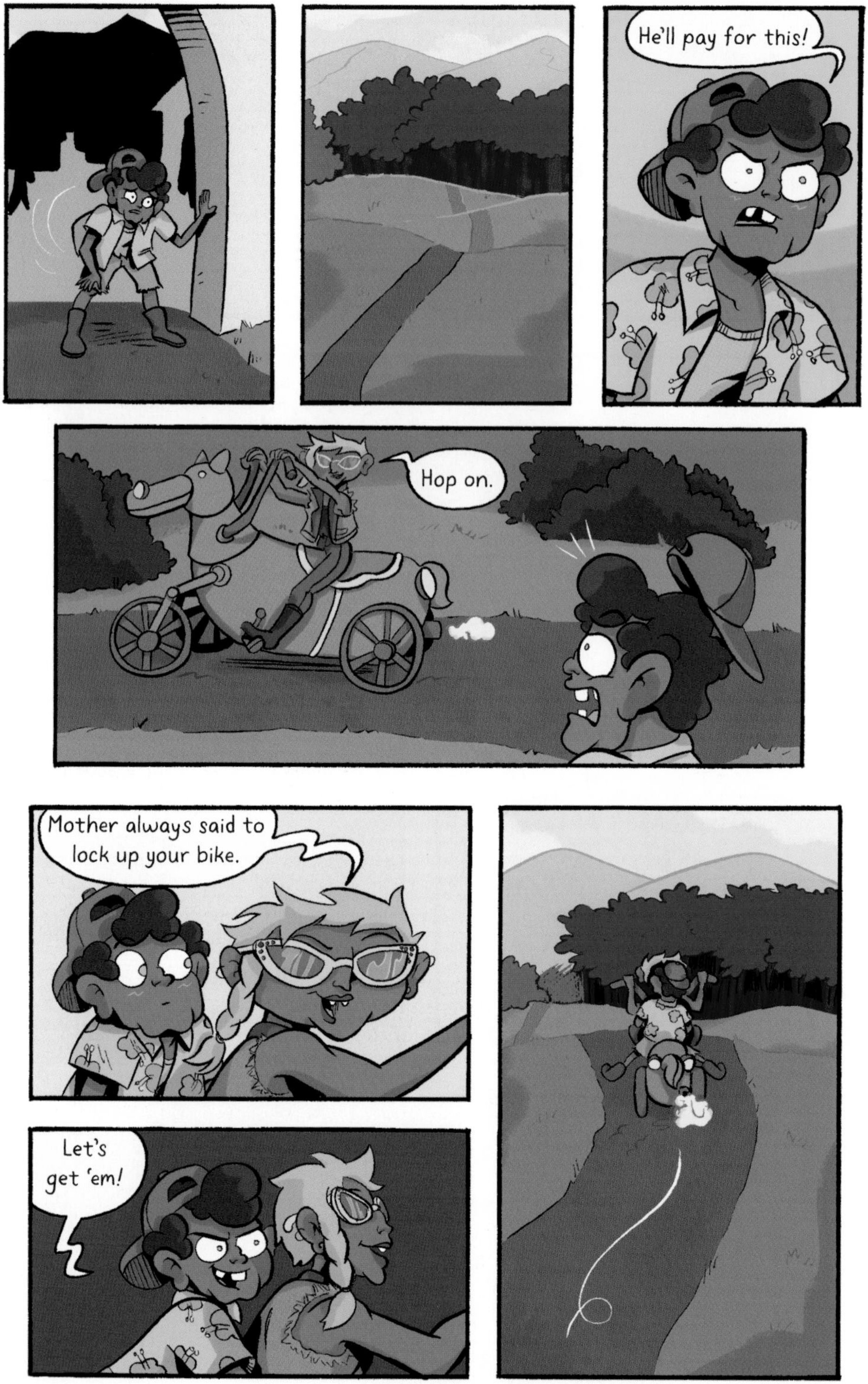
He'll pay for this!
Hop on.
Mother always said to lock up your bike.
Let's get 'em!

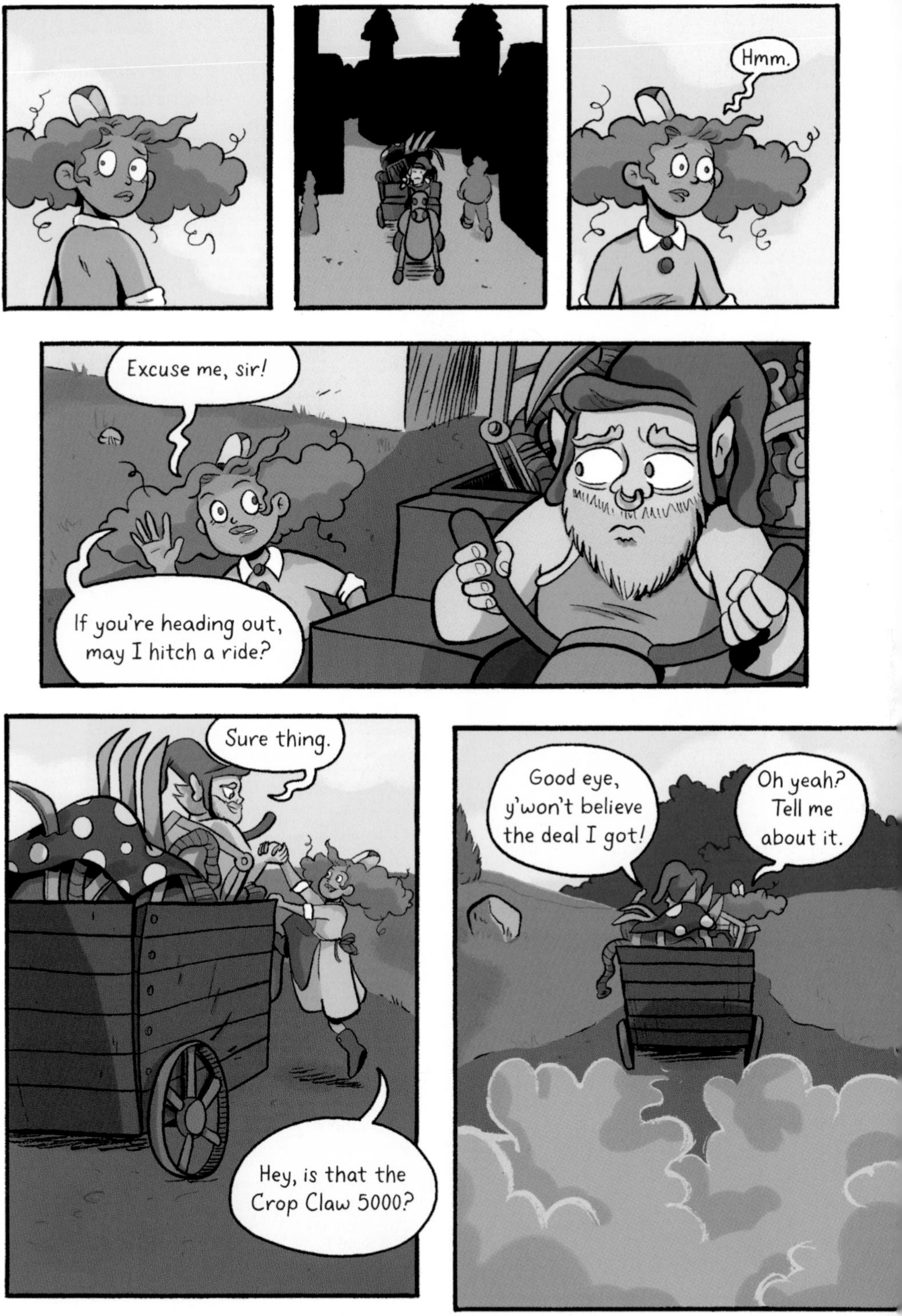
Hmm.
Excuse me, sir!
If you're heading out, may I hitch a ride?
Sure thing.
Hey, is that the Crop Claw 5000?
Good eye, y'won't believe the deal I got!
Oh yeah? Tell me about it.

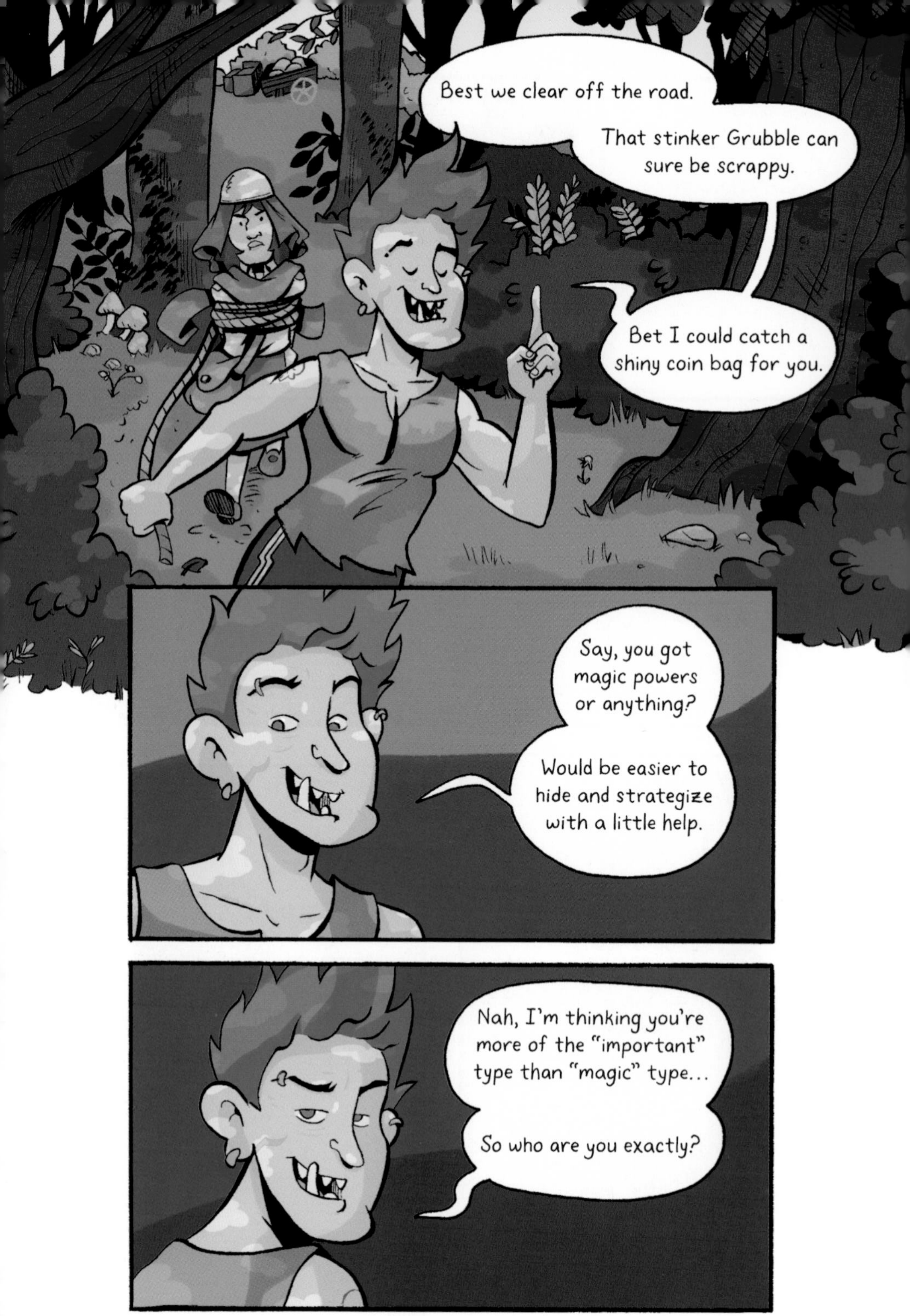
Best we clear off the road.
That stinker Grubble can sure be scrappy.
Bet I could catch a shiny coin bag for you.
Say, you got magic powers or anything?
Would be easier to hide and strategize with a little help.
Nah, I'm thinking you're more of the "important" type than "magic" type...
So who are you exactly?

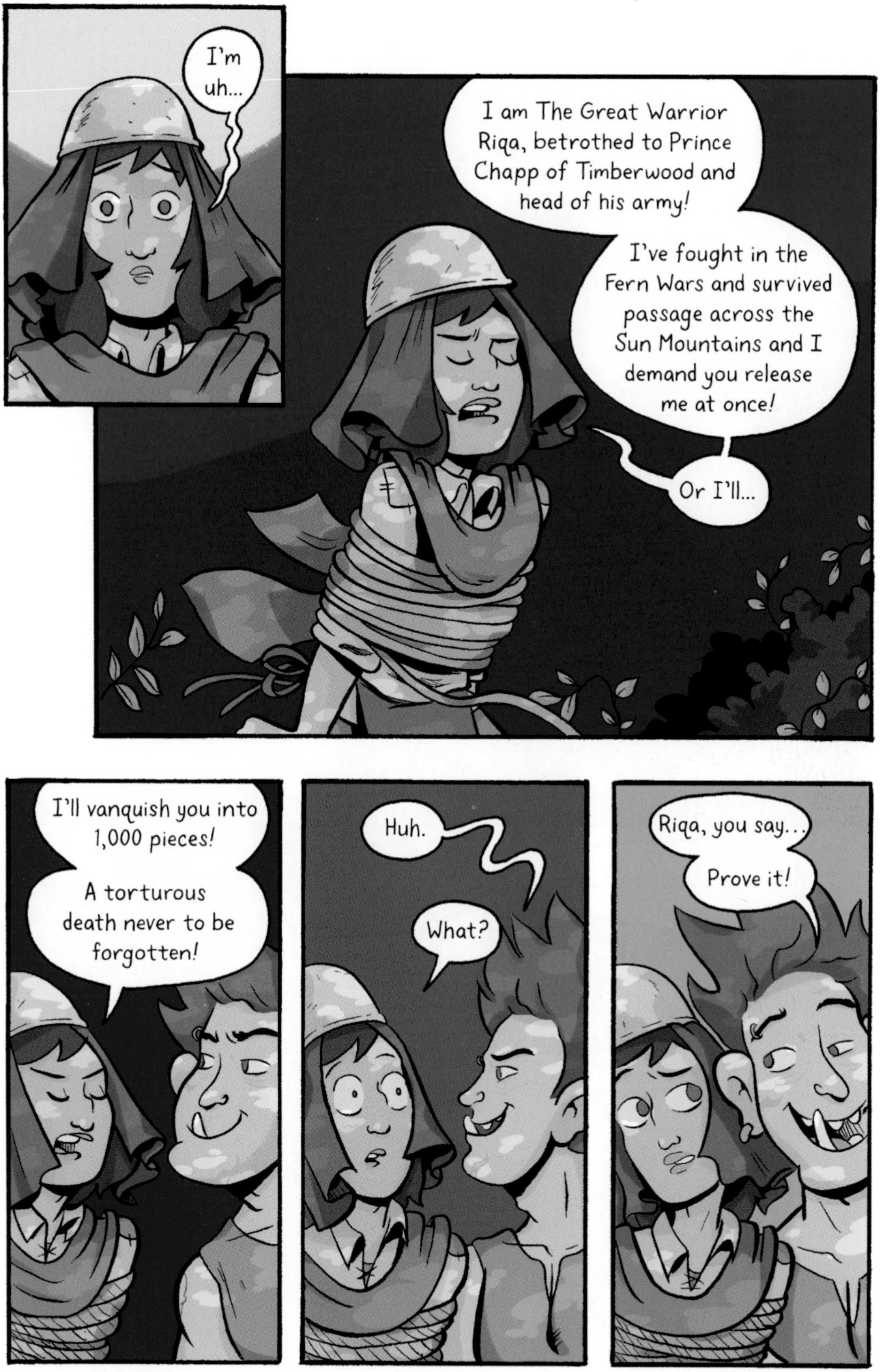
I'm uh...
I am The Great Warrior Riqa, betrothed to Prince Chapp of Timberwood and head of his army!
I've fought in the Fern Wars and survived passage across the Sun Mountains and I demand you release me at once!
Or I'll...
I'll vanquish you into 1,000 pieces!
A torturous death never to be forgotten!
Huh.
What?
Riqa, you say...
Prove it!

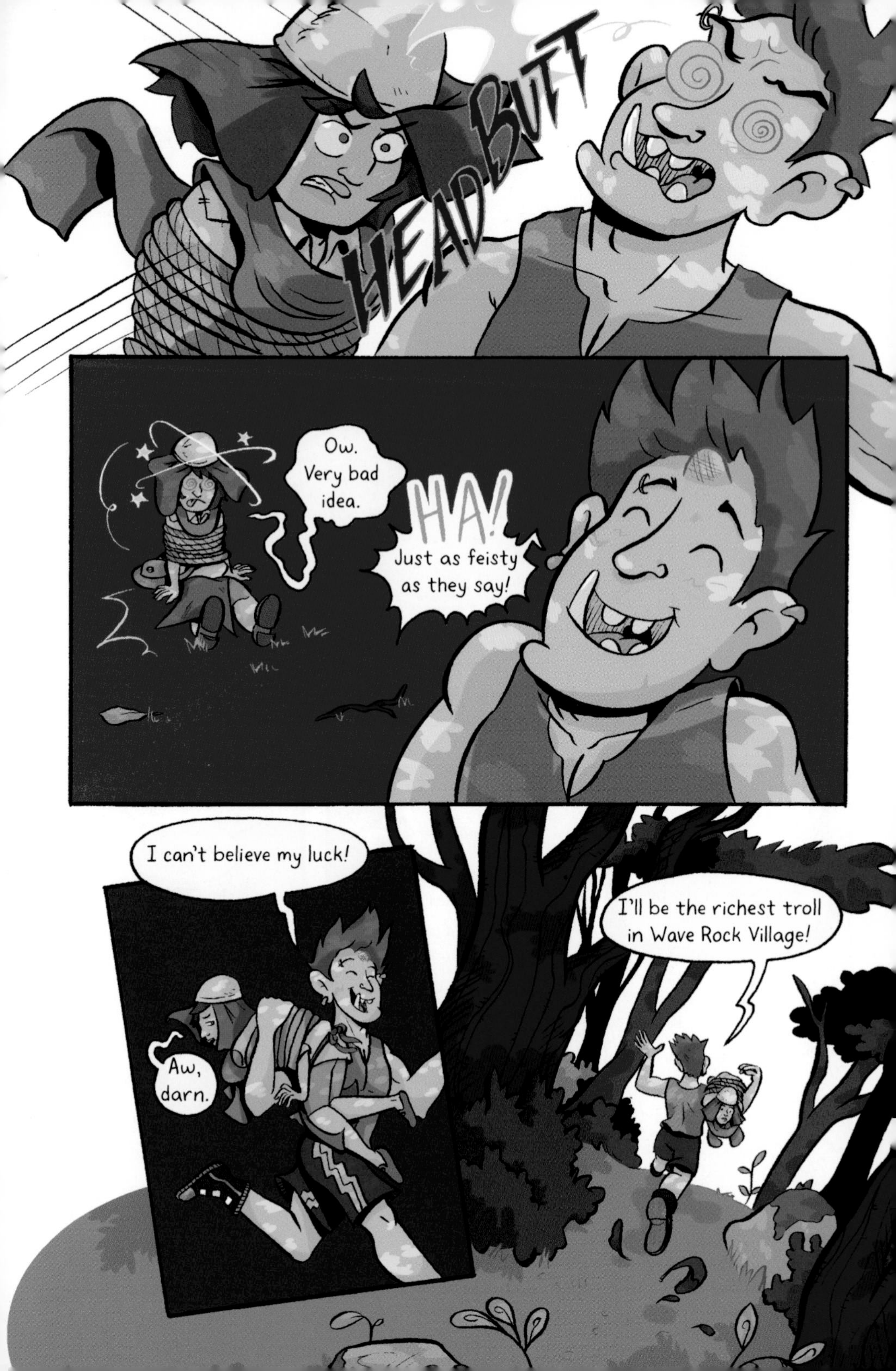
HEAD BUTT
Ow. Very bad idea.
HA!
Just as feisty as they say!
I can't believe my luck!
Aw, darn.
I'll be the richest troll in Wave Rock Village!

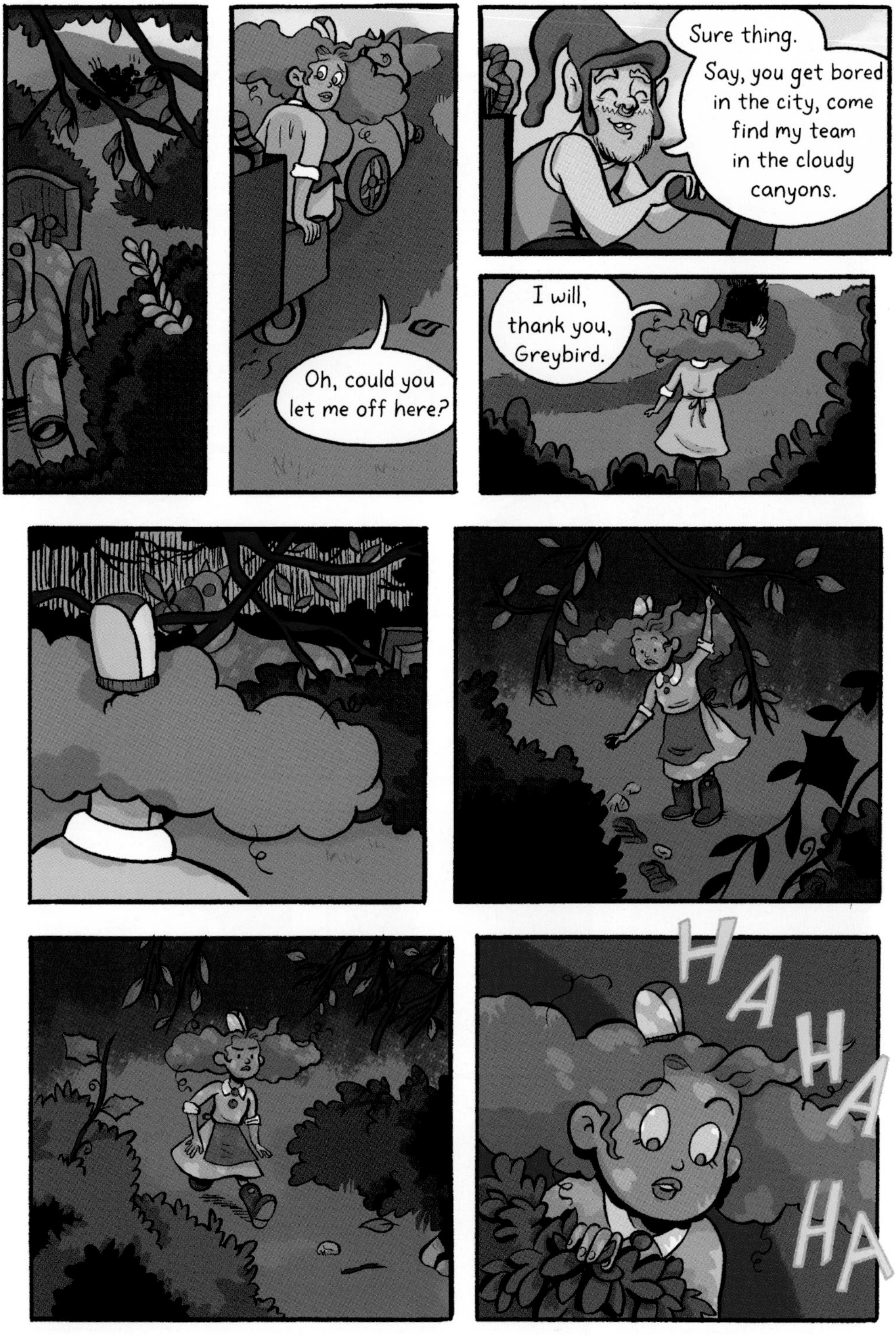
Oh, could you let me off here?
Sure thing.
Say, you get bored in the city, come find my team in the cloudy canyons.
I will, thank you, Greybird.
HAHAHA
HAHA

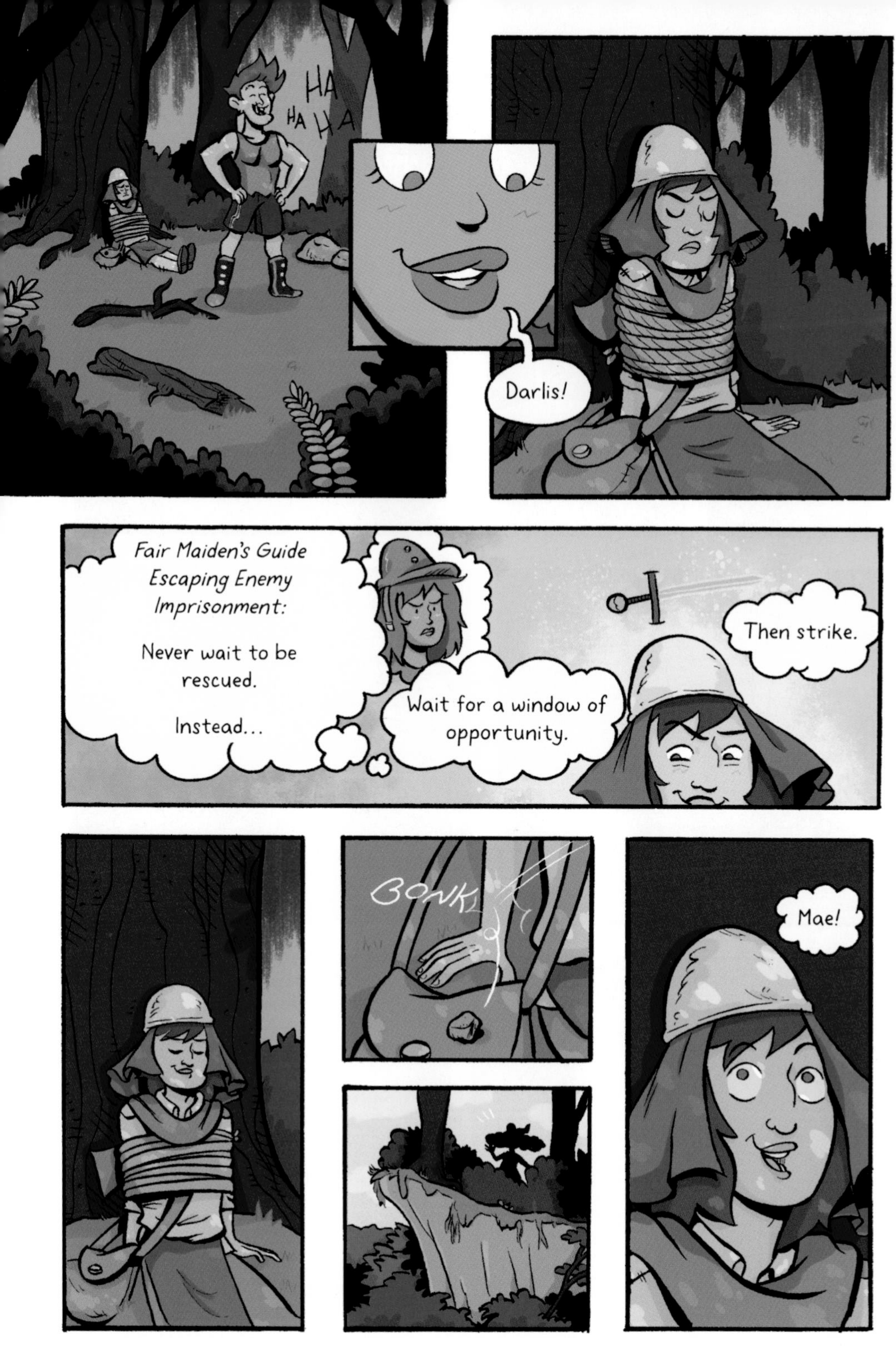
HA
HA HA
Darlis!
Fair Maiden's Guide Escaping Enemy Imprisonment:
Never wait to be rescued.
Instead...
Wait for a window of opportunity.
Then strike.
BONK
Mae!

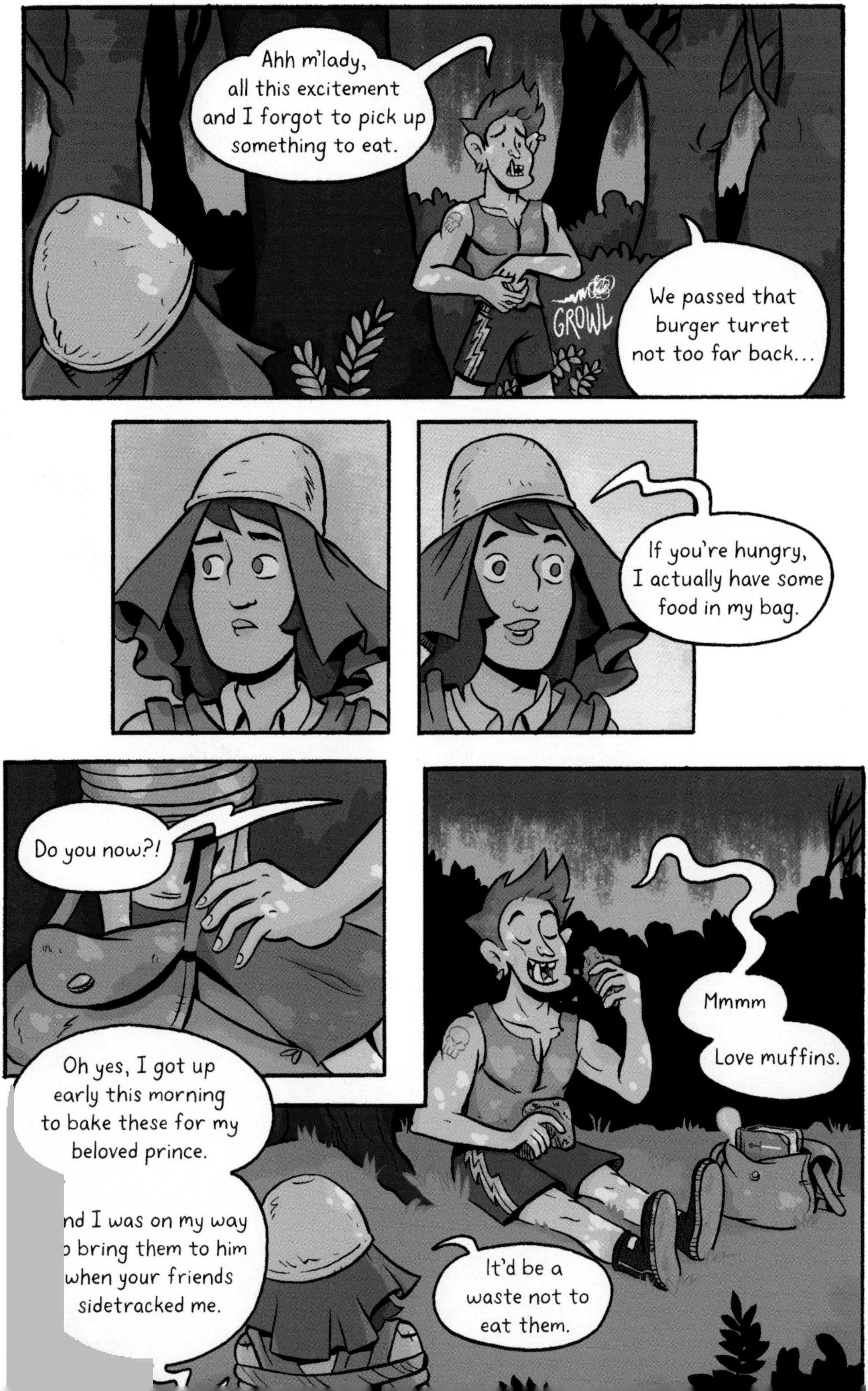
Ahh m'lady, all this excitement and I forgot to pick up something to eat.
GROWL
We passed that burger turret not too far back...
If you're hungry, I actually have some food in my bag.
Do you now?!
Oh yes, I got up early this morning to bake these for my beloved prince.
nd I was on my way
bring them to him when your friends sidetracked me.
Mmmm
Love muffins.
It'd be a waste not to eat them.

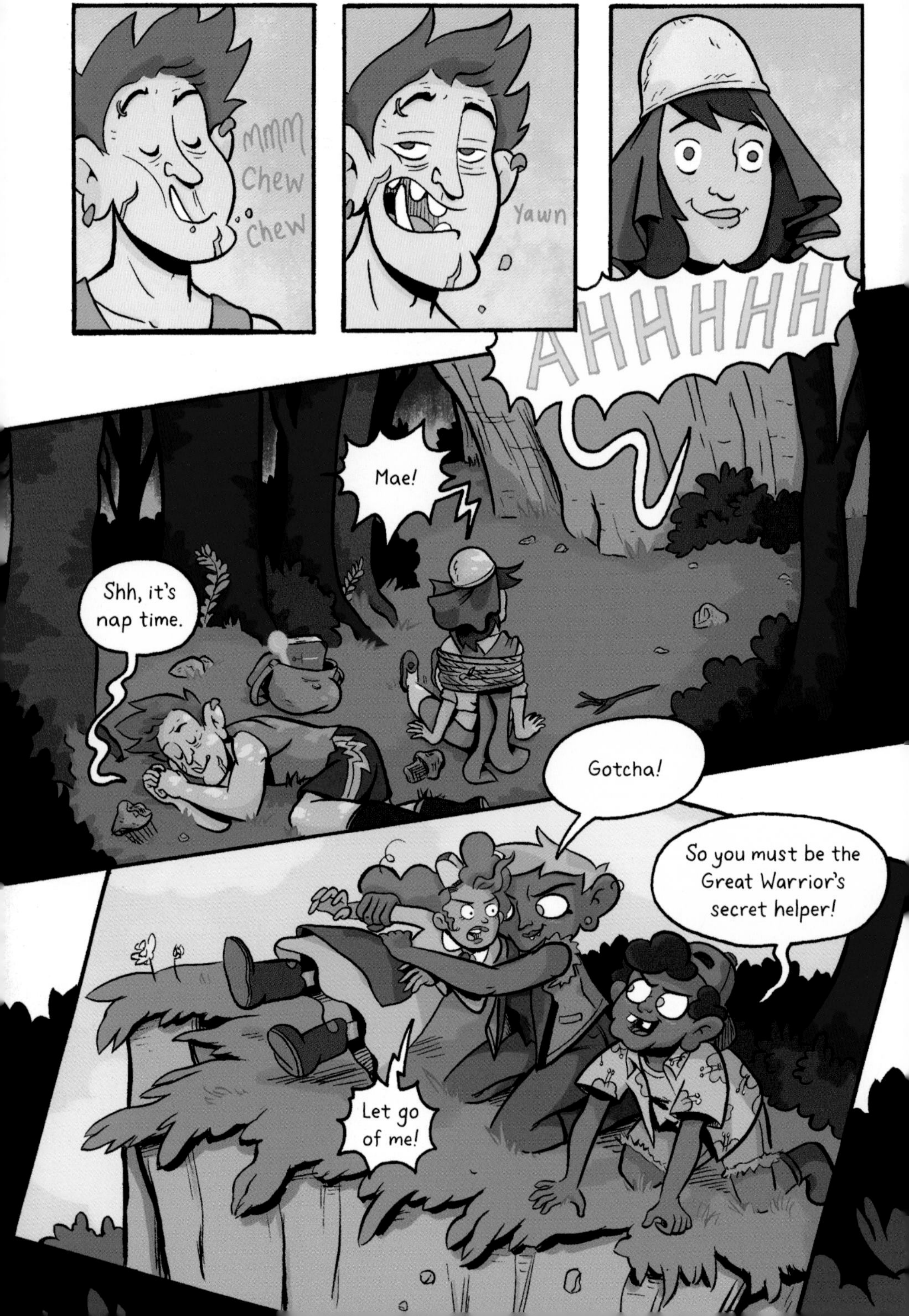
MMM
Chew
Chew
Yawn
AHHHHH
Mae!
Shh, it's nap time.
Gotcha!
So you must be the Great Warrior's secret helper!
Let go of me!

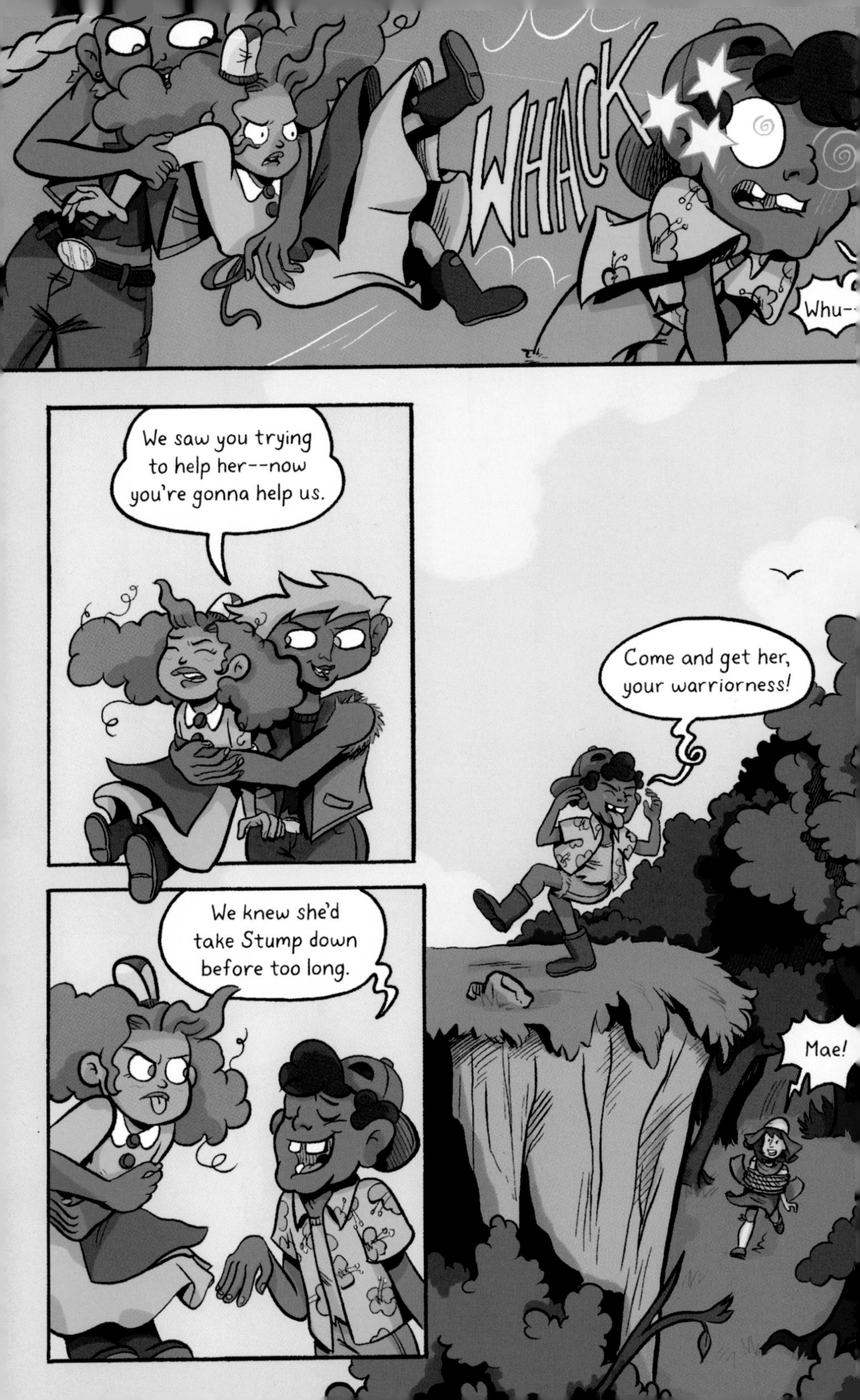
WHACK
Whu--
We saw you trying to help her--now you're gonna help us.
We knew she'd take Stump down before too long.
Come and get her, your warriorness!
Mae!

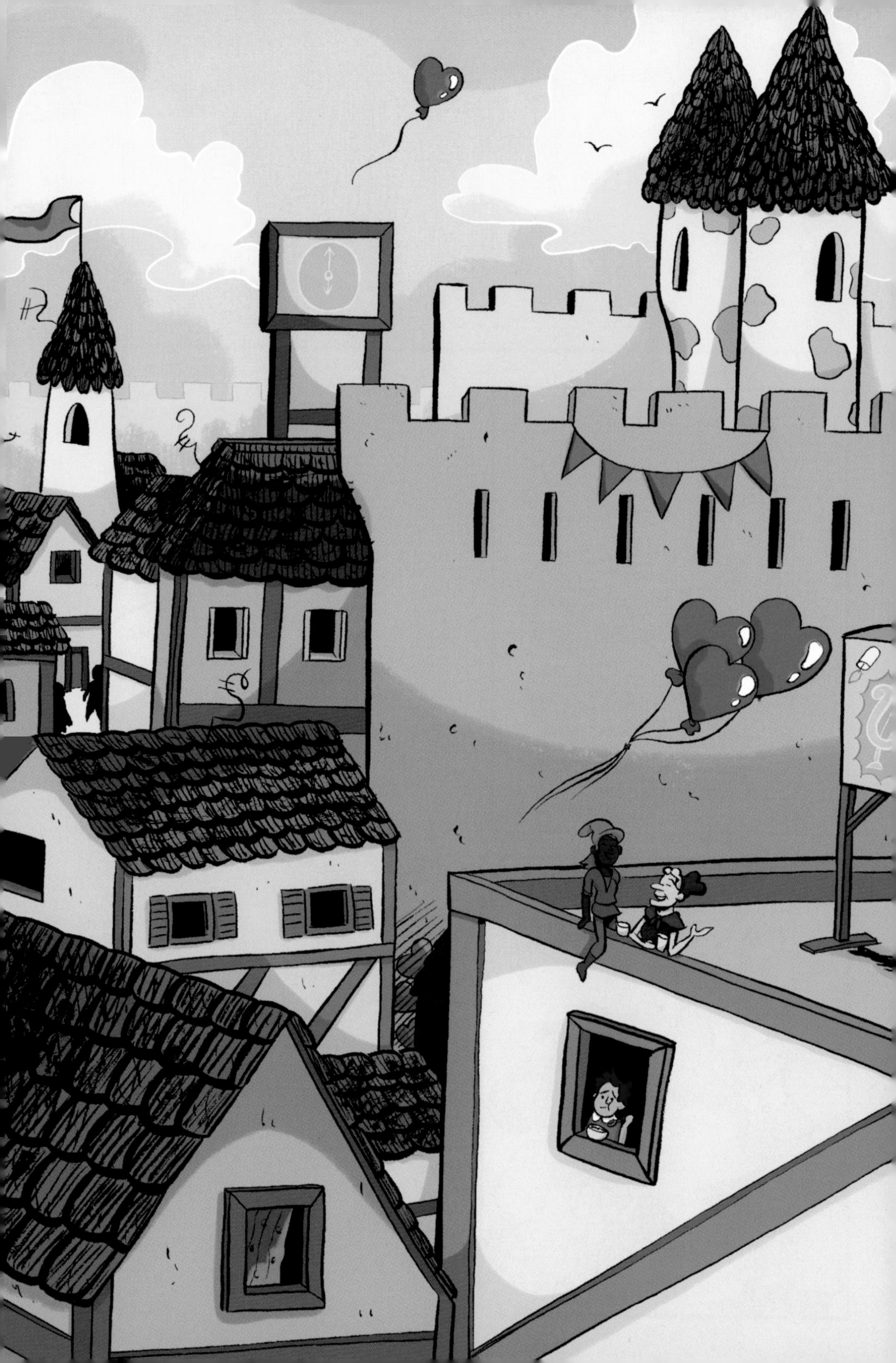

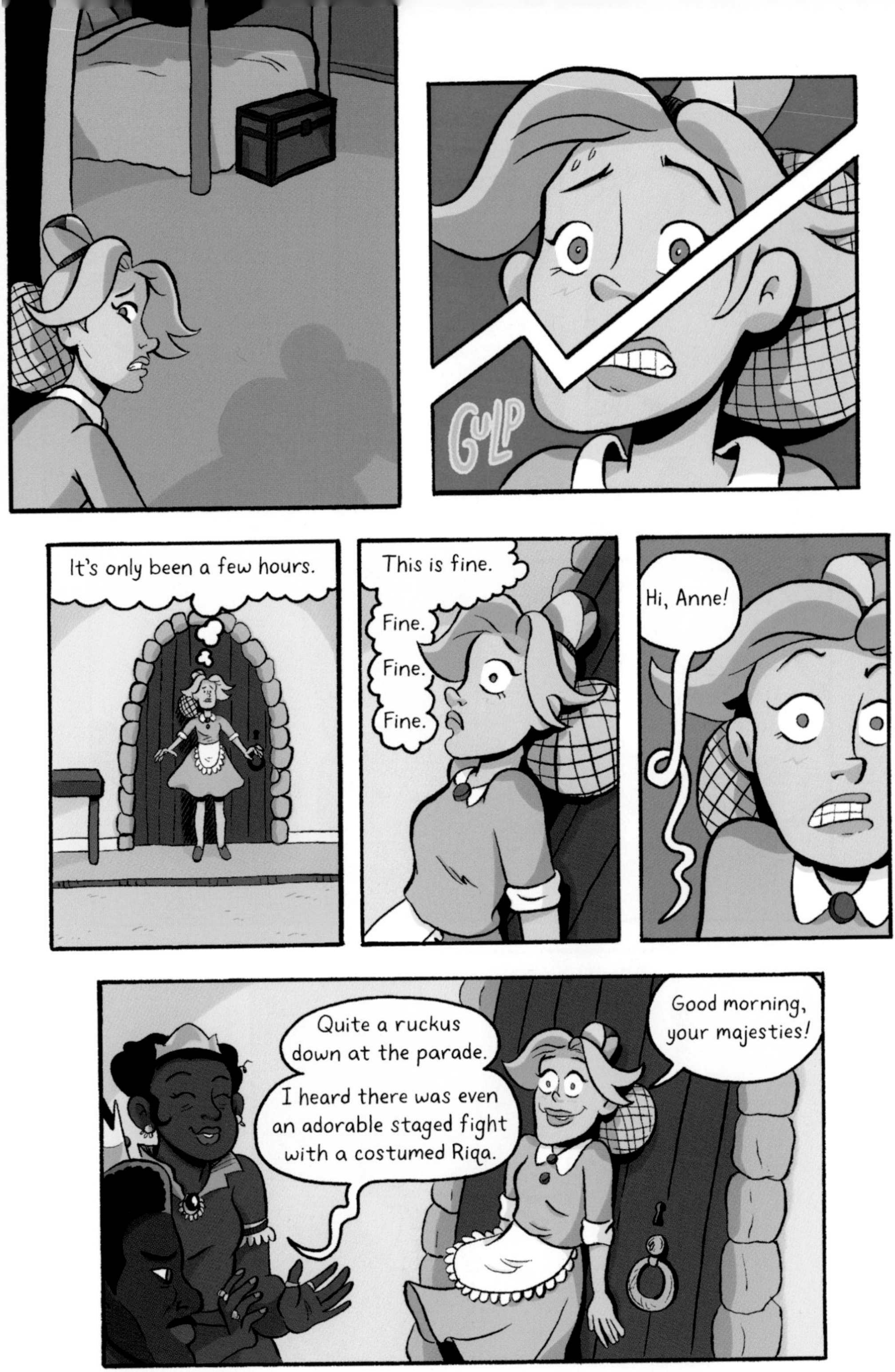
GULP
It's only been a few hours.
This is fine.
Fine.
Fine.
Fine.
Hi, Anne!
Good morning, your majesties!
Quite a ruckus down at the parade.
I heard there was even an adorable staged fight with a costumed Riqa.

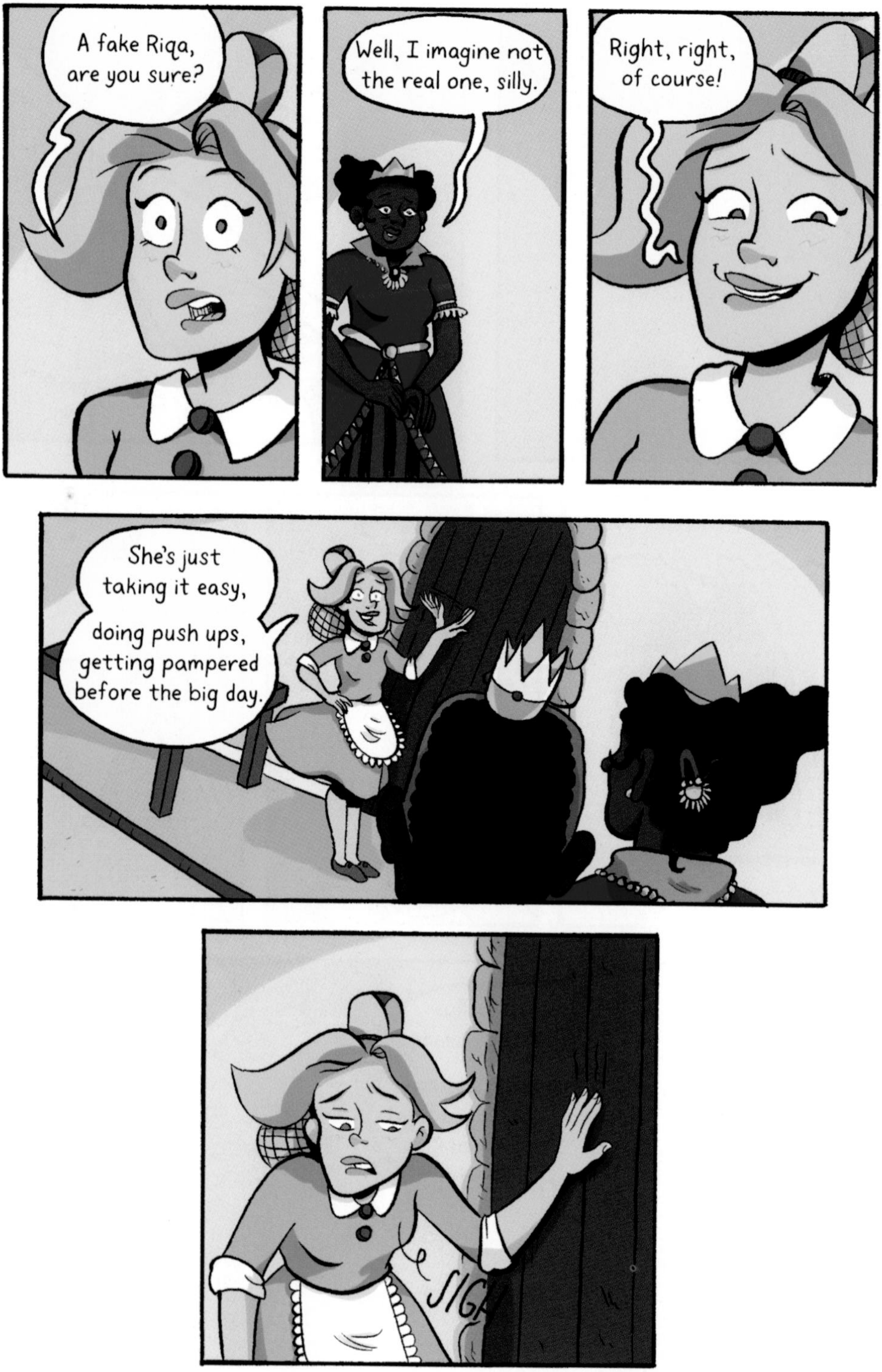
A fake Riqa, are you sure?
Well, I imagine not the real one, silly.
Right, right, of course!
She's just taking it easy,
doing push ups, getting pampered before the big day.
SIG

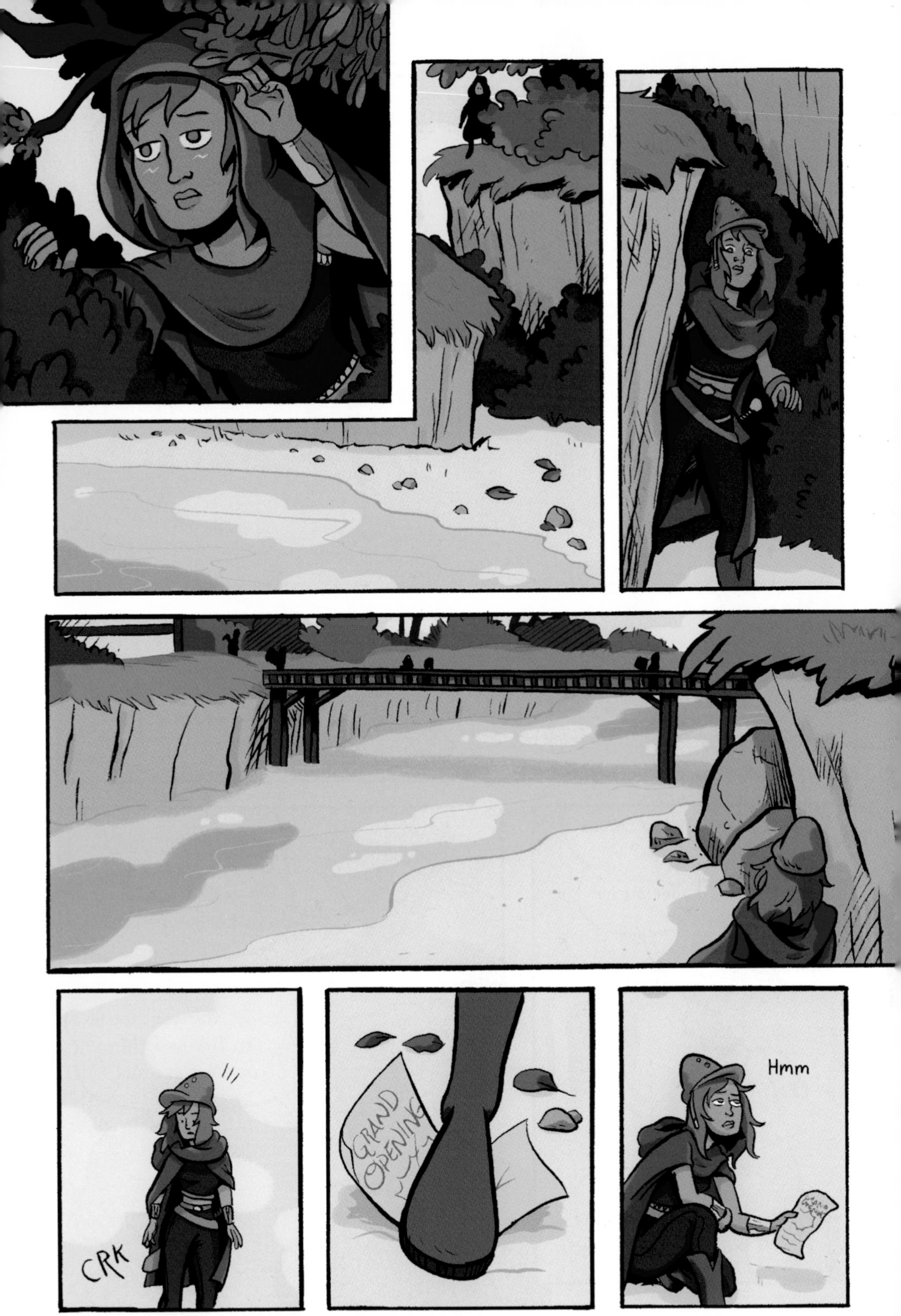
CRK
GRAND OPENING
Hmm

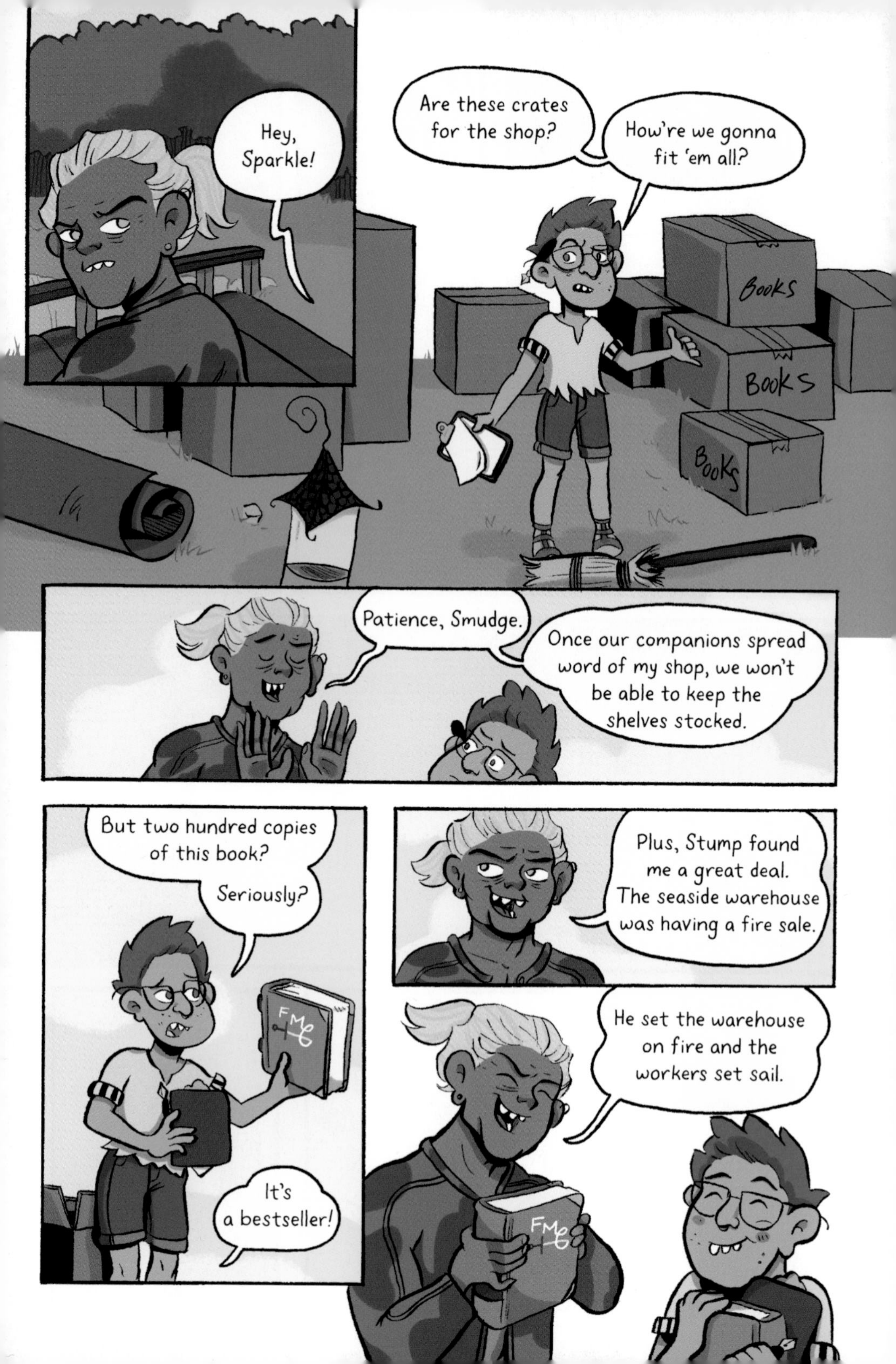
Hey, Sparkle!
Are these crates for the shop?
How're we gonna fit 'em all?
Books
Books
Books
Patience, Smudge.
Once our companions spread word of my shop, we won't be able to keep the shelves stocked.
But two hundred copies of this book?
Seriously?
It's a bestseller!
Plus, Stump found me a great deal. The seaside warehouse was having a fire sale.
He set the warehouse on fire and the workers set sail.

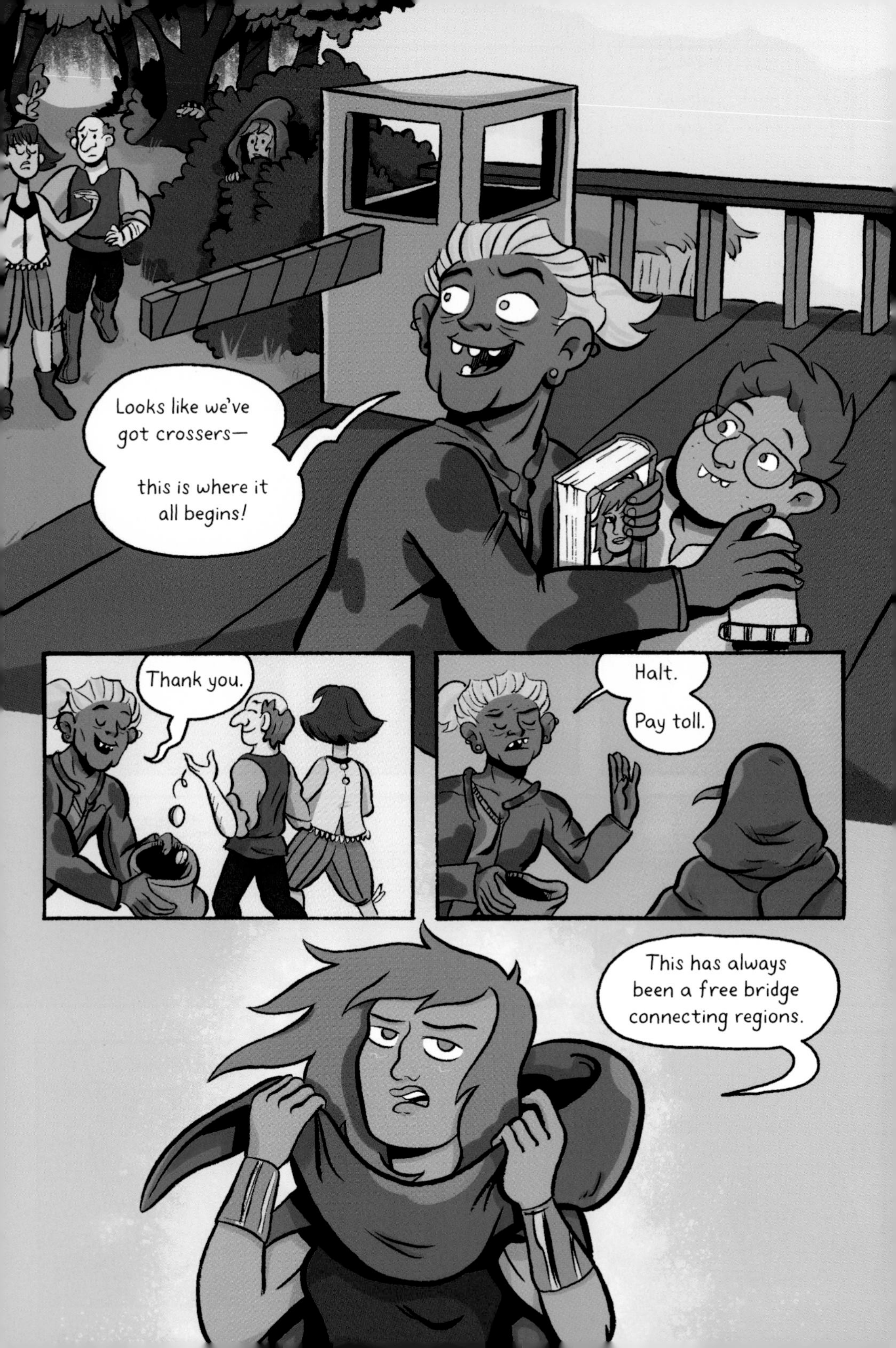
Looks like we've got crossers—
this is where it all begins!
Thank you.
Halt.
Pay toll.
This has always been a free bridge connecting regions.

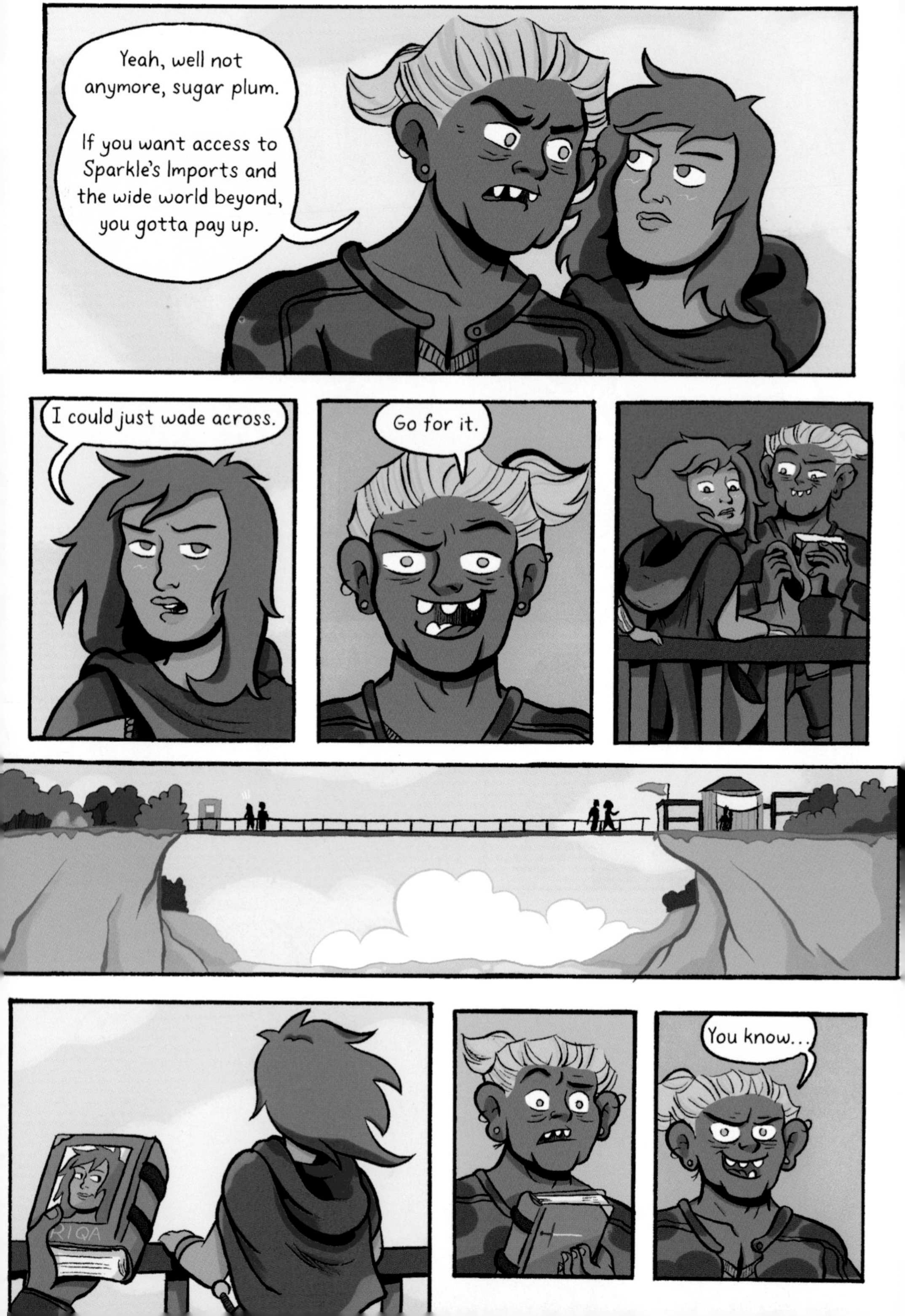
Yeah, well not anymore, sugar plum.
If you want access to Sparkle's Imports and the wide world beyond, you gotta pay up.
I could just wade across.
Go for it.
RIQA
You know...

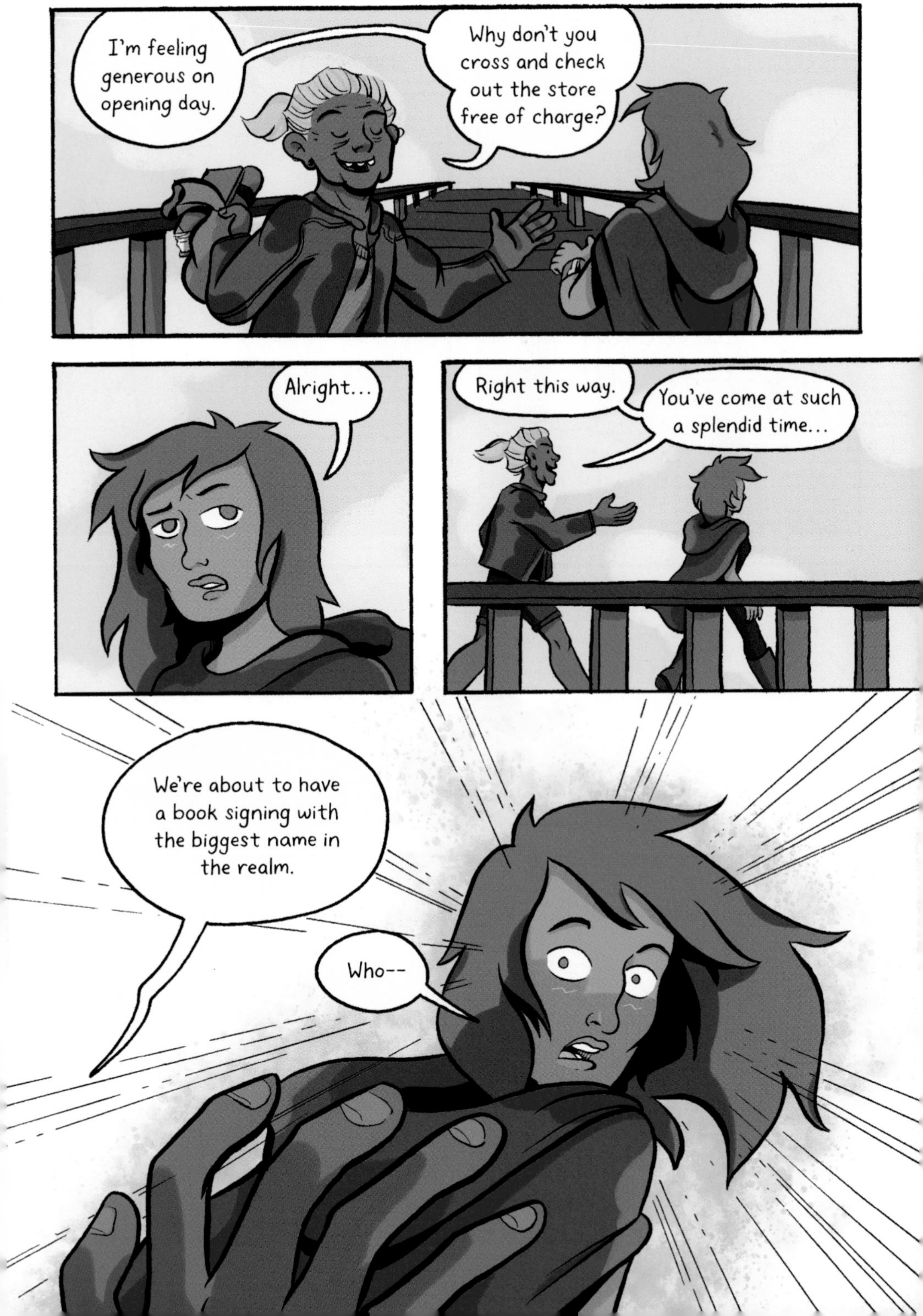
I'm feeling generous on opening day.
Why don't you cross and check out the store free of charge?
Alright...
Right this way.
You've come at such a splendid time...
We're about to have a book signing with the biggest name in the realm.
Who--

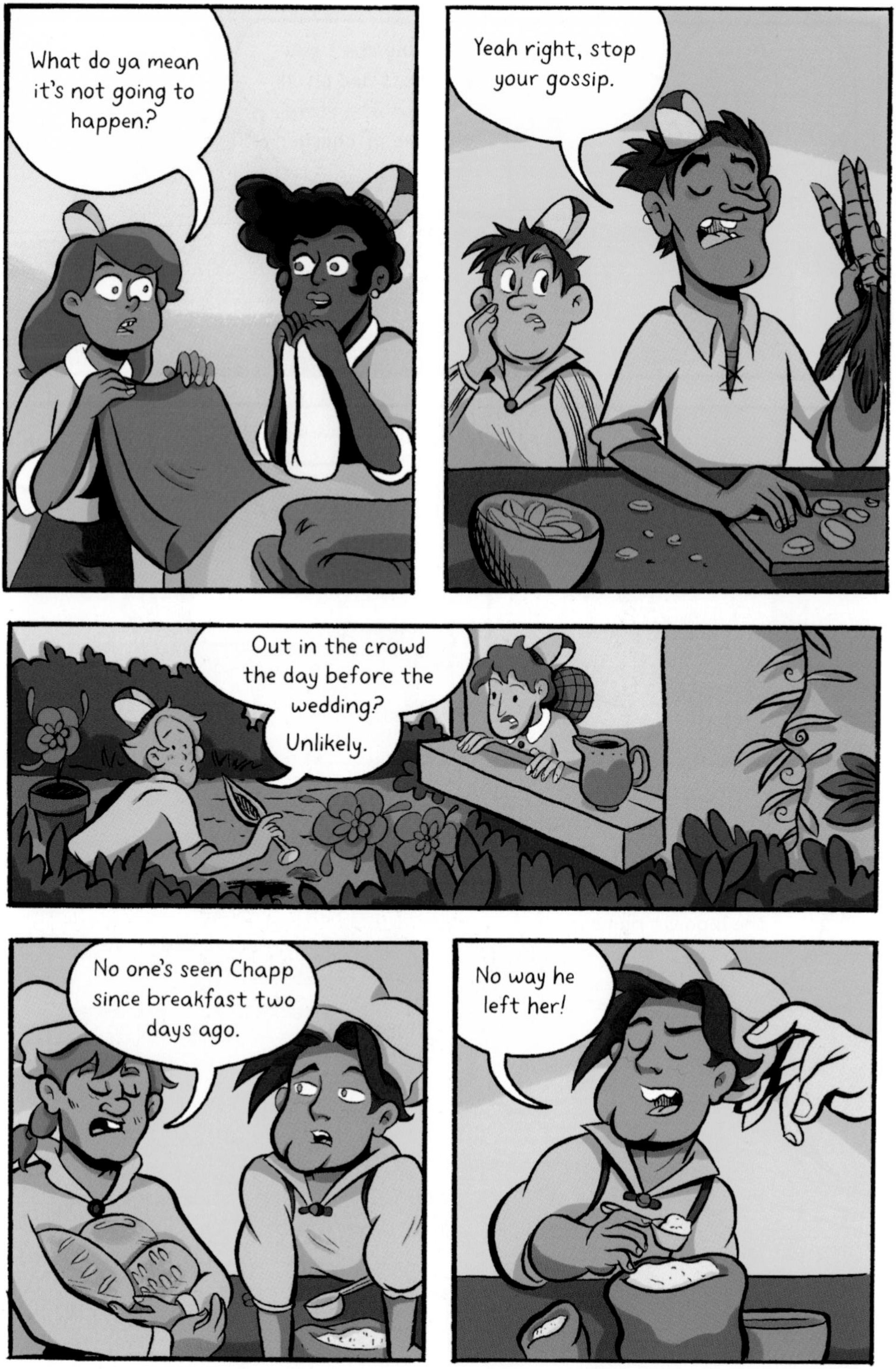
What do ya mean it's not going to happen?
Yeah right, stop your gossip.
Out in the crowd the day before the wedding?
Unlikely.
No one's seen Chapp since breakfast two days ago.
No way he left her!

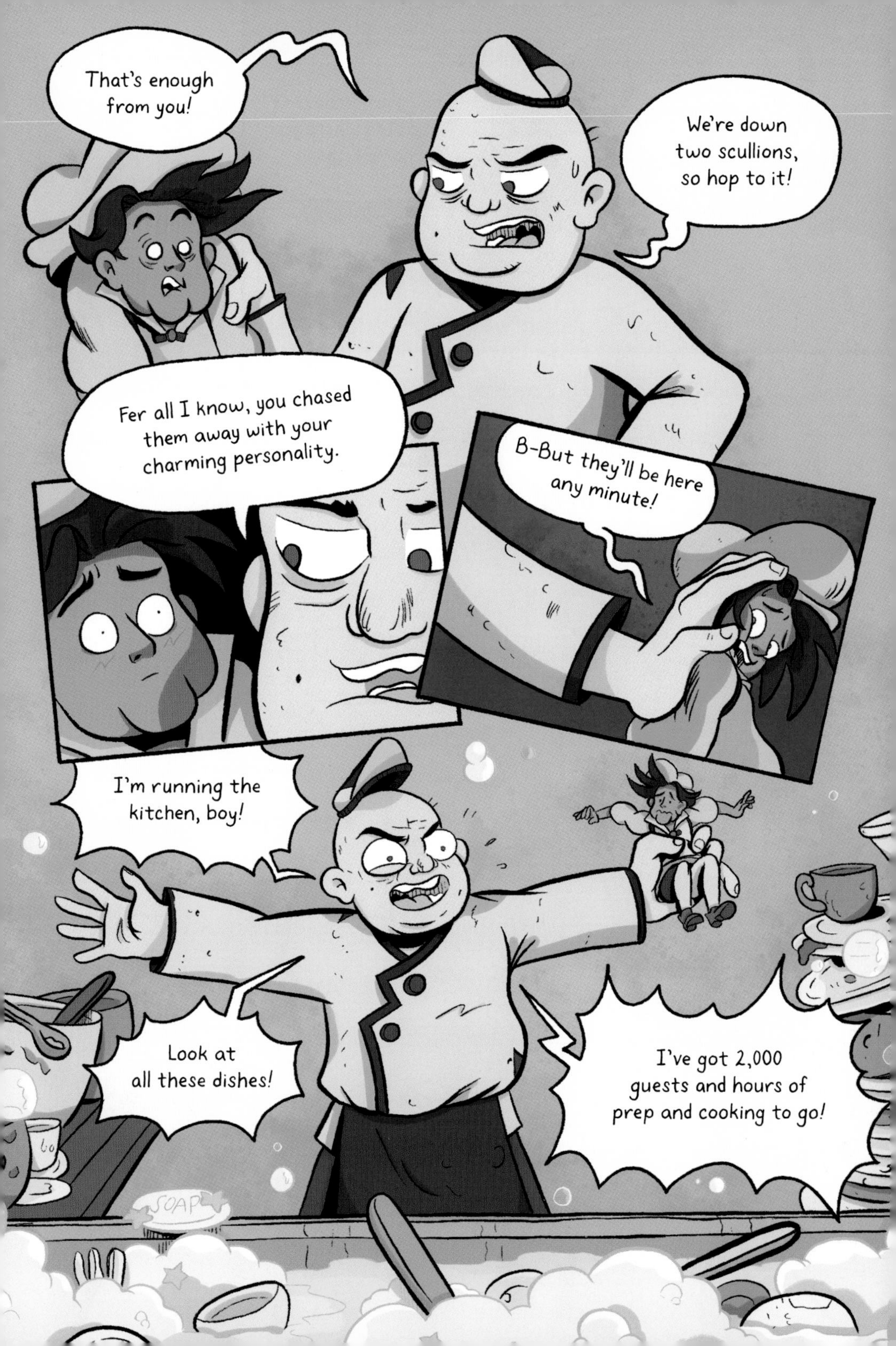
That's enough from you!
We're down two scullions, so hop to it!
Fer all I know, you chased them away with your charming personality.
B-But they'll be here any minute!
I'm running the kitchen, boy!
Look at all these dishes!
I've got 2,000 guests and hours of prep and cooking to go!
SOAP

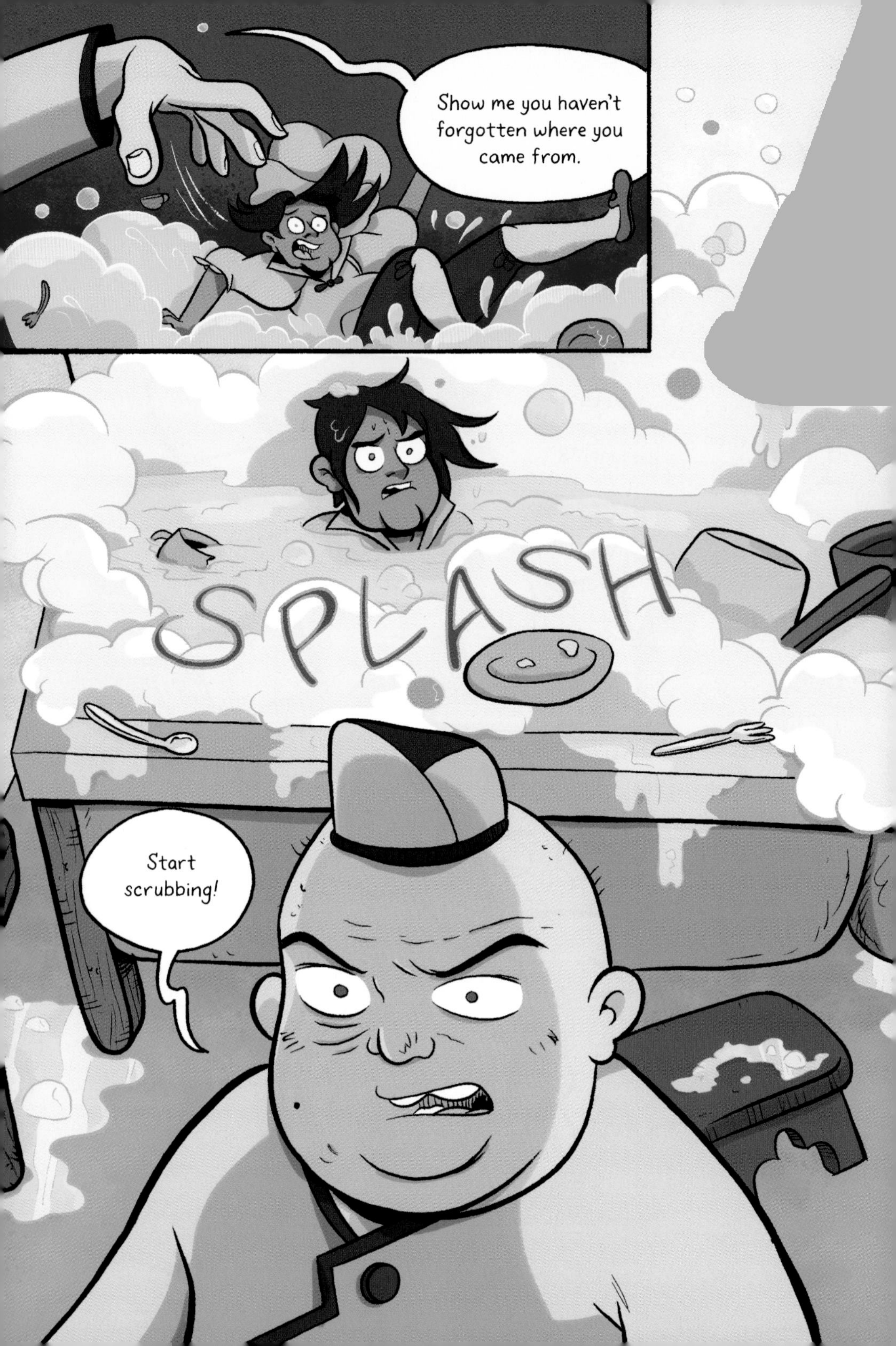
Show me you haven't forgotten where you came from.
SPLASH
Start scrubbing!

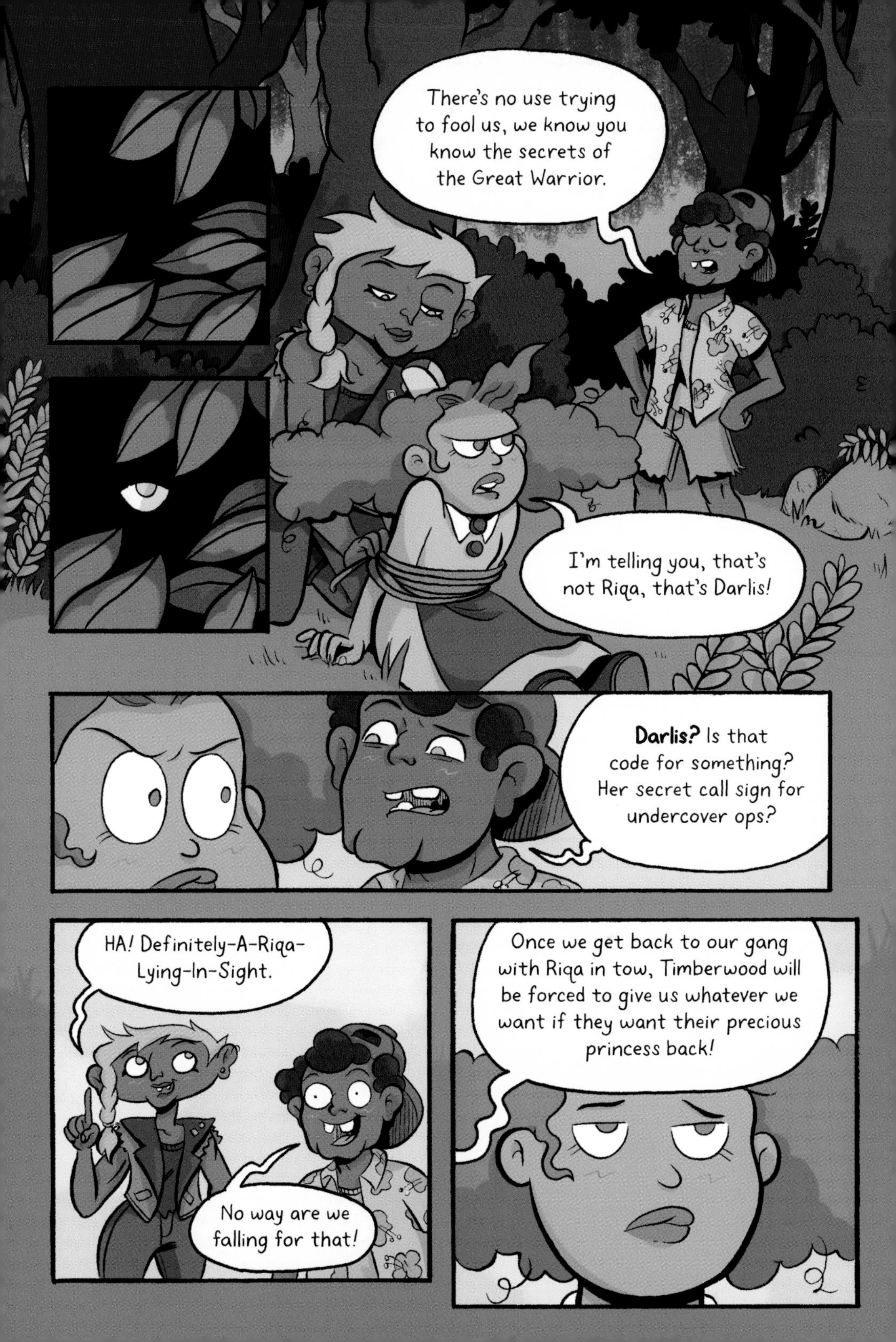
There's no use trying to fool us, we know you know the secrets of the Great Warrior.
I'm telling you, that's not Riqa, that's Darlis!
Darlis? Is that code for something? Her secret call sign for undercover ops?
HA! Definitely-A-Riqa-Lying-In-Sight.
No way are we falling for that!
Once we get back to our gang with Riqa in tow, Timberwood will be forced to give us whatever we want if they want their precious princess back!

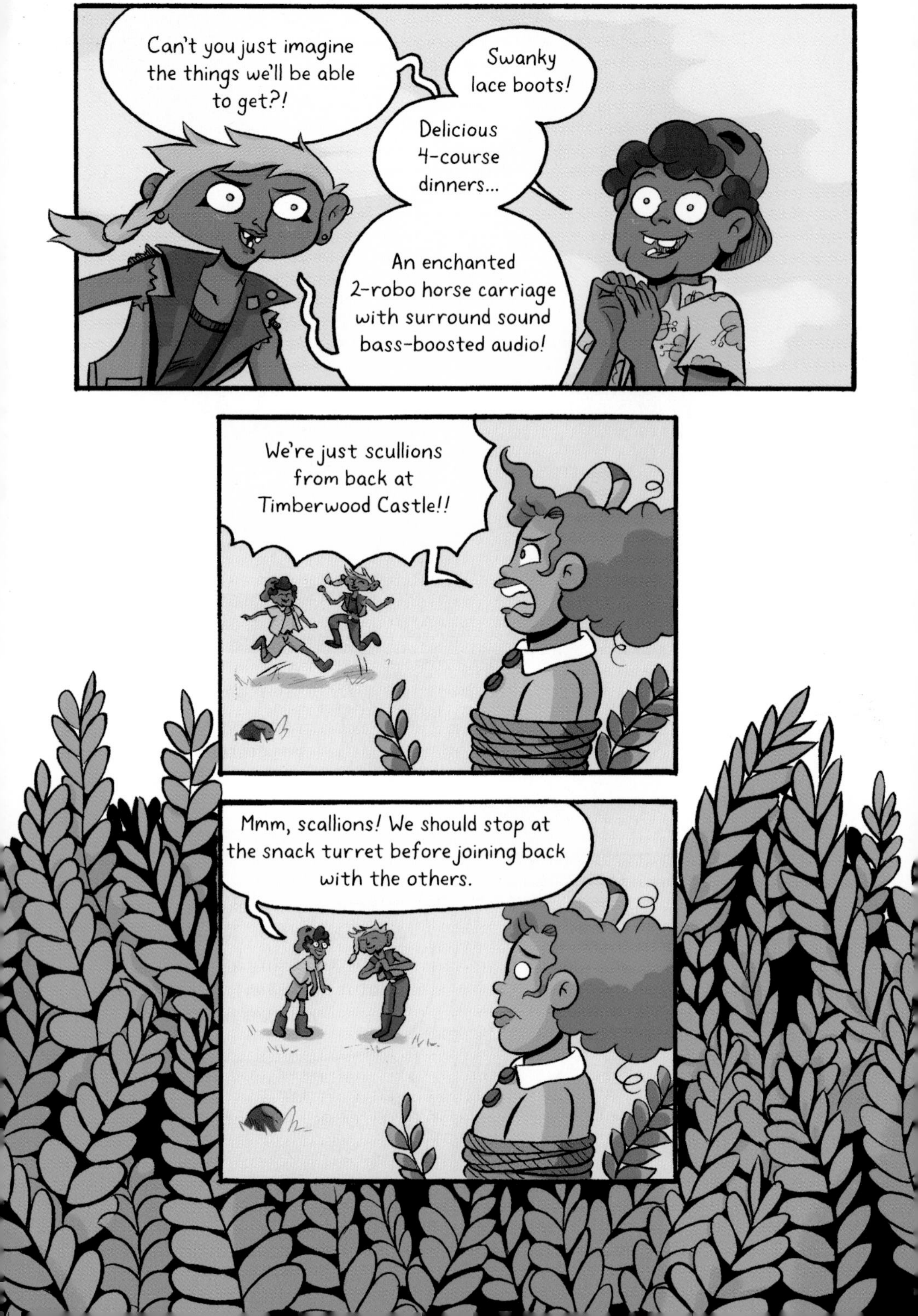
Can't you just imagine the things we'll be able to get?!
Swanky lace boots!
Delicious 4-course dinners...
An enchanted 2-robo horse carriage with surround sound bass-boosted audio!
We're just scullions from back at Timberwood Castle!!
Mmm, scallions! We should stop at the snack turret before joining back with the others.

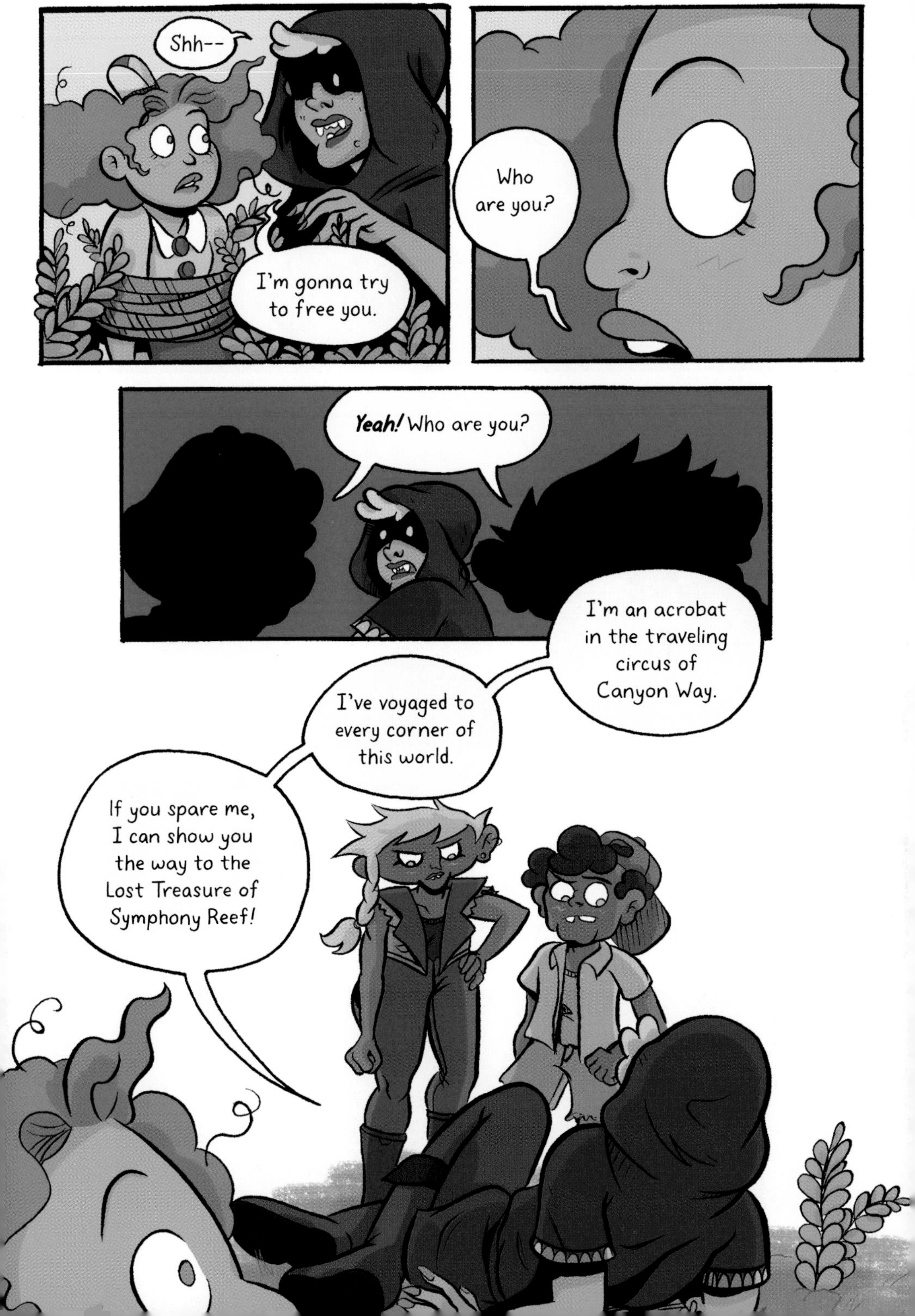
Shh--
I'm gonna try to free you.
Who are you?
Yeah! Who are you?
I'm an acrobat in the traveling circus of Canyon Way.
I've voyaged to every corner of this world.
If you spare me, I can show you the way to the Lost Treasure of Symphony Reef!

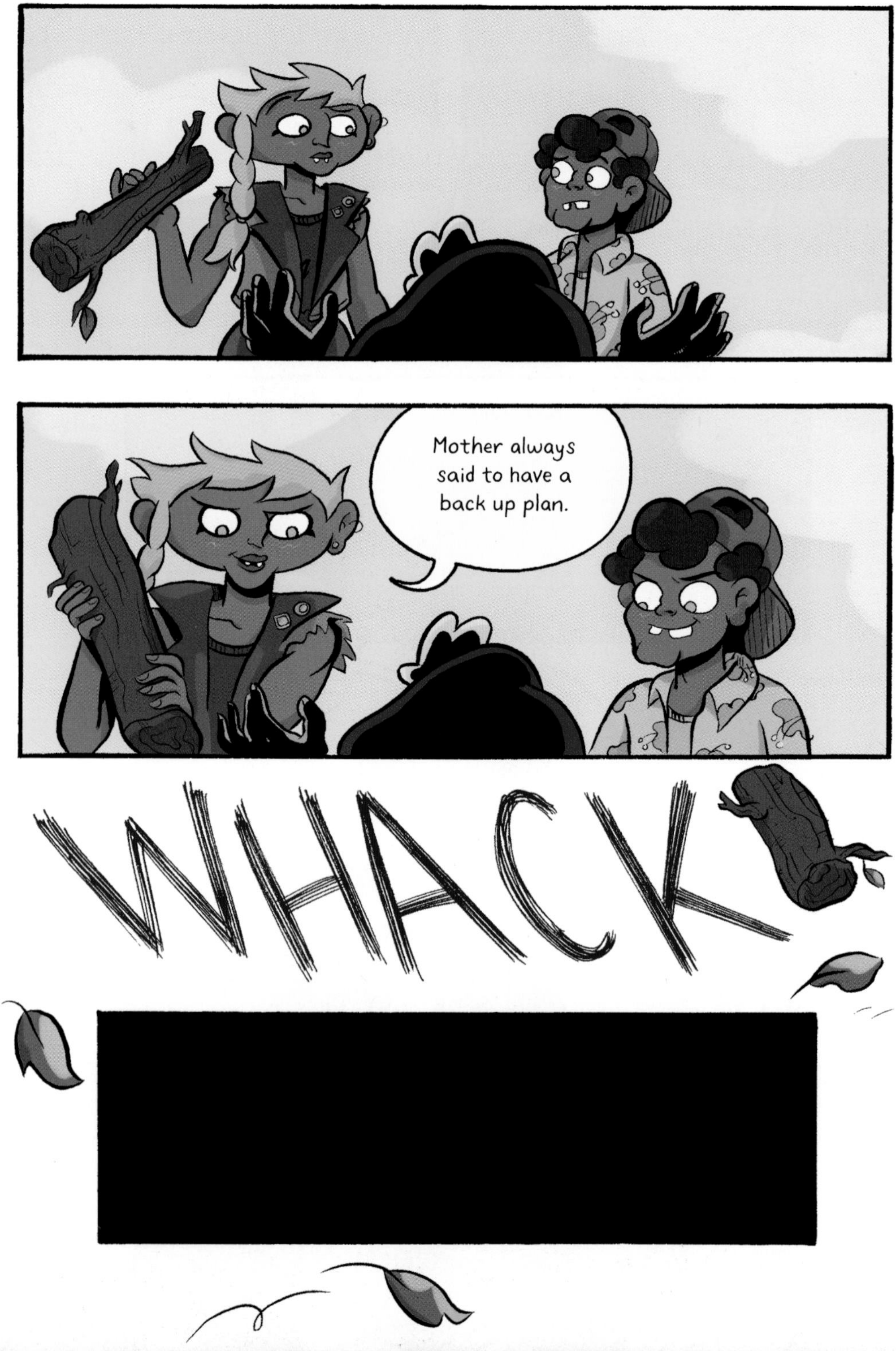
Mother always said to have a back up plan.
WHACK

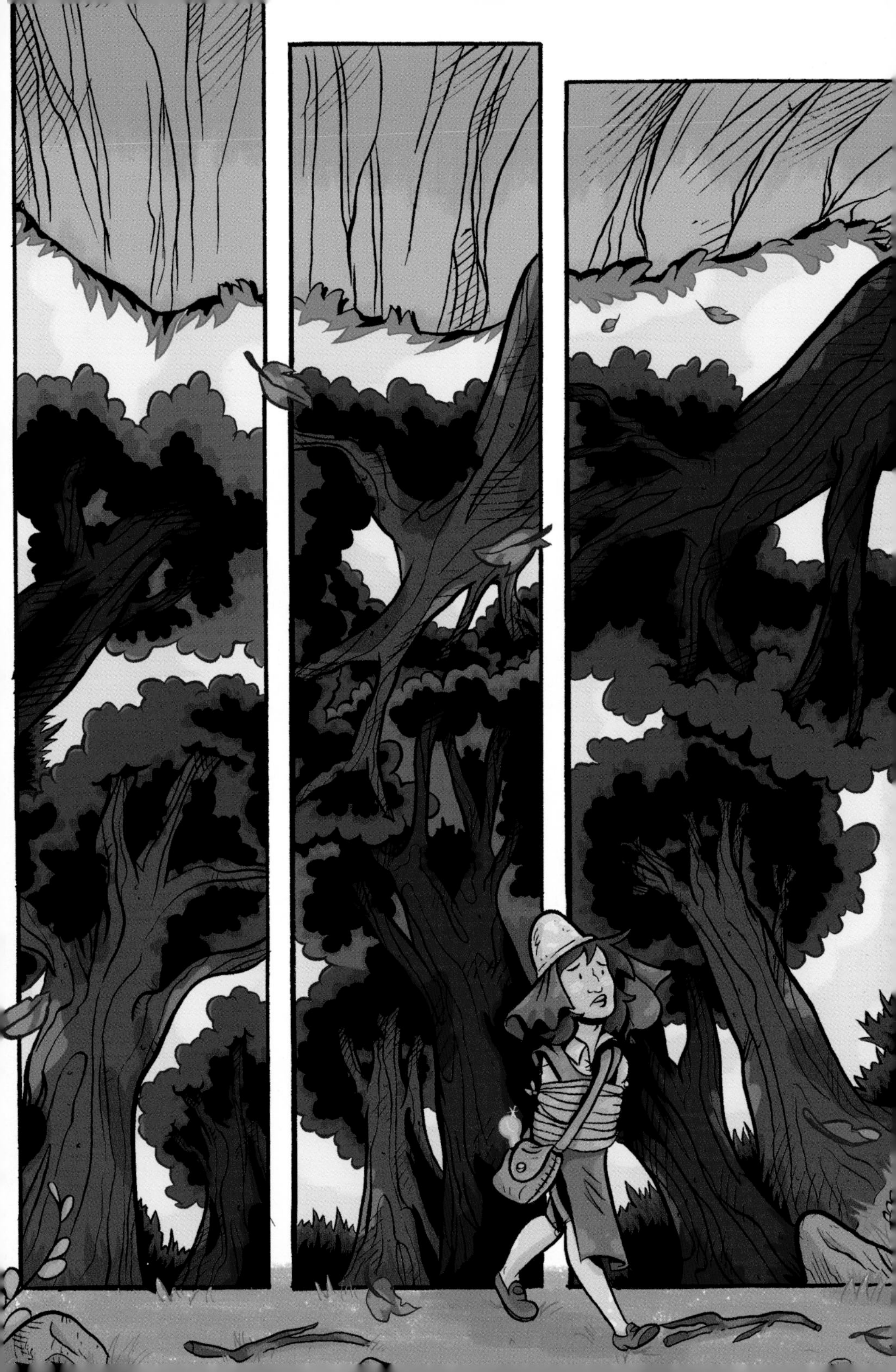

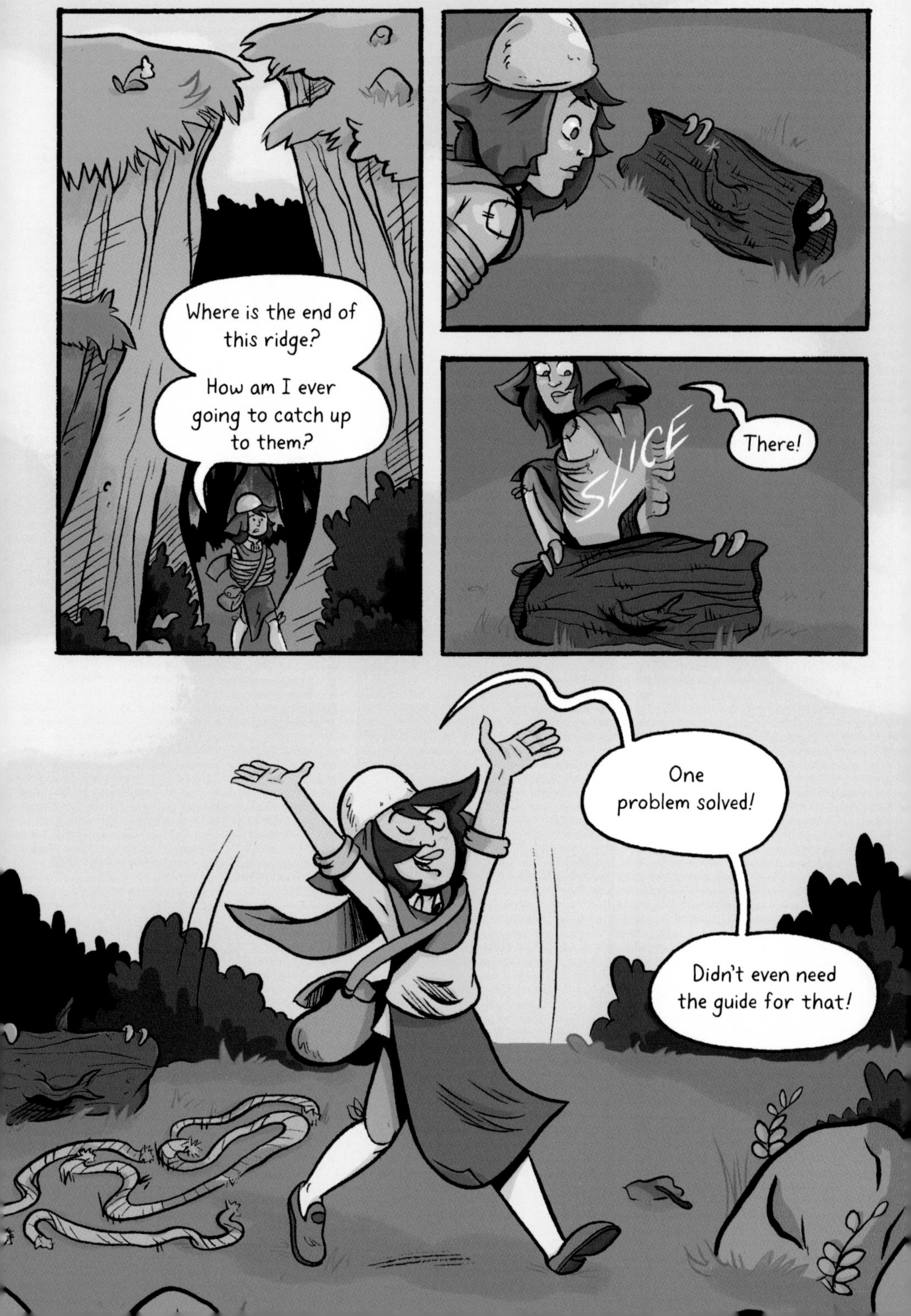
Where is the end of this ridge?
How am I ever going to catch up to them?
SLICE
There!
One problem solved!
Didn't even need the guide for that!

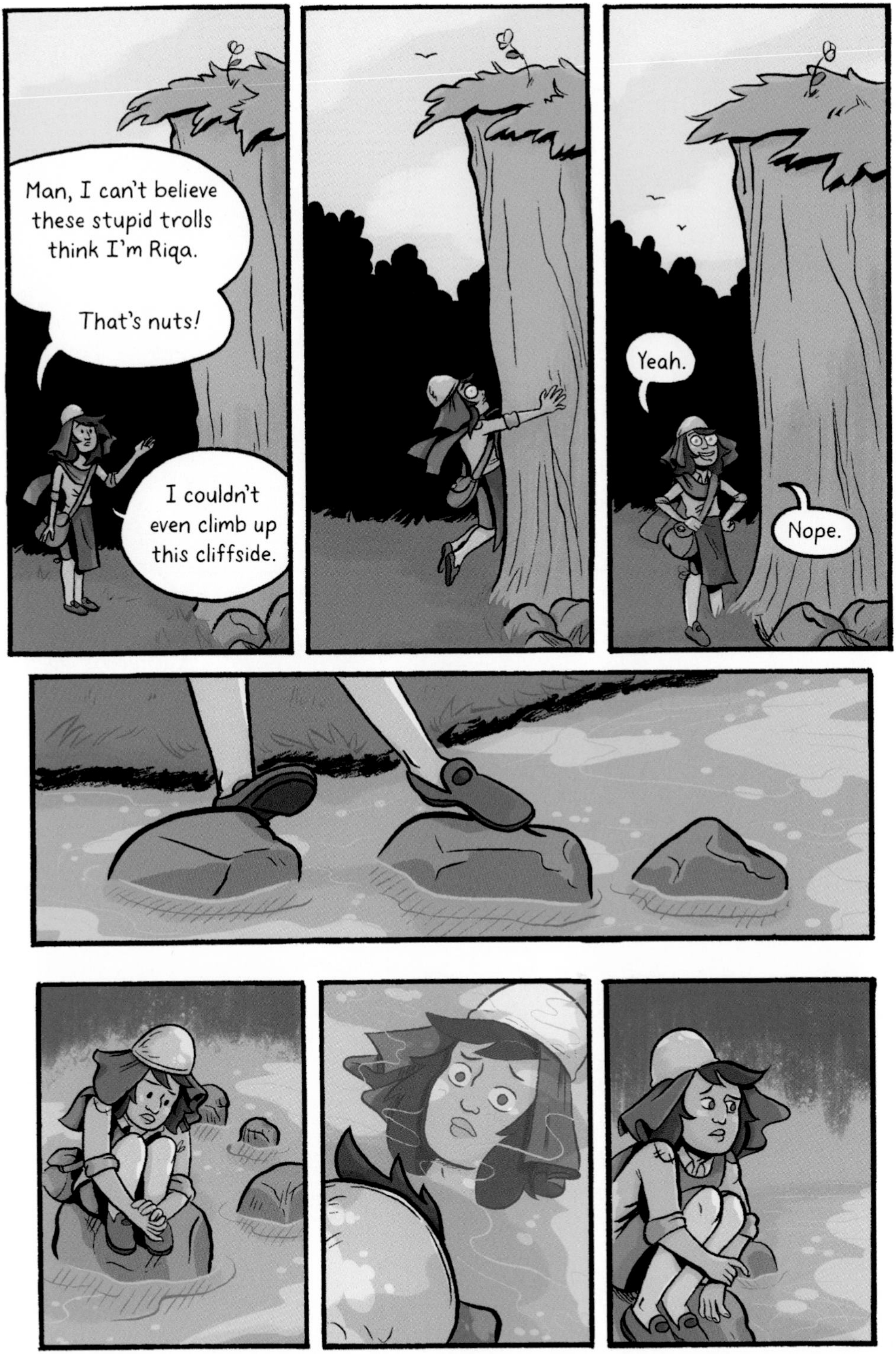
Man, I can't believe these stupid trolls think I'm Riqa.
That's nuts!
I couldn't even climb up this cliffside.
Yeah.
Nope.

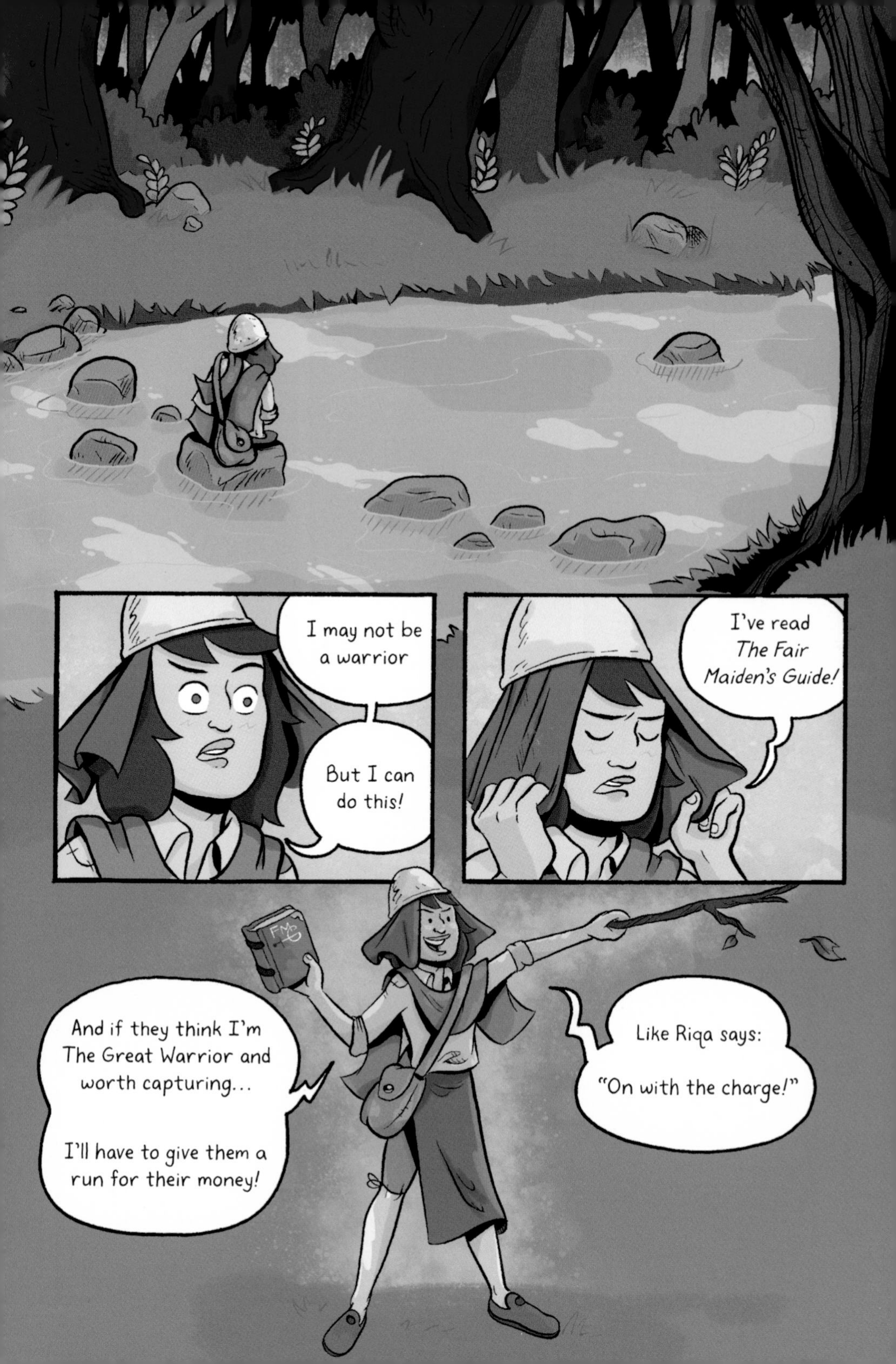
I may not be a warrior
But I can do this!
I've read *The Fair Maiden's Guide!*
And if they think I'm The Great Warrior and worth capturing...
I'll have to give them a run for their money!
Like Riqa says:
"On with the charge!"

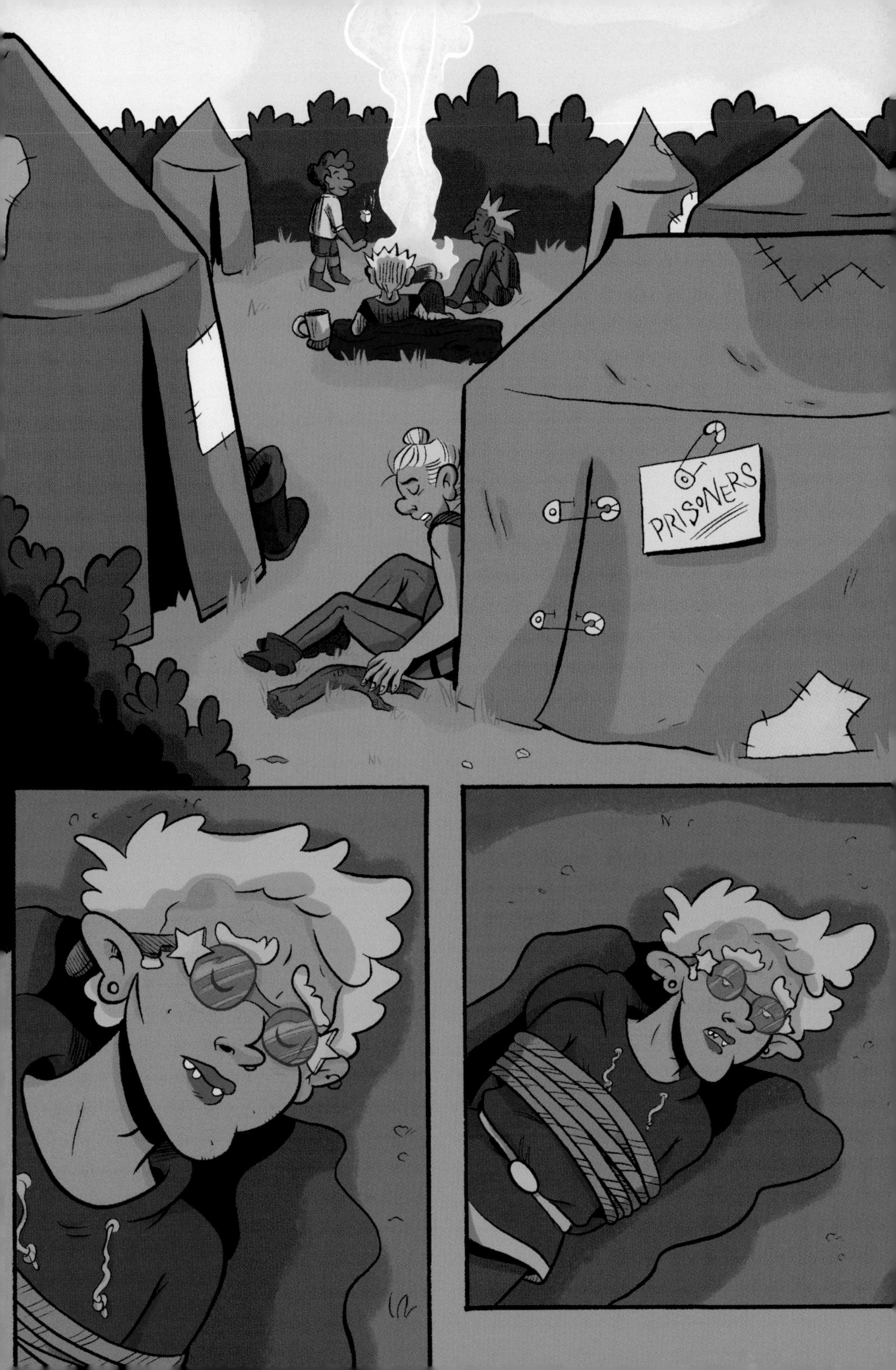
PRISONERS

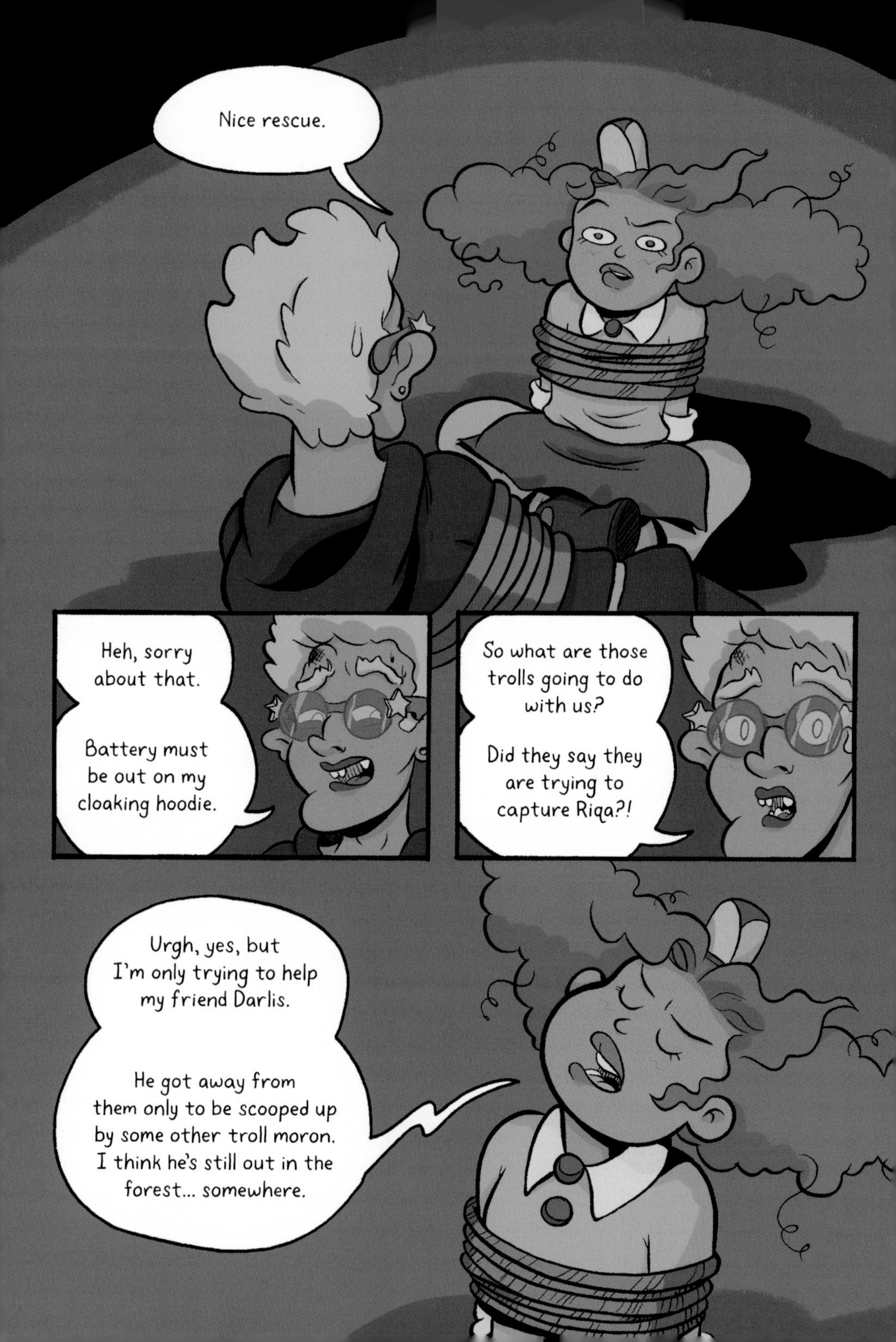
Nice rescue.
Heh, sorry about that.
Battery must be out on my cloaking hoodie.
So what are those trolls going to do with us?
Did they say they are trying to capture Riqa?!
Urgh, yes, but I'm only trying to help my friend Darlis.
He got away from them only to be scooped up by some other troll moron. I think he's still out in the forest... somewhere.

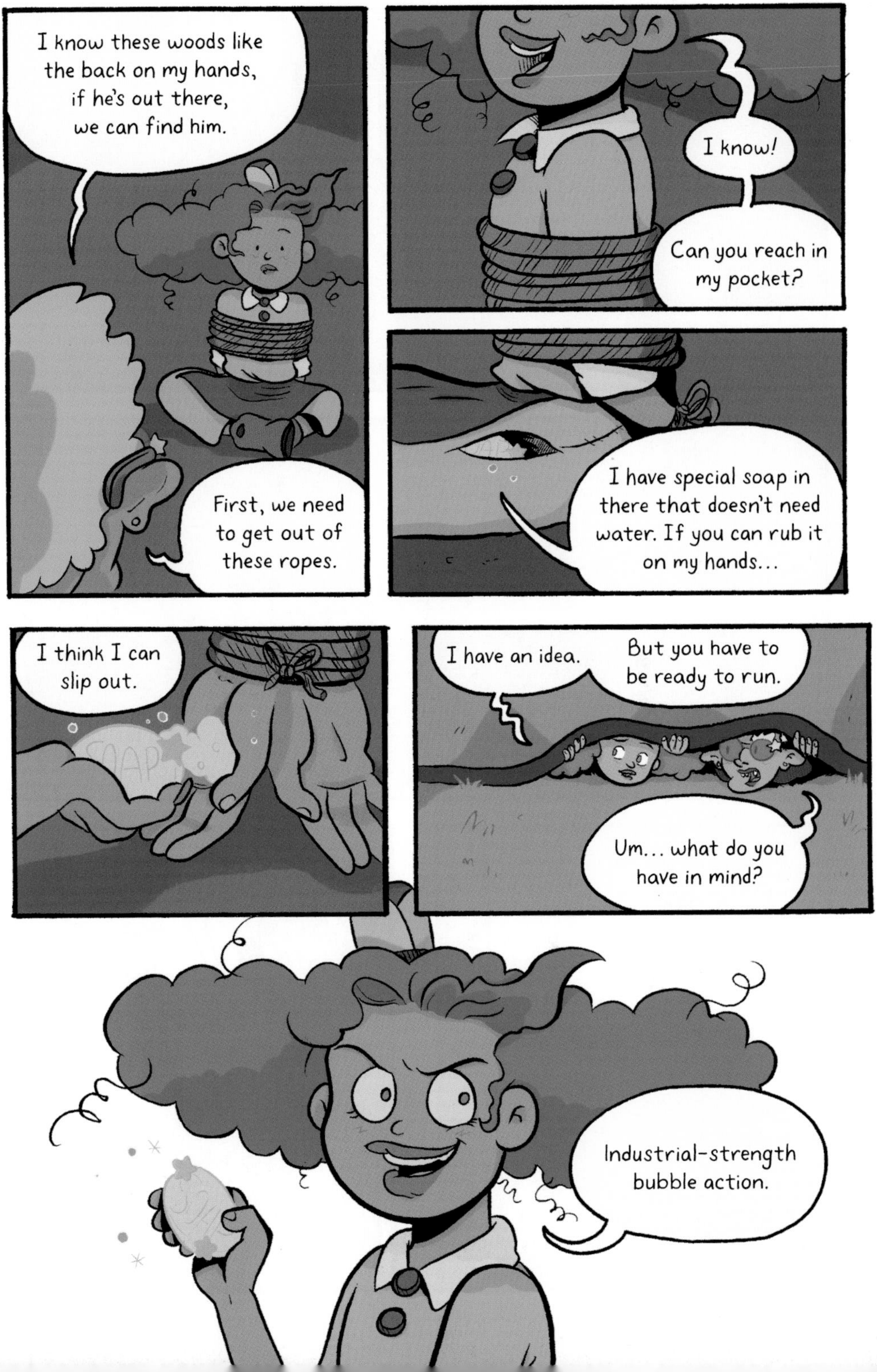

I know these woods like the back on my hands, if he's out there, we can find him.
First, we need to get out of these ropes.
I know!
Can you reach in my pocket?
I have special soap in there that doesn't need water. If you can rub it on my hands...
I think I can slip out.
SOAP
I have an idea.
But you have to be ready to run.
Um... what do you have in mind?
Industrial-strength bubble action.

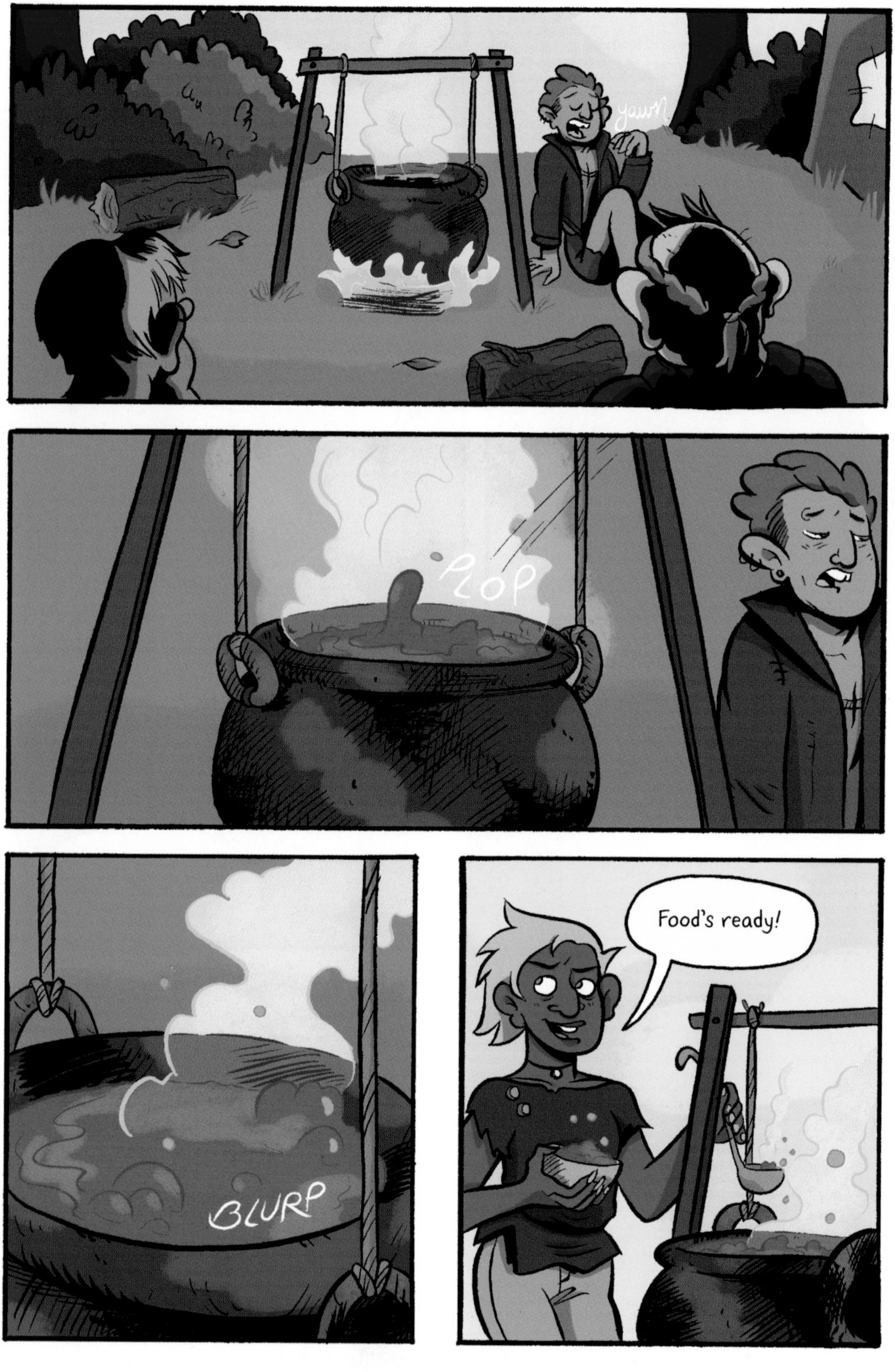

yawn
PLOP
BLURP
Food's ready!

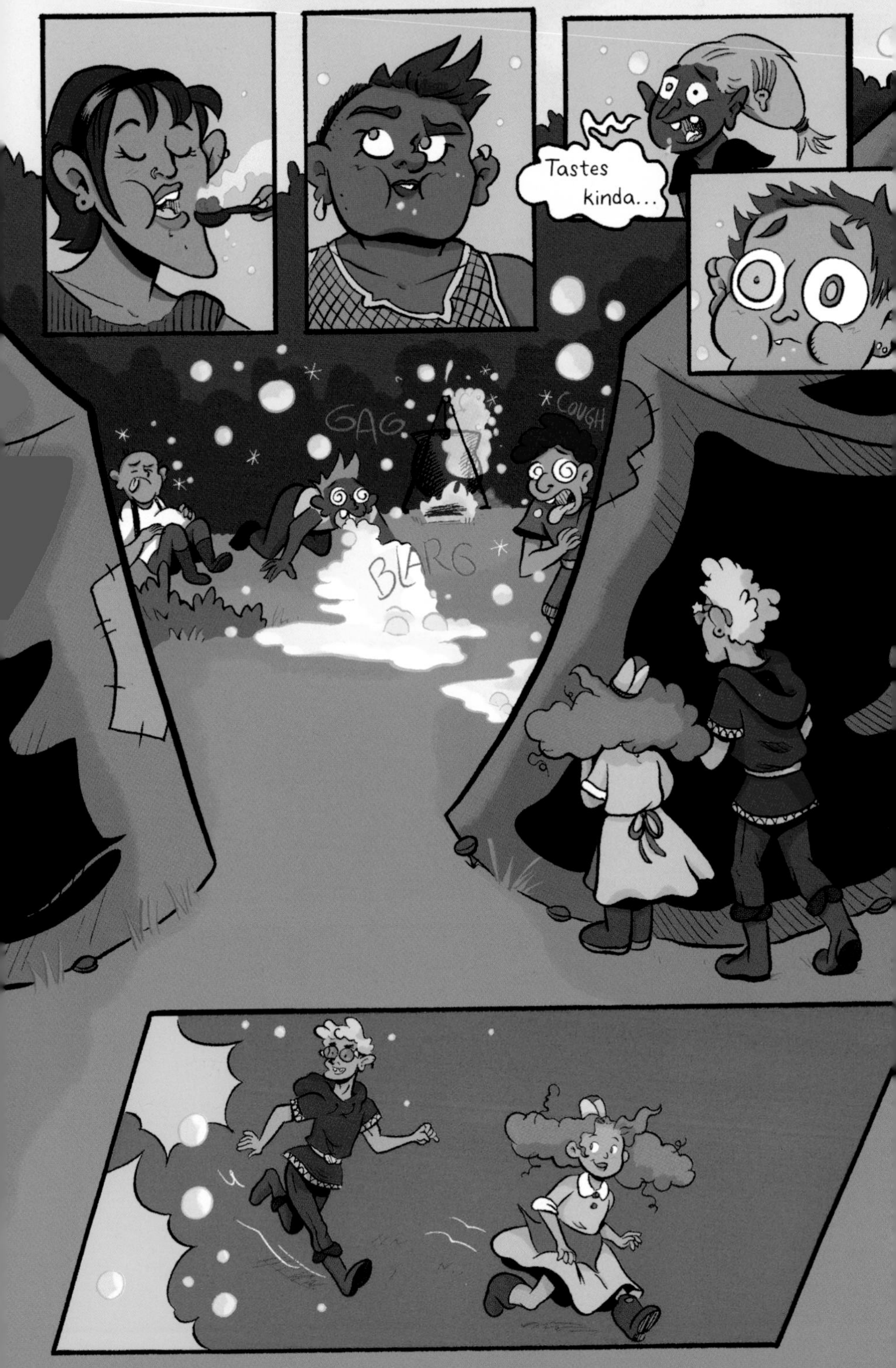
Tastes
kinda...
GAG
COUGH
BLARG

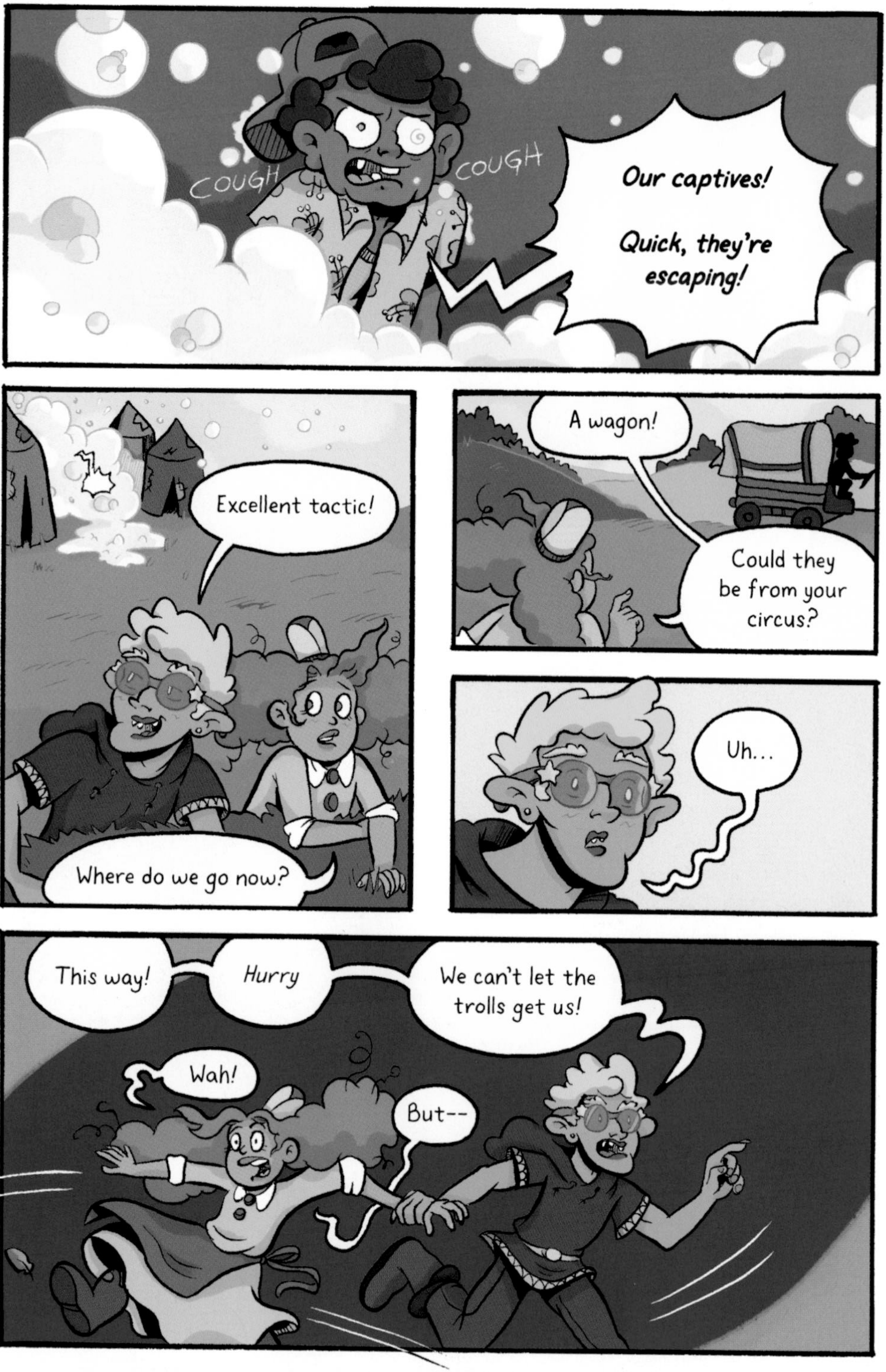
COUGH
COUGH
Our captives!
Quick, they're escaping!
Excellent tactic!
Where do we go now?
A wagon!
Could they be from your circus?
Uh...
This way!
Hurry
We can't let the trolls get us!
Wah!
But--

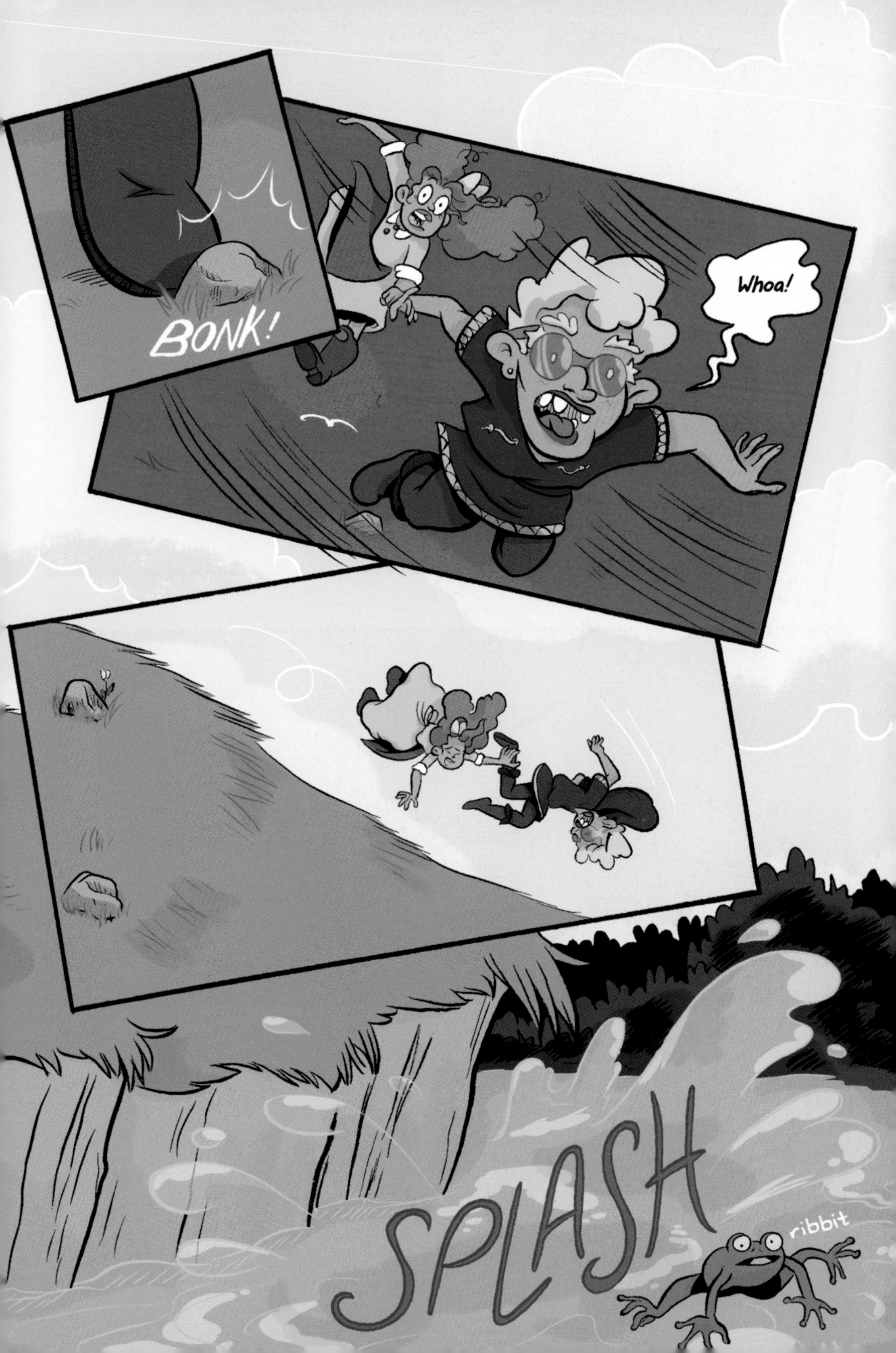
BONK!
Whoa!
SPLASH
ribbit

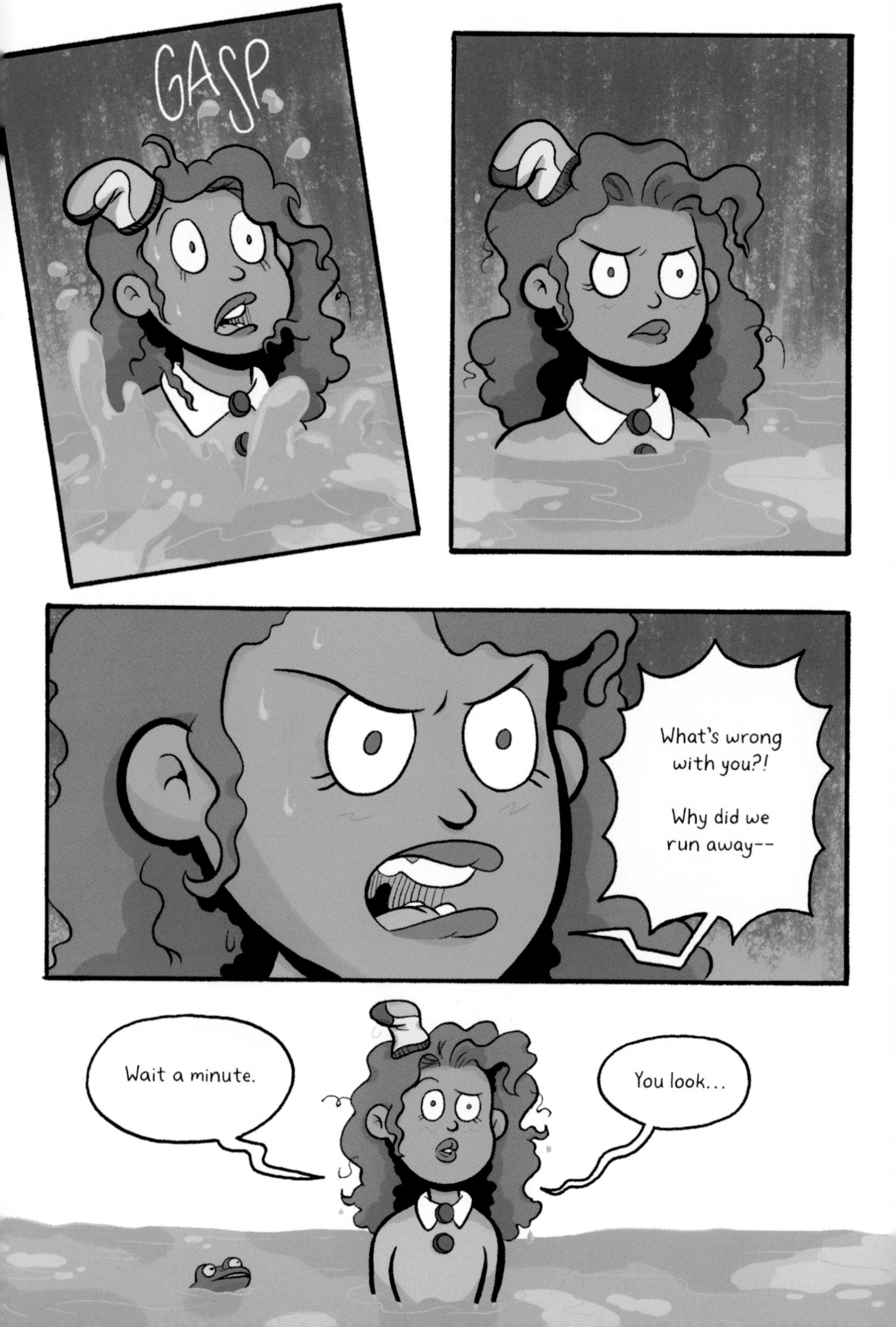
GASP
What's wrong with you?!
Why did we run away--
Wait a minute.
You look...

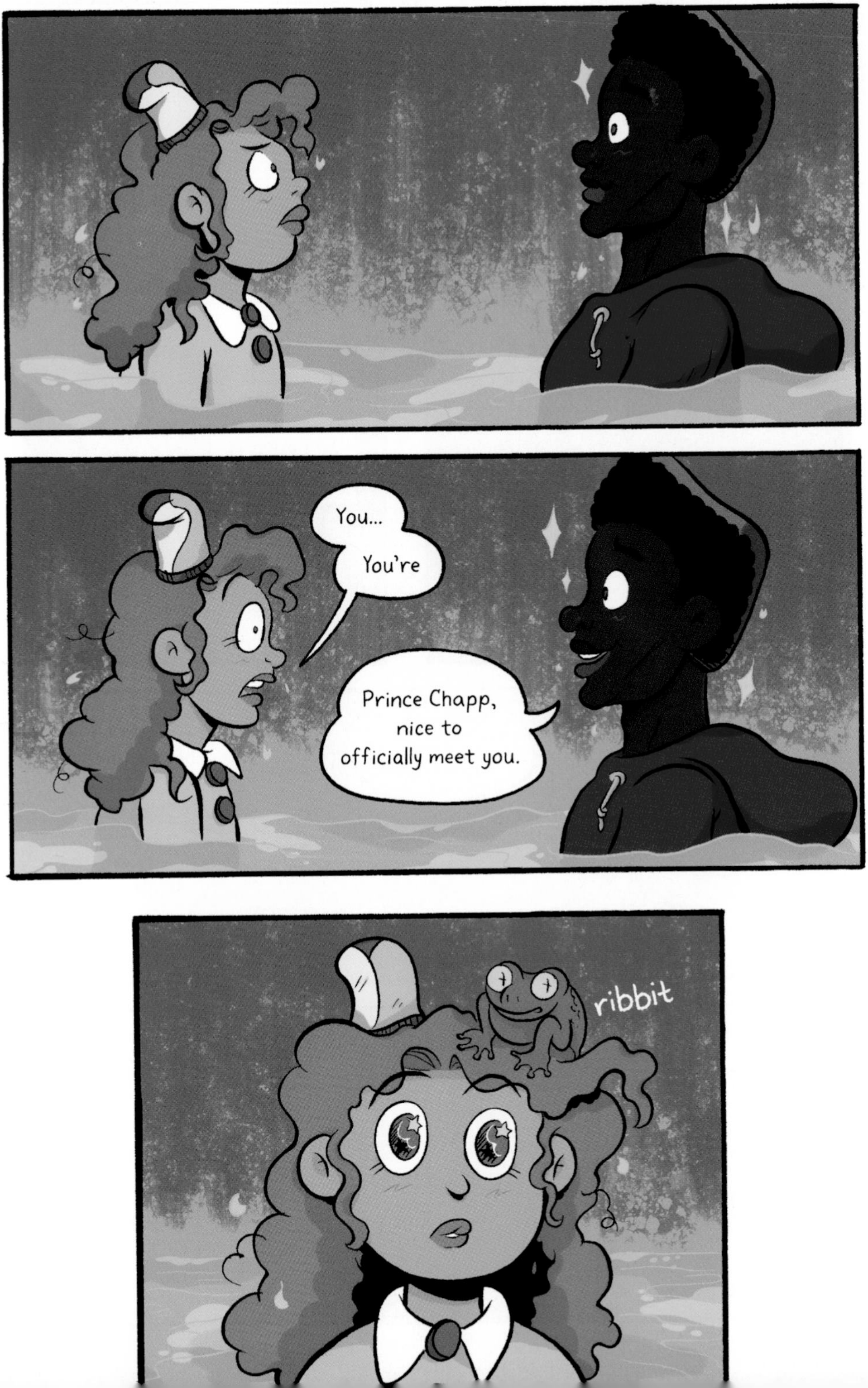
You...
You're
Prince Chapp, nice to officially meet you.
ribbit

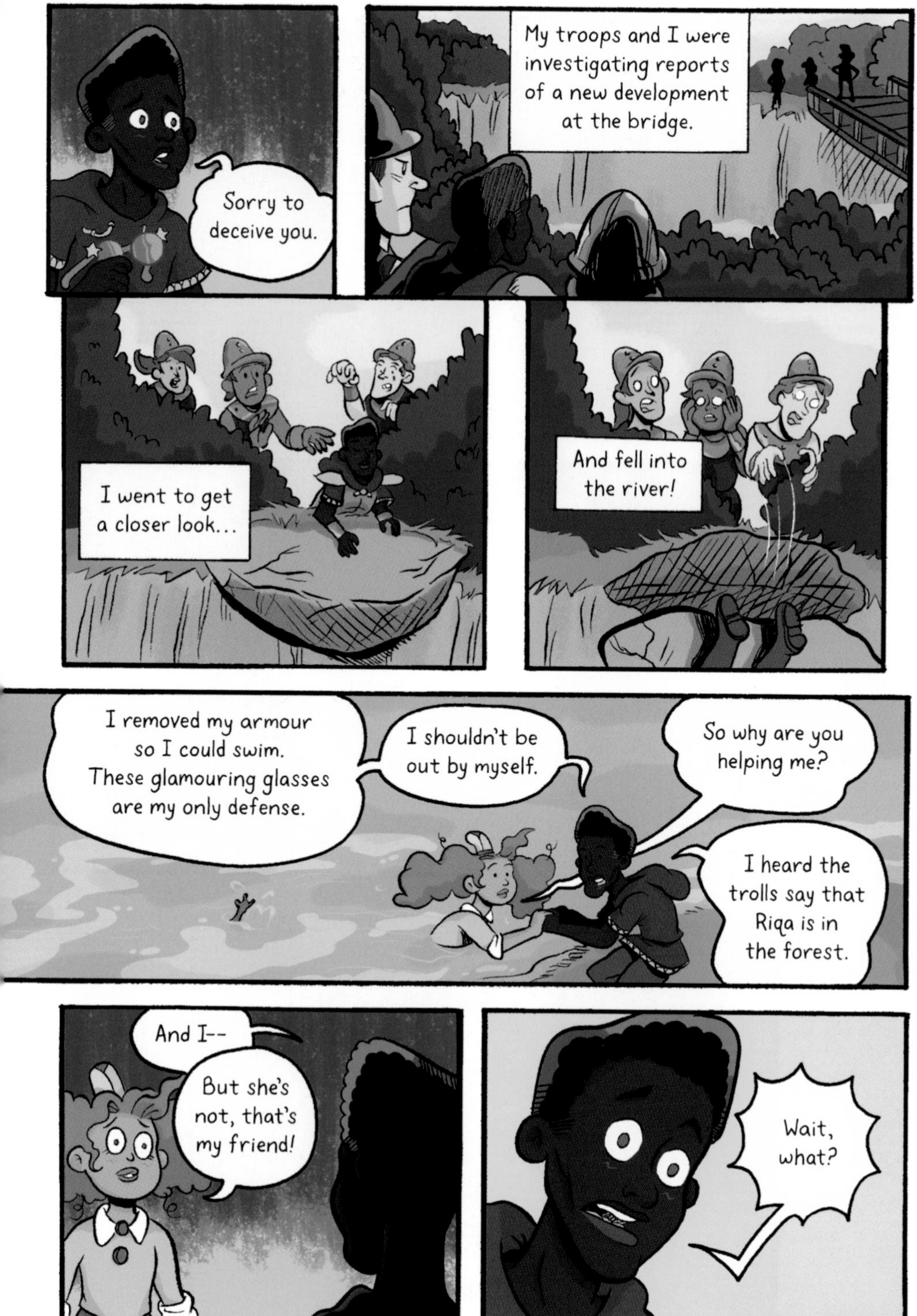
Sorry to deceive you.
My troops and I were investigating reports of a new development at the bridge.
I went to get a closer look...
And fell into the river!
I removed my armour so I could swim. These glamouring glasses are my only defense.
I shouldn't be out by myself.
So why are you helping me?
I heard the trolls say that Riqa is in the forest.
And I--
But she's not, that's my friend!
Wait, what?

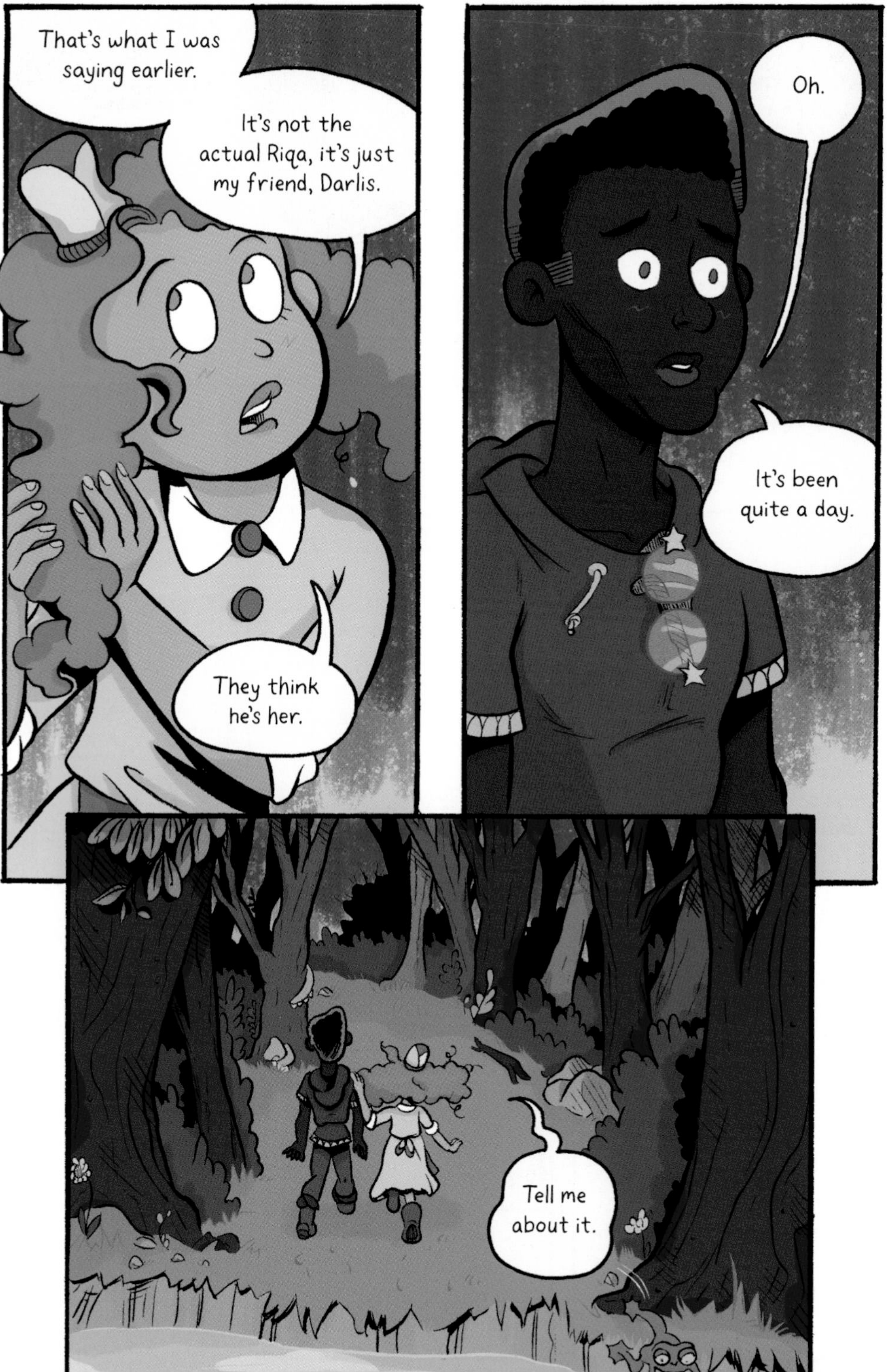
That's what I was saying earlier.
It's not the actual Riqa, it's just my friend, Darlis.
They think he's her.
Oh.
It's been quite a day.
Tell me about it.

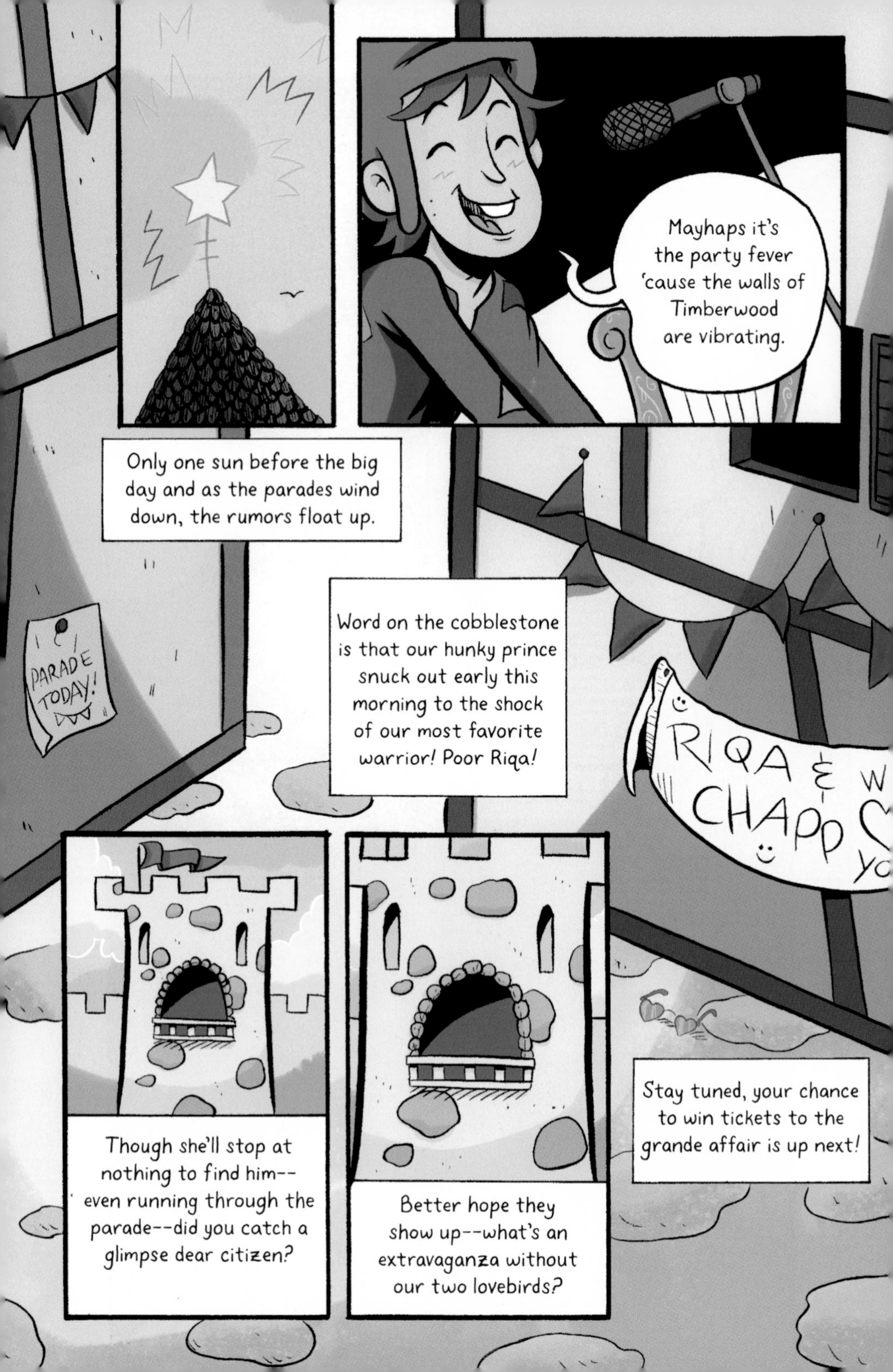
Mayhaps it's the party fever 'cause the walls of Timberwood are vibrating.
Only one sun before the big day and as the parades wind down, the rumors float up.
PARADE TODAY!
Word on the cobblestone is that our hunky prince snuck out early this morning to the shock of our most favorite warrior! Poor Riqa!
RIQA & CHAPP
Though she'll stop at nothing to find him--even running through the parade--did you catch a glimpse dear citizen?
Better hope they show up--what's an extravaganza without our two lovebirds?
Stay tuned, your chance to win tickets to the grande affair is up next!

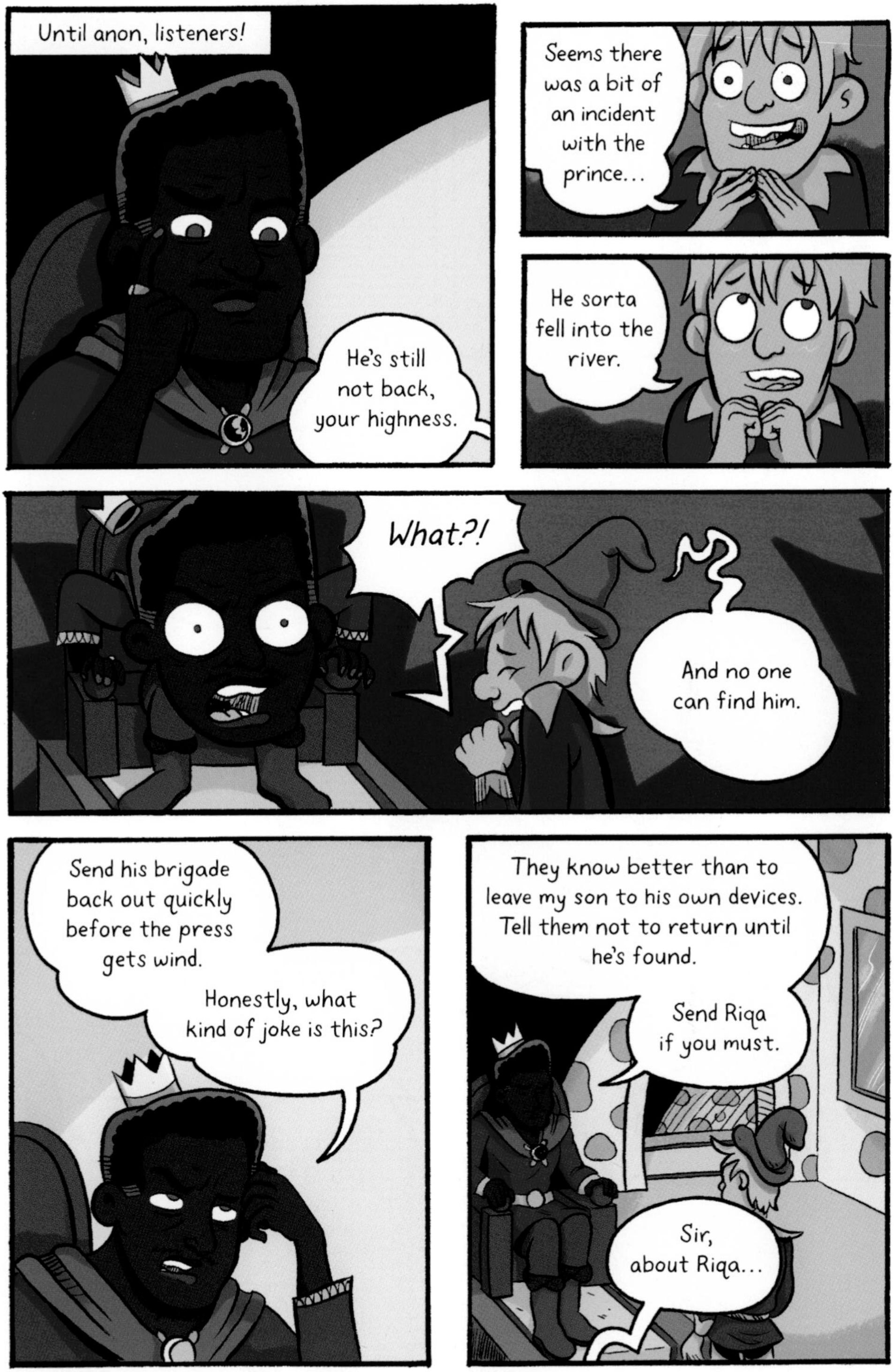
Until anon, listeners!
He's still not back, your highness.
Seems there was a bit of an incident with the prince...
He sorta fell into the river.
What?!
And no one can find him.
Send his brigade back out quickly before the press gets wind.
Honestly, what kind of joke is this?
They know better than to leave my son to his own devices. Tell them not to return until he's found.
Send Riqa if you must.
Sir, about Riqa...

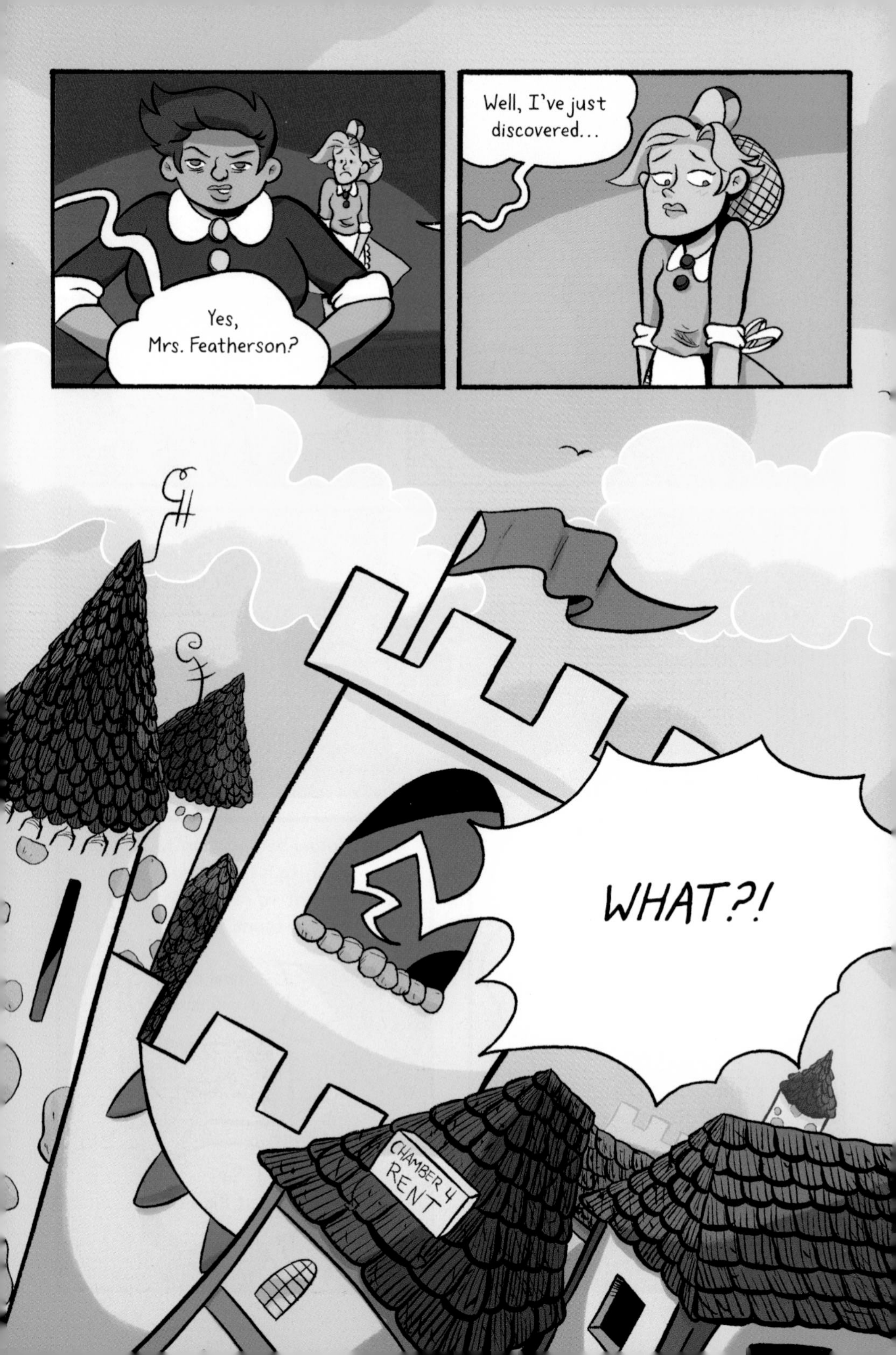
Yes,
Mrs. Featherson?
Well, I've just
discovered...
WHAT?!
CHAMBER 4
RENT

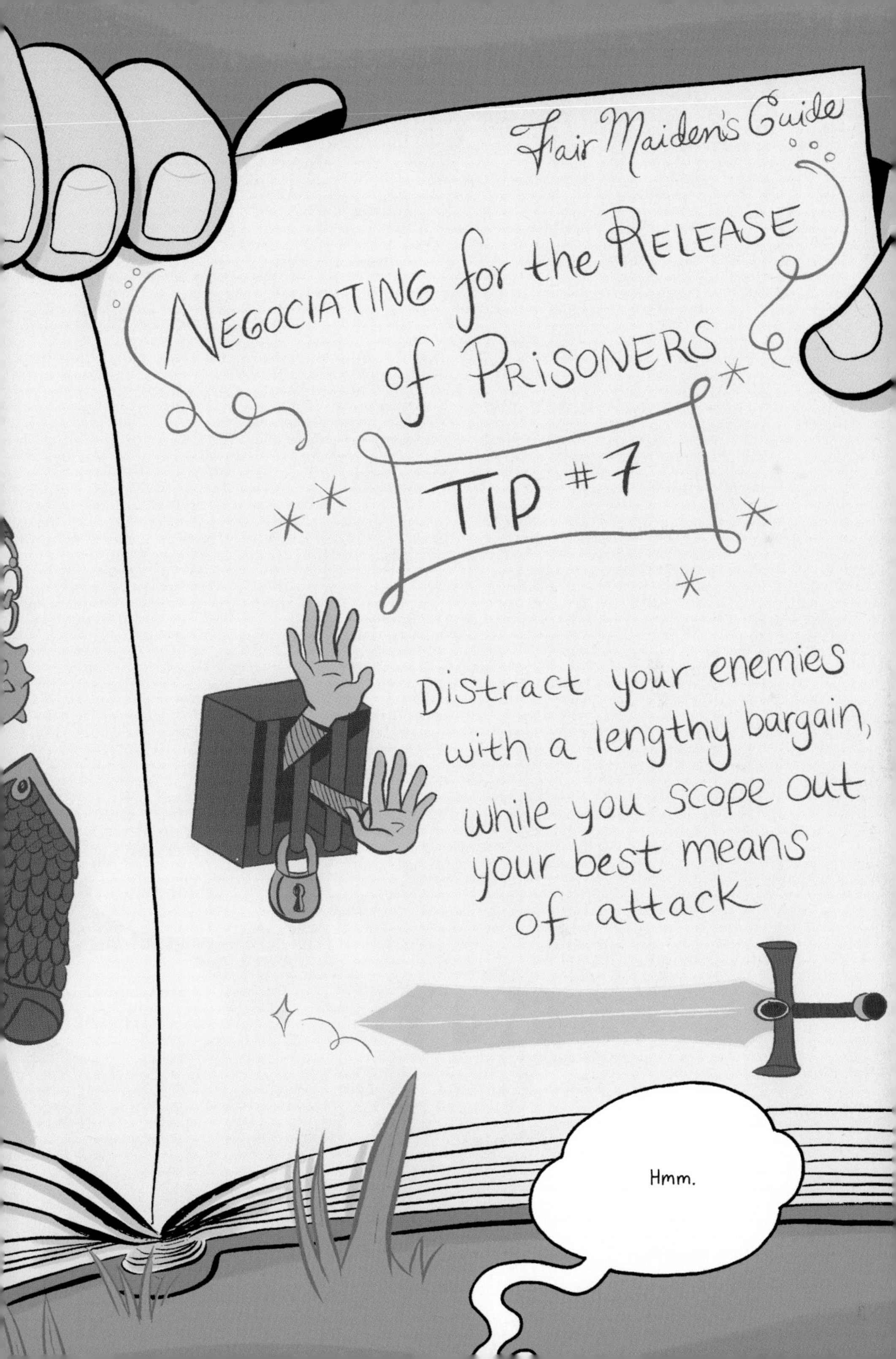
Fair Maiden's Guide
Negociating for the Release of Prisoners
Tip #7
Distract your enemies with a lengthy bargain, while you scope out your best means of attack
Hmm.

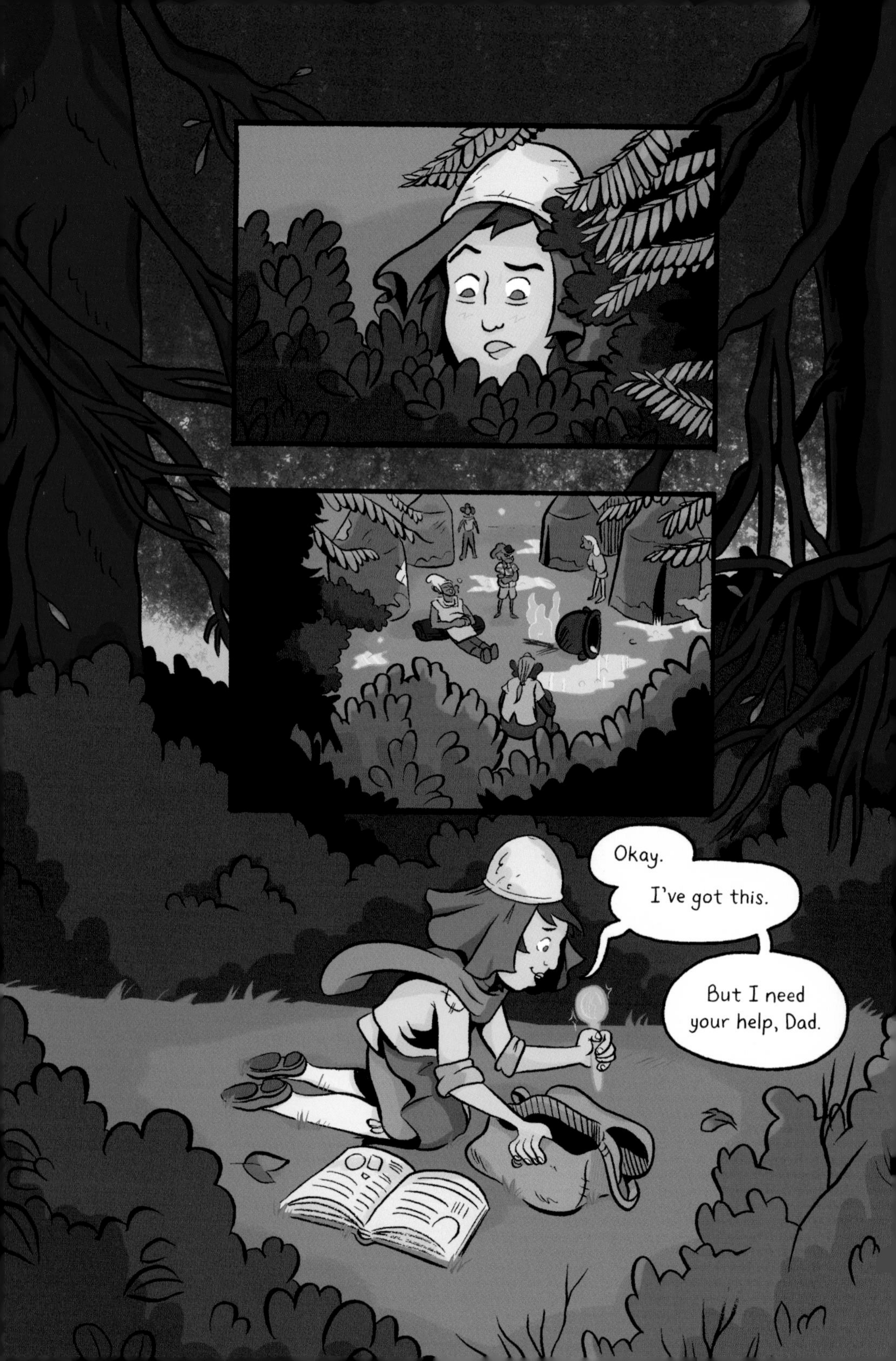
Okay.
I've got this.
But I need your help, Dad.

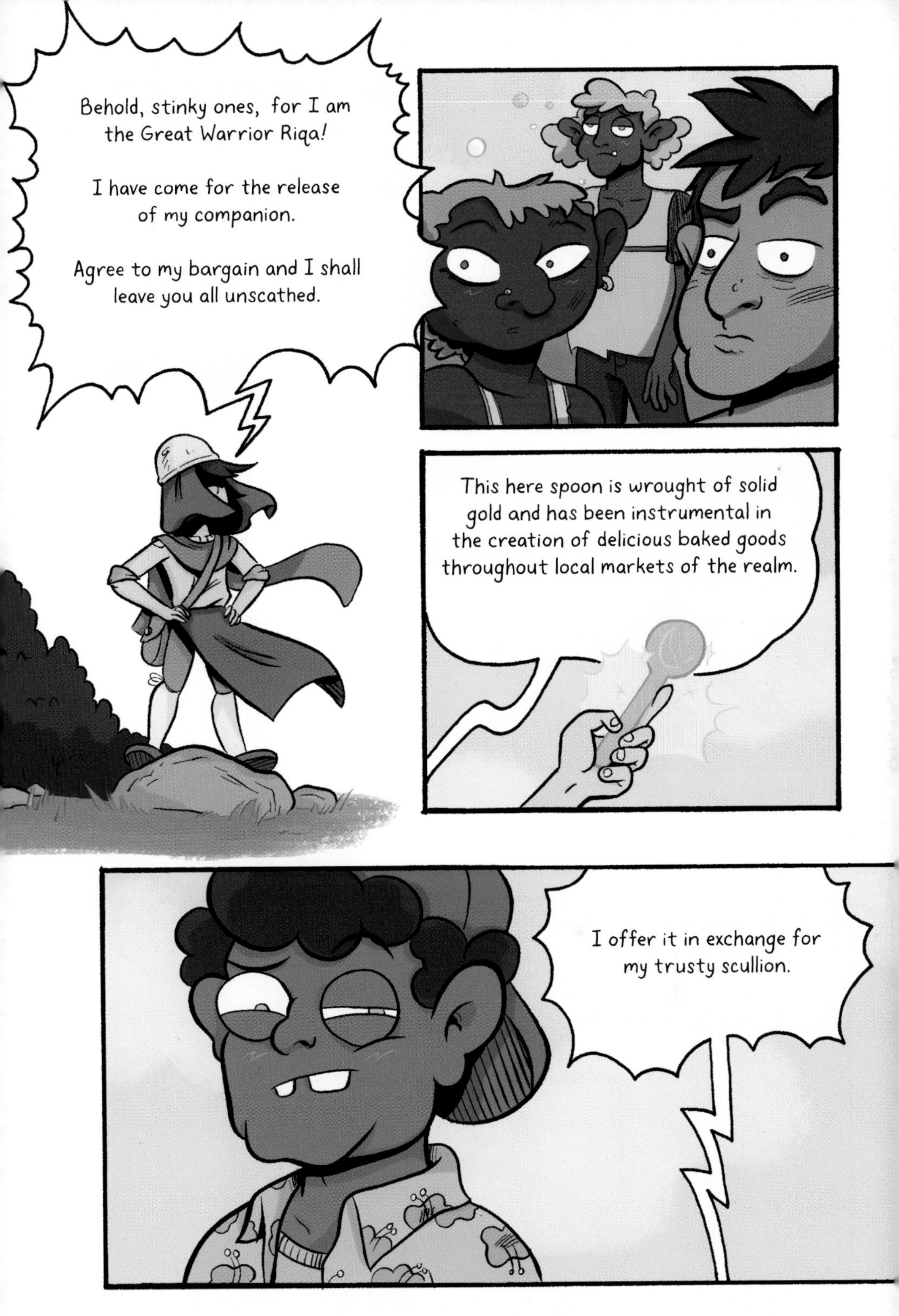
Behold, stinky ones, for I am the Great Warrior Riqa!
I have come for the release of my companion.
Agree to my bargain and I shall leave you all unscathed.
This here spoon is wrought of solid gold and has been instrumental in the creation of delicious baked goods throughout local markets of the realm.
I offer it in exchange for my trusty scullion.

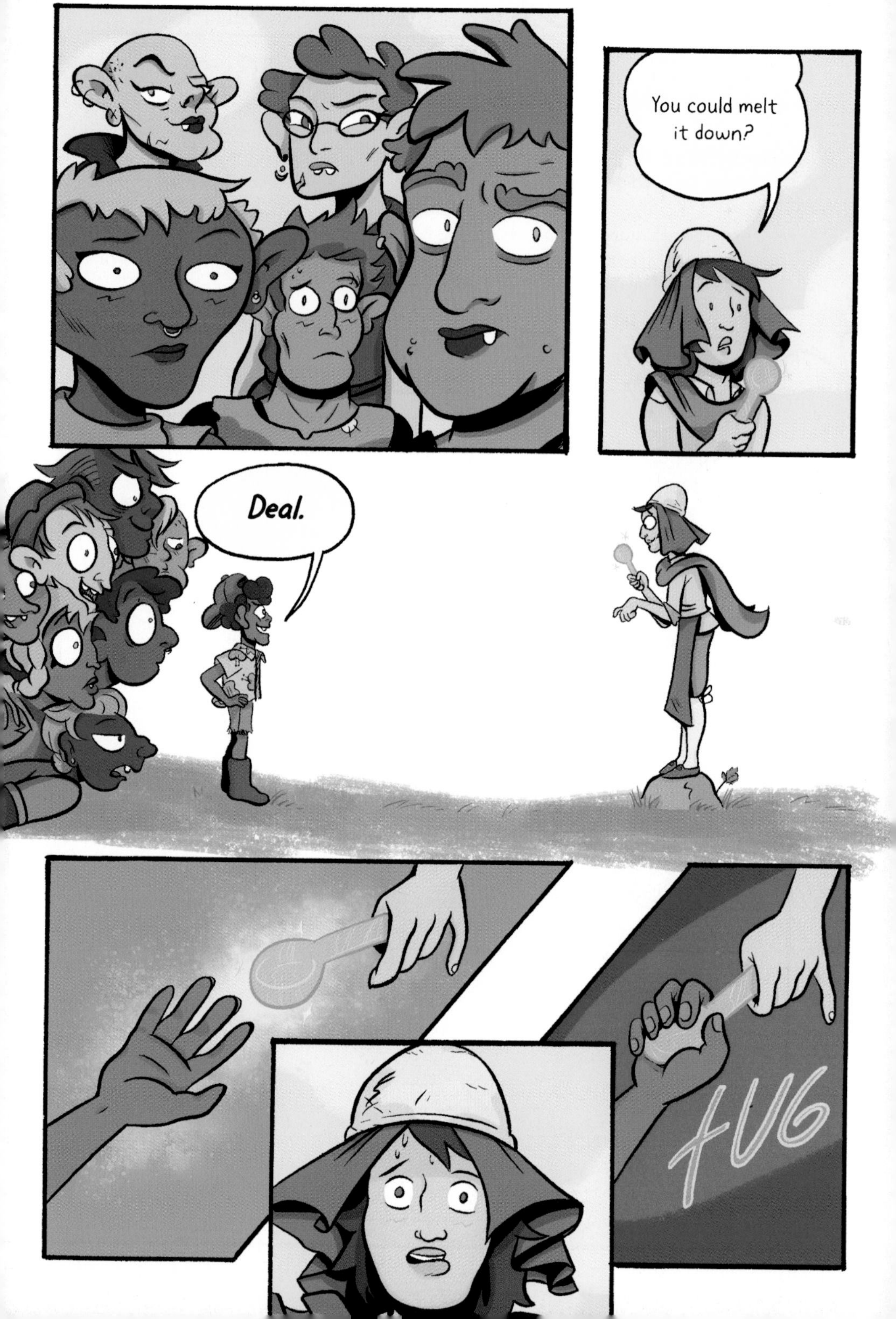
You could melt it down?
Deal.
TUG

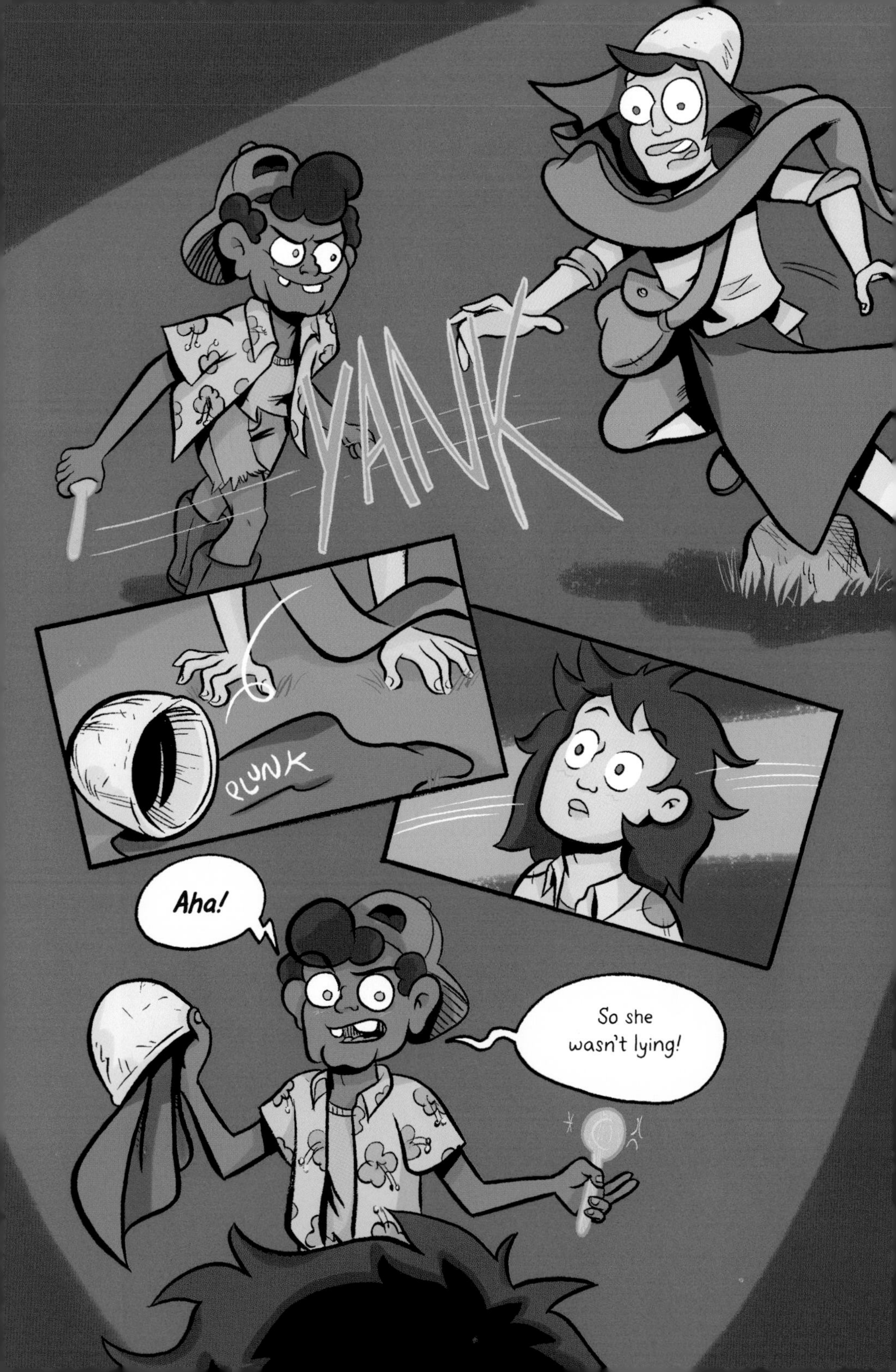
YANK
PLUNK
Aha!
So she wasn't lying!

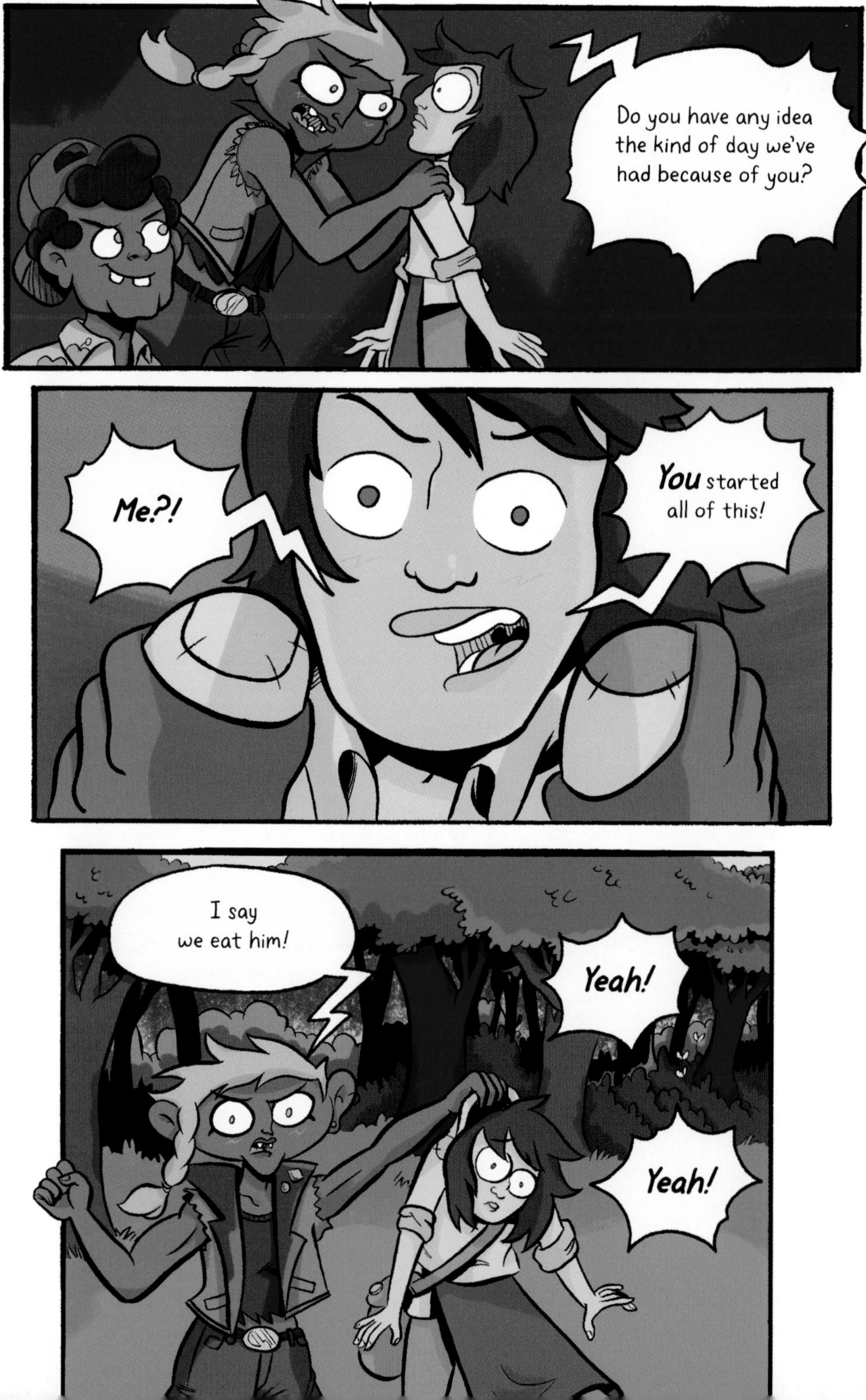
Do you have any idea the kind of day we've had because of you?
Me?!
You started all of this!
I say we eat him!
Yeah!
Yeah!

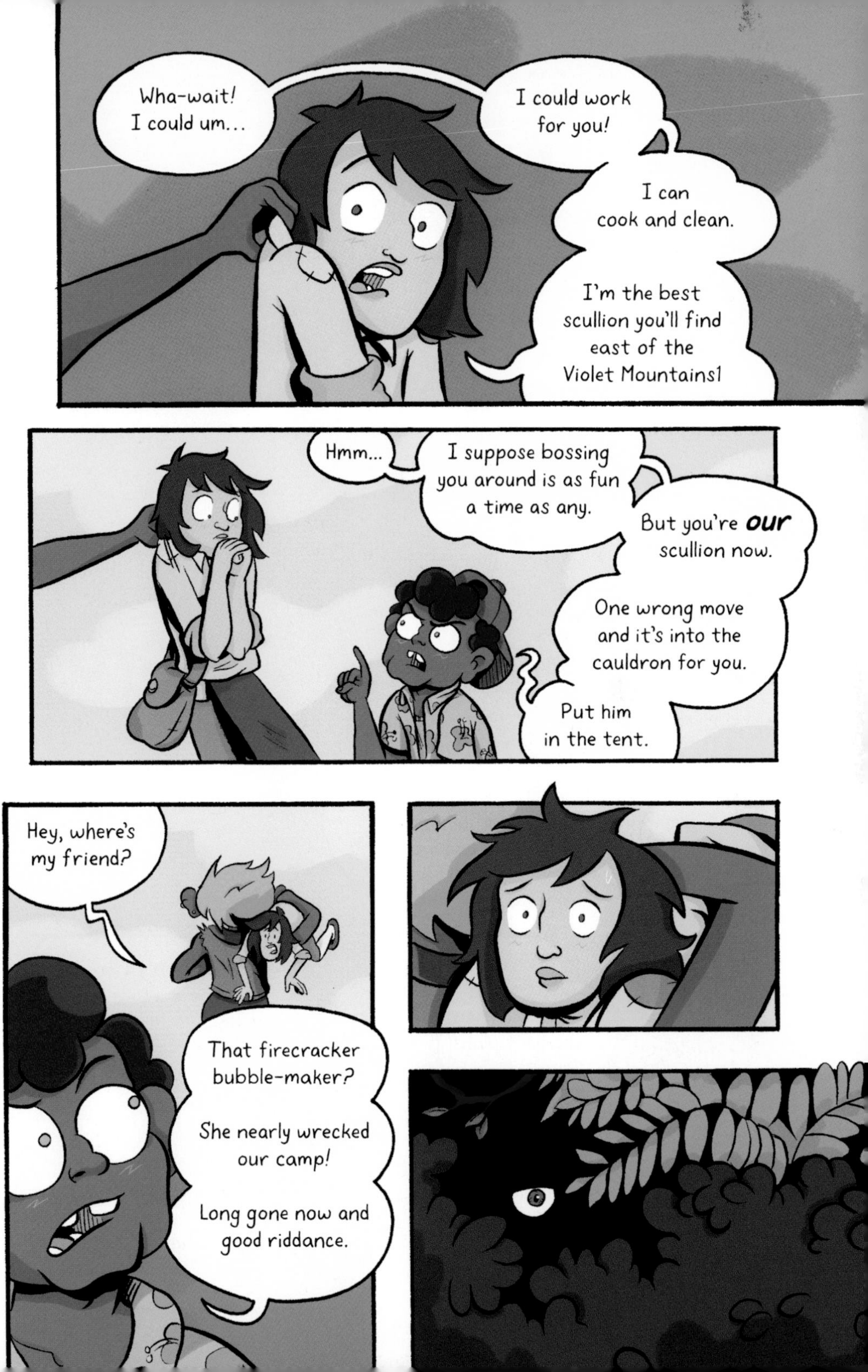

Wha-wait! I could um...
I could work for you!
I can cook and clean.
I'm the best scullion you'll find east of the Violet Mountains1
Hmm...
I suppose bossing you around is as fun a time as any.
But you're **our** scullion now.
One wrong move and it's into the cauldron for you.
Put him in the tent.
Hey, where's my friend?
That firecracker bubble-maker?
She nearly wrecked our camp!
Long gone now and good riddance.

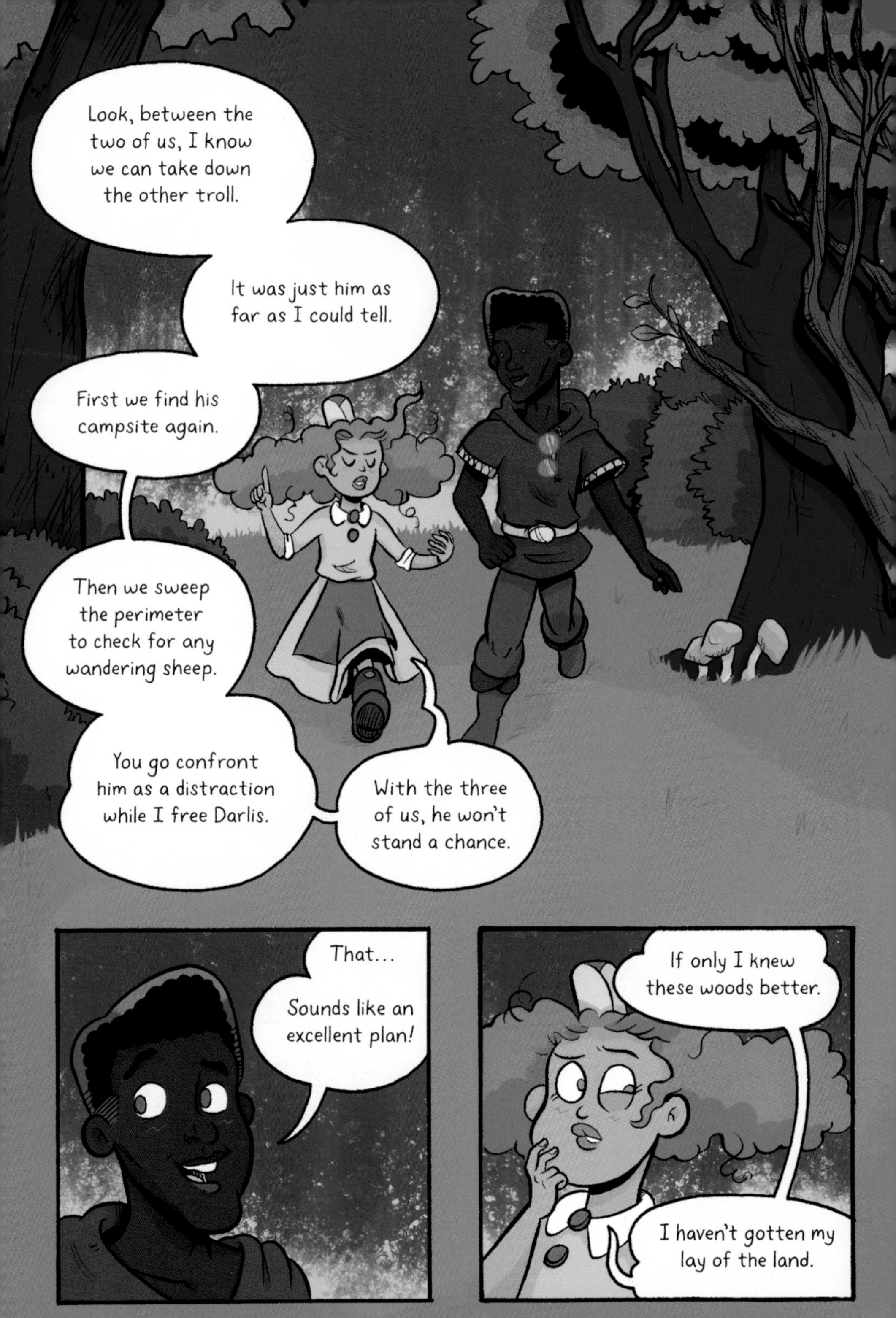
Look, between the two of us, I know we can take down the other troll.
It was just him as far as I could tell.
First we find his campsite again.
Then we sweep the perimeter to check for any wandering sheep.
You go confront him as a distraction while I free Darlis.
With the three of us, he won't stand a chance.
That...
Sounds like an excellent plan!
If only I knew these woods better.
I haven't gotten my lay of the land.

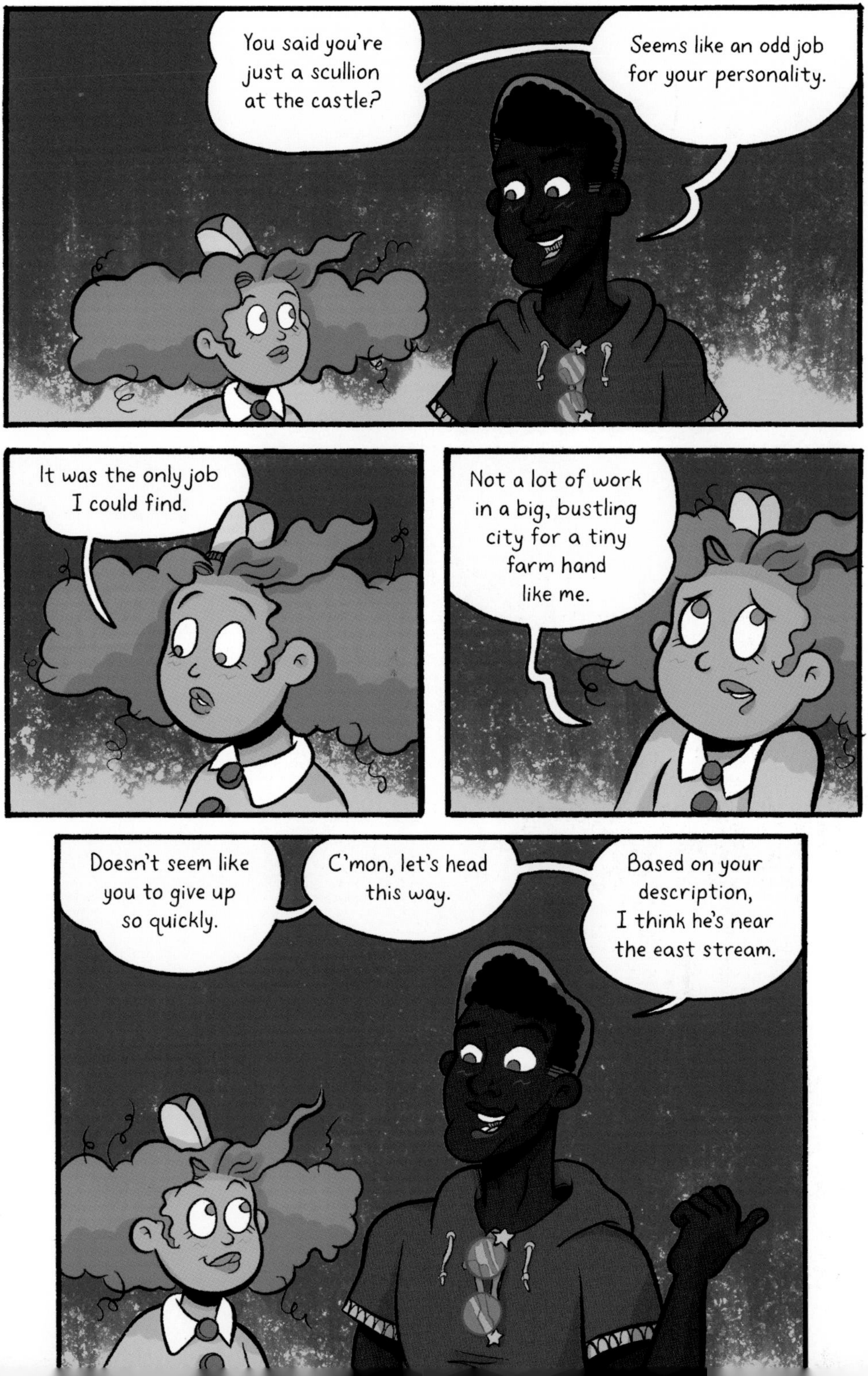
You said you're just a scullion at the castle?
Seems like an odd job for your personality.
It was the only job I could find.
Not a lot of work in a big, bustling city for a tiny farm hand like me.
Doesn't seem like you to give up so quickly.
C'mon, let's head this way.
Based on your description, I think he's near the east stream.

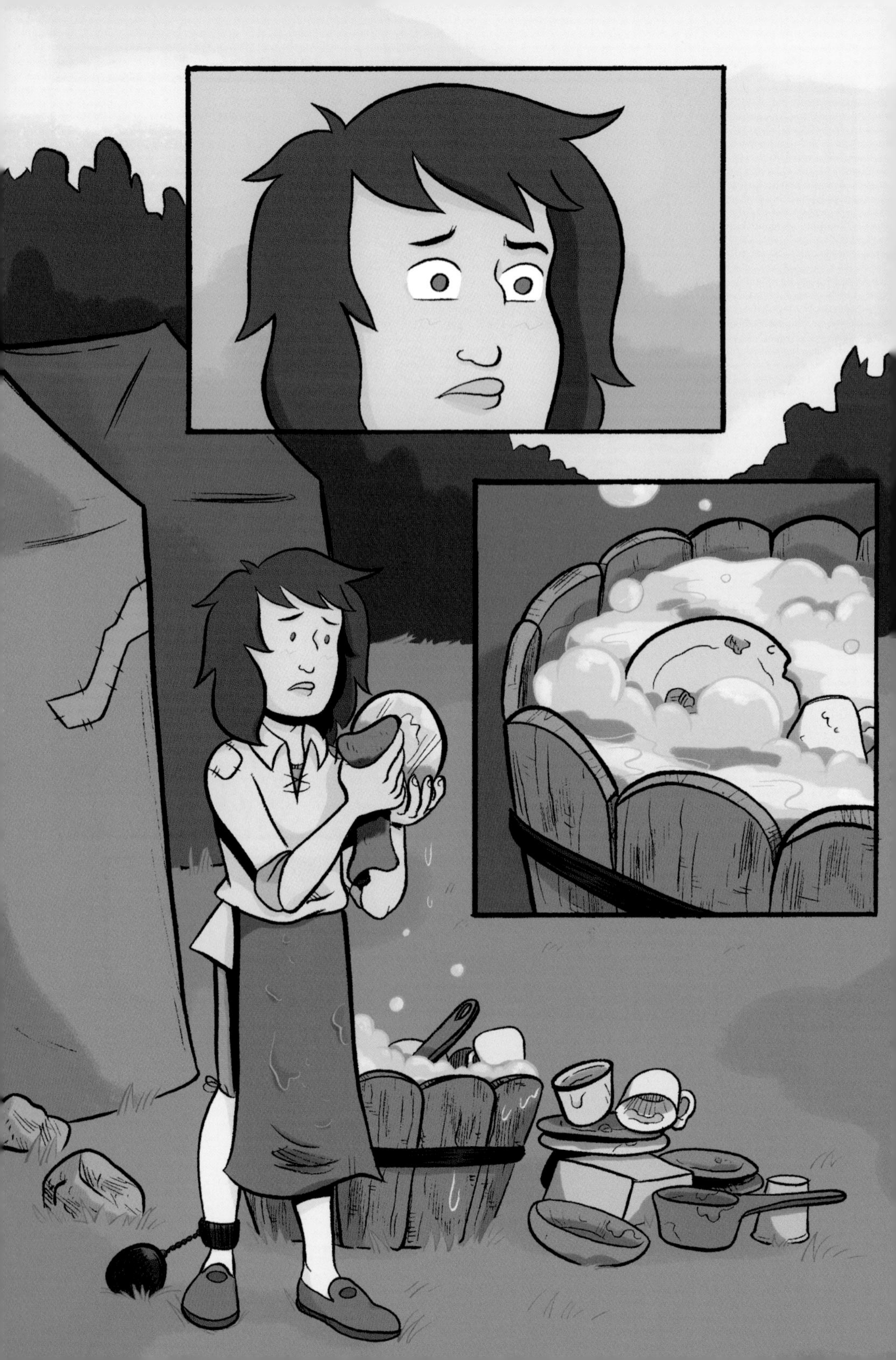

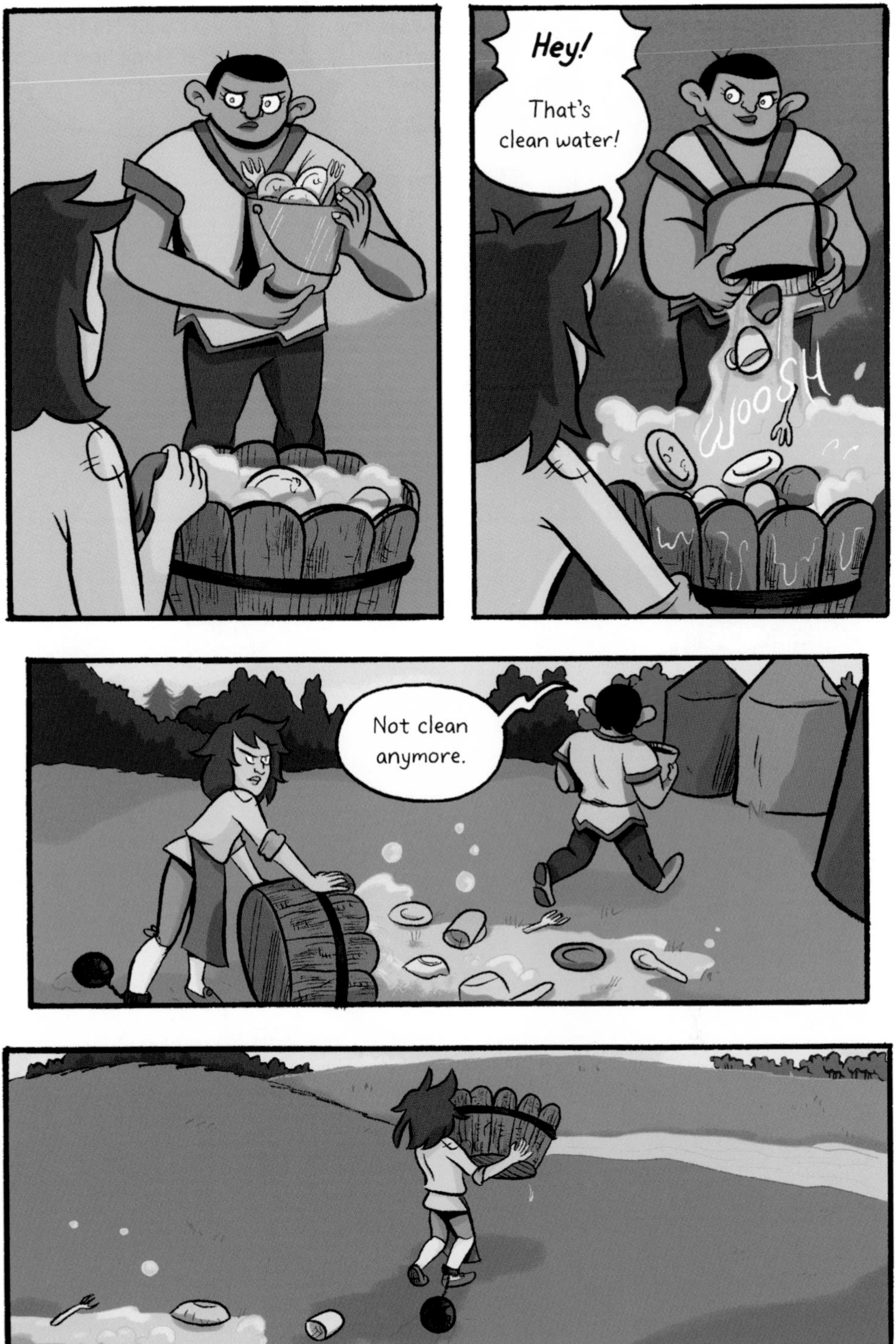
Hey!
That's clean water!
WOOSH
Not clean anymore.

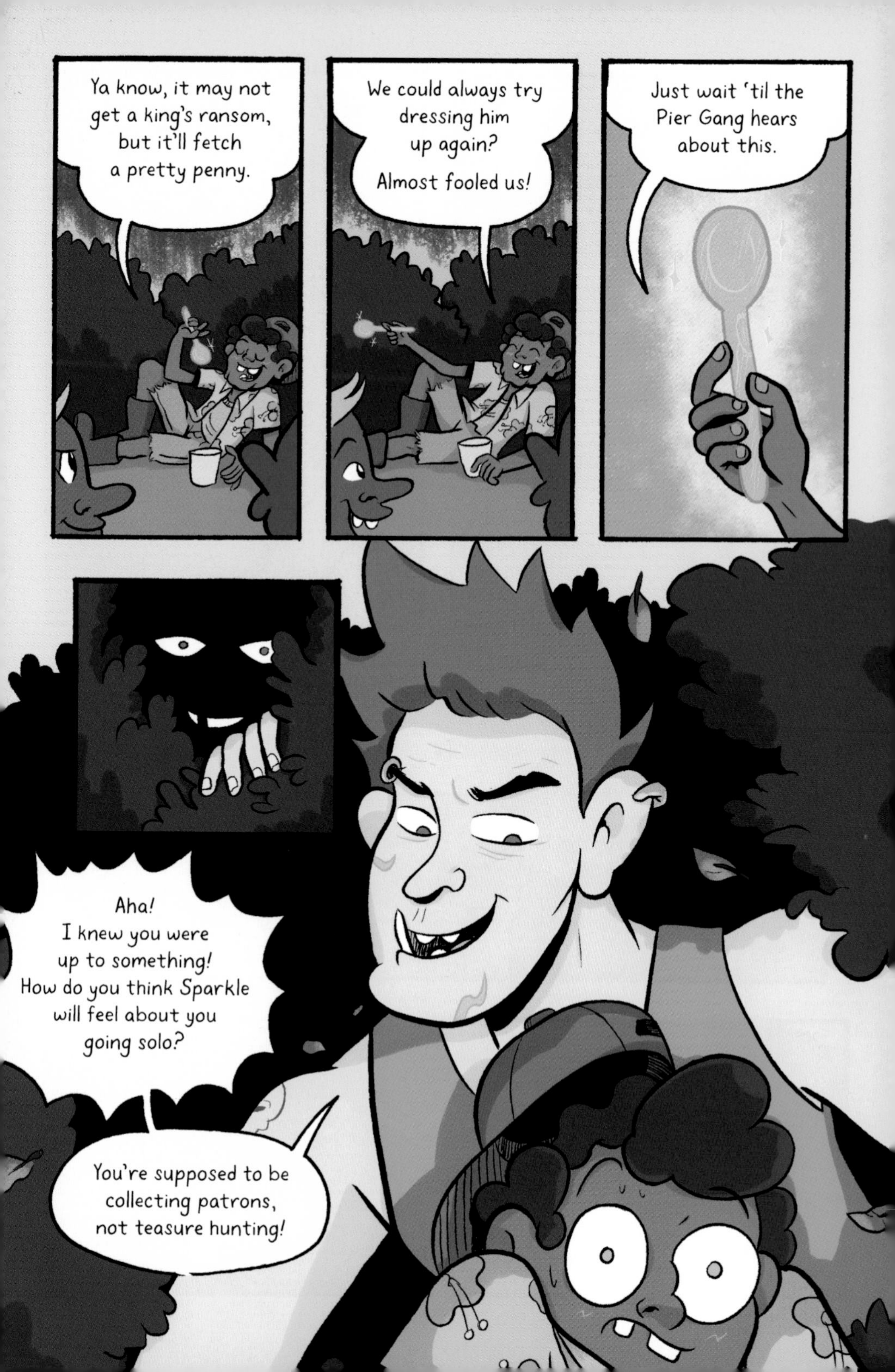
Ya know, it may not get a king's ransom, but it'll fetch a pretty penny.
We could always try dressing him up again?
Almost fooled us!
Just wait 'til the Pier Gang hears about this.
Aha! I knew you were up to something! How do you think Sparkle will feel about you going solo?
You're supposed to be collecting patrons, not teasure hunting!

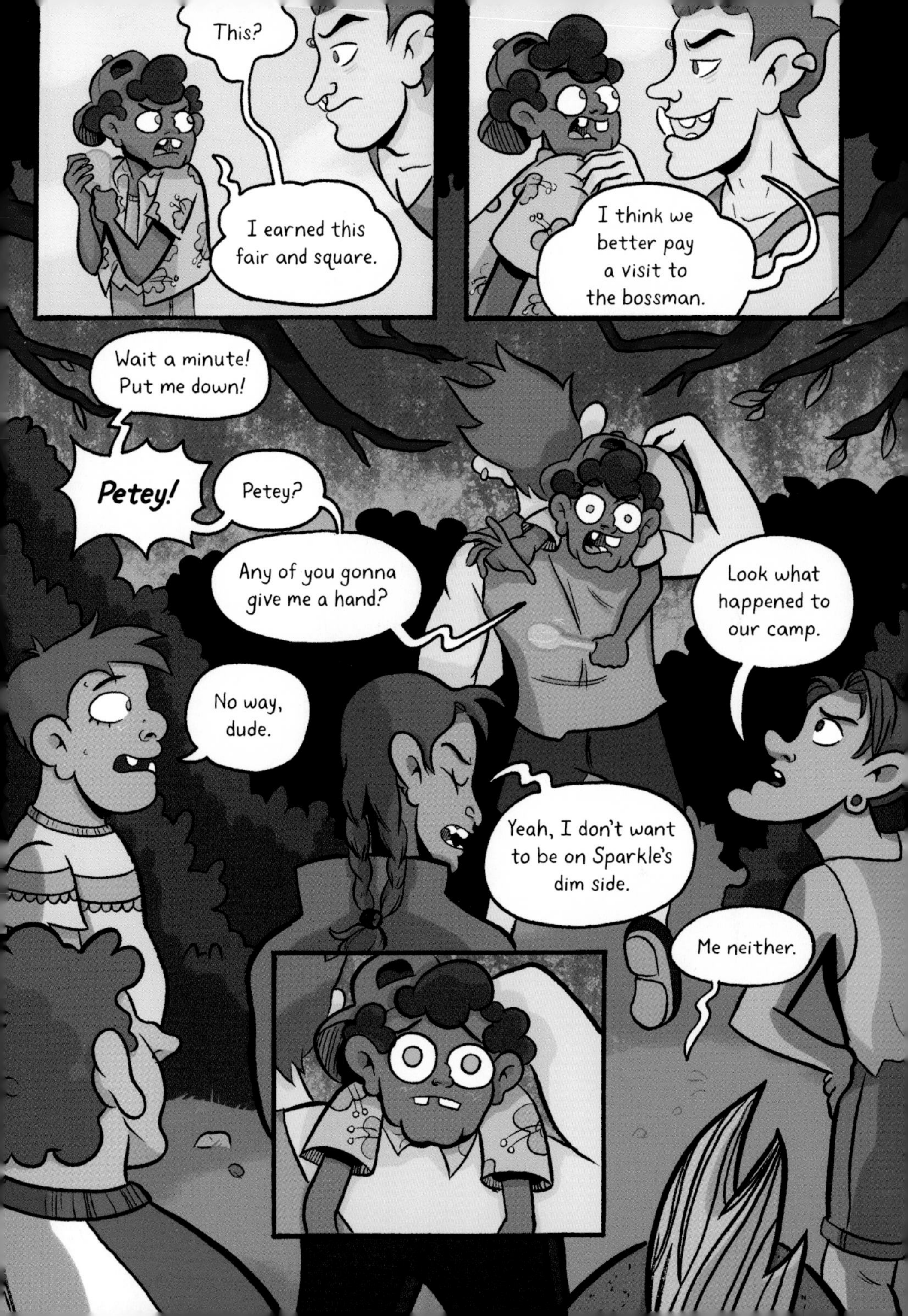
This?
I earned this fair and square.
I think we better pay a visit to the bossman.
Wait a minute! Put me down!
Petey!
Petey?
Any of you gonna give me a hand?
Look what happened to our camp.
No way, dude.
Yeah, I don't want to be on Sparkle's dim side.
Me neither.

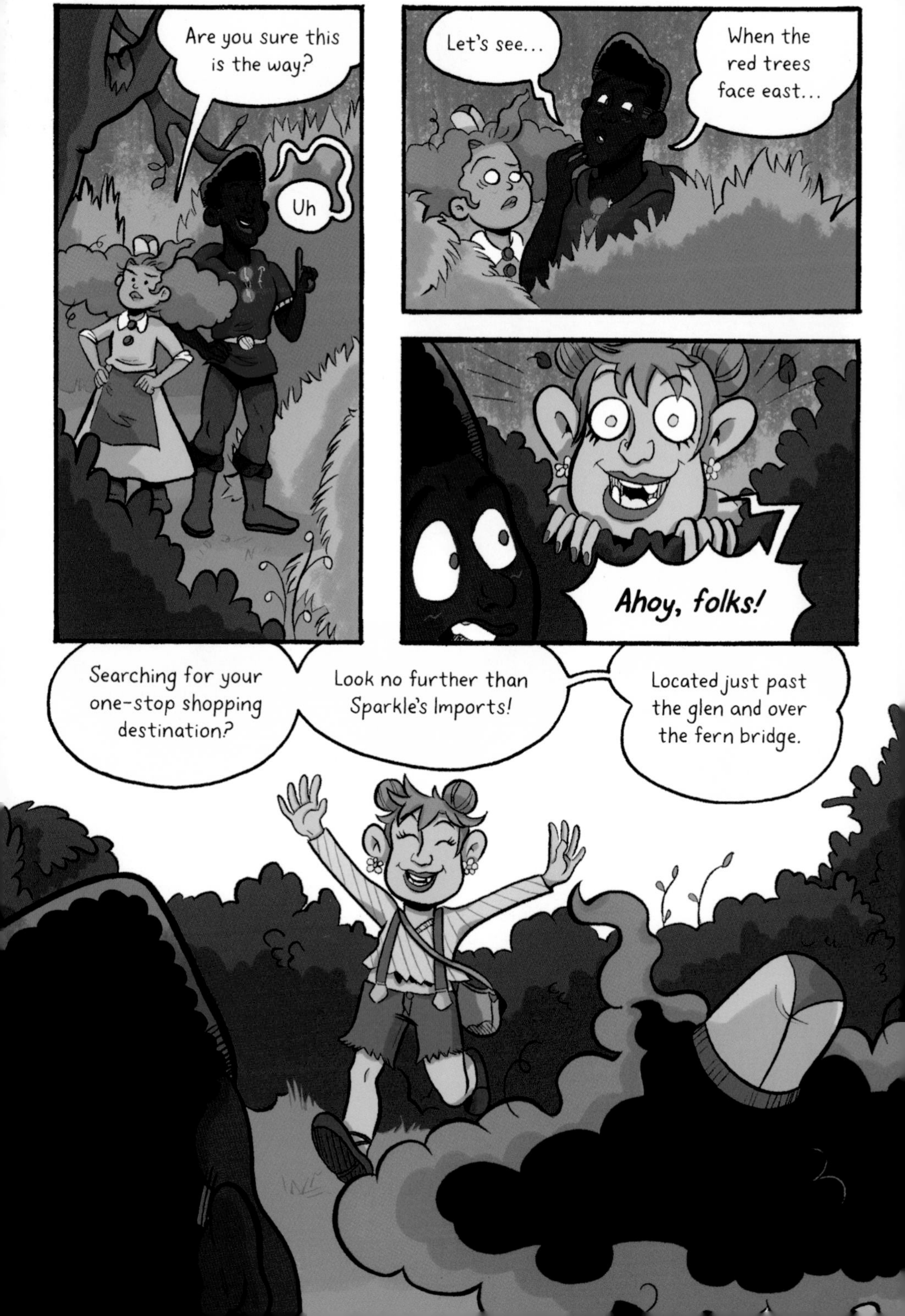

Are you sure this is the way?
Uh
Let's see...
When the red trees face east...
Ahoy, folks!
Searching for your one-stop shopping destination?
Look no further than Sparkle's Imports!
Located just past the glen and over the fern bridge.

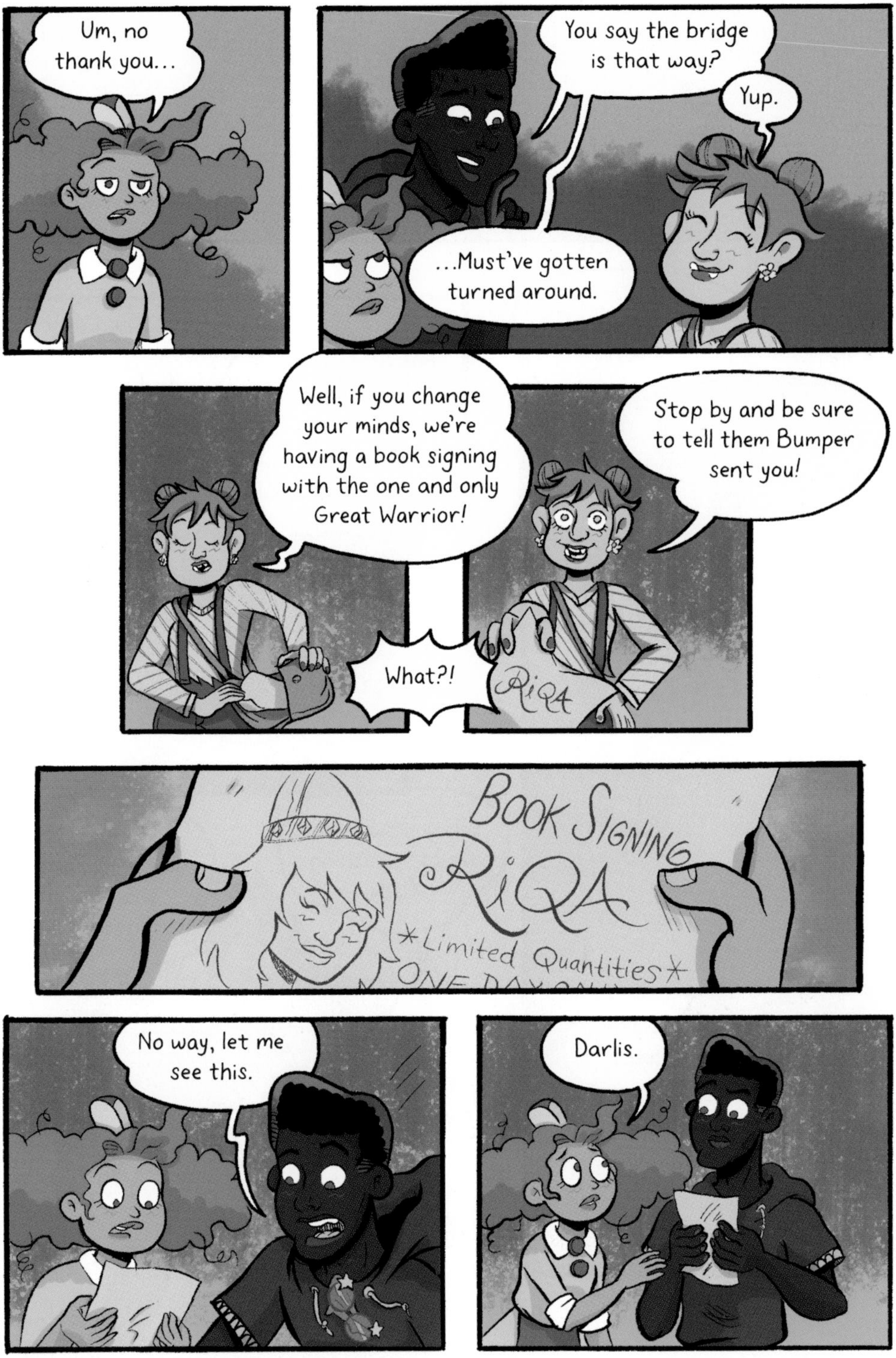
Um, no thank you…
You say the bridge is that way?
Yup.
…Must've gotten turned around.
Well, if you change your minds, we're having a book signing with the one and only Great Warrior!
Stop by and be sure to tell them Bumper sent you!
What?!
RiQA
Book Signing
RiQA
Limited Quantities
No way, let me see this.
Darlis.

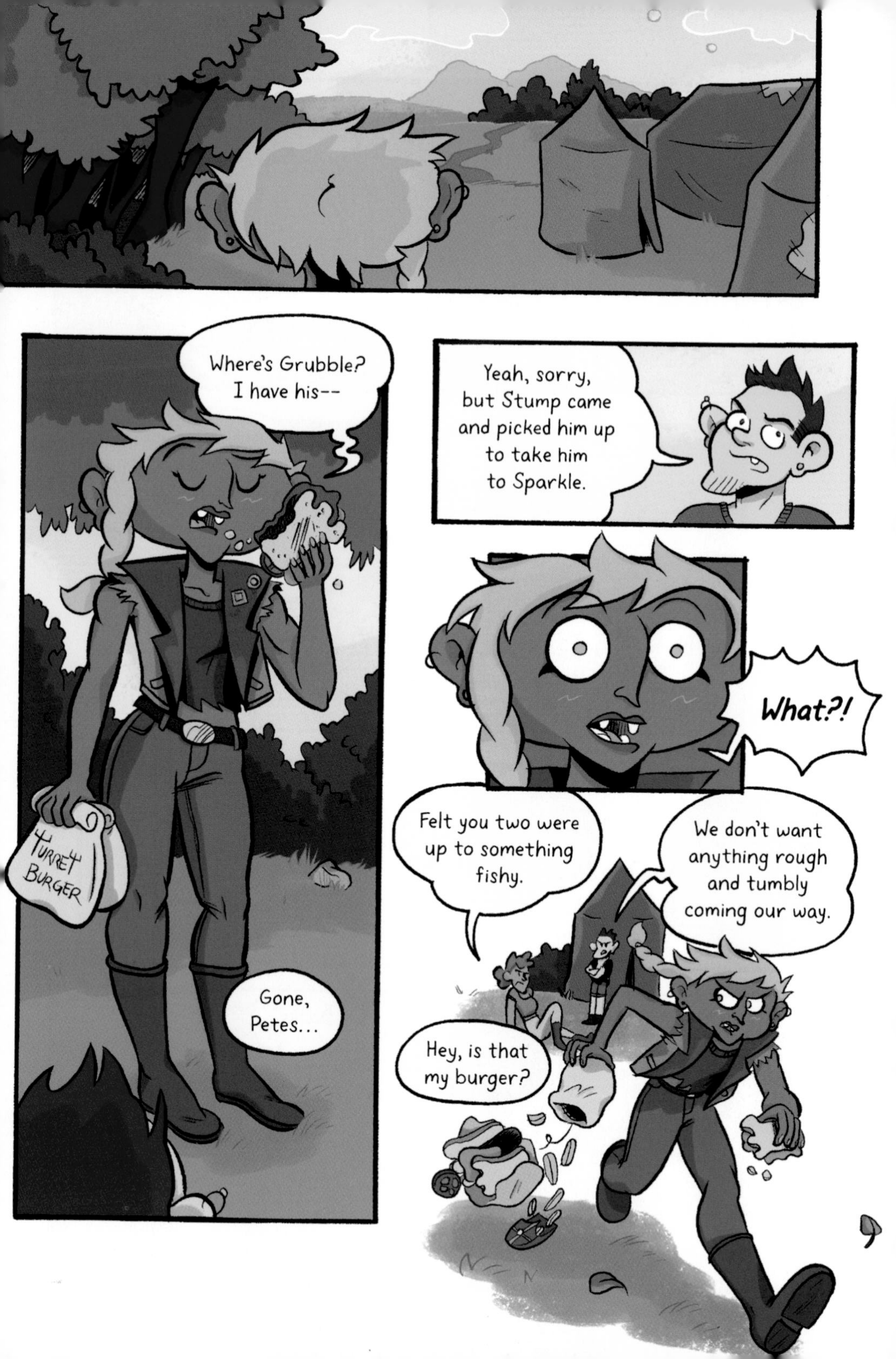
Where's Grubble? I have his--
Yeah, sorry, but Stump came and picked him up to take him to Sparkle.
What?!
Gone, Petes...
Felt you two were up to something fishy.
We don't want anything rough and tumbly coming our way.
Hey, is that my burger?
TURRET BURGER

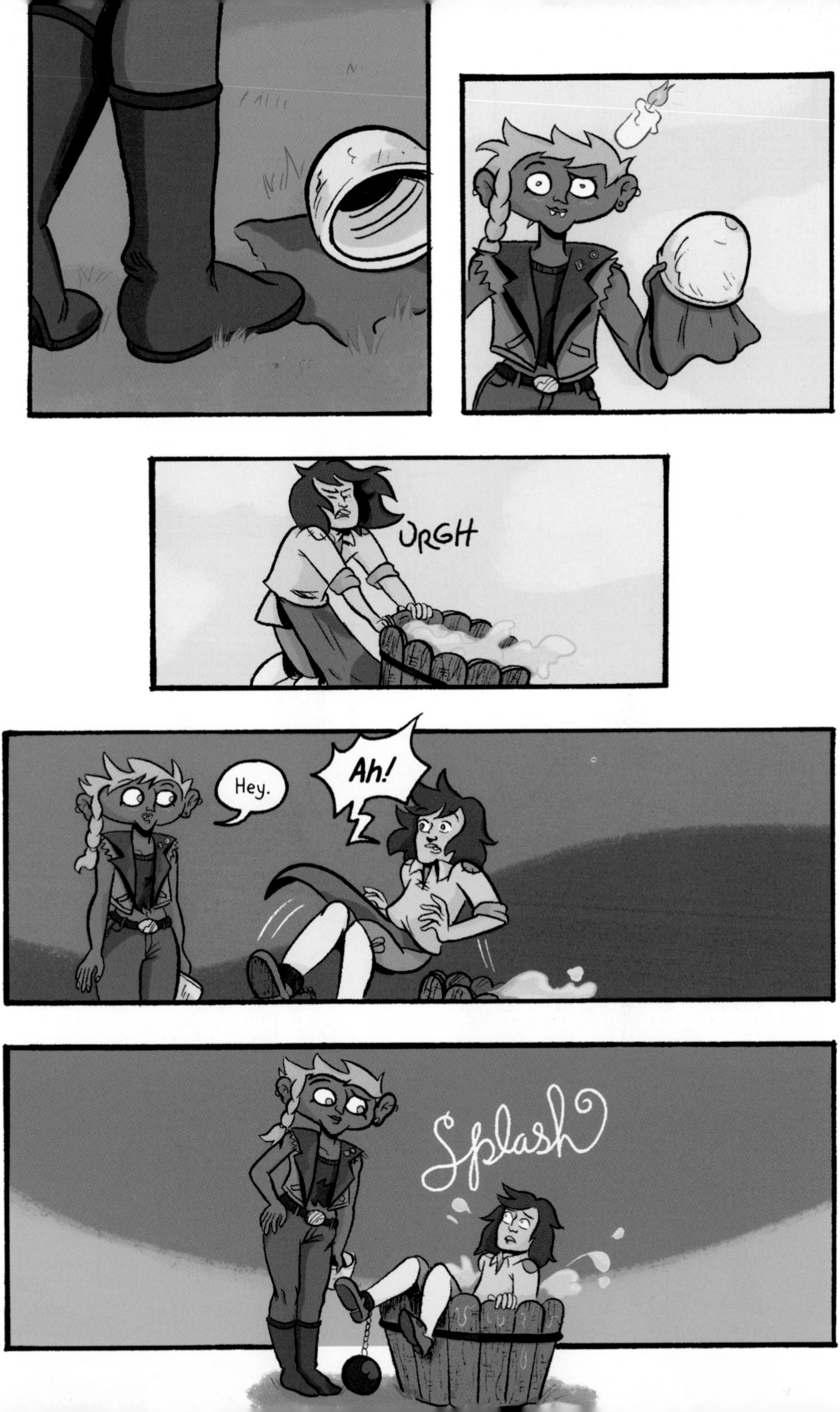
URGH
Hey.
Ah!
Splash

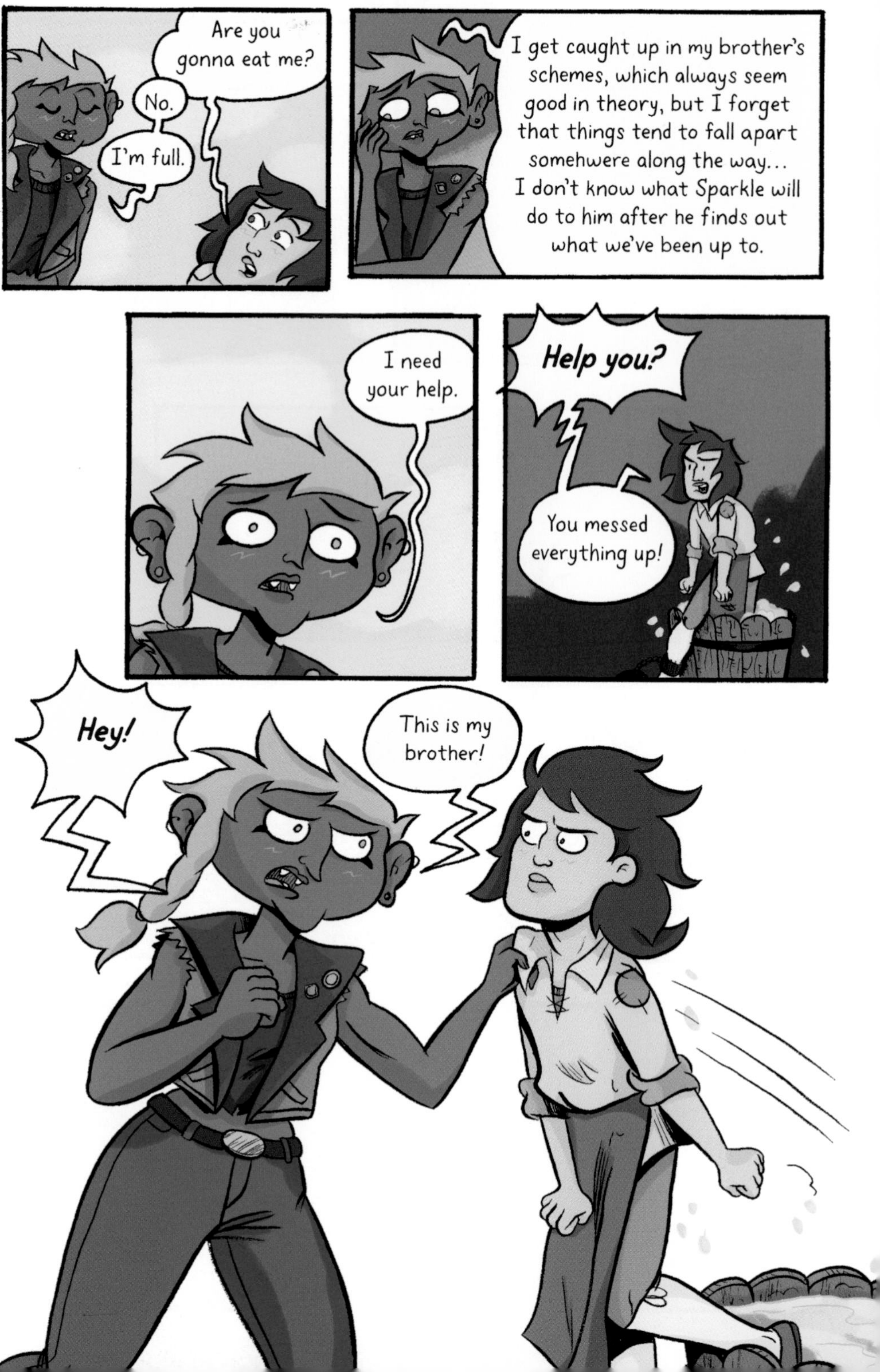
Are you gonna eat me?
No.
I'm full.
I get caught up in my brother's schemes, which always seem good in theory, but I forget that things tend to fall apart somehwere along the way... I don't know what Sparkle will do to him after he finds out what we've been up to.
I need your help.
Help you?
You messed everything up!
Hey!
This is my brother!

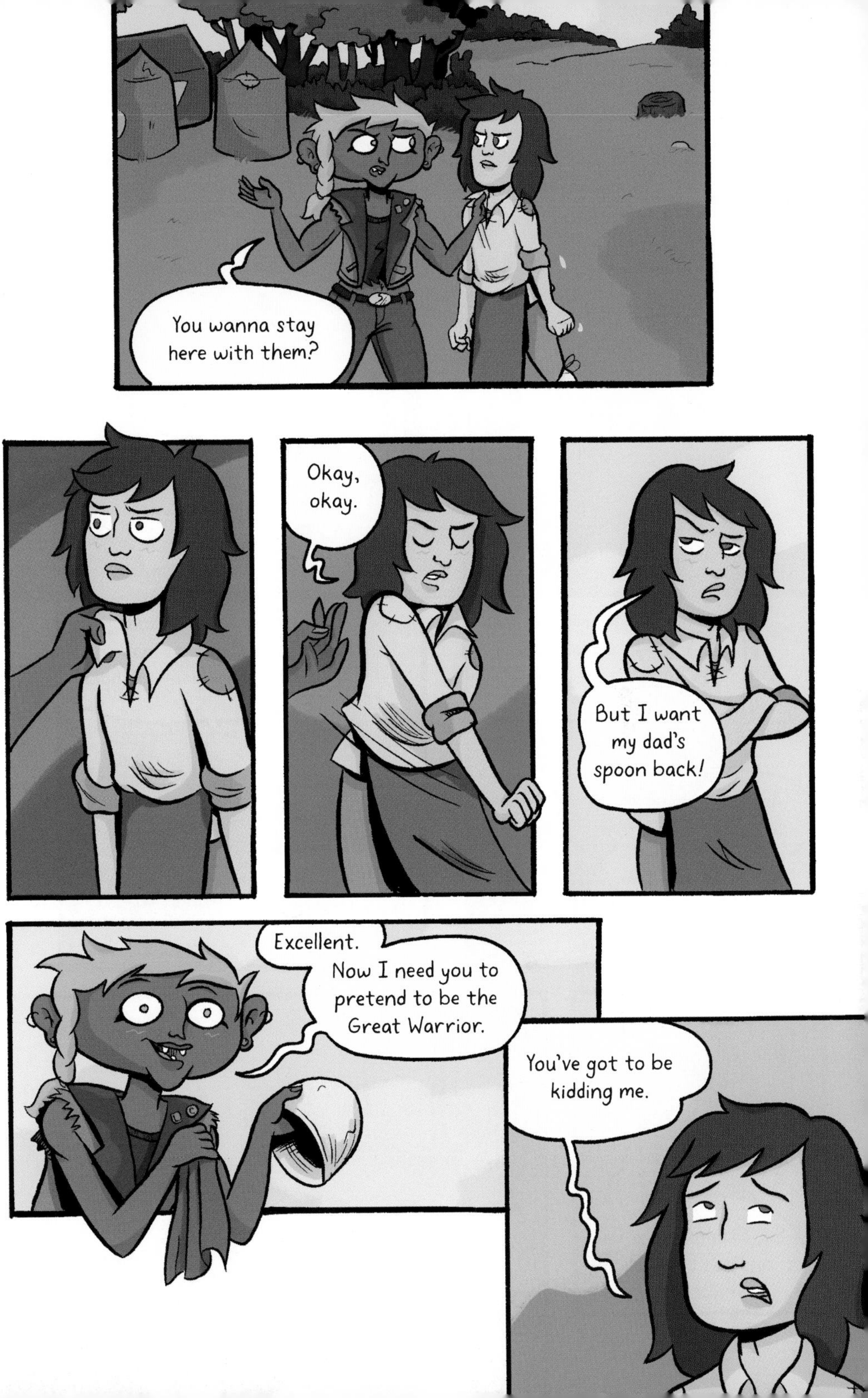
You wanna stay here with them?
Okay, okay.
But I want my dad's spoon back!
Excellent.
Now I need you to pretend to be the Great Warrior.
You've got to be kidding me.

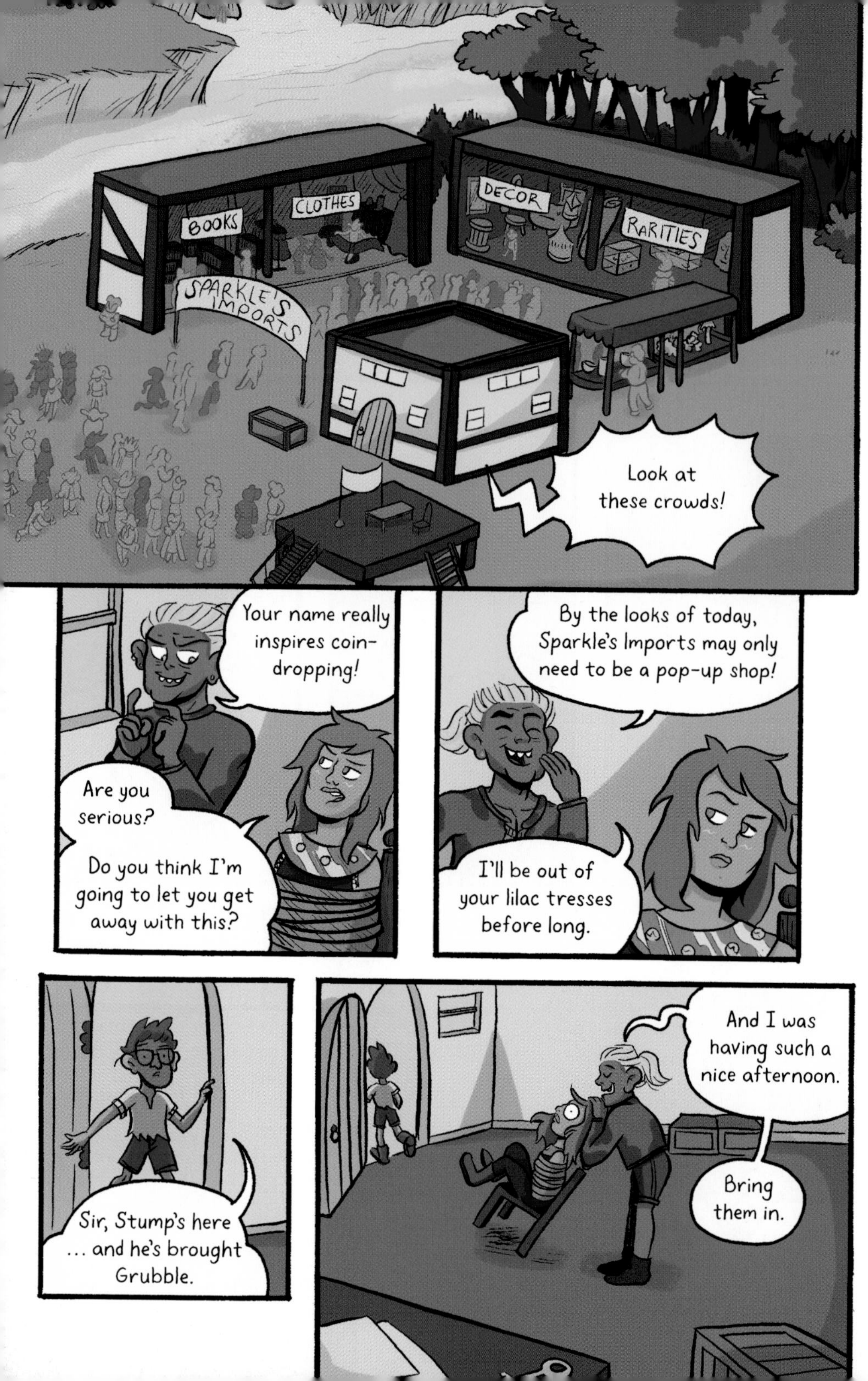
BOOKS
CLOTHES
DECOR
RARITIES
SPARKLE'S IMPORTS
Look at these crowds!
Your name really inspires coin-dropping!
Are you serious?
Do you think I'm going to let you get away with this?
By the looks of today, Sparkle's Imports may only need to be a pop-up shop!
I'll be out of your lilac tresses before long.
Sir, Stump's here ... and he's brought Grubble.
And I was having such a nice afternoon.
Bring them in.

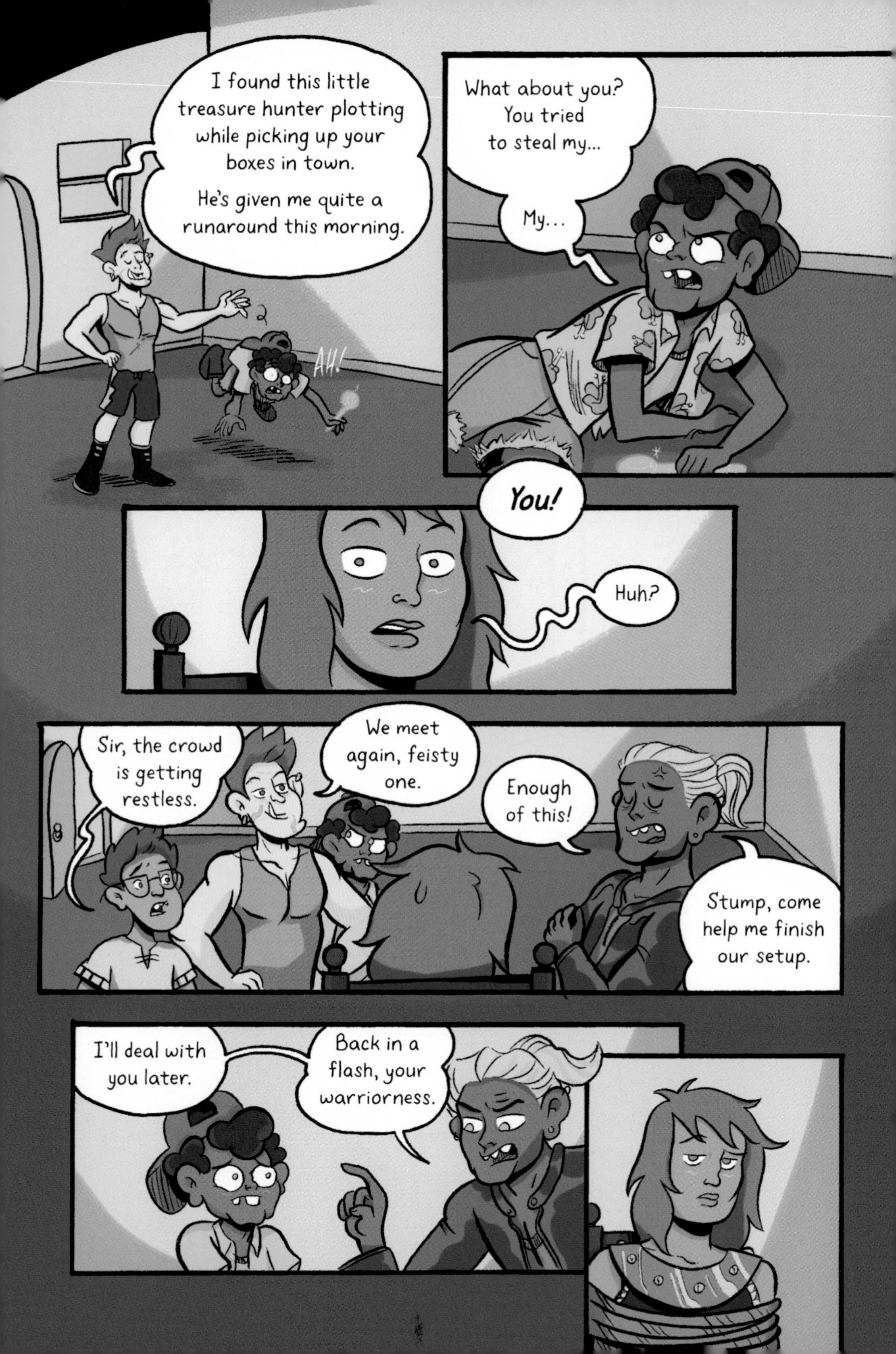
I found this little treasure hunter plotting while picking up your boxes in town.
He's given me quite a runaround this morning.
AH!
What about you? You tried to steal my...
My...
You!
Huh?
Sir, the crowd is getting restless.
We meet again, feisty one.
Enough of this!
Stump, come help me finish our setup.
I'll deal with you later.
Back in a flash, your warriorness.

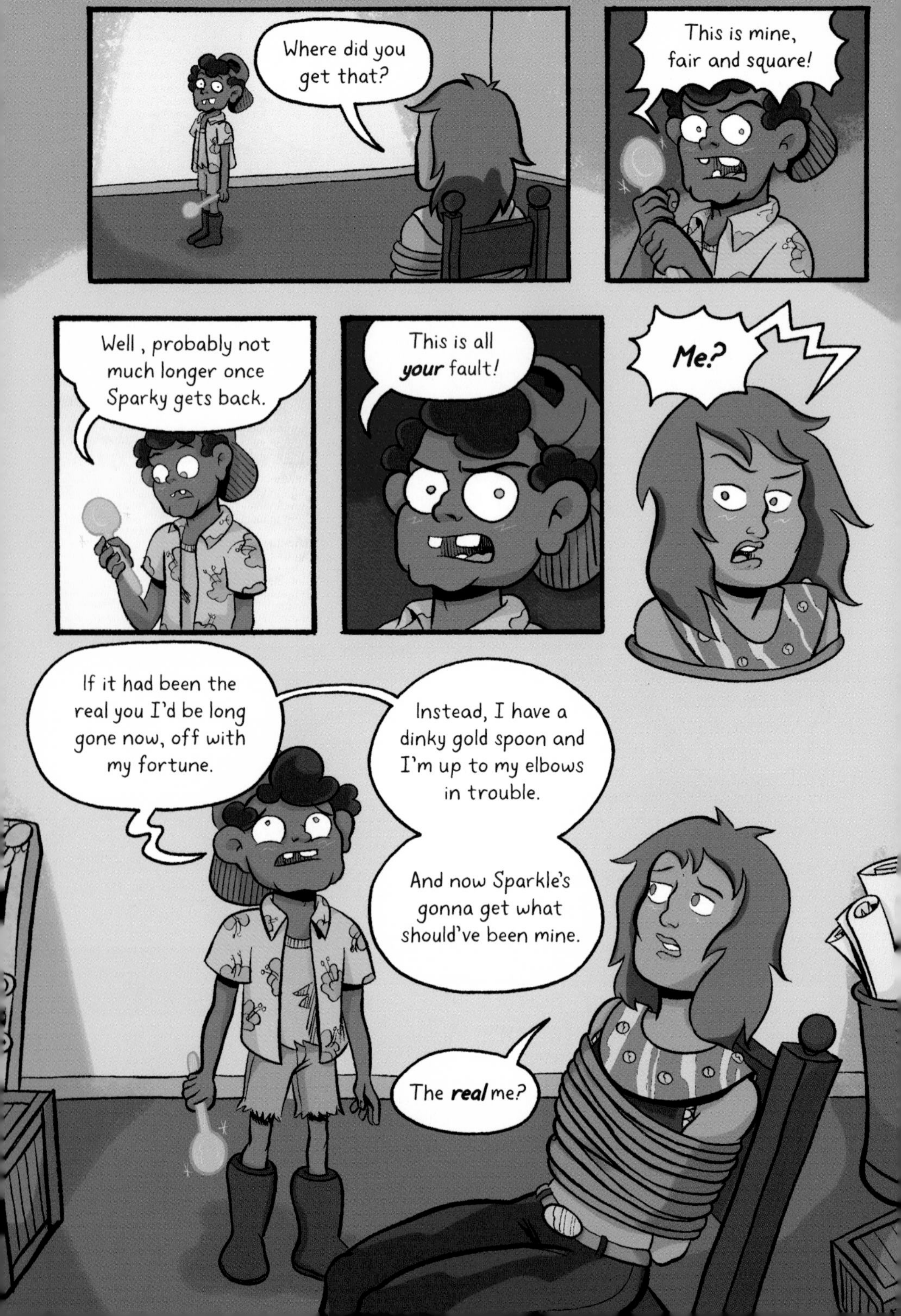
Where did you get that?
This is mine, fair and square!
Well , probably not much longer once Sparky gets back.
This is all **your** fault!
Me?
If it had been the real you I'd be long gone now, off with my fortune.
Instead, I have a dinky gold spoon and I'm up to my elbows in trouble.
And now Sparkle's gonna get what should've been mine.
The **real** me?

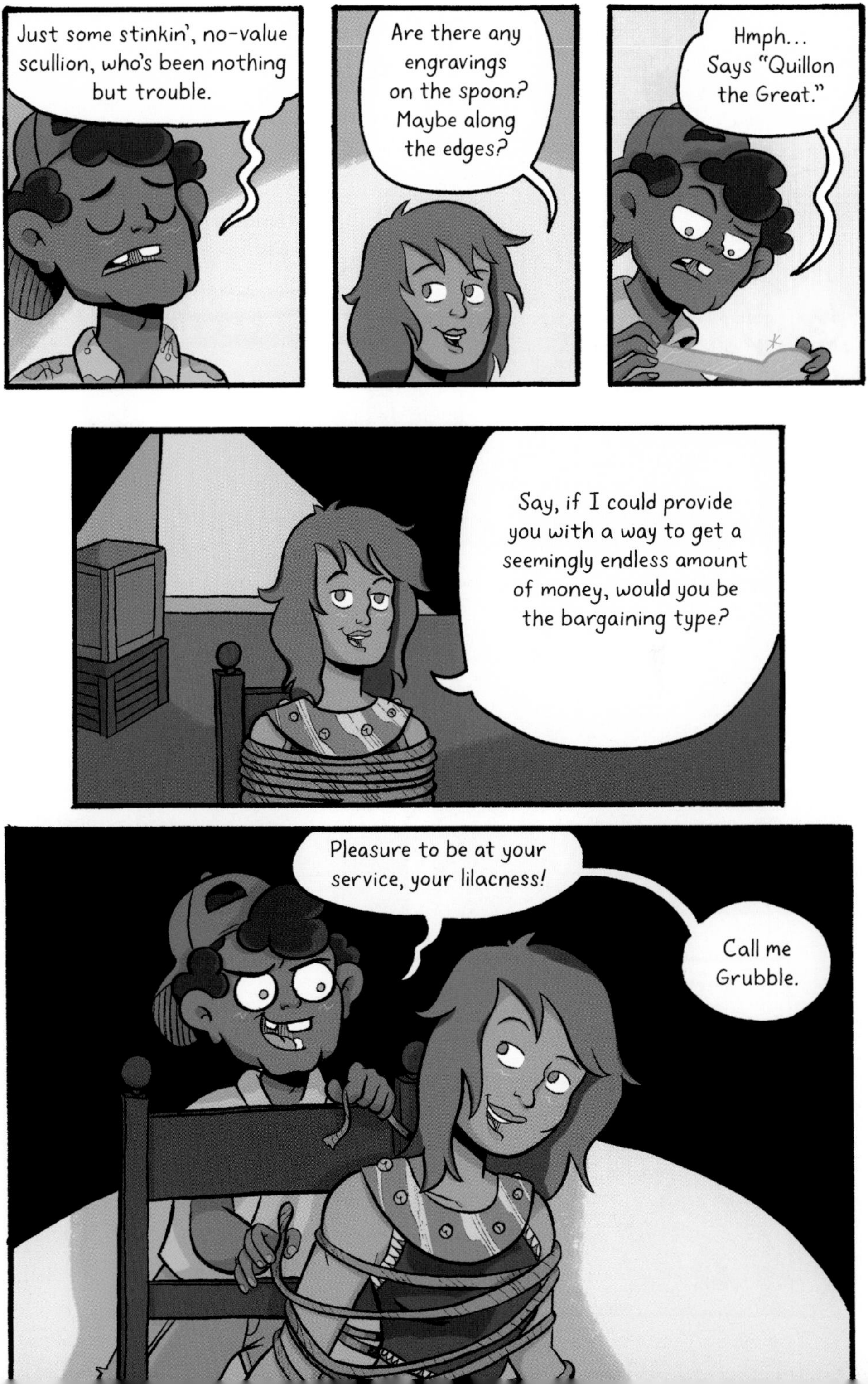
Just some stinkin', no-value scullion, who's been nothing but trouble.
Are there any engravings on the spoon? Maybe along the edges?
Hmph... Says "Quillon the Great."
Say, if I could provide you with a way to get a seemingly endless amount of money, would you be the bargaining type?
Pleasure to be at your service, your lilacness!
Call me Grubble.

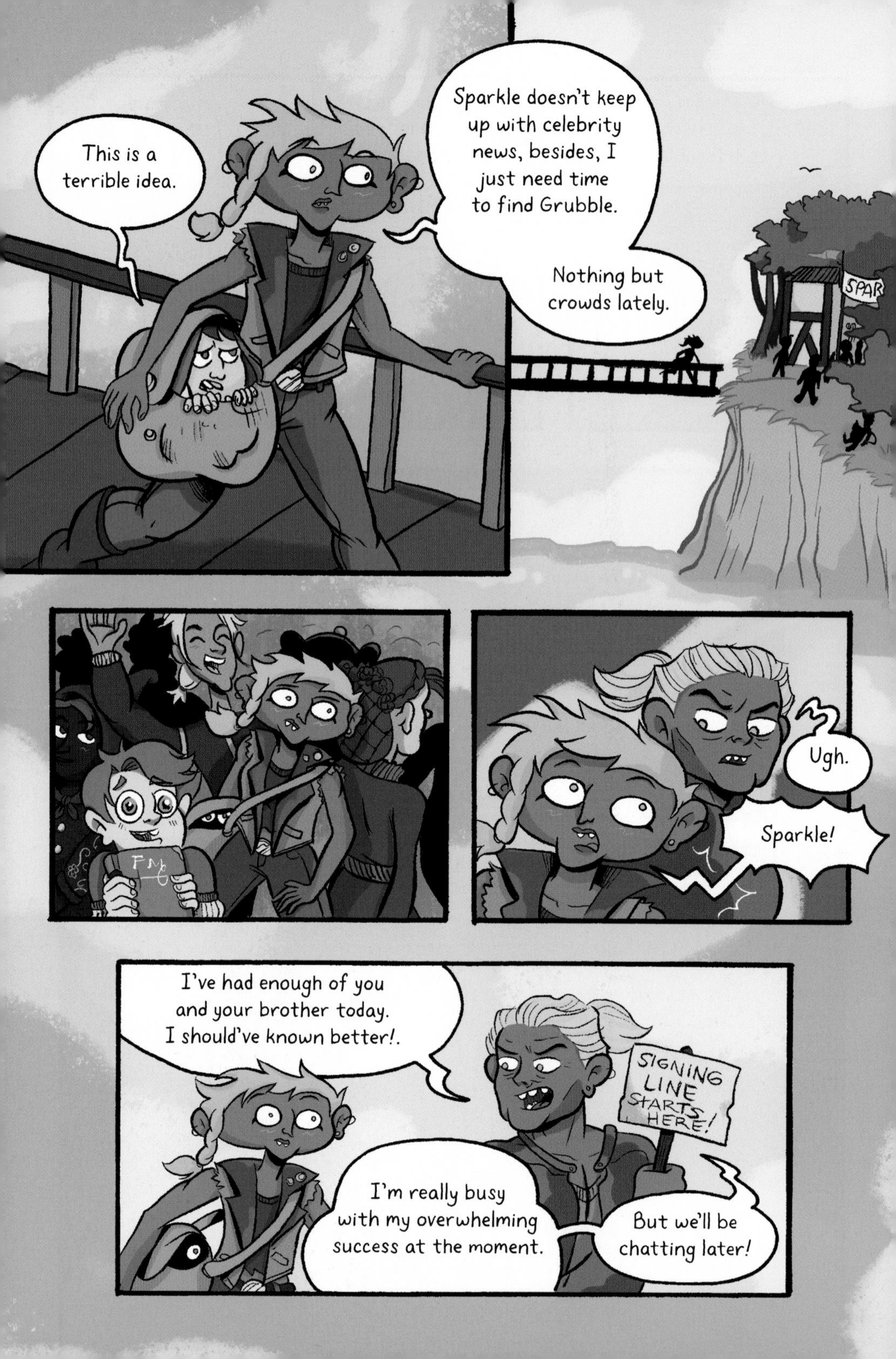
This is a terrible idea.
Sparkle doesn't keep up with celebrity news, besides, I just need time to find Grubble.
Nothing but crowds lately.
SPAR
Ugh.
Sparkle!
I've had enough of you and your brother today. I should've known better!.
SIGNING LINE STARTS HERE!
I'm really busy with my overwhelming success at the moment.
But we'll be chatting later!

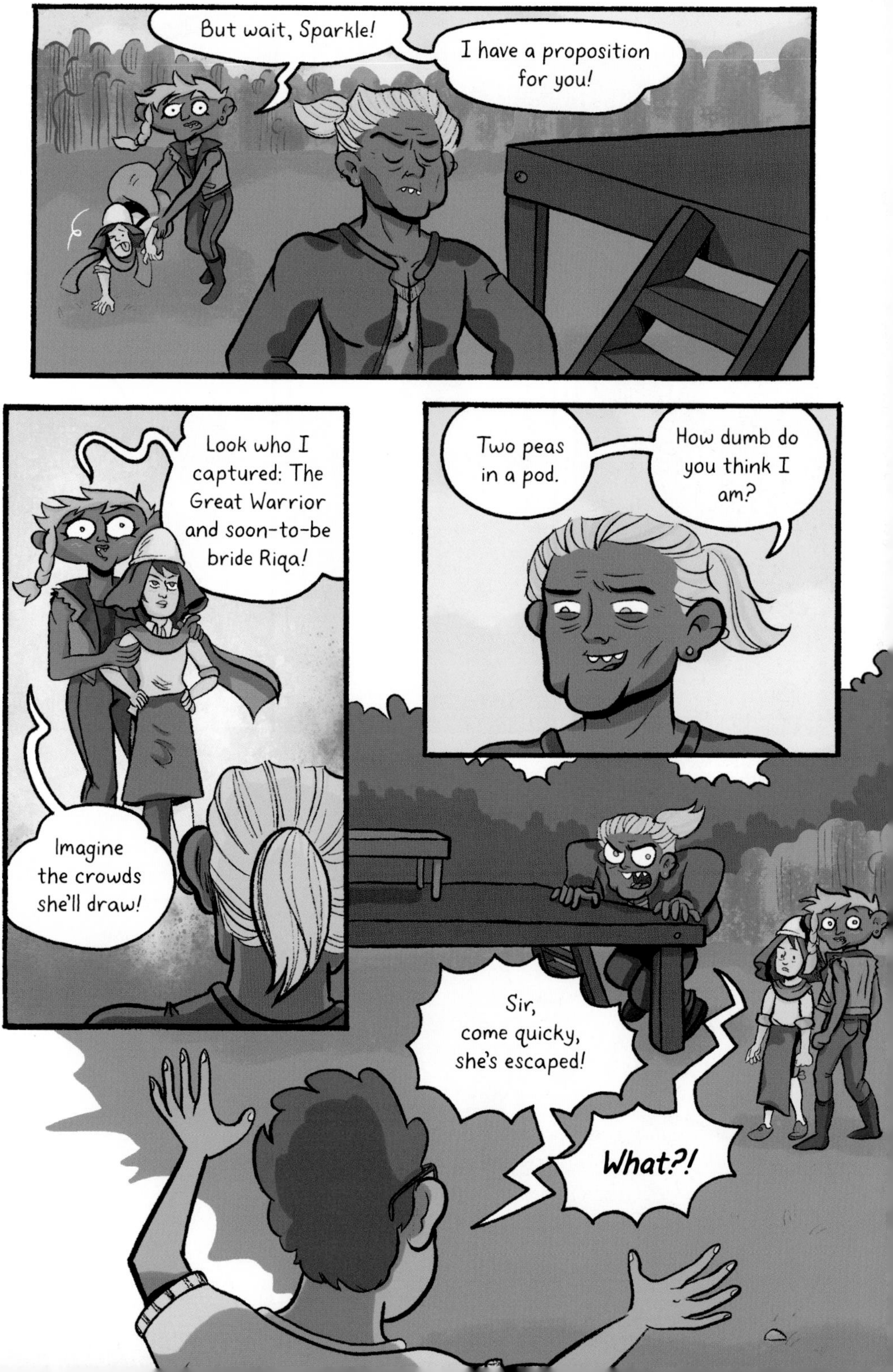
But wait, Sparkle!
I have a proposition for you!
Look who I captured: The Great Warrior and soon-to-be bride Riqa!
Imagine the crowds she'll draw!
Two peas in a pod.
How dumb do you think I am?
Sir, come quicky, she's escaped!
What?!

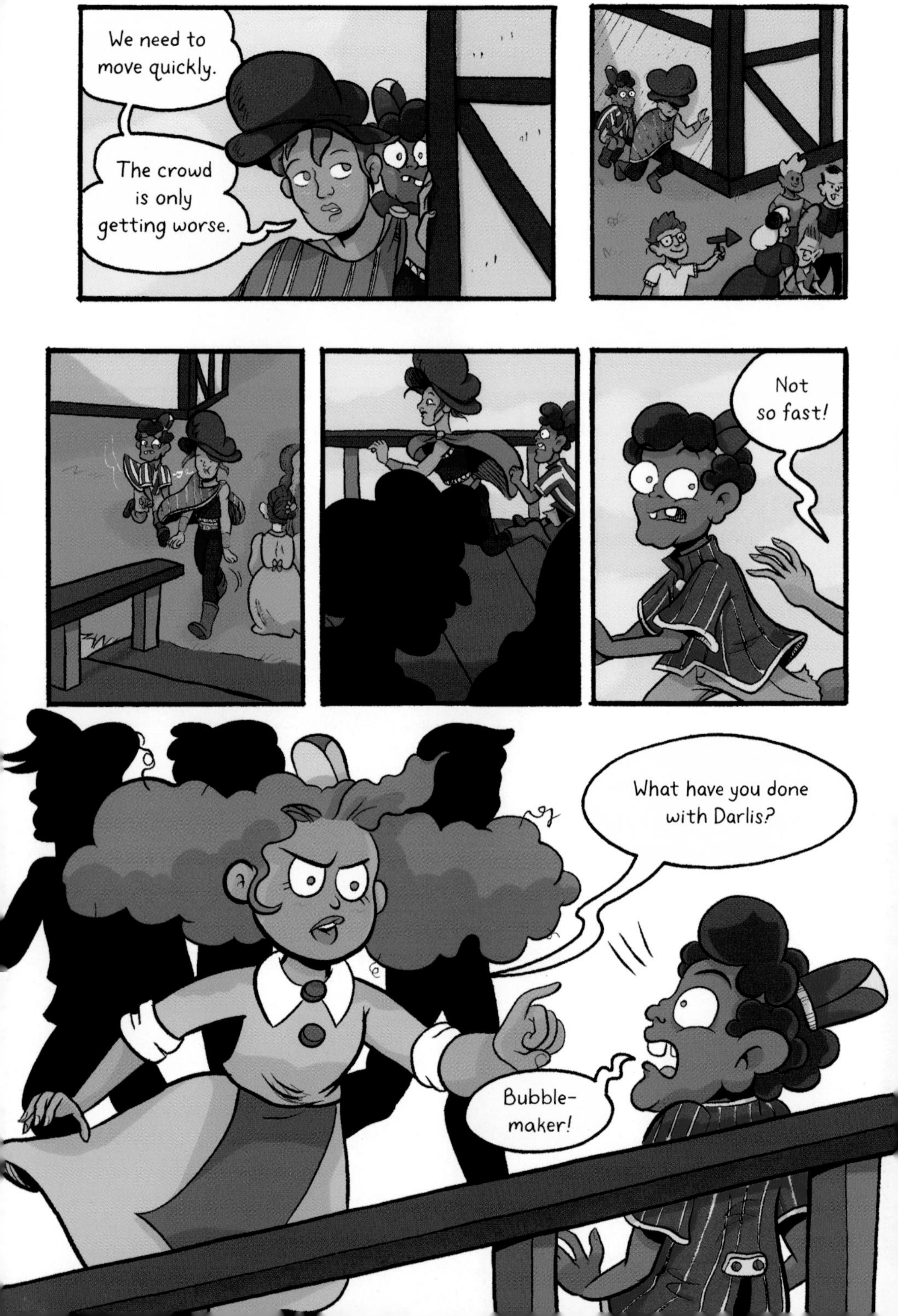
We need to move quickly.
The crowd is only getting worse.
Not so fast!
What have you done with Darlis?
Bubble-maker!

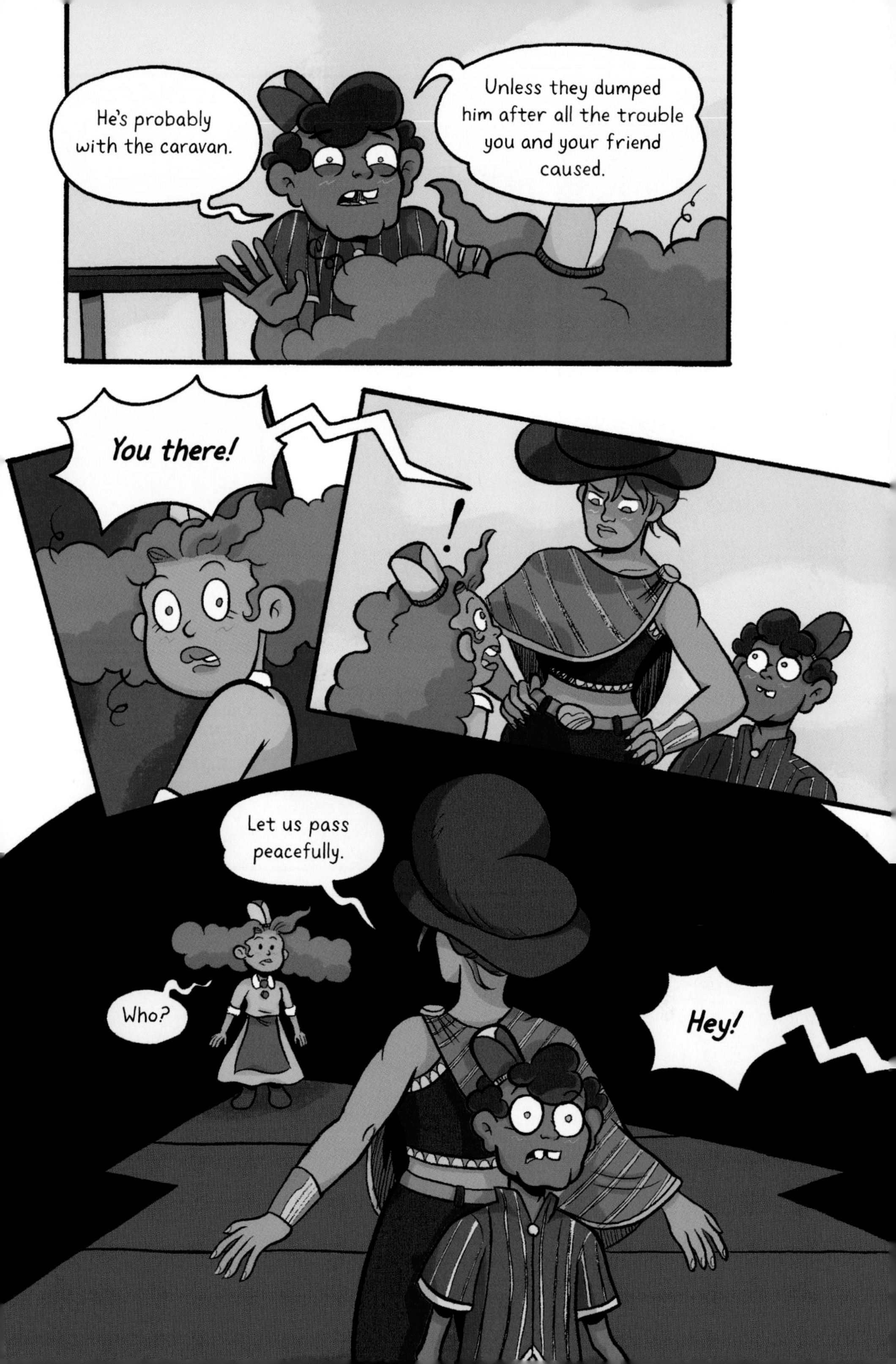
He's probably with the caravan.
Unless they dumped him after all the trouble you and your friend caused.
You there!
!
Let us pass peacefully.
Who?
Hey!

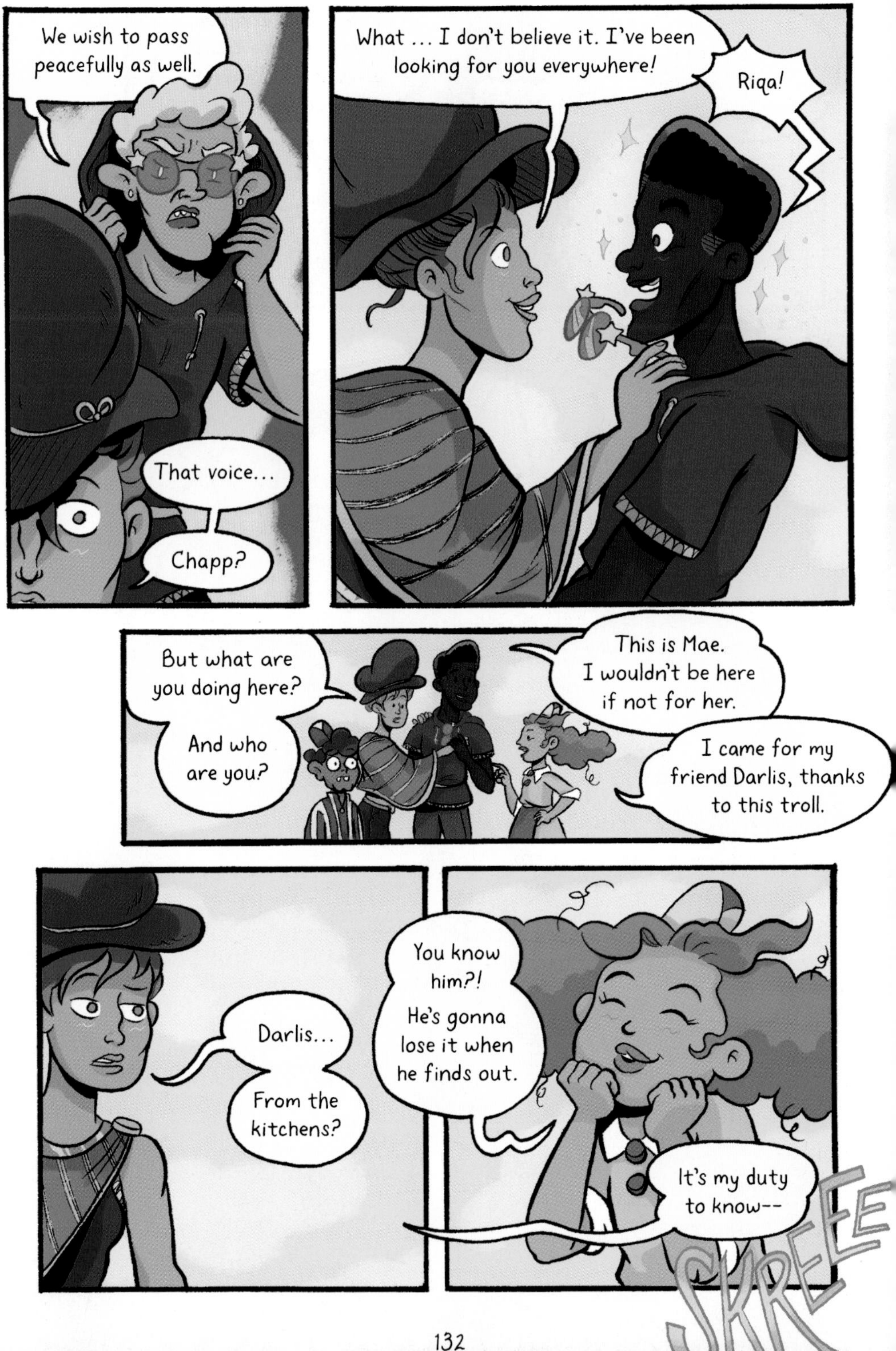
We wish to pass peacefully as well.
That voice...
Chapp?
What ... I don't believe it. I've been looking for you everywhere!
Riqa!
But what are you doing here?
And who are you?
This is Mae. I wouldn't be here if not for her.
I came for my friend Darlis, thanks to this troll.
Darlis...
From the kitchens?
You know him?!
He's gonna lose it when he finds out.
It's my duty to know--
SKREEE

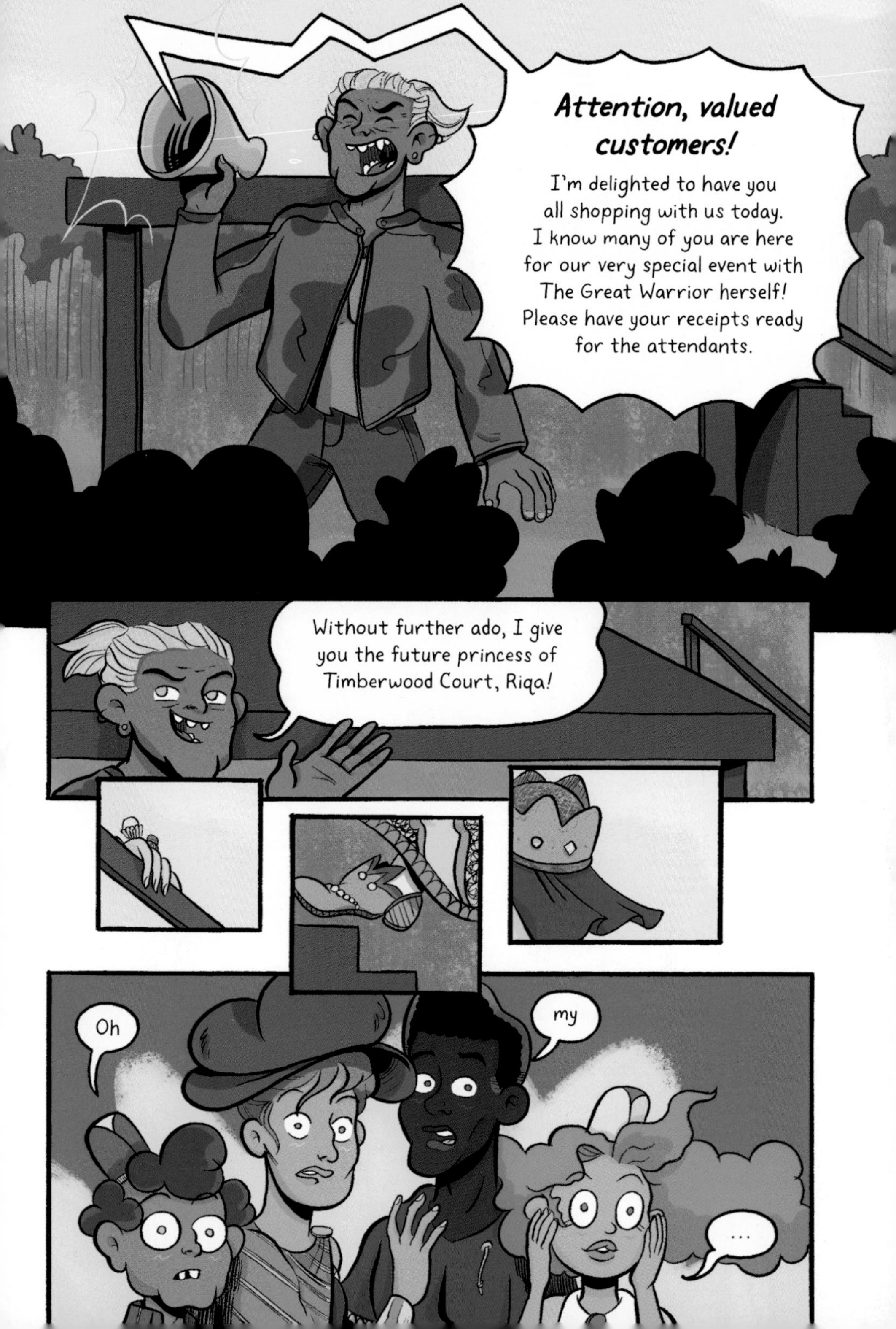
Attention, valued customers!
I'm delighted to have you all shopping with us today. I know many of you are here for our very special event with The Great Warrior herself! Please have your receipts ready for the attendants.
Without further ado, I give you the future princess of Timberwood Court, Riqa!
Oh
my
...

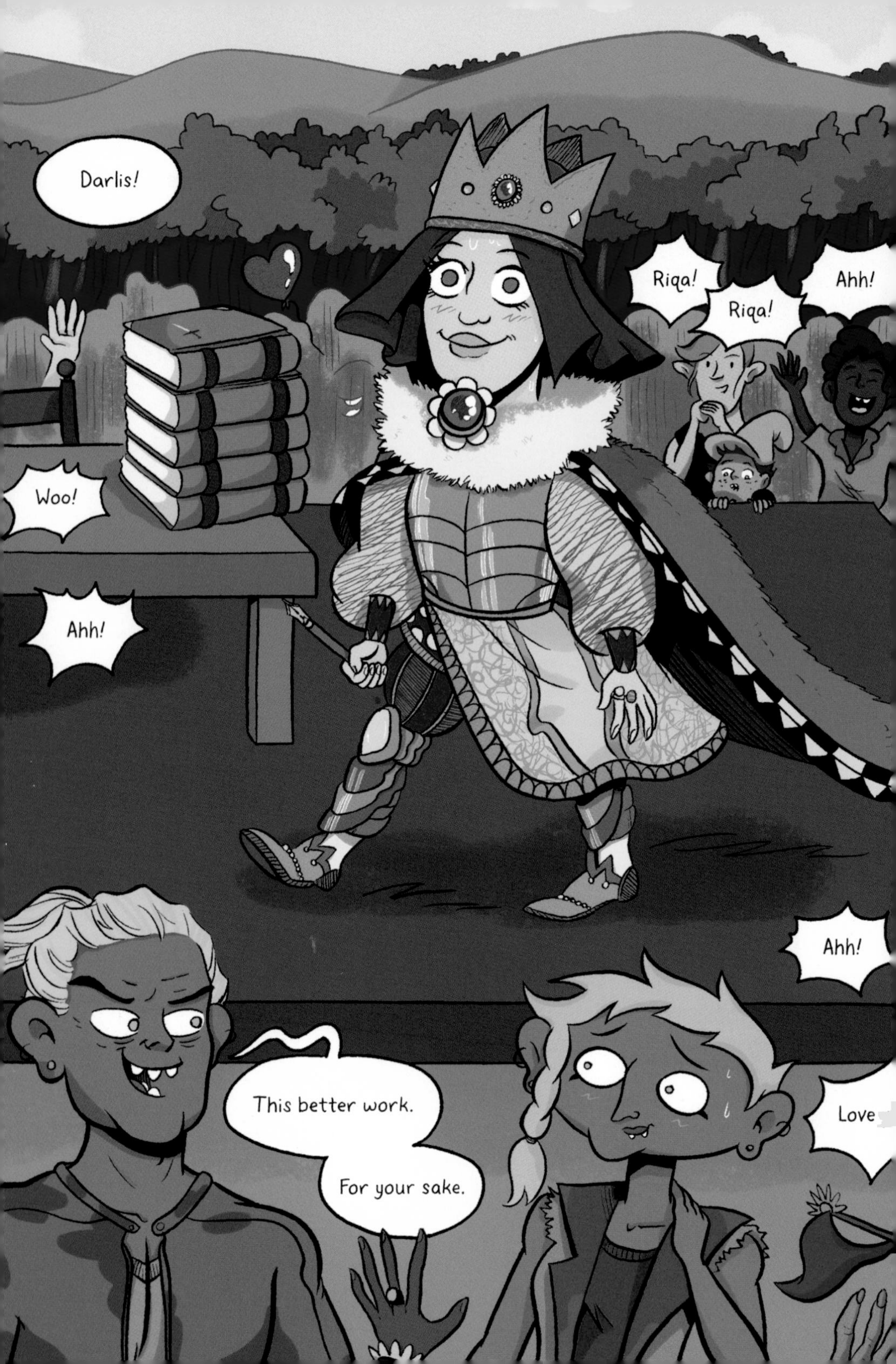
Darlis!
Riqa!
Riqa!
Ahh!
Woo!
Ahh!
Ahh!
This better work.
For your sake.
Love

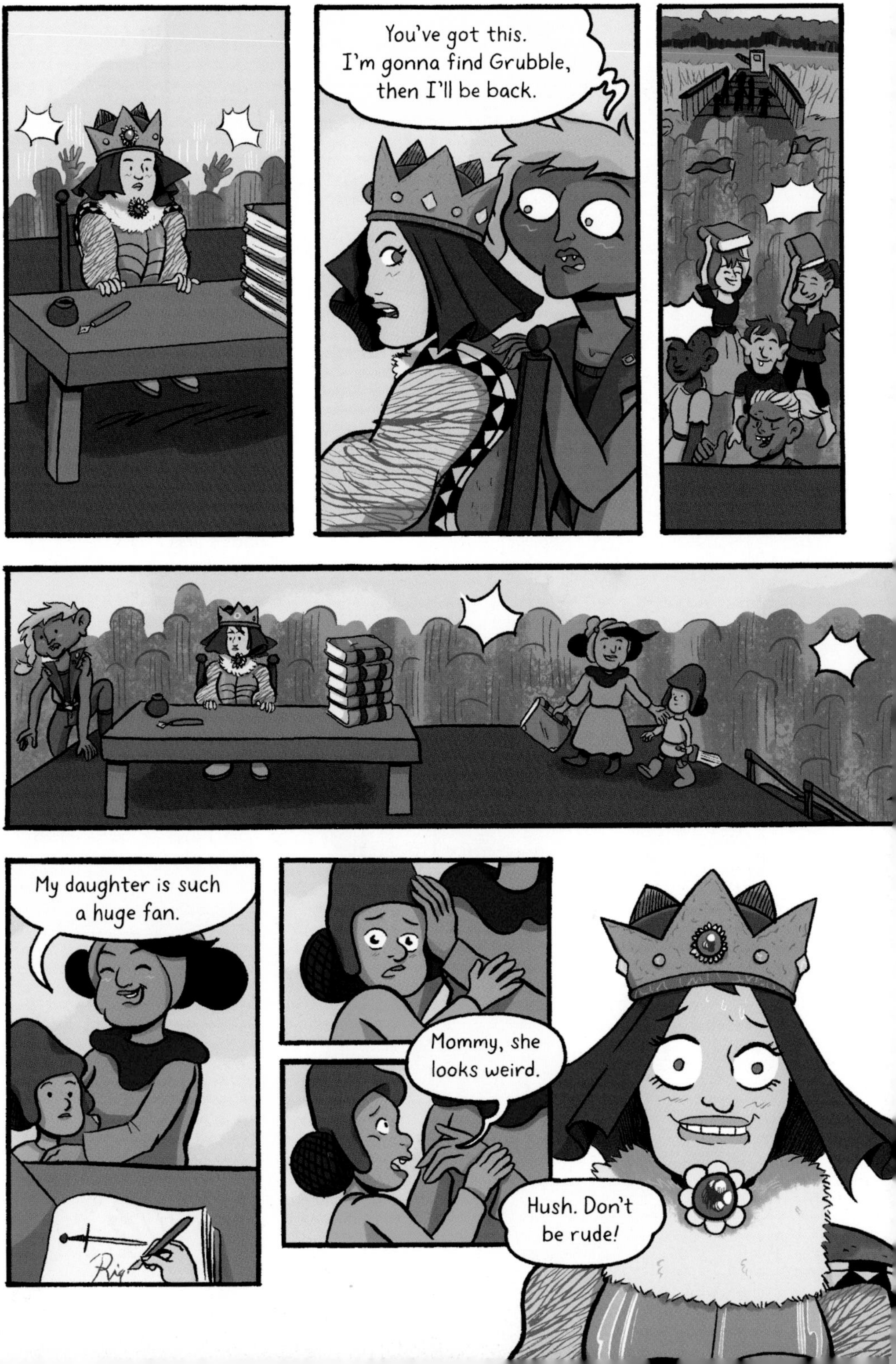
You've got this.
I'm gonna find Grubble,
then I'll be back.
My daughter is such
a huge fan.
Mommy, she
looks weird.
Hush. Don't
be rude!

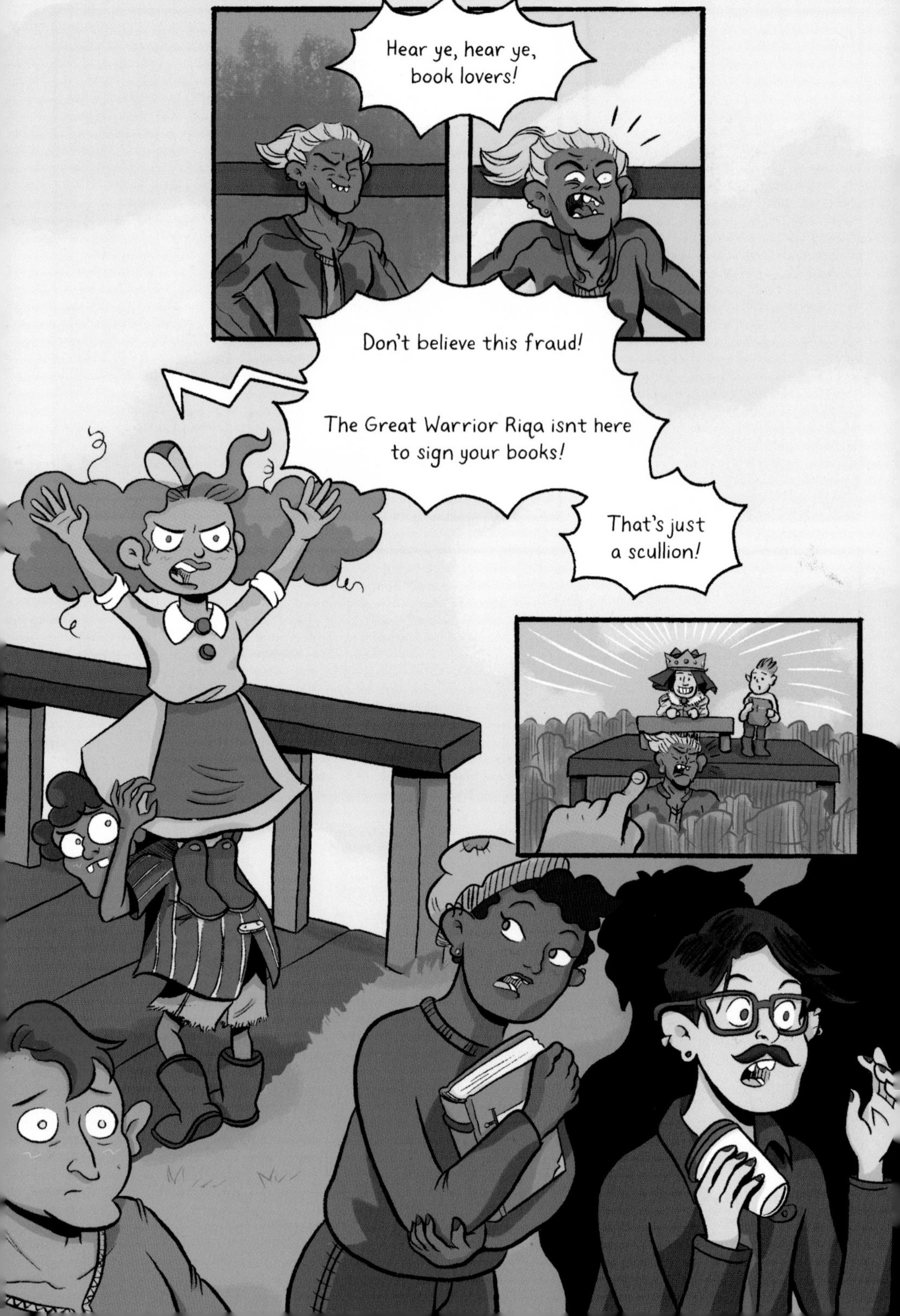

Hear ye, hear ye, book lovers!
Don't believe this fraud!
The Great Warrior Riqa isnt here to sign your books!
That's just a scullion!

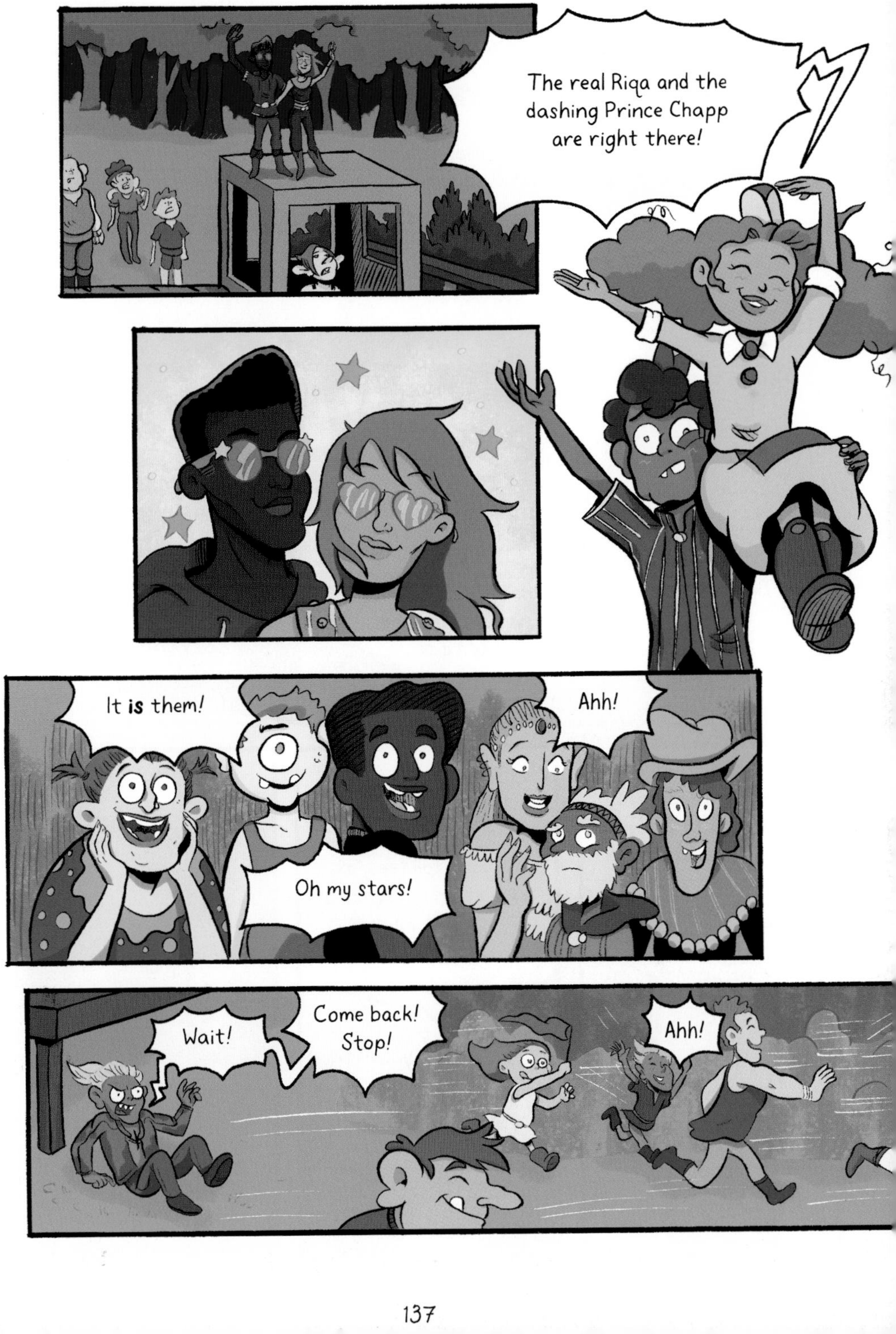

The real Riqa and the dashing Prince Chapp are right there!
It **is** them!
Ahh!
Oh my stars!
Wait!
Come back! Stop!
Ahh!

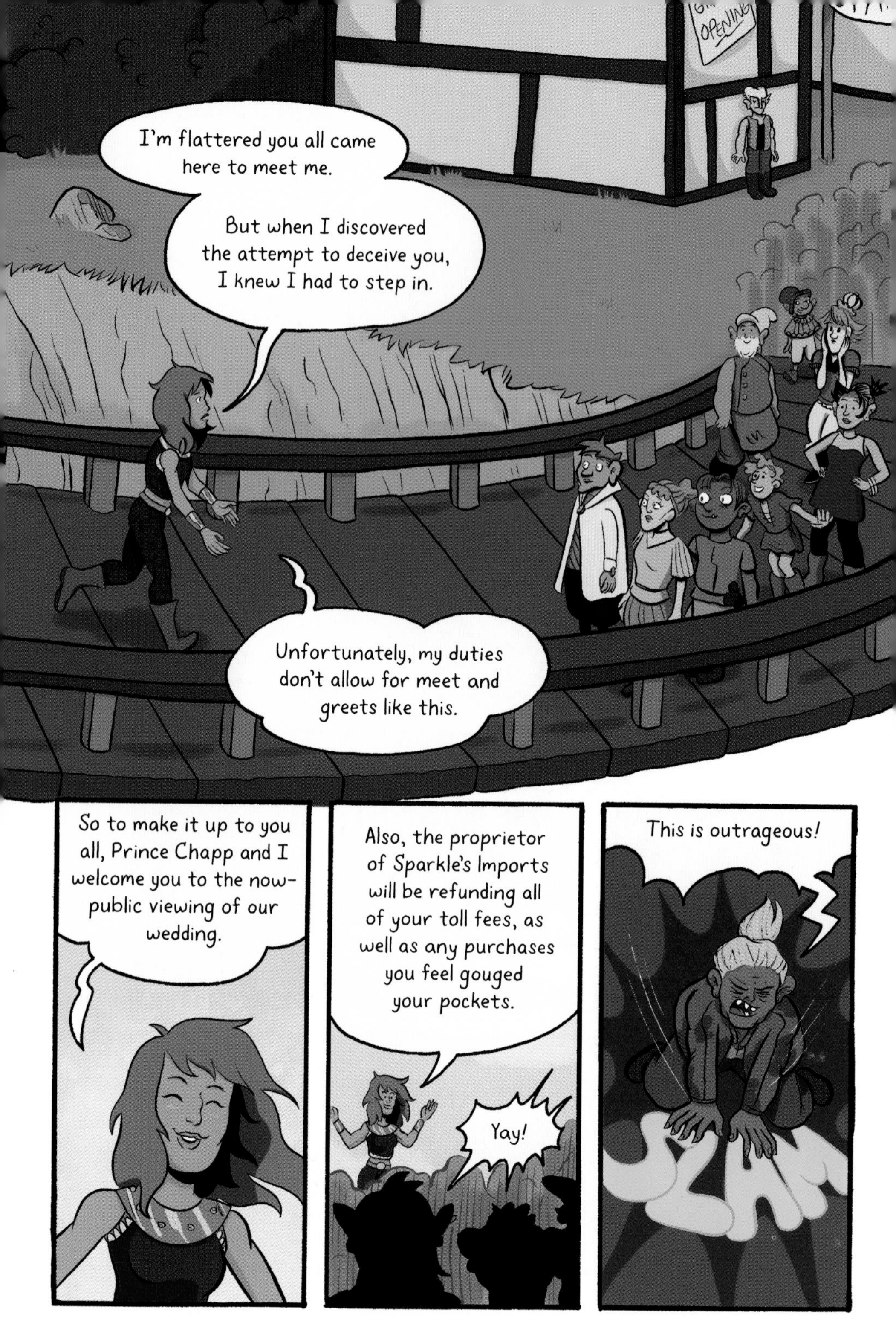
GRAND OPENING
I'm flattered you all came here to meet me.
But when I discovered the attempt to deceive you, I knew I had to step in.
Unfortunately, my duties don't allow for meet and greets like this.
So to make it up to you all, Prince Chapp and I welcome you to the now-public viewing of our wedding.
Also, the proprietor of Sparkle's Imports will be refunding all of your toll fees, as well as any purchases you feel gouged your pockets.
Yay!
This is outrageous!
SLAM

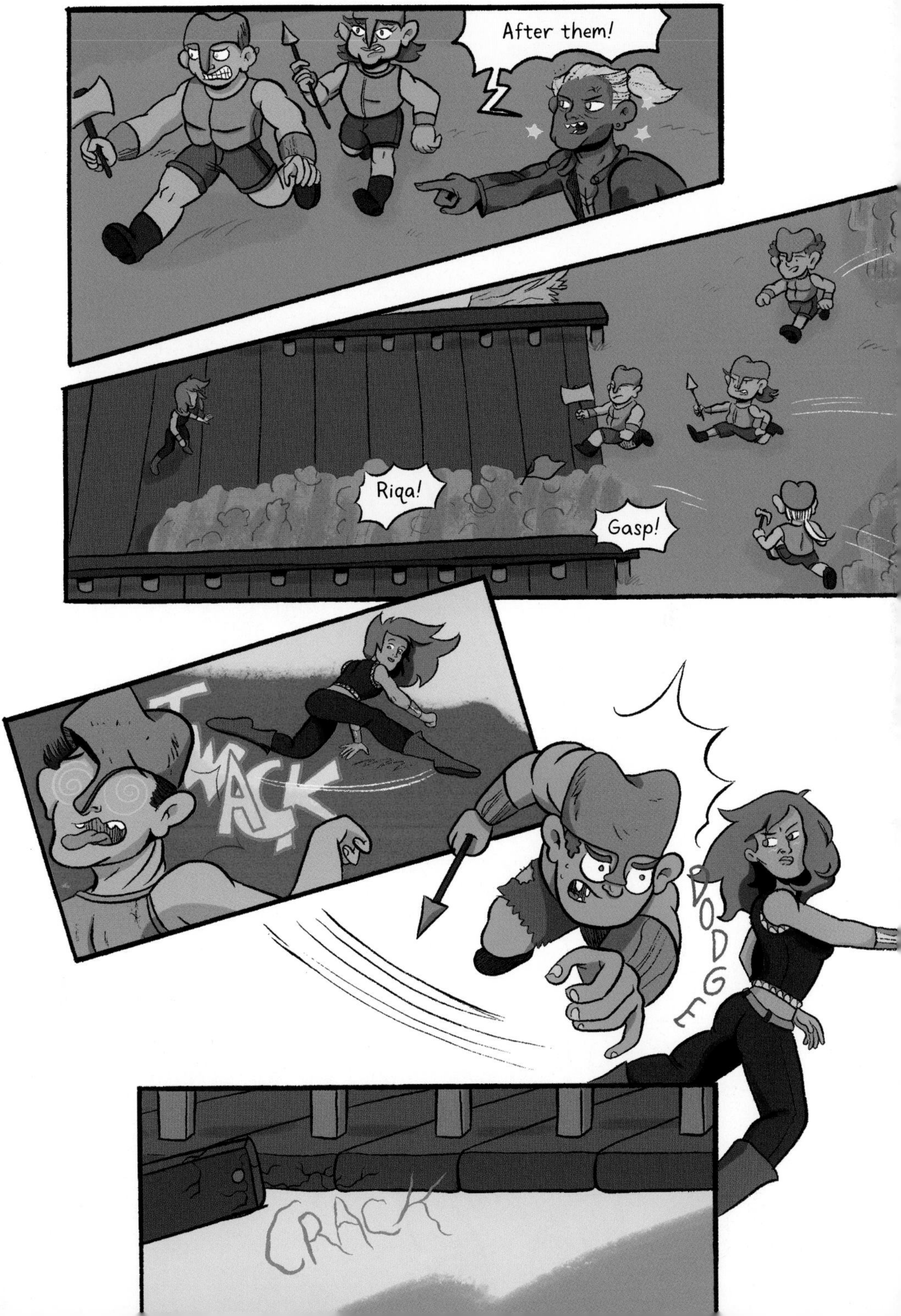
After them!
Riqa!
Gasp!
THWACK
DODGE
CRACK

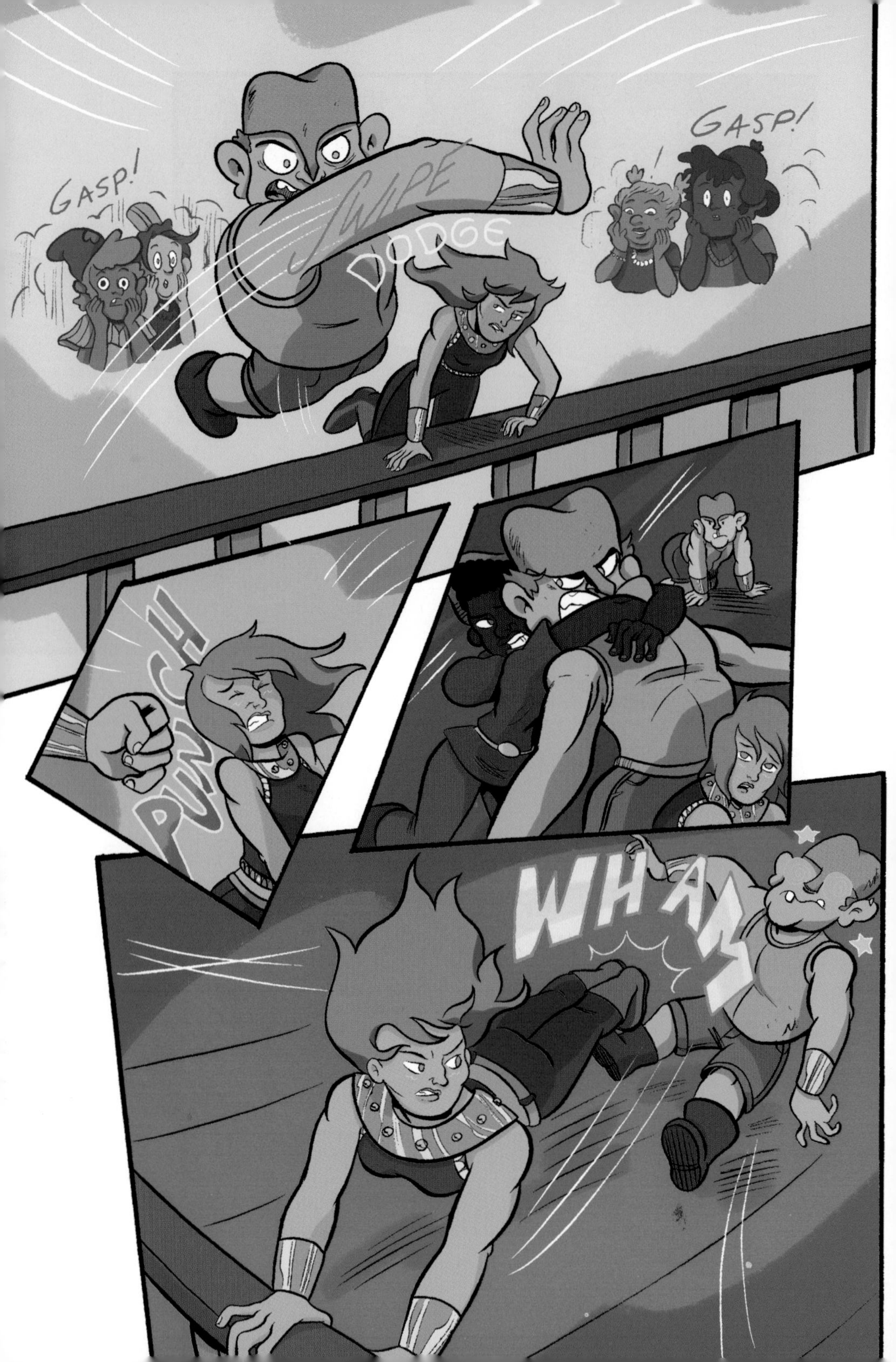
GASP!
SWIPE
DODGE
GASP!
PUNCH
WHAM

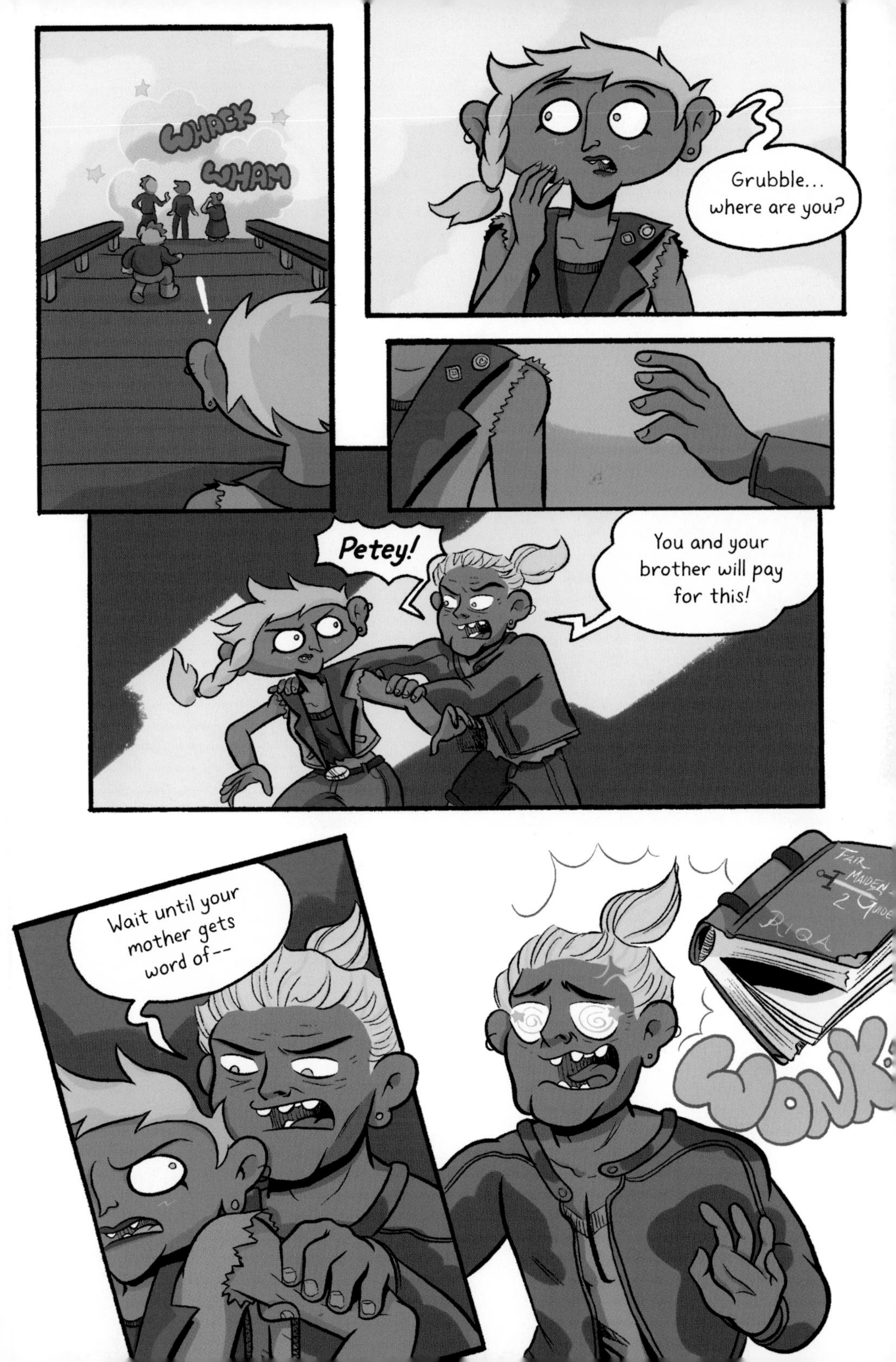
WHACK
WHAM
!
Grubble... where are you?
Petey!
You and your brother will pay for this!
Wait until your mother gets word of--
WONK
FAIR MAIDEN 2 GUIDE

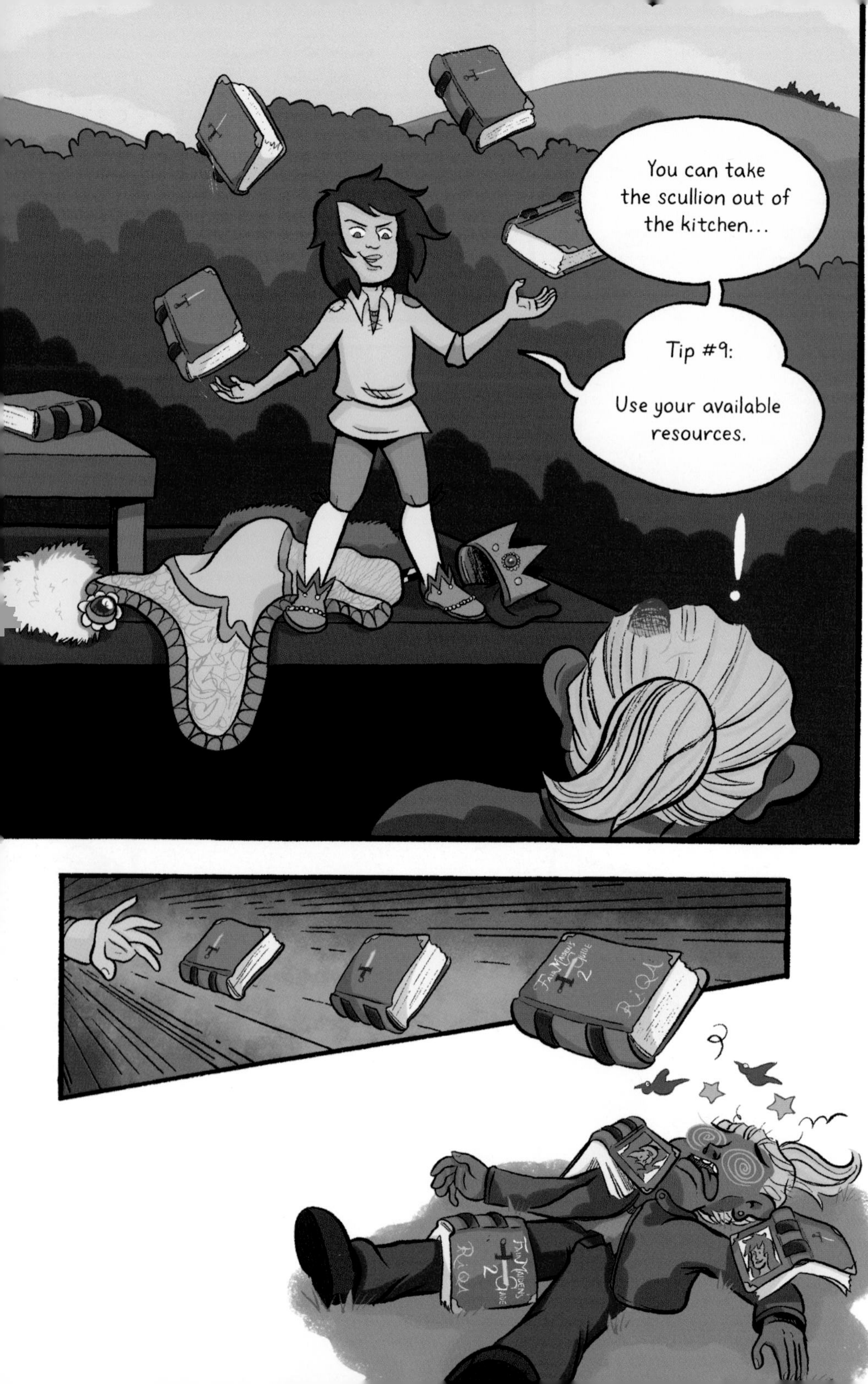

You can take the scullion out of the kitchen...
Tip #9:
Use your available resources.
!

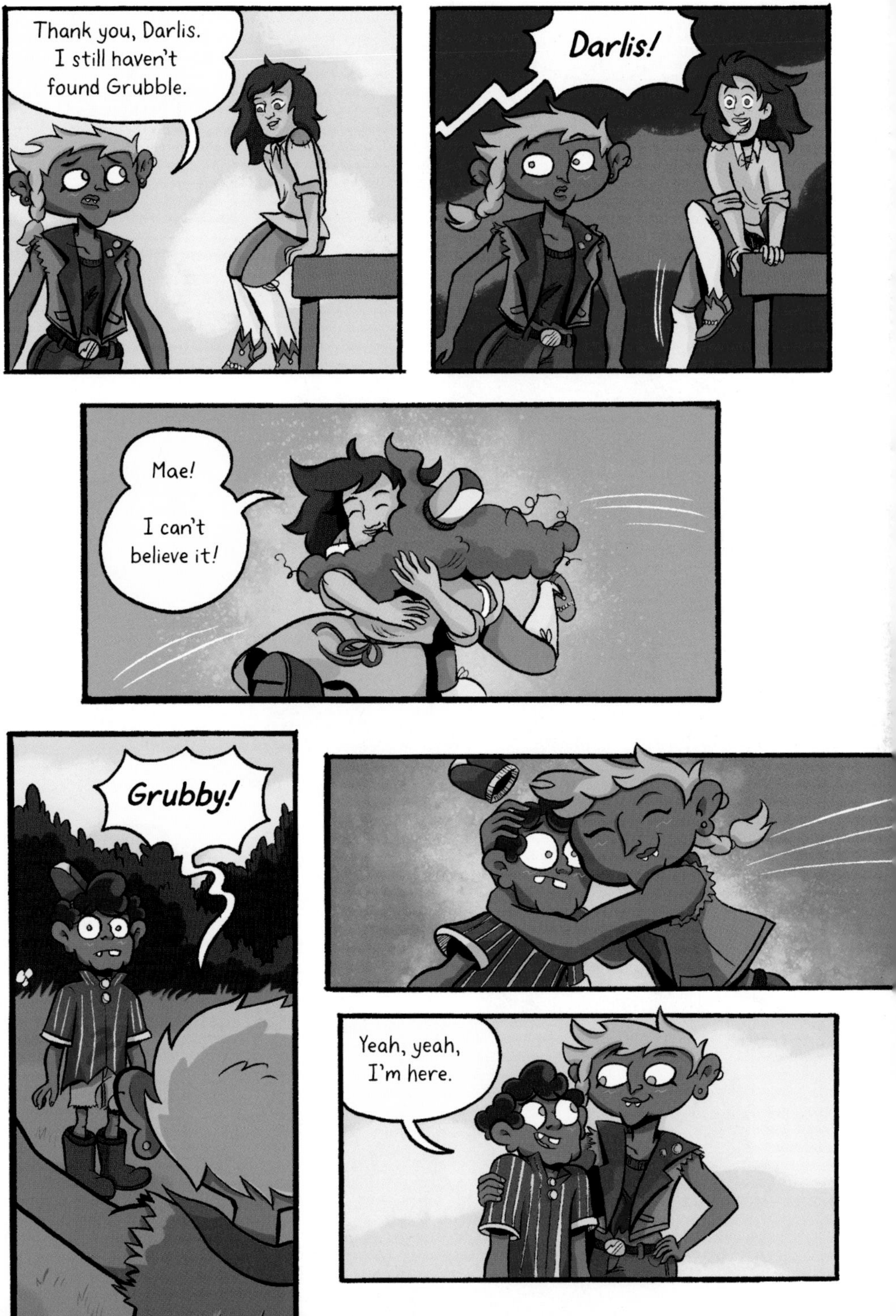
Thank you, Darlis. I still haven't found Grubble.
Darlis!
Mae!
I can't believe it!
Grubby!
Yeah, yeah, I'm here.

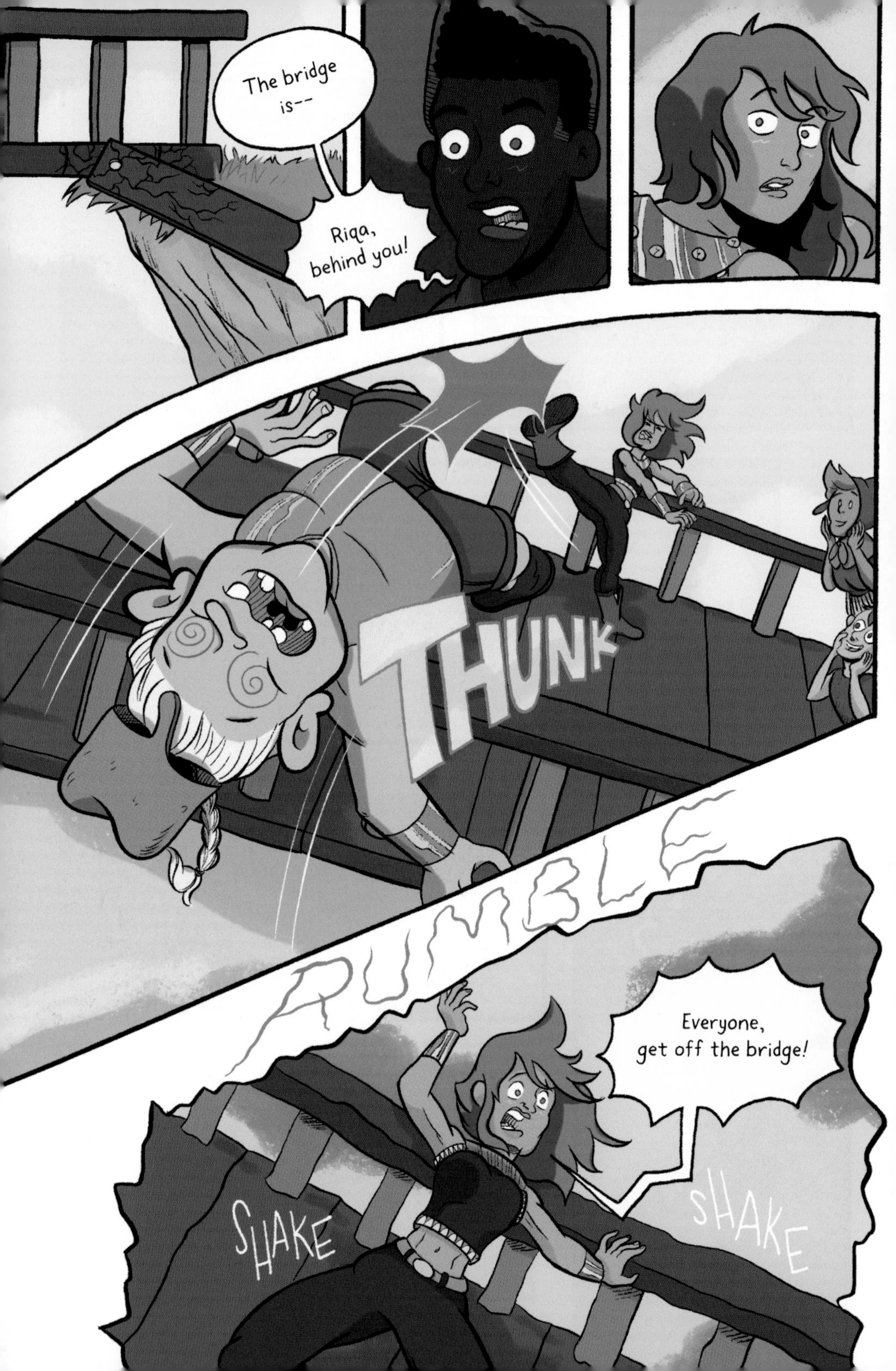
The bridge is--
Riqa, behind you!
THUNK
RUMBLE
Everyone, get off the bridge!
SHAKE
SHAKE

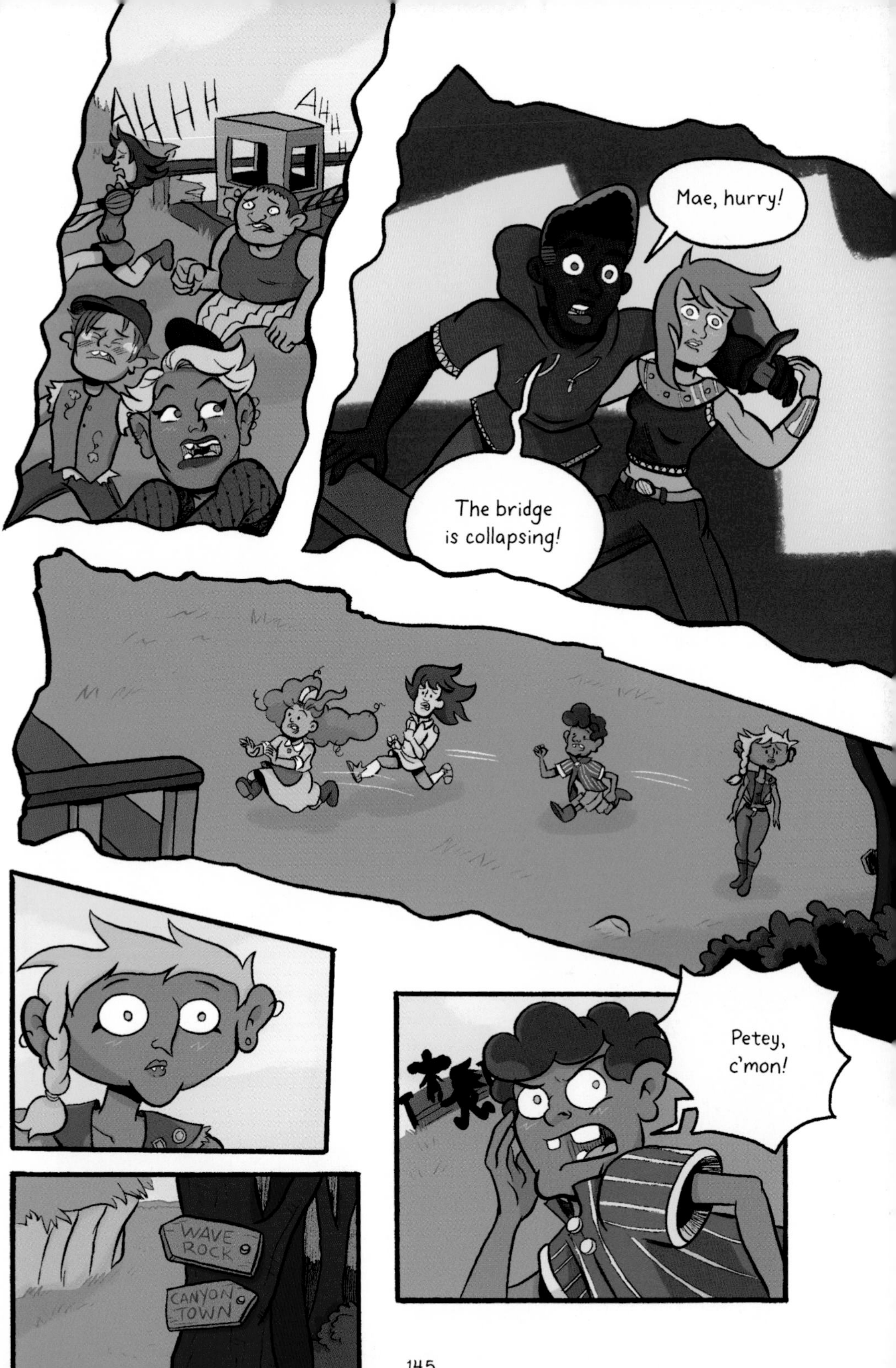
AHHHH
AHHH
Mae, hurry!
The bridge is collapsing!
Petey, c'mon!
WAVE ROCK
CANYON TOWN

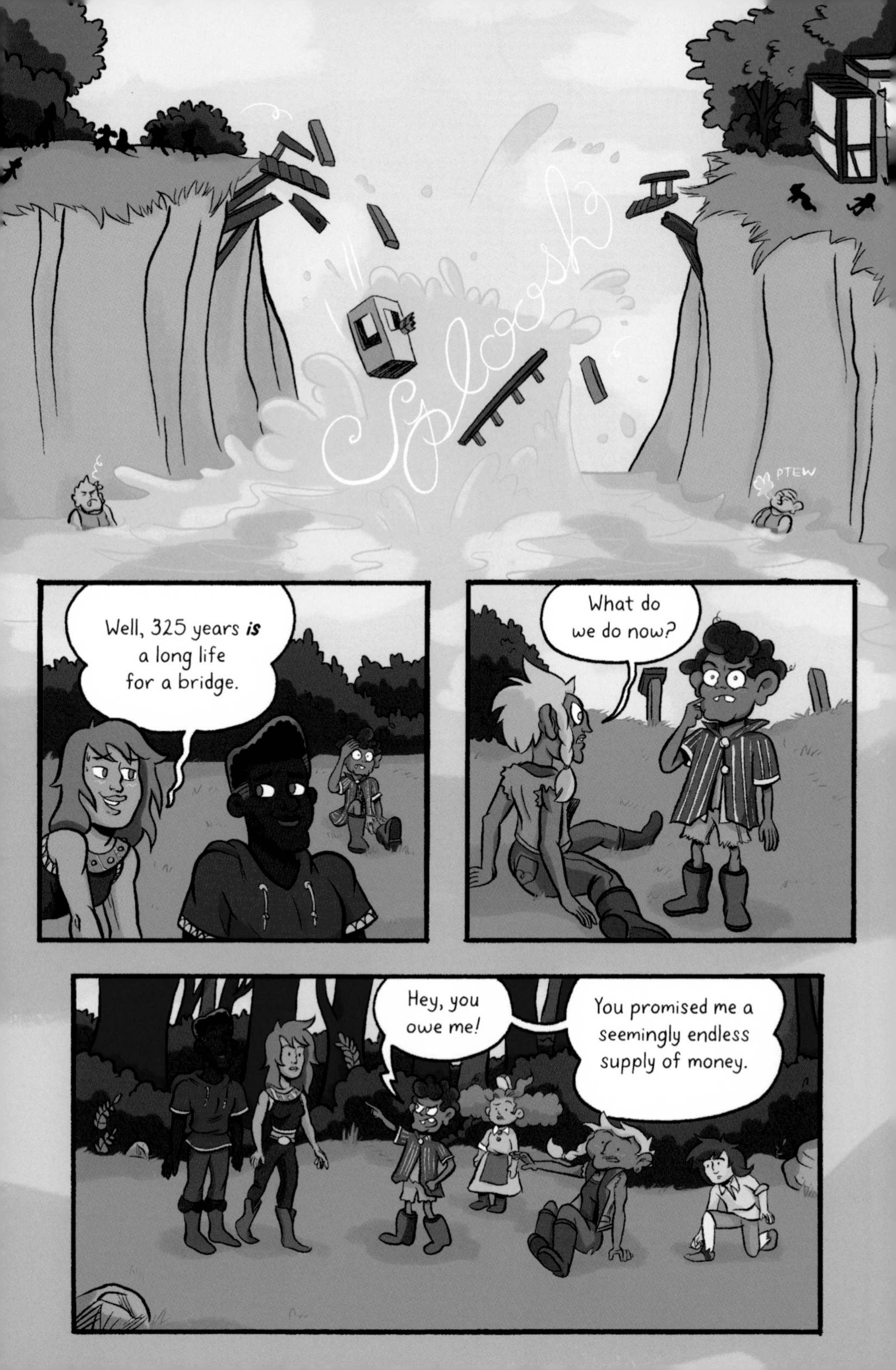
Sploosh
PTEW
Well, 325 years **is** a long life for a bridge.
What do we do now?
Hey, you owe me!
You promised me a seemingly endless supply of money.

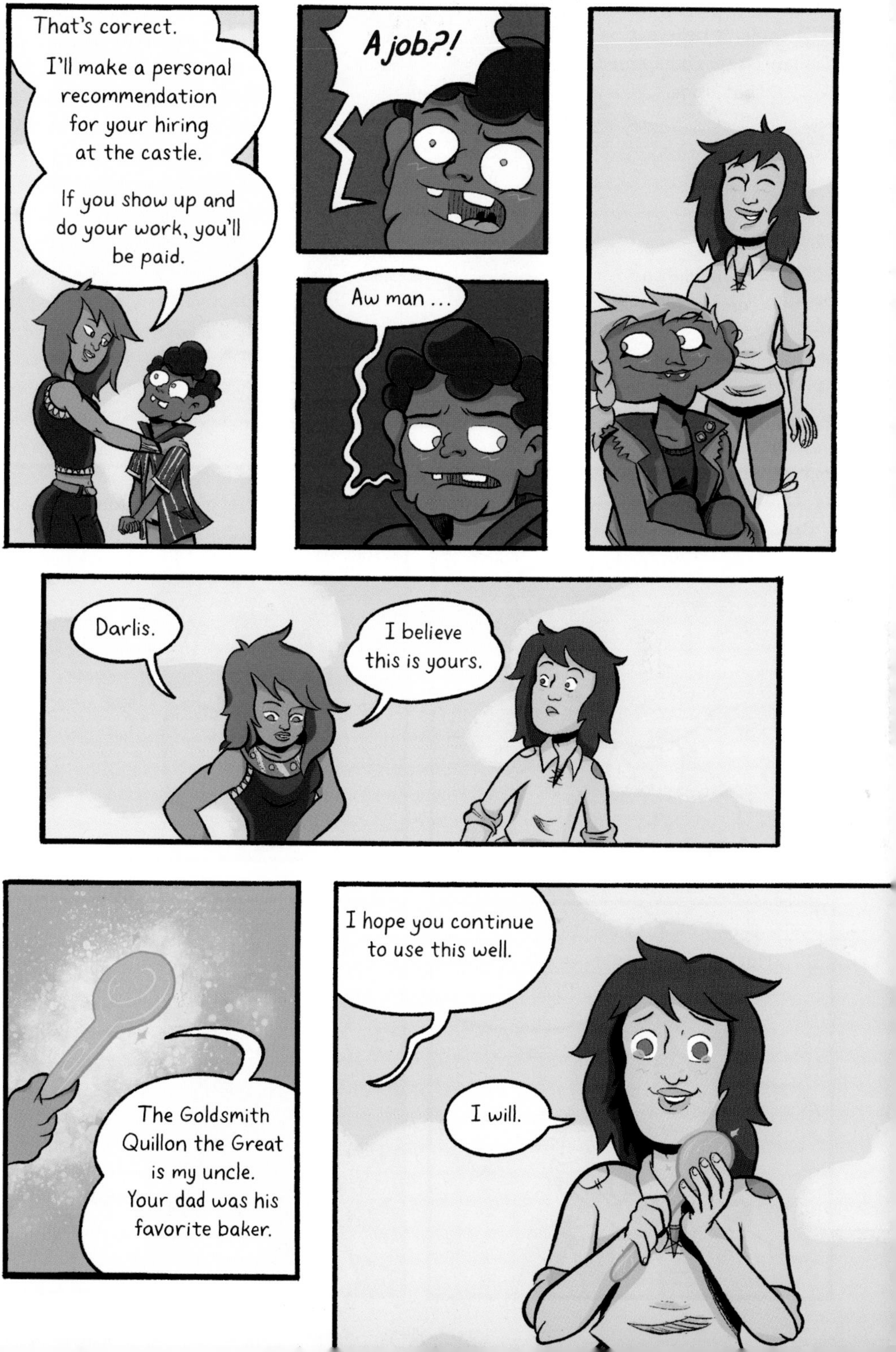

That's correct.
I'll make a personal recommendation for your hiring at the castle.
If you show up and do your work, you'll be paid.
A job?!
Aw man ...
Darlis.
I believe this is yours.
The Goldsmith Quillon the Great is my uncle. Your dad was his favorite baker.
I hope you continue to use this well.
I will.

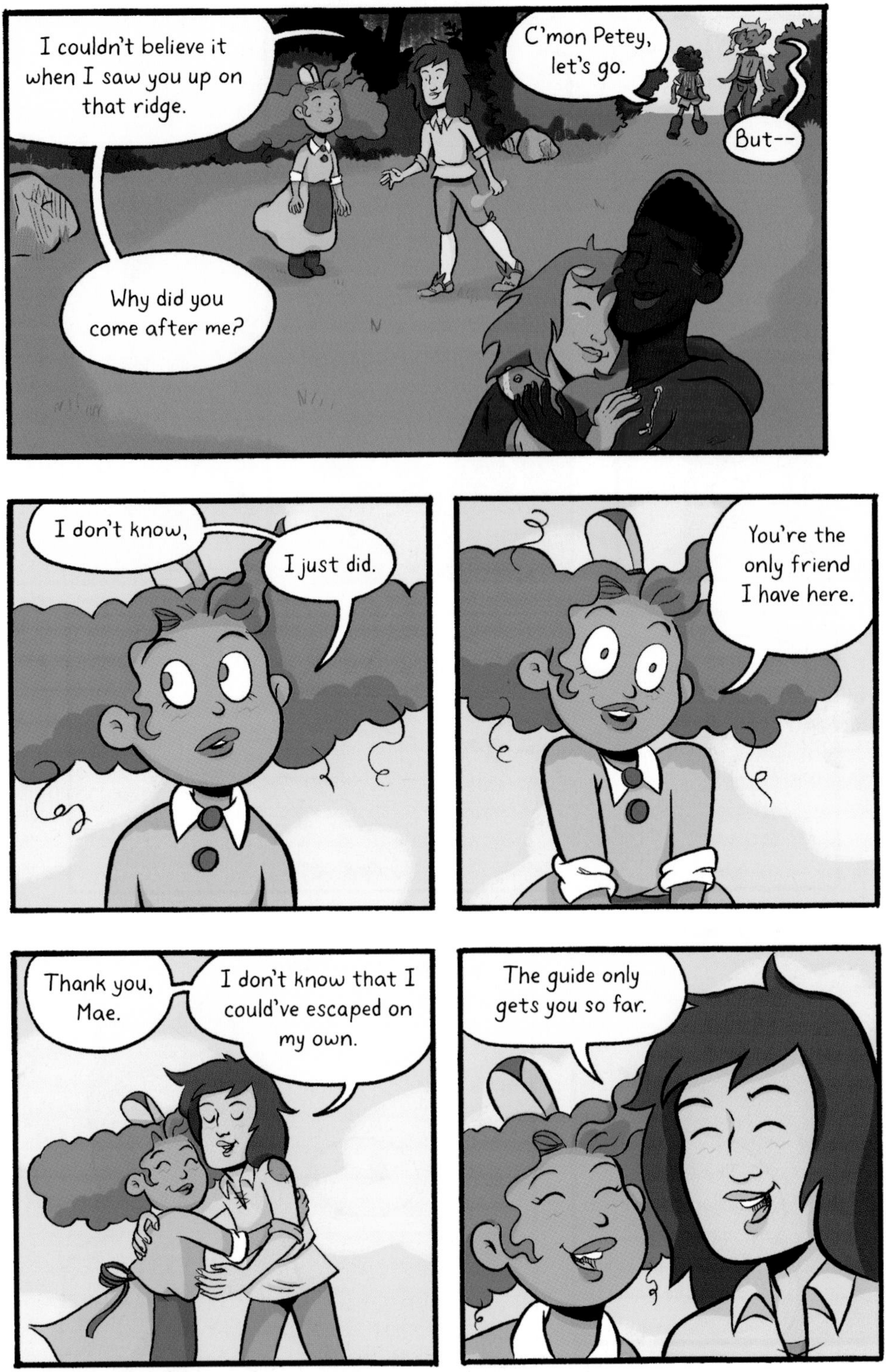
I couldn't believe it when I saw you up on that ridge.
Why did you come after me?
C'mon Petey, let's go.
But--
I don't know,
I just did.
You're the only friend I have here.
Thank you, Mae.
I don't know that I could've escaped on my own.
The guide only gets you so far.

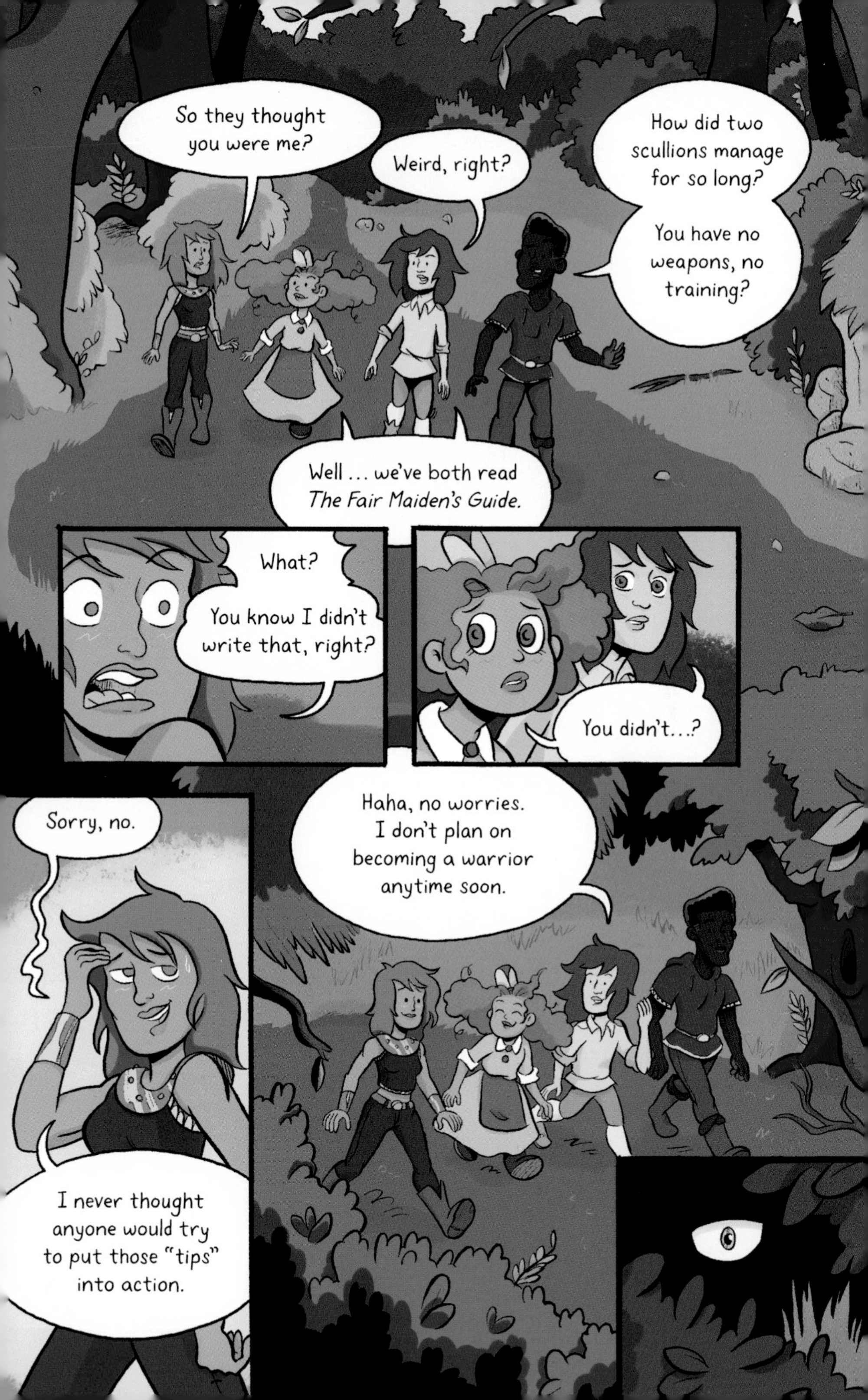

So they thought you were me?
Weird, right?
How did two scullions manage for so long?
You have no weapons, no training?
Well ... we've both read *The Fair Maiden's Guide.*
What?
You know I didn't write that, right?
You didn't...?
Sorry, no.
Haha, no worries. I don't plan on becoming a warrior anytime soon.
I never thought anyone would try to put those "tips" into action.

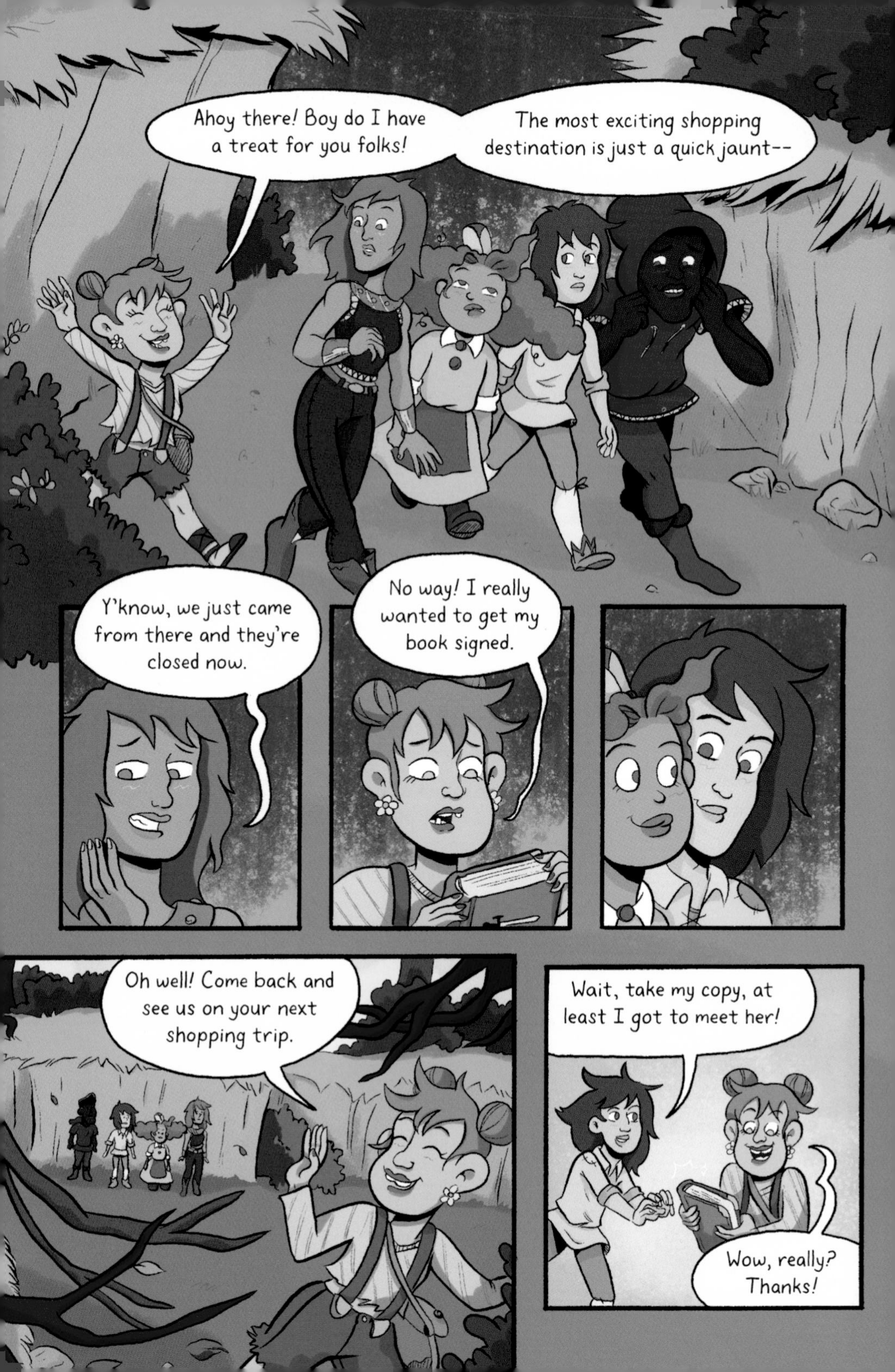
Ahoy there! Boy do I have a treat for you folks!
The most exciting shopping destination is just a quick jaunt--
Y'know, we just came from there and they're closed now.
No way! I really wanted to get my book signed.
Oh well! Come back and see us on your next shopping trip.
Wait, take my copy, at least I got to meet her!
Wow, really? Thanks!

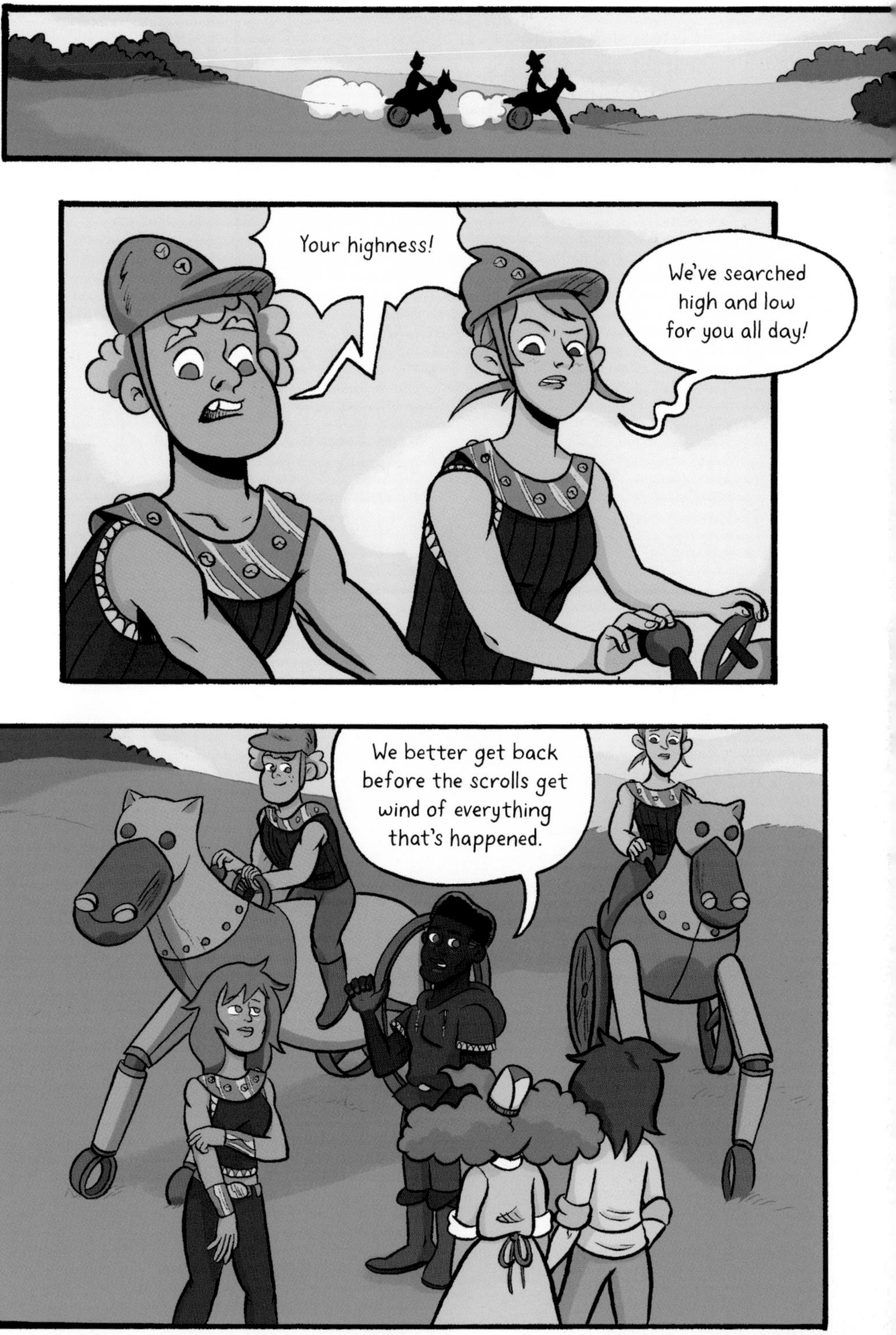
Your highness!
We've searched high and low for you all day!
We better get back before the scrolls get wind of everything that's happened.

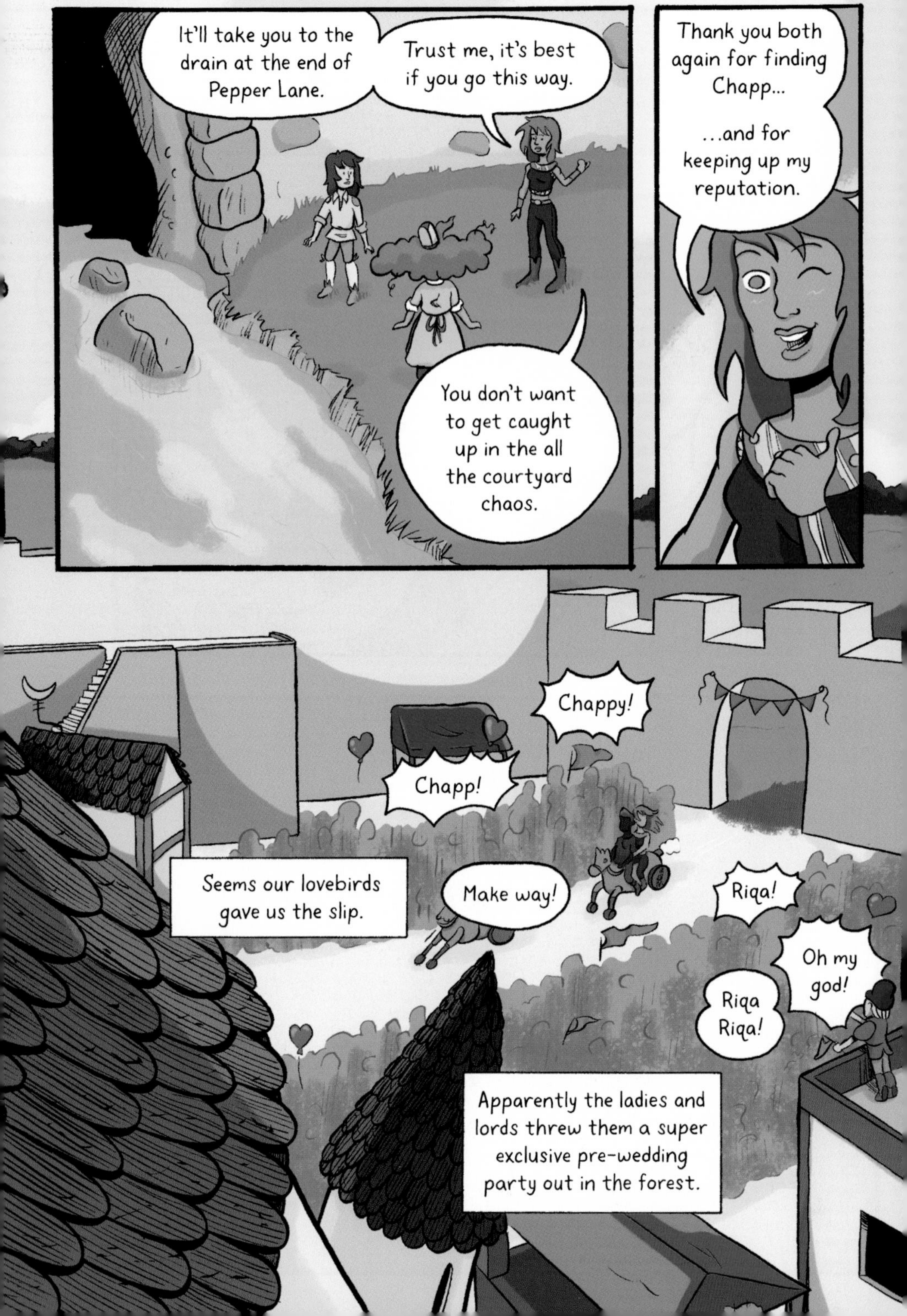
It'll take you to the drain at the end of Pepper Lane.
Trust me, it's best if you go this way.
You don't want to get caught up in the all the courtyard chaos.
Thank you both again for finding Chapp...
...and for keeping up my reputation.
Seems our lovebirds gave us the slip.
Chappy!
Chapp!
Make way!
Riqa!
Oh my god!
Riqa Riqa!
Apparently the ladies and lords threw them a super exclusive pre-wedding party out in the forest.

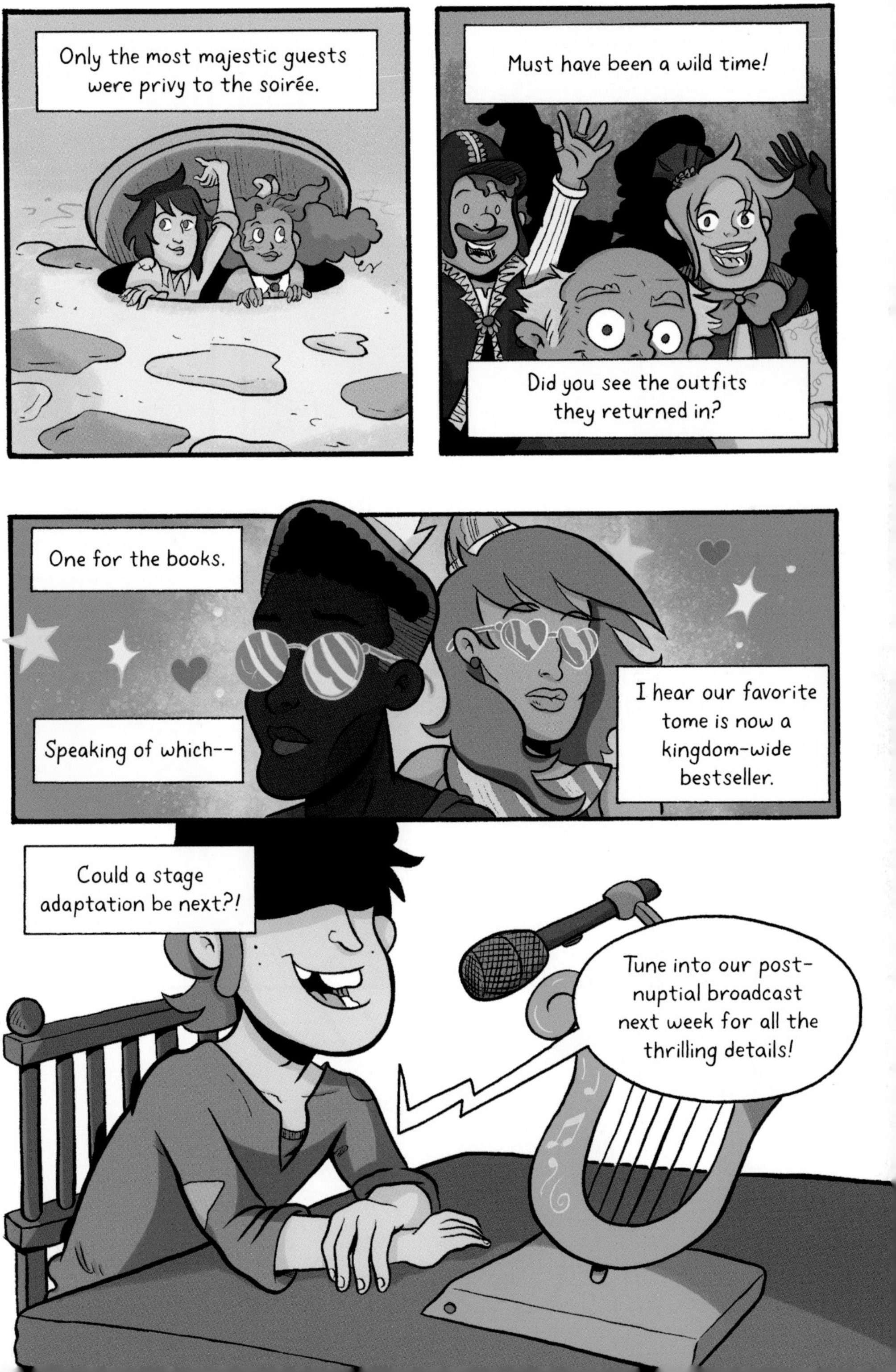
Only the most majestic guests were privy to the soirée.
Must have been a wild time!
Did you see the outfits they returned in?
One for the books.
Speaking of which--
I hear our favorite tome is now a kingdom-wide bestseller.
Could a stage adaptation be next?!
Tune into our post-nuptial broadcast next week for all the thrilling details!

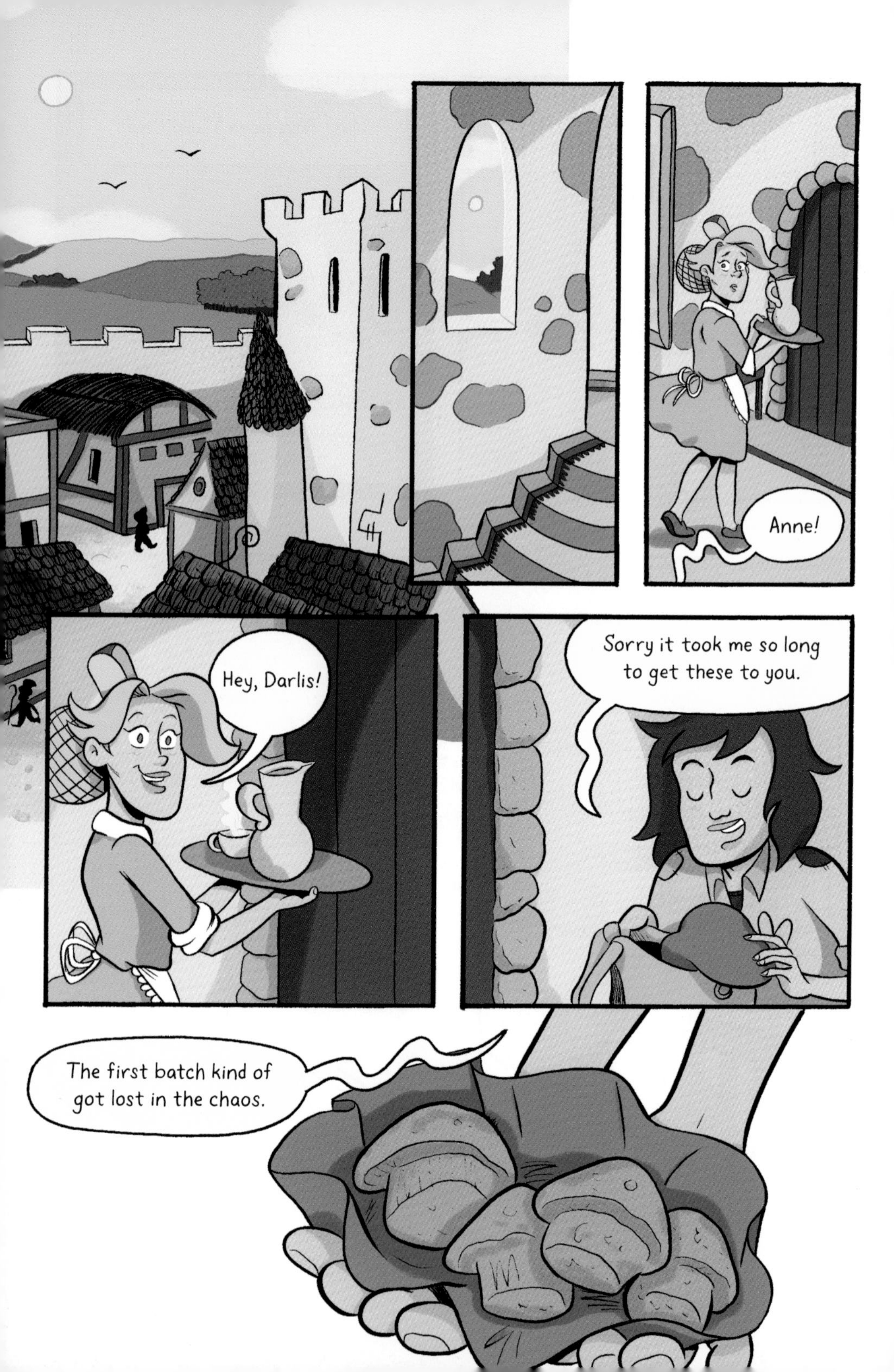
Anne!
Hey, Darlis!
Sorry it took me so long to get these to you.
The first batch kind of got lost in the chaos.

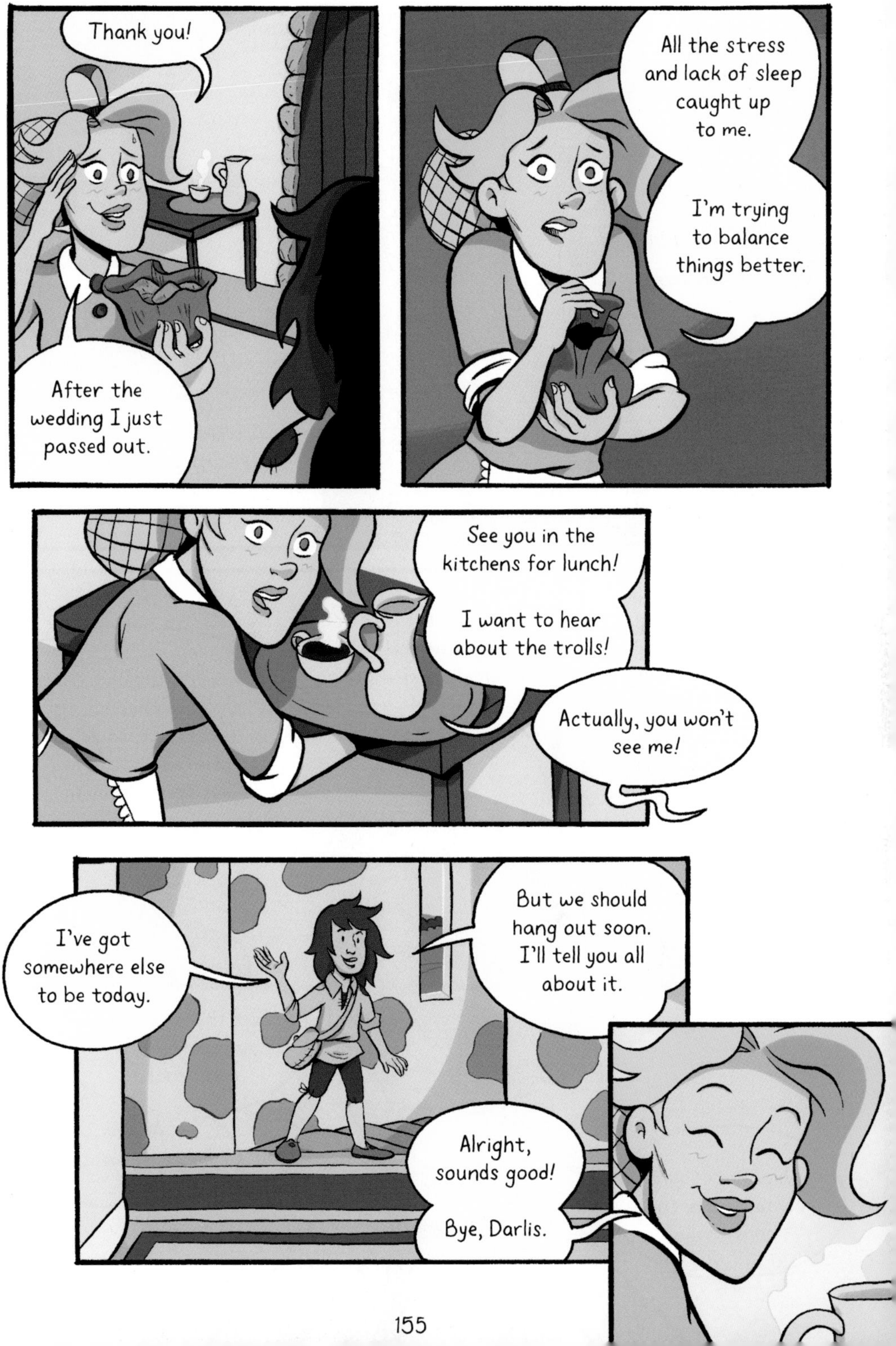
Thank you!
After the wedding I just passed out.
All the stress and lack of sleep caught up to me.
I'm trying to balance things better.
See you in the kitchens for lunch!
I want to hear about the trolls!
Actually, you won't see me!
I've got somewhere else to be today.
But we should hang out soon. I'll tell you all about it.
Alright, sounds good!
Bye, Darlis.

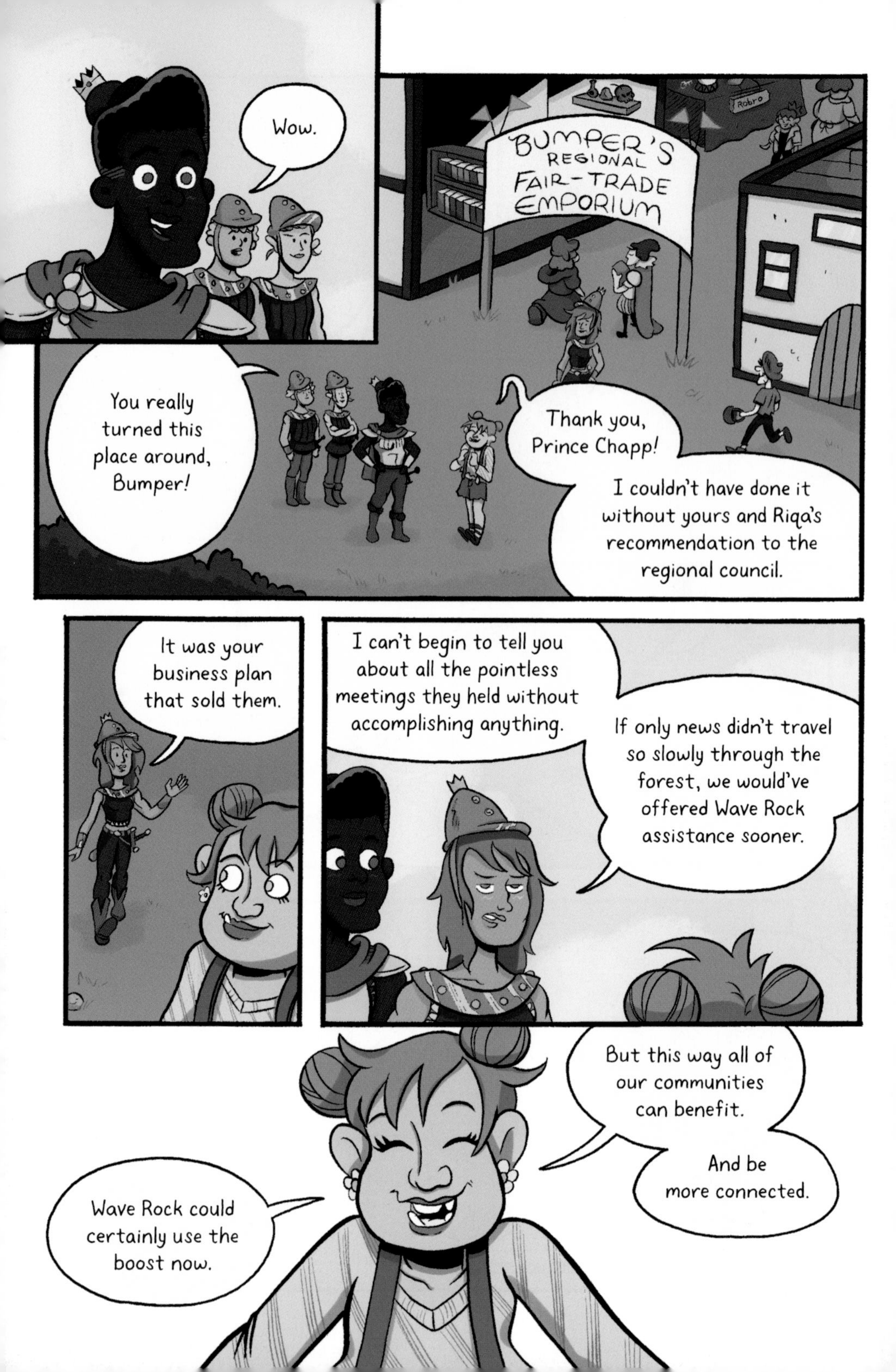
Wow.
BUMPER'S REGIONAL FAIR-TRADE EMPORIUM
Robro
You really turned this place around, Bumper!
Thank you, Prince Chapp!
I couldn't have done it without yours and Riqa's recommendation to the regional council.
It was your business plan that sold them.
I can't begin to tell you about all the pointless meetings they held without accomplishing anything.
If only news didn't travel so slowly through the forest, we would've offered Wave Rock assistance sooner.
But this way all of our communities can benefit.
And be more connected.
Wave Rock could certainly use the boost now.

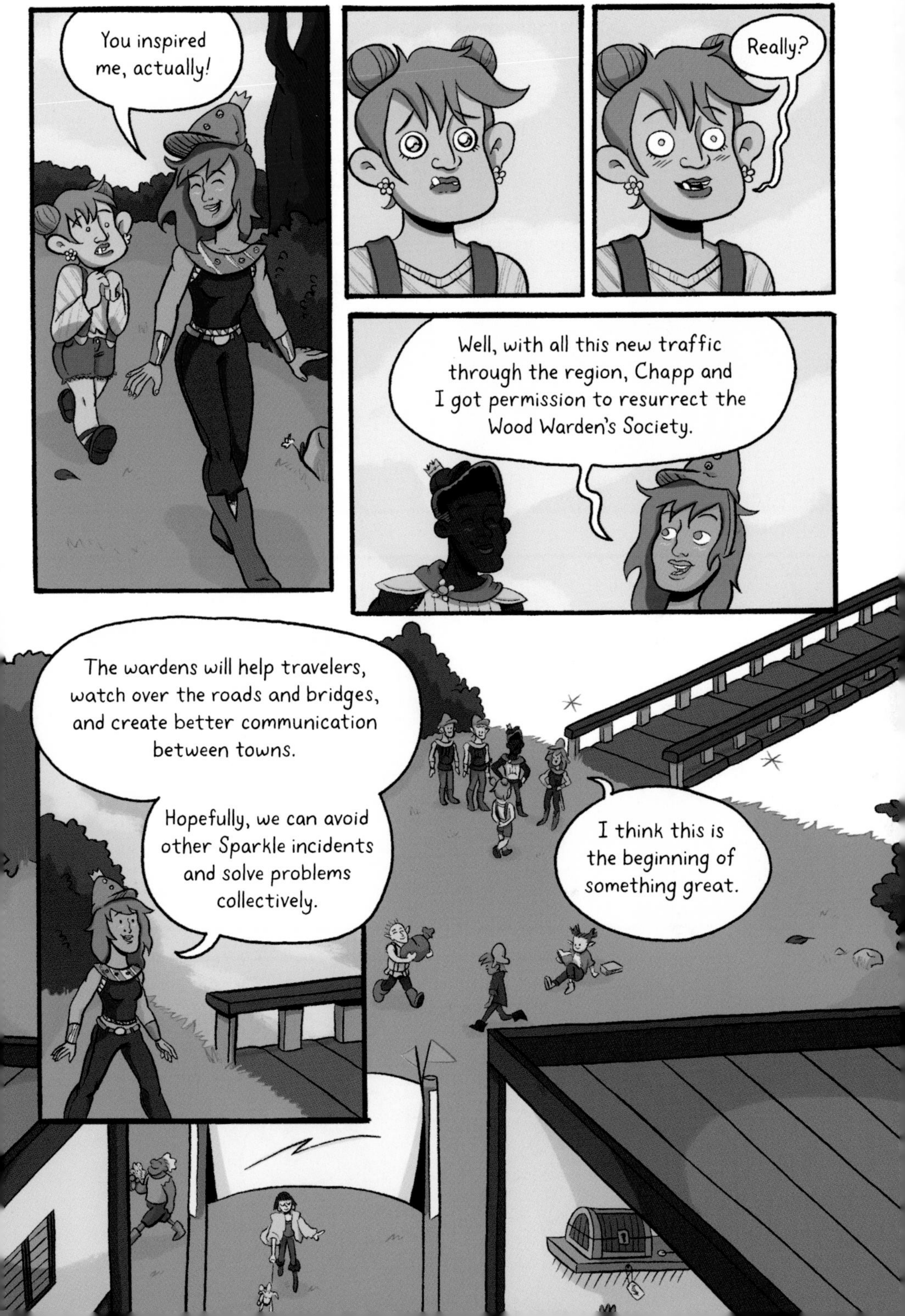
You inspired me, actually!
Really?
Well, with all this new traffic through the region, Chapp and I got permission to resurrect the Wood Warden's Society.
The wardens will help travelers, watch over the roads and bridges, and create better communication between towns.
Hopefully, we can avoid other Sparkle incidents and solve problems collectively.
I think this is the beginning of something great.

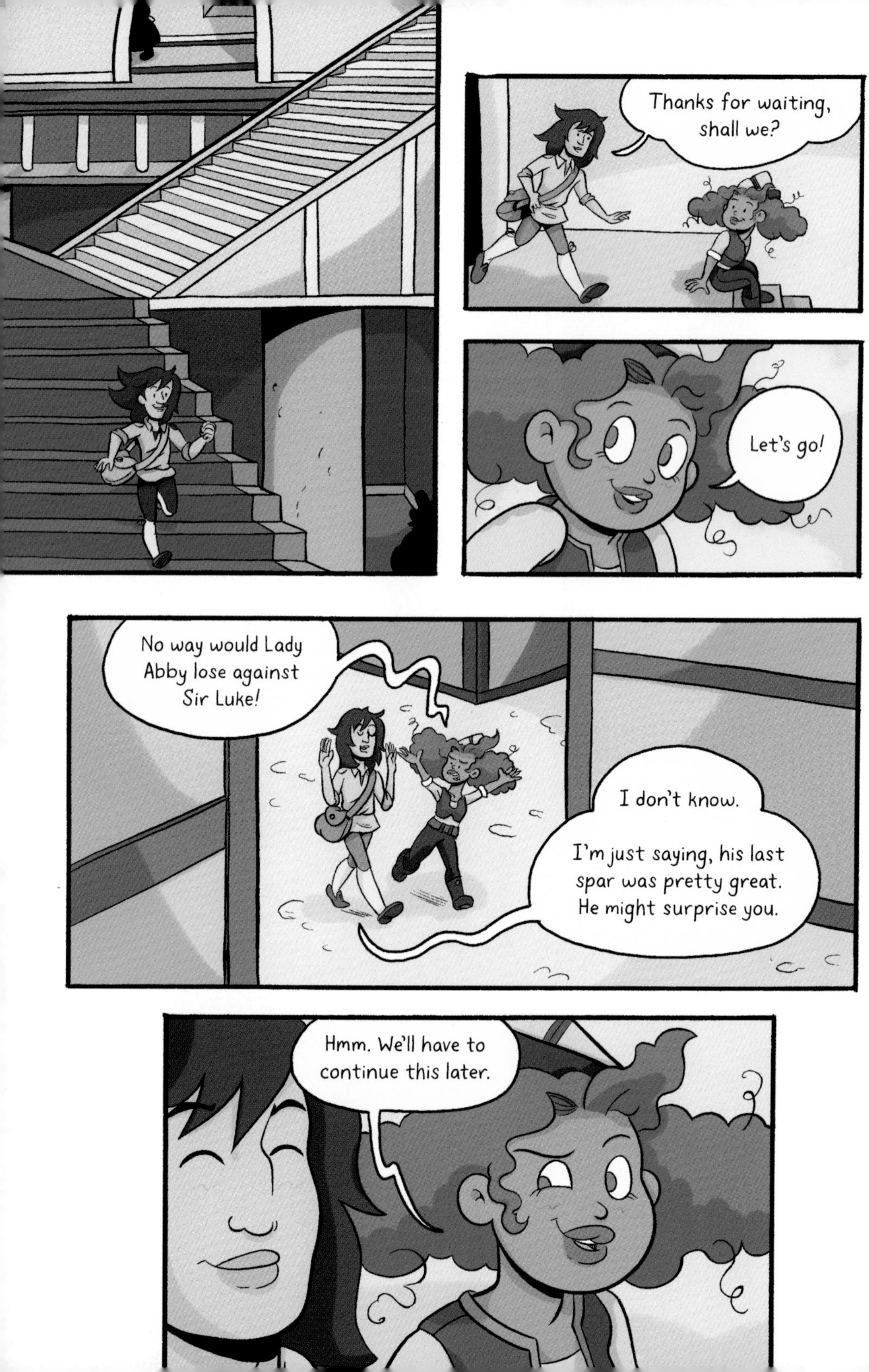

Thanks for waiting, shall we?
Let's go!
No way would Lady Abby lose against Sir Luke!
I don't know.
I'm just saying, his last spar was pretty great. He might surprise you.
Hmm. We'll have to continue this later.

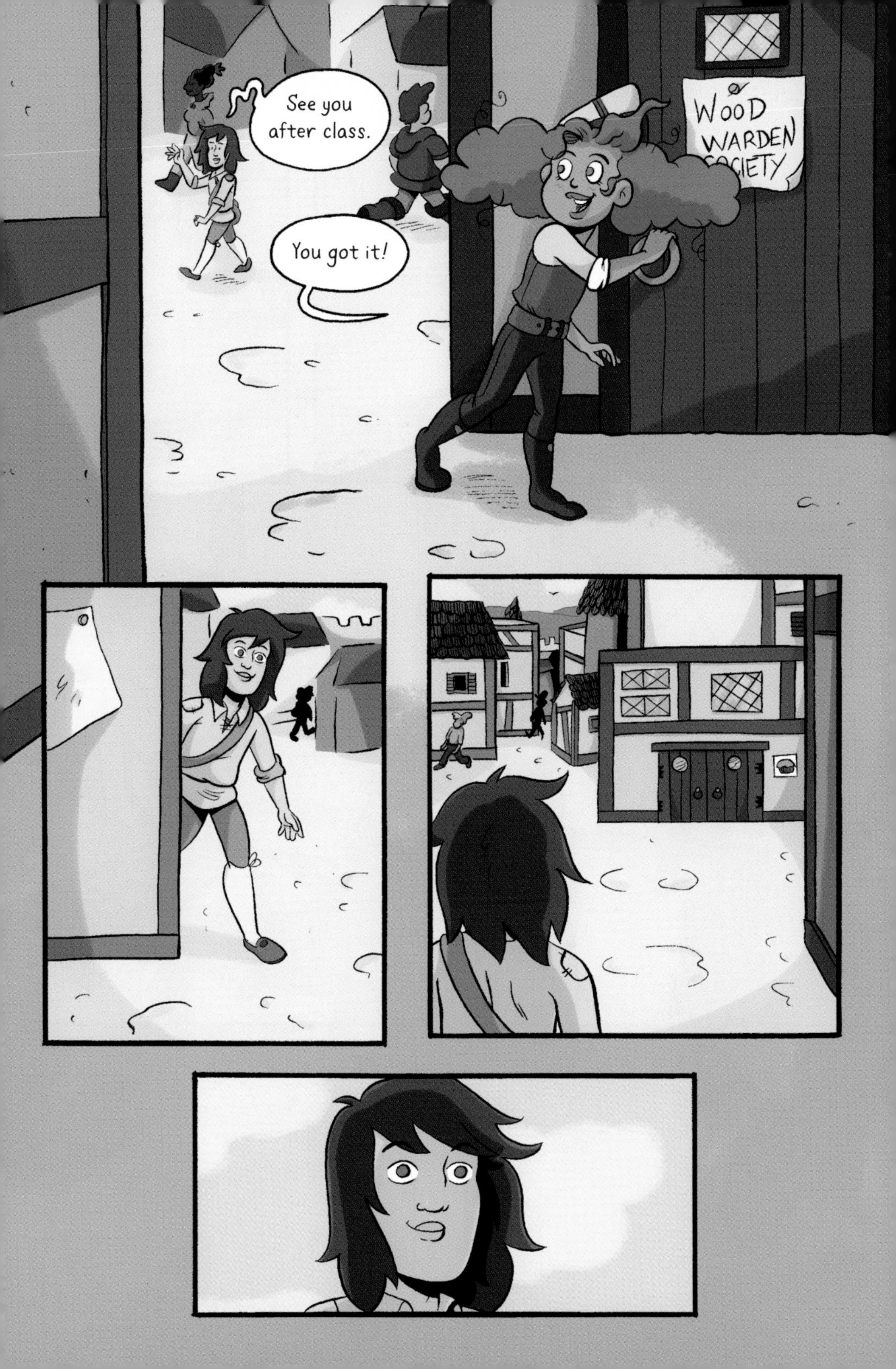
WOOD WARDEN SOCIETY
See you after class.
You got it!

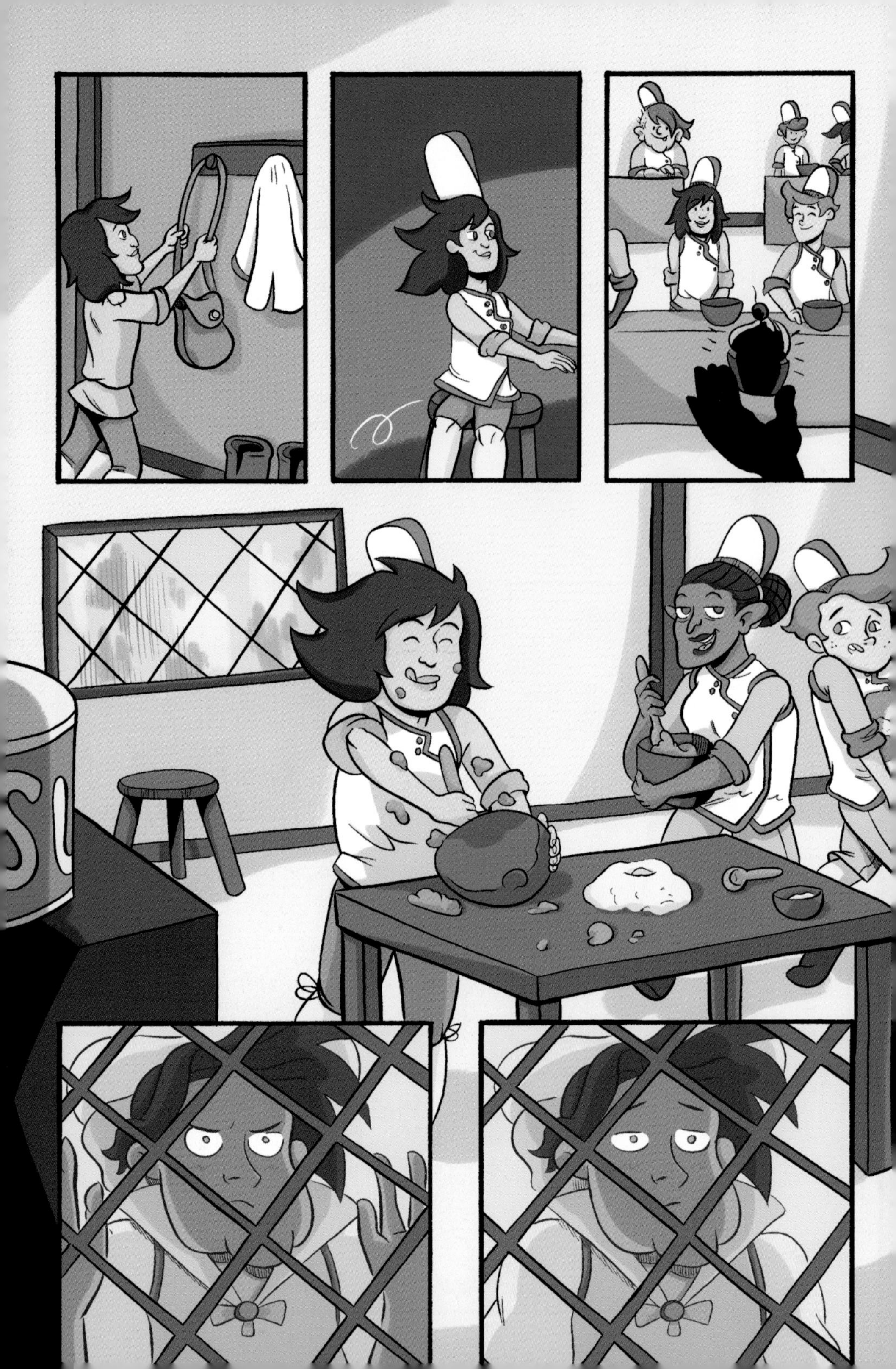

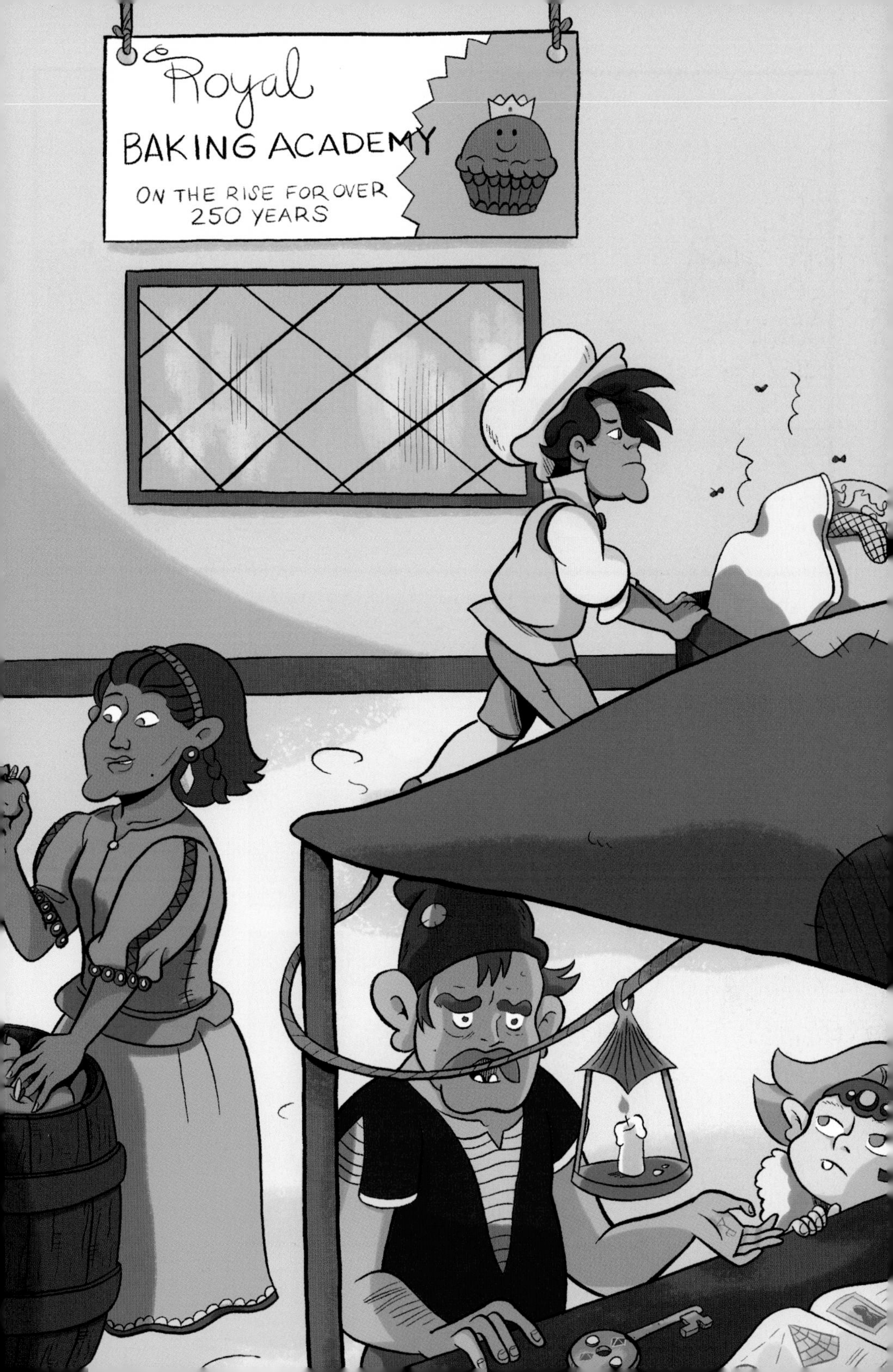
Royal
BAKING ACADEMY
ON THE RISE FOR OVER
250 YEARS

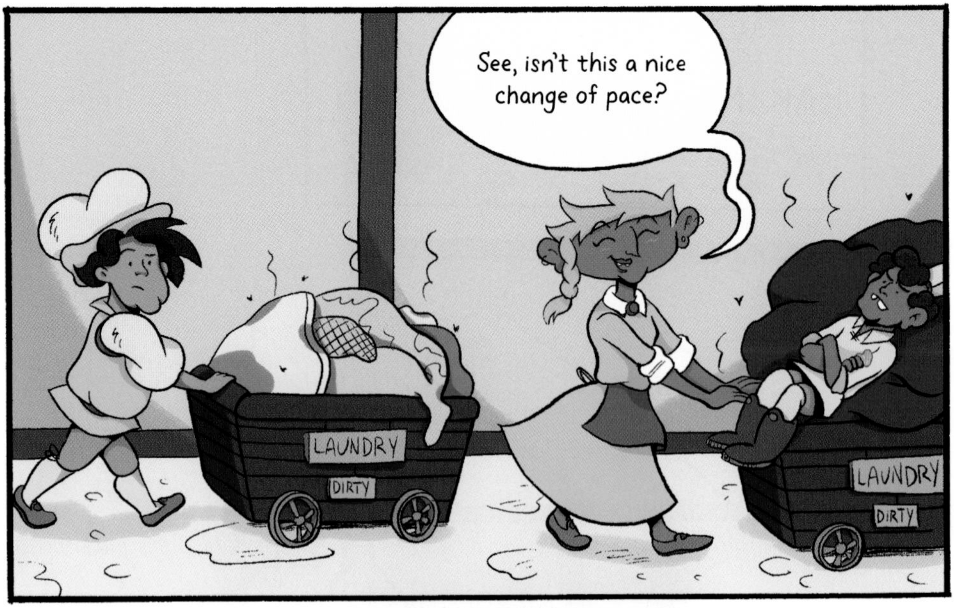
See, isn't this a nice change of pace?
LAUNDRY
DIRTY
LAUNDRY
DIRTY

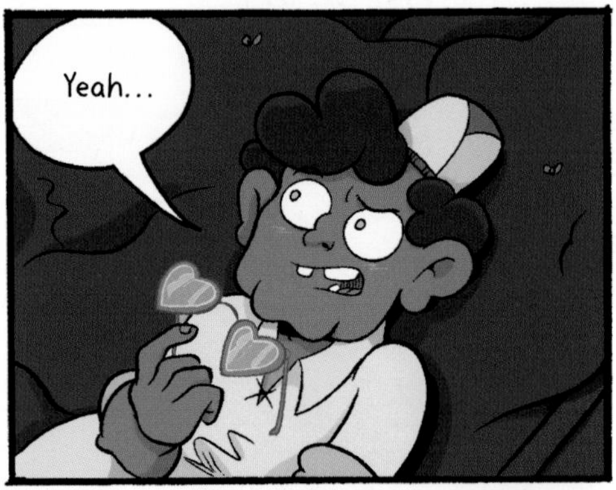
Yeah...

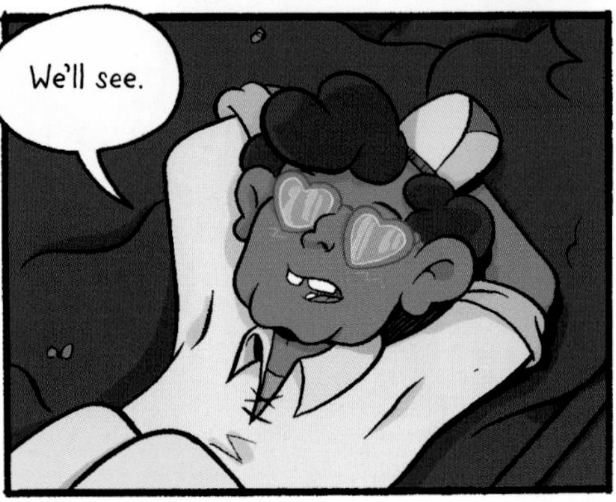
We'll see.

the end!

There are so many people who supported me and *SCULLION* along the way:

Thank you to my wonderful editors, Hazel Newlevant, for taking a chance on me at the very beginning, and Amanda Meadows, for helping me cross the finish line. And the crew at Oni Press for getting it out into the world.

Kelly Sonnack, for looking out for me and being the world's best agent.

Dave Roman, Sophie Yanow, and Jason Lutes, for your thoughtful perspective, encouragement, and guidance when this book was my thesis at The Center for Cartoon Studies.

My CCS work family and friends.

Tony Cliff, for coloring advice when it felt insurmountable. Steve, Whiteley, and Jess for flatting at the speed of light.

Super friends Ashley, Tillie, Dan, Daryl, Luke, Robyn, and Steve. And my family, always.

Thank you all!

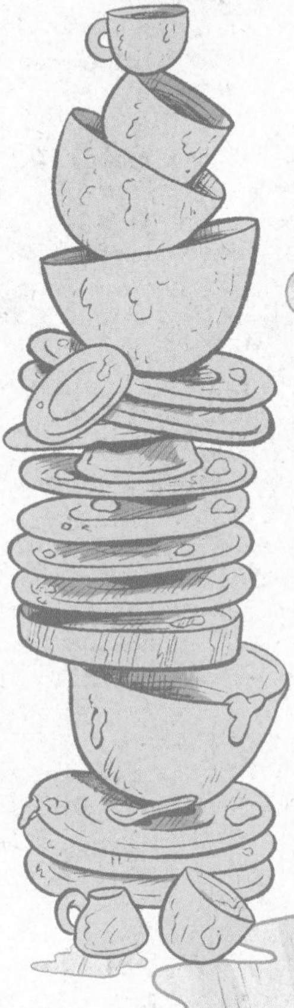

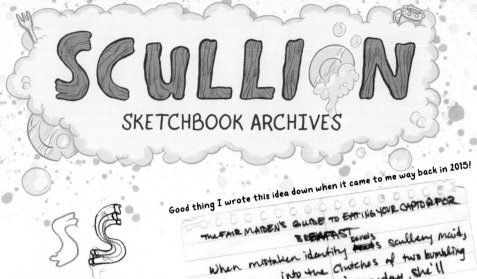

SCULLION

SKETCHBOOK ARCHIVES

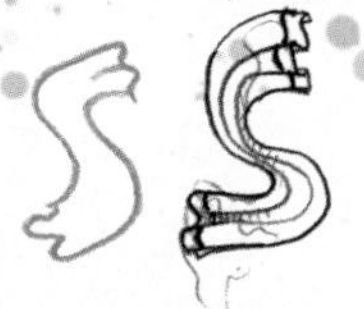

A wet towel for the SCULLION 'S' didn't quite work for me.

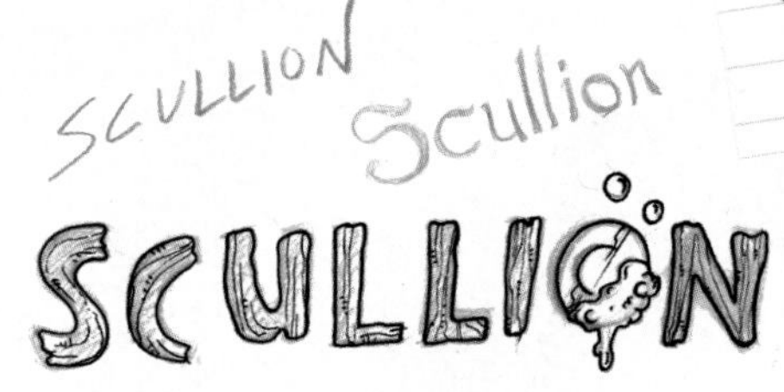

SCULLION
Scullion
SCULLION

Good thing I wrote this idea down when it came to me way back in 2015!

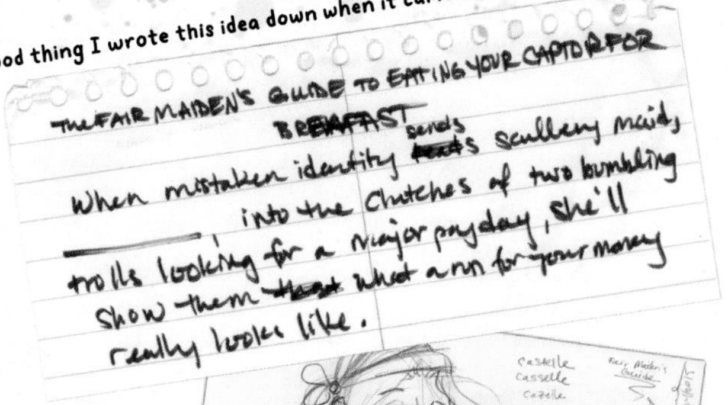

THE FAIR MAIDEN'S GUIDE TO EATING YOUR CAPTOR FOR BREAKFAST

When mistaken identity sends scullery maid, ____, into the clutches of two bumbling trolls looking for a major payday, she'll show them what a run for your money really looks like.

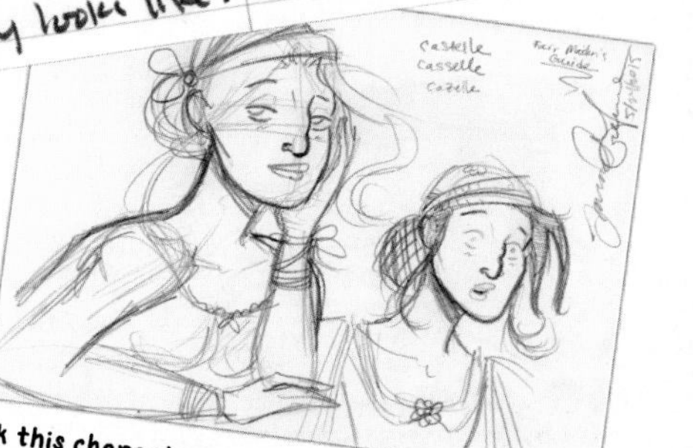

Casselle
Casselle
Cazelle

I think this character morphed into Darlis, Mae, and Riqa.

Something really clicked with these sketches!

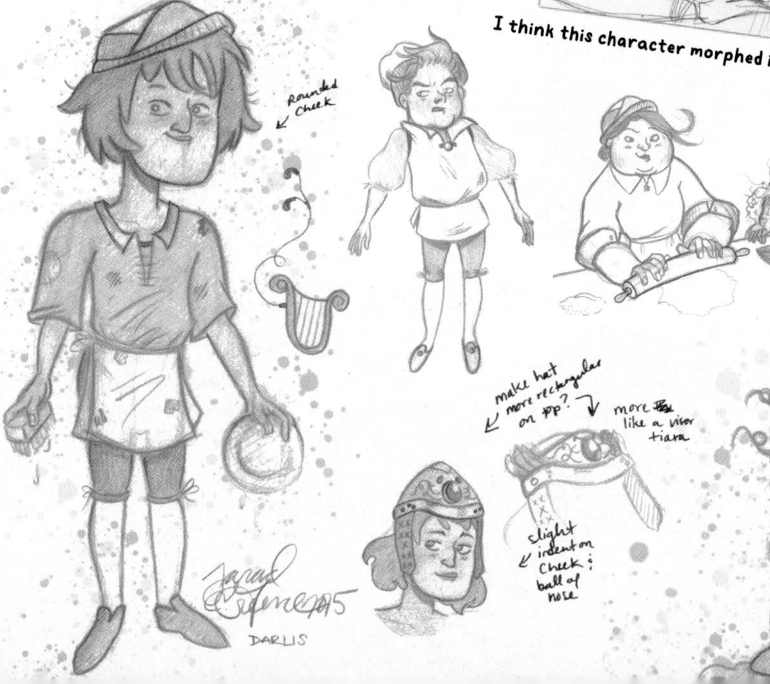

Rounded Cheek
make hat more rectangular on pp?
more like a visor tiara
slight indent on cheek; ball of nose
DARLIS

So cute!
I love this sketch of Mae!

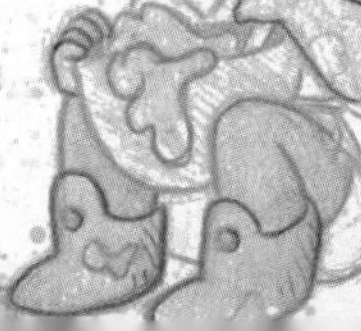

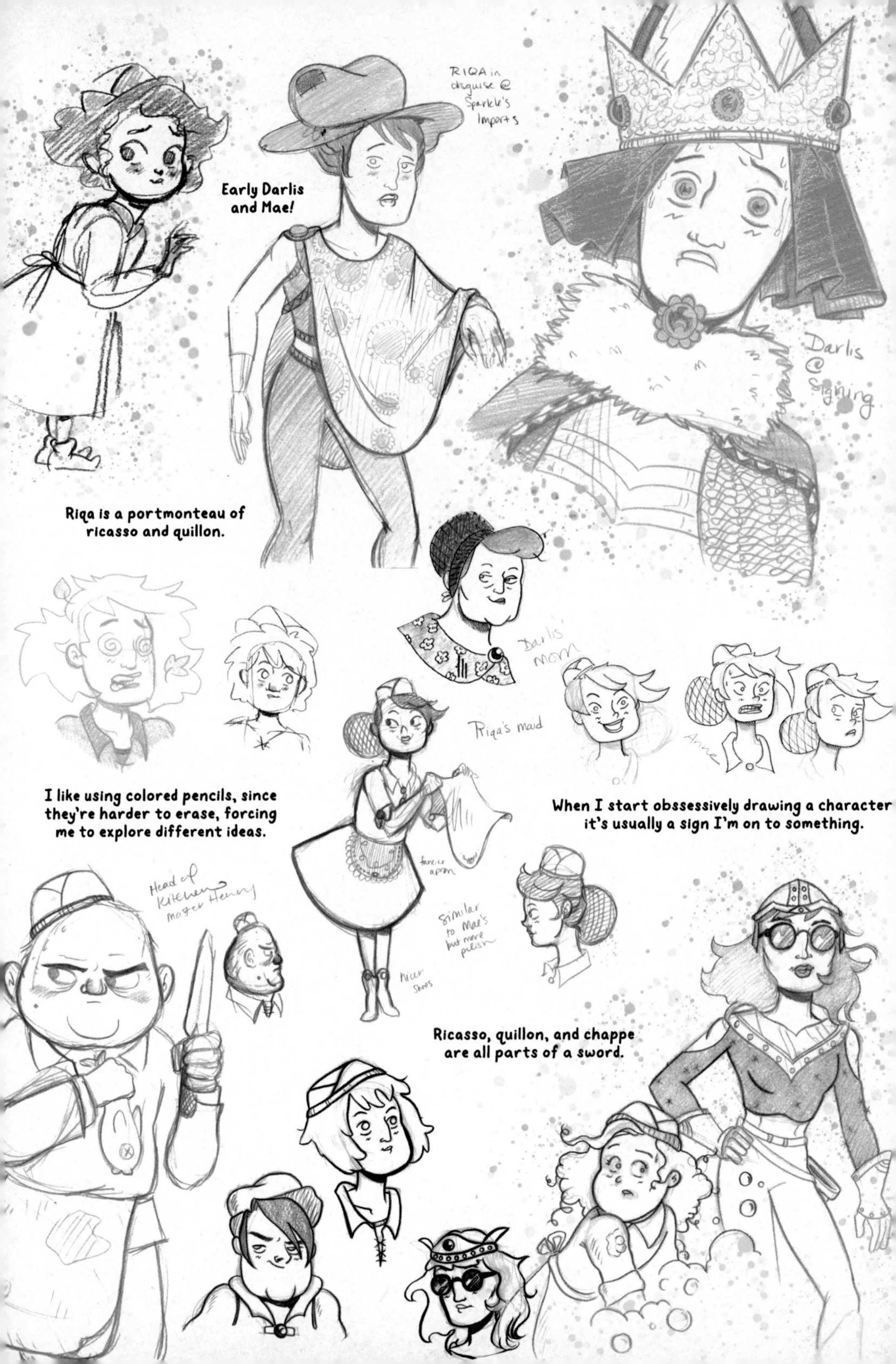
RIQA in disguise @ Sparkle's Imports
Darlis @ Signing
Darlis' mom
Riqa's maid
Anne
fancier apron
similar to Mae's but more polish
nicer shoes
Head of Kitchen Master Henry

Early Darlis and Mae!

Riqa is a portmonteau of ricasso and quillon.

I like using colored pencils, since they're harder to erase, forcing me to explore different ideas.

When I start obsessively drawing a character it's usually a sign I'm on to something.

Ricasso, quillon, and chappe are all parts of a sword.

This didn't seem like enough of a disguise.

Glamourized Chappe

Smudge was named after my friends' cat.

thaps as gnome?

A better disguise!

close

SMUDGE

Reality...?

Larger? More intimidating since solo?

SPARKLE

swim trunk-esque?

maybe show knee?

Bumper was the last character I designed.

Stump

If you can believe it, my original draft did not contain Sparkle, Stump, Bumper, or the Imports Shoppe! And originally Riqa rescued Darlis from the trolls!

Grubble in disguise

Grubble & Petey

I drew so many trolls before finding my Grubble and Petey.

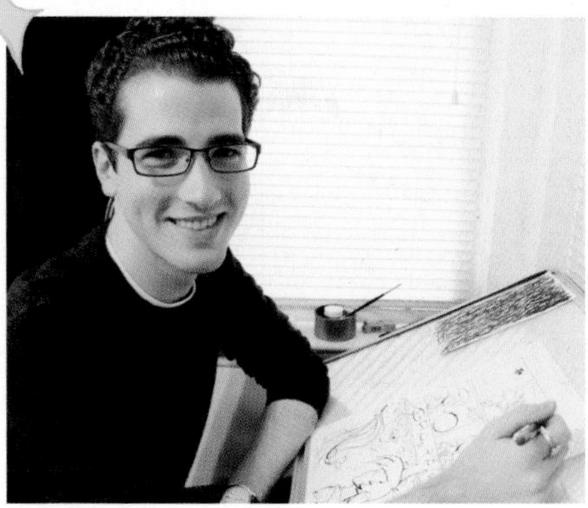

Jarad Greene is a cartoonist who loves creating fantasy, adventure, and memoir comics for kids and young adults. After many years in humid and sunny cities in Florida and South Carolina, Jarad currently finds himself in the foggy and peculiar train town of White River Junction, Vermont, where he works for The Center for Cartoon Studies. He does love to bake, but isn't too fond of doing the dishes. He's been told he looks a bit like Tom Hanks, or maybe a Jonas brother, but he has yet to be chased by the paparazzi... or trolls. Take a peek at what's on his desk @JaradGreene.

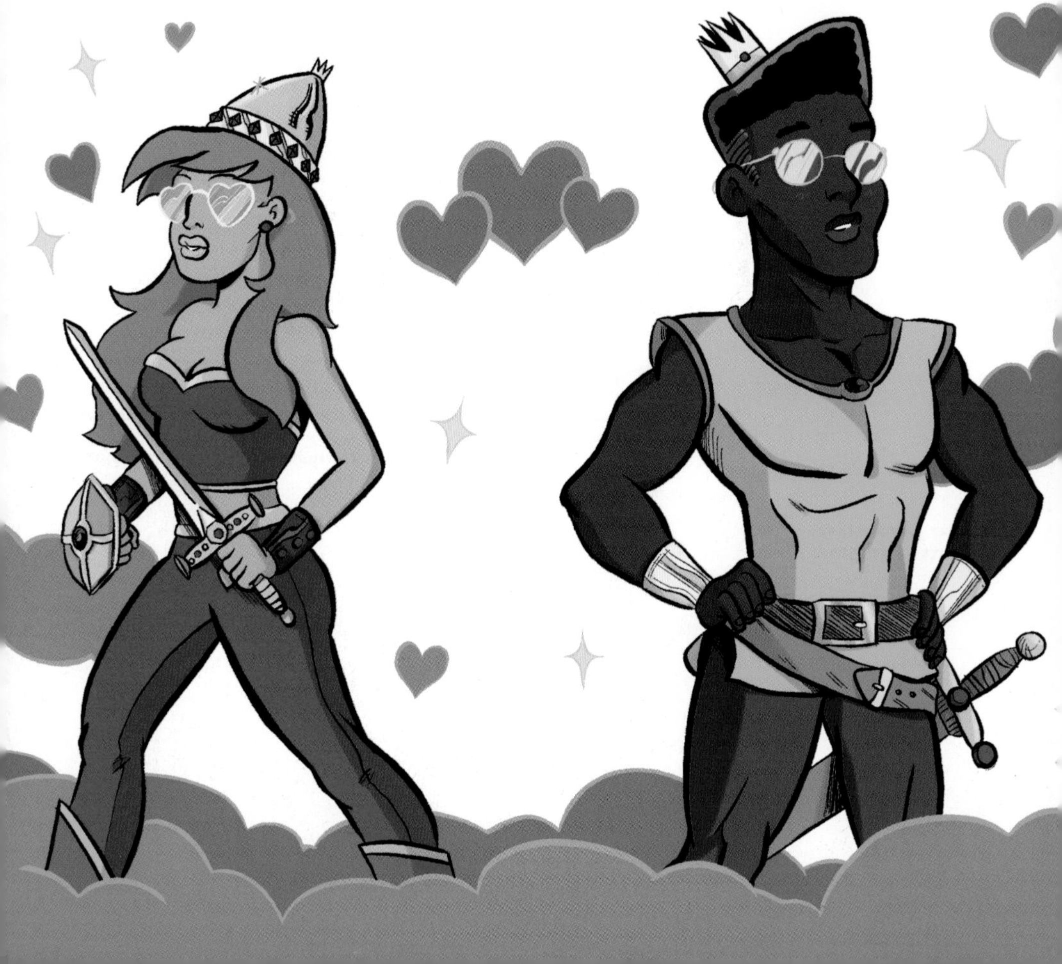